About the Author

Internationally recognized blogger, author, and podcaster Shannon Ables founded the blog *The Simply Luxurious Life* in 2009 and debuted the podcast *The Simple Sophisticate* in 2014. She writes and teaches about true contentment and how shifting the focus to quality rather than quantity in every area of our lives elevates the everyday, regardless of one's age, income, gender, or relationship status.

Her first book, *Choosing the Simply Luxurious Life: A Modern Woman's Guide*, describes the foundation of the simply luxurious life — one that prioritizes quality over quantity in each of our endeavors: curating our passions and talents; building healthy, strong relationships; being sensible about our finances; curating a signature personal style; maintaining fitness in mind and body; traveling well; creating an inviting sanctuary; and entertaining with ease. An entire chapter explains how to indulge your inner Francophile.

Shannon's second book, *Living the Simply Luxurious Life: Making Your Everydays Extraordinary and Discovering Your Best Self*, offers the tools to tailor your everydays so that you can live your best life, utilizing your strengths to reach your full potential — a truly singular and individual journey.

Shannon is a retired public education teacher. After earning a Master's in Education degree in Language Arts Secondary Education, she taught AP Language and Composition for the final ten years of her twenty-year teaching tenure. During her undergraduate studies to earn a bachelor's degree in English, with a minor in history, she sought out courses in British literature and history, and studied for a time in Angers, France. The French and British cultures inspire much of the content on *The Simply Luxurious Life* blog and continue to pique her curiosity.

Shannon has lived in Bend, Oregon, since 2015, with her two boys (gentleman pups) Oscar (2005–2021) and Norman, both depicted on the cover of this book. During the summer of 2019, Shannon found and purchased the house that she fondly named Le Papillon.

Also by Shannon Ables

Choosing the Simply Luxurious Life: A Modern Woman's Guide

Living the Simply Luxurious Life: Making Your Everydays Extraordinary and Discovering Your Best Self

Find Shannon here:

Blog: https://thesimplyluxuriouslife.com and the shortened url: http://tsll.co
Podcast: *The Simple Sophisticate*: https://thesimplyluxuriouslife.com/tsllpodcast
Instagram: @thesimplyluxuriouslife
podcast Instagram: @thesimplesophisticatepodcast
Facebook: /thesimplyluxuriouslifeblog
Twitter: @simplyluxurious
YouTube: https://youtube.com/shannonables
Website: https://shannonables.com

The Road to Le Papillon
Daily Meditations on True Contentment

Shannon Ables

Simply Luxurious Publishing
Bend, Oregon

Copyright © 2022 by Shannon Ables.

All rights reserved. No part of this publication may be reproduced, distributed or transmitted in any form or by any means, including photocopying, recording, or other electronic or mechanical methods, without the prior written permission of the publisher, except in the case of brief quotations embodied in critical reviews and certain other noncommercial uses permitted by copyright law. For permission requests, write to the publisher, addressed "Attention: Permissions Coordinator," at the email address below.

Simply Luxurious Publishing
www.thesimplyluxuriouslife.com

Book layout ©2022 BookDesignTemplates.com
Illustrations by Sarah Löcker
Cover layout by Dash Creative

Ordering Information:
Quantity sales. Special discounts are available on quantity purchases by independent book shops, associations, and others. For details, contact the "The Simply Luxurious Life, Inc." at info@thesimplyluxuriouslife.com.

The Road to Le Papillon: Daily Meditations on True Contentment/ Shannon Ables. — 1st ed.
ISBN: 978-1-7369672-3-2 (hardback)

To my great Aunt Betty, whose unwavering confidence in me I will carry with me always. Thank you for making this book possible.

To my sweet, gentleman boy Oscar. Thank you for breaking my heart open. I hold you in it always.

To the readers of TSLL's weekly newsletter over the past twelve years, thank you for the encouragement to bring forth what you hold in your hands.

And now, there really is a different kind of freedom. That's why we take risks, right? And why we say yes to things, because you never know what beautiful gift is awaiting when you do.

— Laura Dern

The caterpillar grows wings during a period of isolation. Remember that the next time you're alone.

Contents

Introduction		11
January	Let Go of What Doesn't Work, and Embrace the Unknown	17
February	Be Yourself Fully, but Stay Vulnerable	53
March	Embrace Patience, Healing, and Growth	87
April	Speak Up, Communicate Well, Set Boundaries	125
May	Love Mother Nature	163
June	Let Your Curiosity Expand the Everyday and Open Your Mind	203
July	The Gifts of France: Awakening, Savoring, and Being True to Oneself	243
August	Be Playful as You Create and Explore	281
September	Be Strong and Soft, and Think Critically	323
October	Lead with Your Humanity as You Pursue Knowledge, Understanding, Bravery, and Kindness	365
November	Explore and Discover Yourself and the World	401
December	Find Peace, Calm, and Sanctuary: Become a Butterfly	441
Conclusion		479
Epilogue		483
Quick Guide to Recommended Books		487
Quick Guide to Recommended Musical Selections		491
Acknowledgments		493

Introduction

Spiritual awakening can be compared to the butterfly breaking free from the confinement of its cocoon ... While the cocoon may feel safe and warm, we all reach a point where it becomes too constricting and we are ready to break free and find our wings ... A spiritual awakening is nature's way of helping us achieve our full potential.
—Richard Paterson, "8 Signs You May Be Having a Spiritual Awakening"

Paterson also writes, "Living simply, spending time in nature, enjoying good company, paying attention to the present moment and making time to do the things we love doing — all cost nothing and help connect us with our happy, unconditioned selves."

The journey of self-discovery is one that brings us back to ourselves. Our true selves. As Richard Paterson describes it, our *unconditioned* selves. When all the cultural programming, all the expectations of others and the world — ideas we have gladly or unknowingly accepted — wash away, we are reintroduced to our true self.

Le Papillon (The Butterfly) is the name I chose for my house and garden in Bend, Oregon. The name encompasses both tangible and intangible truths about my life journey to discover what true contentment is and how to ensure it is part of my everyday life. I set out on the road to Le Papillon the moment I was born — unconsciously, of course. Consciously, the journey began when I sat down on December 26, 2009, to begin writing *Simply Luxurious*, which was what I then called my blog.

On August 23, 2019, I signed the mortgage papers and gained the keys to my sanctuary. The Craftsman-style house, only three years old, small in square footage, but made large with an abundance of natural light and tall, vaulted ceilings, is paired perfectly with a tidy *potager*-inspired garden, intertwining perennials and shrubs with vegetables and fruit.

Le Papillon is my sanctuary, a place where I can create and rest peacefully, a place to gather friends, a place to be fully Shannon. In Bend, Oregon, I am a few footsteps away from the wilderness and Mother Nature's splendid four seasons — a connection and daily reminder of the fundamentals of life. Another essential ingredient in my life of contentment at Le Papillon: daily interactions with my neighbors — face-to-face chats, waves of hello and nods of heads while enjoying a stroll, the neighborhood children stopping by to pet Norman and Oscar while I dig in the dirt, smiles of shared appreciation of our small, quiet neighborhood.

Having a house of my own enables me to relax, to create, to make fewer decisions based on "have to" and more based on "want to." The pace and melody of the life I love living enable me to give my best and to act most genuinely in my personal and professional lives, secure in the stability that comes from knowing my home is mine (with a fixed monthly payment). The pride of place I feel in my house and garden serves as an active counterpoint to my ongoing journey. That journey, with all its twists and turns, eventually led me to move beyond what sheltered me from experiencing a full life and encouraged me to seek the full potential of my existence. I worked for this by moving beyond simply being aware to being *fully curious*.

The art of living well, focusing on a life of quality over quantity in all arenas, is dynamic; it requires us to be fluid and to face unknowns. Yet equally and most significantly, it is an art that brings daily contentment and joyful moments shared with others. It liberates us from the *should*s of life and instead guides us toward the rich goodness of what it means to fully live our one and only life.

In June 2010, I began writing a free weekly newsletter and sending it out each Friday morning to subscribers of TSLL (my blog's name had by then become *The Simply Luxurious Life*). I published my first book, *Choosing the Simply Luxurious Life: A Modern Woman's Guide*, in 2014, and a follow-up volume, *Living the Simply Luxurious Life: Making Your Everydays Extraordinary and Discovering Your Best Self*, four years later.

My subscriber list had grown to 15,000 readers in June 2020, and I shifted temporarily to a monthly delivery of the newsletter due to the pandemic, which caused school schedules to shift frequently from one month to the next, but not without heeding the words of my subscribers urging me to do something with the letters included in each issue — more than 500 in all.

I have tried to make this new book about being. The skill of cultivating true contentment consists of a beautiful mosaic of thoughtfully chosen behaviors and skills, many of which I share in my second book. We must know these skills, apply them, and exercise them until they become habits, freeing our mind to be present and open to the beautiful spontaneity of life. Then, when we have clarity about and some command of the key components of living well, even if we are still on the road to embodying them fully, we need to concentrate simply on being. Both Kurt Vonnegut and the Dalai Lama remind us that we are human *beings*, after all, not human *doings*.

The Road to Papillon is divided into twelve sections, each focused on a contemplative monthly theme and based on an arena of my life that has been a key part of my journey. There are as many entries as there are days in the year. Begin reading on today's date, or start on January 1, or read here and there, wherever your eye and interest are drawn based on the themes. My hope is that what you discover will offer inspiration for your unique journey to your own version of Le Papillon, whether that is a

Introduction

home, a degree, a job, a relationship, or some other important personal goal.

The clarity we gain about our lives simplifies our answer when the big questions arrive — whether to marry, whom to marry, whether to invest in education, whether to start a new business, to travel, to move, to have children, to leave a career to which you have dedicated years of your life. We can gain that clarity only if we live consciously, awake in the world around us each and every day. Many people go through life doing as they think they *should*, doing what is applauded, and avoiding confrontation or friction. However, after a while, just conforming to others' ideals will dull our brightness and degrade our gifts. We will start to ache, and we may not know why.

The aching is a plea from your most sincere you: It is *begging* to be shared with the world. I can acknowledge now that my aching began when I was in graduate school and at the end of my student-teaching tenure, an experience that had gone exceedingly well and that confirmed for me that I had made the right decision in becoming a secondary language-arts teacher. My then mentor teacher shared with me what the chair of the department had told her when I interviewed for the program: "I don't know if she really wants to be a teacher."

I can't say what had given him that impression, but in my heart of hearts, if I am being completely honest, it was true: I never really wanted to be a teacher. I wanted to be around the written word, analytical thinking, and brilliant literature written by people far smarter than me. I wanted to be around the craft of writing, a medium of expression that seemed magical, and teaching was the only way I could imagine that would also allow for a stable income and time for doing what I loved.

After twenty years of teaching, a career that began in September 2001, when 9/11 shook the country, and ended as the 2020 pandemic seemed to start to ease in the United States in the spring of 2021, I handed in my resignation papers. Not because I didn't enjoy teaching — the interaction with blossoming young minds, being up close and personal with literary classics, teaching rhetoric, the art of effective communication and argument — but because I loved something else, writing, more than I ever imagined I could and finally could pursue it with stability. Le Papillon is my stability.

The Road to Le Papillon is a map for living a life of true contentment each and every day. It is a guide for navigating the uncertainties of life, elevating your experiences and personal interactions, and growing into the person you are capable of becoming along the way.

Your Le Papillon may also be a house of your own, but it need not be. Maybe you already own your home but have not found true peace in your daily life. Maybe you love the freedom of renting but have not found out what to do with all the freedom you have in your life. Maybe it is not a

The Road to Le Papillon

matter of your living situation. Perhaps relationships you have forged pull you down and mute a voice inside you, and you hope one day to find the strength to share what you feel. Or maybe the traditional structures — whether within school, work, or family life — constrict or bind in a way you cannot explain without seeming to hurt those you love, but you know you must find a way to communicate your needs with kindness, yet with strength, in order to live a life that soothes your being.

As you arrive at your unique Le Papillon, you will cross the threshold into a life you love living each day, one that keeps you in the present moment, soaking up all that life has given, and you will pinch yourself, wondering how you could be so lucky.

A note on the pages that follow

Each month opens with an introduction based on the month's theme, an intimate glimpse into my personal world, my life journey. Following the introduction, daily entries share reflections on the month's theme. Each concludes with a bottom-line statement — a thought of the day, an action to ponder — to help you nurture your own unique contentment.

Punctuating the end of each daily entry are two codas:

Petit plaisir A simple pleasure to savor during your everydays, inspired by my own everyday routines enjoyed over the course of the past few years. Listeners of the podcast *The Simple Sophisticate* will recognize this feature; at the end of each episode, I share a book, a film, a show, a recipe — anything that is likely to satiate your sophisticated taste.

Explore further A link to a related post from *The Simply Luxurious Life* blog. If you are reading this in the ebook format, simply copy and paste the URL shared into your browser (preceded by https://). If you are reading a hard copy of the book or listening to the audio book, just type in the link (preceded by https://). Either way, you will be taken directly to the full, detailed post.

A note on the inclusion of suggested musical selections

Who hears music feels his solitude
Peopled at once.

— Robert Browning

Introduction

Jazz entered my life when I was a teenager. I was partly influenced by the ubiquitous saxophone solo in 80's pop music ever-present during my childhood played on the radio while riding in the backseat of the car with my parents, but also by my Great Uncle Rufus, who played early- and mid-20th-century big band numbers and jazz on his record player when we would visit him and my Great Aunt Betty. I was introduced to the jazz classics — Louis Armstrong, Ella Fitzgerald, and then, through my own exploration, Miles Davis's album *Kind of Blue*, just to name the first of many musicians I have enjoyed over the years. "So What" became my ringtone for a while, as an anthem to trusting my journey. The syncopation and the seemingly improvised musical riffs, one of the primary components of jazz music, captured my ear and have held my interest ever since, especially when I need to let my hair down, kick off my shoes, pour a glass of wine, and just celebrate being alive.

Classical music took longer to come into my life, only because I — like many people, I suspect — was intimidated by the appearance of a sophistication I knew I did not have. It turns out that sophistication is not what was needed, but simply curiosity. When I finally had the courage to explore it, I never turned back.

Clemency Burton-Hill writes exquisitely and refreshingly of the joys of classical listening in her book *Year of Wonder: Classical Music to Enjoy Day by Day*: "Classical composers are no different from other writers of music, or any creative artist: all they are doing, in their own way, is seeking to get down on paper something they think and feel — which in turn makes others think and feel. It is an exercise in human connection — and generosity — that might seem complex on the page when you look at all those black notes, but comes down to something exquisitely simple . . . Music's very *raison d'être* is to be brought to life, to be experienced in time, to be *listened* to. In other words, these composers want to talk to you."

As I will share in more detail in a couple of entries in November, my students indirectly introduced me to classical music, as they were musicians who played many different instruments in high school and local regional symphonies and orchestras; they learned how to turn the notes on the page into harmonies that spontaneously moved one to smiles, to applause, and to deep appreciation of the magic of the music and how it can speak to us. I went to their concerts and saw their talents outside of the English and social studies classroom. I became the student, and they became the teachers in those moments when I wanted to learn more. *How do you say Haydn? What is an adagio? What is the proper pronunciation of concerto?*

Admittedly, I also continued to gravitate toward jazz and classical music because, while both include songs with words, in most cases lyrics are absent. I am able to interpret the notes played as I need or desire at any moment in my life. Both genres of music became the background in my classroom during my years as a teacher, played during the five to seven minutes between classes and while students worked quietly together or on their own during class. While I wasn't the "cool" teacher with my selections, I tried to offer a space that kept me grounded and calm during the busyness of the school day; hopefully, it did the same for even just a few students during a time of chaos or confusion in their lives.

For this book, I have hand-selected each musical entry. I have no expectations that you will become a jazz or a classical music lover. My suggestions offer an opportunity to be present in your day, to celebrate or relax or savor whatever might be going on. Hopefully, the selections will elevate these moments even more, as they do for me when they play in the background as the soundtrack of my daily life.

January

Let Go of What Doesn't Work, and Embrace the Unknown

January

As readers of my previous books know, I believe we are very much the curators of our unique and simply luxurious life. Achieving such a life is a conscious pursuit, something we cultivate. It also takes time, as we continue to have new experiences and gain new understandings of the world and ourselves: what we love and value, what we need to distance ourselves from, and the default behaviors we need to refrain from that are not serving us well. Living a simply luxurious life is about choosing wisely, welcoming what elevates the overall quality of our lives, and letting go of what does not.

If you refuse to stop searching, refuse to ignore your curiosity, and refuse to let go of what you know you will find if you don't give up, it will happen — most likely when you are least expecting it. And before you know it, you will feel that the path you are meant to travel, the life you are meant to live, is choosing you. Then, as David Whyte describes in *The Three Marriages: Reimagining Work, Self and Relationship*, the only question remaining is "Will you respond?"

> Being smitten by a path, a direction, an intuited possibility, no matter the territory it crosses, we can feel, in youth or at any threshold, as if life has found us at last. Beginning a courtship with a work . . . demands a fierce attention to understand what it is we belong to in the world. But to start the difficult path to what we want, we also have to be serious about what we want.
>
> Following this path through increasing levels of seriousness, we reach a certain threshold where our freedom to choose seems to disappear and is replaced by an understanding that we were made for the world in a very particular way and that this way of being is at bottom nonnegotiable. Like the mountain or the sky, it just *is*. It is as if we choose and choose until there is actually no choice at all . . . The only question is whether you will respond.

What a beautiful arrival and a reason to celebrate. Let's get started.

January 1
The Formula for True Success

I think in a broad sense, happiness and success is really just being able to do what you want and make a living off of it in the simplest way.
— Martha Beck

When I came across this quote from an interview with life coach Martha Beck, I stopped to reread it. I wanted to frame it, because it solidifies the idea that it is not an abundance of money that determines one's success, or even following a very specific, prescribed path, but rather finding what you love doing and doing it sufficiently well to be paid enough to live comfortably.

So simple, no? Possible, yes! Easy, not necessarily. Doing what you want and being paid for it — aka the path to happiness and success — is simple in definition, but not so simple in execution. The good news, however, is that if you are willing to put in the time to figure out what makes you come alive or, as Dr. Jeanne Lamonte says, to "find a job in which your neurosis is constructive," you must persevere until you can make a living doing it. It takes time and investing in yourself, but it is absolutely possible.

Before discovering blogging, I would not have been able to describe the peace people find when they enjoy what they are doing. Why? Because I wasn't doing it — the elusive thing that puts me into that magical state of "flow," a term coined by psychologist Mihaly Csikszentmihalyi to mean a sense of fluidity, complete immersion, deep focus, and immunity to distraction. Once I began blogging, I finally experienced that flow state and became lost in it each day. Pursuing this goal is worth the effort, because what you discover will be your peace, your calm, your deepest joy, a fundamental pillar of your contentment.

The first step is to discover what you love doing and can offer to people to make their lives better. The second step is to work your tail off while having patience.

Petit plaisir Listen to the Vienna New Year's Concert as a way to transition gently and with an abundance of courage and hope into the new year.

Explore further thesimplyluxuriouslife.com/january1 (the benefits of classical music)

January 2
The Value of Determination

Happy new year! I am a day late, I know, but you deserve to continue celebrating. However the year began for you — blissful and calm or harried — there are still 364 days to get it right. If you are determined to make this a wonderful year, you most certainly will do so. We draw to us what we believe we deserve. If you are resolute in your determination to exude positive energy each day, I can promise that you will attract more positive experiences than disappointing ones.

January

Often when a new year arrives, I greet it from a small rental cottage at the Oregon coast. With the boys (my dogs) in tow, I welcome the new year with multiple walks a day on the sand, thankful for the opportunity to slow down my mind, take in the ocean air, and reenergize. I pack my wellies, pop by the local grocer, make sure I have books, notebooks, and journal, my favorite pajamas and oversized sweaters. Once I arrive and get settled, I rarely look at the clock except to coordinate with the open hours of local grocers, the bookshop, and a few small boutiques. I go to sleep when I am tired and awake when I am rested, resetting my body clock and beginning the new year with a restored body and mind.

A ritual for the start of the new year need not be expensive or even take you away from your home. The ritual itself affirms that something new has begun, that new opportunities are present. Giving ourselves space between the old and the new year allows a deep breath of life to circulate and energize us for experiences yet to be revealed.

Whether you create a ritual that takes you away from home or one in which you snuggle in at your sanctuary, take two or three days or a week off to set your determination for a sure-footed journey toward life-changing contentment.

Petit plaisir Greet each person you pass with a smile, and exchange an enthusiastic wish for a "Happy New Year!" (that may just be the friendly Oregonian in me, so precede at your own comfort level).

Explore further thesimplyluxuriouslife.com/january2 (the three fundamental components of a strong state of social well-being)

January 3
Growth and Continual Learning

Some of the most helpful, direction-changing, or life-affirming lessons I have learned have come from reading biographies, memoirs, and philosophical books. Beatrix Potter's life journey taught me many things and confirmed a fundamental element of living simply luxuriously: Refuse to follow societal nudgings or expectations if you do not like what they require and what they will offer. Julia Child's life taught me an abundance of life-truths; a necessary and reassuring one was that often an initial rejection is a test to determine your true desire.

And Benjamin Hoff's *The Tao of Pooh* underscored the gift we receive when we regularly take the time to be entirely on our own: "Music is the space between the notes — emptiness cleans out the messy mind and charges up the batteries of spiritual energies — Loneliness actually begins when all the spaces are full and the TV gets turned on to make it go away. The power of a clear mind is beyond description."

Some lessons can be hard to learn. But if we are resilient in our determination *to* learn, we will be given opportunities to acquire the knowledge we seek.

Part of me wishes I could live for centuries. My curiosity constantly uncovers new knowledge or insights, and each time I learn something new, I come upon a new unknown that piques my curiosity further, in a cycle that could continue endlessly.

To be fair, the learning process is not always fun. At times, it can be frustrating and even scary. Learning to appreciate our good health may require a brief dance with the reality of death (hopefully a momentary one). To learn our value and understand our truest gifts, we may have to experience extreme limitation, often created by our ignorance of our choices.

However, lessons need not be experienced as negative in order for us to learn. We can pick up a book on an intriguing topic, take an online course on something we wish to understand, or have in-depth conversations with people whose work we admire — all of it fuel for our desire to thrive and advance in the direction of our dreams.

Today, consider a gap in your knowledge base. Perhaps it is how to better communicate, or maybe you simply need to understand how to feel more comfortable with your own company. Maybe you need to learn to cook simple, yet delicious meals to meet your new year's goals. Don't wait for knowledge to happen to you; instead, choose to be a student and embark on a journey that is likely to be more enjoyable than you might think.

Petit plaisir Listen to Antonio Vivaldi's Four Seasons: Winter (L'Inverno) to invigorate your morning constitutional. After a long sunrise walk, savor a homemade buttery croissant while engaging in your favorite morning rituals.

Explore further thesimplyluxuriouslife.com/january3 (the importance of rituals)

January 4
Puzzling Out Nature versus Culture

No matter how far you think you've strayed from your true path, the moment you say I'm going to trust myself, I am going to follow my truth, the healing begins.
— Martha Beck

When, in a podcast interview, Martha Beck, author of *The Way of Integrity*, asked, "Does the culture nurture your nature?" I knew I had made the right decision to shift my life into a new chapter. She continued: "As long as the two [one's nature and the culture] go together, then we're in our integrity." For over twenty years, the culture and my nature did not get along, but I was determined to fit into the culture, telling myself I was bringing a touch of Shannon with me. But that's the problem: The world needs more than just "a touch" of who you are.

Often, beautiful puzzles come together in our lives. Such a puzzle can be magnificent, even awe-inspiring, but we are not always meant to be a part of it. Sometimes we have to see when we do not fit within a situation and say, "Another puzzle awaits me. I need to leave what I have been doing and find it or build it." Stepping away from something you have been doing is not easy; the outside world may even judge that you are making an unwise decision. But when your nature is not being tapped, you know you are trying to solve the wrong puzzle.

Such was the case when I made the decision to resign from my final teaching position: I realized that this job was not meant to be my puzzle. The culture wasn't nurturing for my particular understanding and approach to teaching and living well, and I found myself in a fight to maintain my well-being as I tried to perform to the high standard I had set for myself. Thankfully, I was already immersed in another culture (my writing) that did nurture my nature. I was able to see the difference between teaching and writing as they affected my health, my relationships, my mind, my entire well-being.

The pandemic didn't make my life worse; in fact, it was the opposite. Teaching from home, I saw improvements in my health, communications, personal connections — my overall well-being. I told myself I would find my courage to make a change.

Today, ponder the question: Does your culture nurture your nature? If not, rather than criticize the culture, acknowledge the truth you have discovered in the current situation (for example, it might be a puzzle, but one that is not meant to be yours). Then find or build a puzzle to which you can apply your awesome and unique gifts.

Petit plaisir For a late lunch, make a buckwheat galette with prosciutto, Gruyère, and egg and pair it with a glass of chardonnay and a green salad tossed with vinaigrette.

Explore further thesimplyluxuriouslife.com/january4 (a recipe for a buckwheat galette)

January 5
Be Open to Magic

In January 2017, central Oregon was slammed with a deluge of snow, breaking records more than twenty-five years old. Aside from my amazement, I was mesmerized and dazzled by the power of Mother Nature. This experience offers a reminder that life can amaze us. Often we cannot predict the magic that will occur, but the key to recognizing these unexpected events as indeed magical and not blockades or hurdles is to be prepared. The key takeaway I am trying to remember as I move forward is to be prepared to savor and not live in fear when such moments happen.

Regularly shoveling the driveway, having a garage and a house that has heat and pipes that aren't frozen, removing the snow on my roof to prevent damage — doing what I can to prevent the potential negative effects puts the odds in my favor. I also know that there are unknowns that I cannot predict. The good news is that, when we do what we can, when we educate ourselves, when we live in a place that can keep us safe and warm, no matter what Mother Nature brings, we can truly savor such unexpected moments, which have the potential to offer amazing highs and beautiful gifts.

The additional time at home gave me the ability to work entirely in TSLL office: catching up on e-mail, planning the first few months of the year, having time to read more books, *and* finally creating TSLL YouTube channel! I used this unexpected time provided by the snowstorms to dive into what I love, but your choice in such a situation will be unique to you. Maybe you will begin to explore something that, up until now, you have not had time to investigate. Maybe you will read an eye-opening book that will profoundly change your approach to the new year. Or maybe you will dive into the kitchen and bring your friends and family to the table for an amazing meal. Just listen to what is speaking to you and follow where it leads.

Life is full of magic. Stay open to the possibility of it happening, and live in such a way each day that you can see it and savor it.

Petit plaisir Order seeds for a small cottage flower and cutting garden: snapdragons, cosmos, nasturtiums, Prairie Sun black-eyed susans, larkspurs, sunflowers, and cups and saucers.

Explore further thesimplyluxuriouslife.com/january5 (the benefits of gardening)

January 6
Being Brave

Life offers amazing gifts to each of us. Your gifts, while they may bring the same euphoria or excitement as mine, will differ and will arrive at their own times and circumstances. I mention this because knowing what will make another human being happy absolutely is next to impossible. Yes, the more we know the person, the more time we spend with them, and the more opportunities presented to observe them as they go about their days, the sharper will be our perceptions about what makes them come alive. But each of us has our own path for tapping into the unique nature that resides within us all.

We can look to role models and those who have traveled a similar path and observe how their lives unfolded as they learned from their mistakes. This is all to the good, but we cannot expect the same results, the same reactions, the same feelings as the people we observe. Each person brings their unique observations, talents, and experiences with them to make the magic that inspires them to live their best life.

We must be brave enough to realize that while we can seek out advice from others, read books to gain a deeper understanding of a concept, issues, or event, we need to have the courage to create our own path. Along this chosen path, we will use the knowledge we have gained, the wisdom others have provided for us, as well as knowledge from our previous mistakes. But to assume that your life must mimic that of others, no matter how much we respect them, is to stunt the growth your life wants to reveal to you.

Find the courage within yourself, as this new year begins, to forge your own path, dive into your own unique undertakings that perhaps nobody you know has experience with. Trust your instincts and intuition, and proceed with patience. You will not regret this approach, and what you discover may thoroughly surprise you.

Petit plaisir Examine your home budget: Where can you trim? Where is money not being put to good use? Where can it be of more use?

Explore further thesimplyluxuriouslife.com/january6 (money: seven tips for a strong financial foundation)

January 7
Navigating through Struggles

For those of us who endlessly seek answers to life's infinite questions, it can sometimes seem as if the joke is on us. The questions keep coming, even if we find an answer to a previous uncertainty, which makes you wonder, why should you keep seeking? Why not settle for the answers you know and find peace with the unknown?

Fair questions, each one, but I cannot help but accept, based on the progress of my life, that while we may never reach an end to our quest, it will lead us down a path that is, with each answer, more in tune with what we seek, who we truly are, and what we truly need to be genuinely fulfilled.

Sometimes we think we know what will make us happy, only to have what we thought was a certainty pulled out from underneath us, leaving us a puddle on the floor for a moment until we can gather ourselves. At such times, the hindsight that will eventually reveal why such an event happened is not yet available, so we must trust that the universe has a grand plan that may just be better than what we thought we were going to be enjoying.

Life does not give out free rides, absolutely not. But what it does provide is road signs that clarify truths that initially appeared out of focus or unclear; if we have the courage to keep striving forward — not moping, but picking ourselves up and dusting ourselves off, keeping our lives in motion — clarity will gradually arrive. Responding to setbacks is not easy, and you might need to reach out for the hand of a friend or family member to pull you back onto your feet. Believe it or not, life does improve so long as we keep our confidence and awareness of our self-worth strong.

Adverse events would not happen if you weren't strong enough to withstand them. Think about this life-truth during moments of doubt. I have been knocked down more times than I can count, but the benefits always materialize after I pick myself back up and choose to strive forward.

Petit plaisir Look out for Mother Nature's wee creatures: A bird sleeps on my front-door wreath of dried magnolia leaves until tomorrow's sunrise.

Explore further thesimplyluxuriouslife.com/january7 (how to savor everyday moments of kindness)

January 8
Creating Your Dream Life

One of the most fortunate states to attain is to feel content within the life you have created for yourself, regardless of the decisions made by your loved ones for their journey. It is not that you disregard how those around you or those you hope to spend your life with are doing, but you know that whatever these people do, you have a life you can revel in, one in which you feel utterly secure and comfortable, one that you thoroughly enjoy.

Such a state is quite liberating, but it does not just occur. It takes conscious effort, attention, and discipline, and oh, how it is worth it. At the ground level, you cultivate a life around your values, passions, and talents. It takes time to reach this destination, but when you do, you radiate strength, quiet confidence, and a tranquil energy that people gravitate toward.

Today, or sometime in the near future, take a moment to sit down and assess how you are doing in terms of reaching this life milestone. If you don't feel at peace when others don't act as you would prefer in order to fulfill your needs, ask yourself, "What can I do to fill this need for myself?" "What is it that I am seeking?" Perhaps it is companionship, perhaps it is validation. While we understandably may desire the company of others, we can also do ourselves a tremendous favor by being our own best friend: speaking kindly about and to ourselves, taking care of ourselves, putting up necessary healthy boundaries, and seeking out others who respect us.

When you begin to treat yourself well, you refrain more from seeking outside approval because you have realized it was, instead, your own approval all along that you needed. When you reach this point, finding contentment with your life becomes much easier.

Petit plaisir Savor the lavender sunrise while taking an early-morning walk. Notice the different colors Mother Nature paints with from one morning to the next.

Explore further thesimplyluxuriouslife.com/january8 (inspiration for taking up walking)

January 9
Mastering Fear

Recently, I watched Oprah's OWN series *Master Class*, an episode featuring Jane Fonda. She talked about mastering the things we fear, the things that keep our feet stuck in cement, thwarting our ability to grow or overcome challenges and barring us from discovering our true capabilities. Simply put, she said, "When I'm afraid of something, I embrace it. I become its best friend. I know everything I can about it." When we do this, we dissipate the fear because we only fear things when we are uncertain about what they are made of. When we know all the ins and outs of the thing we fear, we can then prepare and deal with it appropriately and effectively.

Life continues to pull the puppet strings, it seems. Sometimes it pulls in a direction we would rather not go, but just as many times (and often more), it offers serendipitous moments that fill us with glee and absolutely astonish us. The irony is that we have more say in determining what life does than we realize.

However, if we rely only on hope, the life we desire will never occur.

Yes, this means that we must constantly be making conscious decisions. Yes, this means we must do the hard work, the research, and not just rely on hearsay. Yes, this means that we will have to be more organized, focused, and clear about what we want to achieve. And yes, most important, this means we must strengthen our emotional intelligence.

You propel yourself toward your destiny when you master your fears. To let fear master you is to deny yourself the beautiful and beyond-belief reality that might exist if only you were to step out of your own way. In other words, choose to be the master of your mind and your emotions. Seek out a counselor in order to invest in your emotional intelligence and mental well-being. Project the image and behavior of a person who is confident yet humble, serene yet strong, and observant as well as compassionate.

Petit plaisir Ease out of your workday and listen to Johann Sebastian Bach's Cello Suite no. 1, Prelude in G major.

Explore further thesimplyluxuriouslife.com/january9 (becoming the master of your mind)

January 10
South-facing Windows

Only three weeks after the shortest day of the year, ample and abundant access to natural sunlight presents a priceless gift.

When I first saw my house, which would become Le Papillon, it was the middle of July. The sun was generous, giving us long summer days, so the idea of how little sunlight would be present in the winter did not immediately enter my mind. Fast-forward six months, and quite the opposite is true: Daylight is more limited, requiring me to savor every drop, every minute of the well-known and beloved Bend's Bluebird Days (days in which the sky is a pristine bluebird blue *sans* a speck of clouds).

What caught my eye upon stepping into my future house were the sloping ceilings, stretching to heights of 15 feet, an ample garden, and a rockery, or rock garden (already landscaped and awaiting my preferences for flowers, herbs, vegetables, and fruits), the open common living space, which made the small (1,500 square foot) house appear far larger than it was, and a garage that opened to the back of the house rather than the front, enabling the front porch (with space for a swing) to be the welcome — a person, not a vehicle, lives here, and one who will share a friendly hello or welcome. What I saw, but did not yet fully appreciate, was the south-facing wall of windows — a total of nine, counting the glass door opening to my private garden porch.

These winter days of beauty and their recharging energy inspire me not only in my creative pursuits, such as writing, but in my excitement for the coming of spring, my reminder of the gifts of Mother Nature, and my understanding of how powerful sunshine can be wherever we find ourselves on our life journey.

Author Austin Kleon suggests we invest in something that "will outlast this." Whatever your "this" is — something hard to deal with, something you did not wish for — his suggestion is worth exploring. However it relates to your own life, what do you want to savor tomorrow and for the rest of your days? Today, your life journey may find you not living the life you hope you will someday live, but your someday can come if you invest today.

I invested in my tomorrows when I purchased Le Papillon, and each day, it surpasses my reasons for doing so. I wanted security, and I received peace of mind. I wanted simple daily living, and I received a muse. I wanted a home to comfort me, and I received a home for sharing love. I wanted a place to create, and I received a place to become.

The south-facing wall of windows gave me rejuvenating energy, little need for man-made energy (to help out Planet Earth), and a reminder that such a simple architectural detail can have profound effects on our well-being. It need not be large, it just needs to be intelligently designed as our minds and our temperaments respond in wondrous ways to the gifts of Mother Nature when we welcome them rather than try to avoid them or shut them out.

Today, find ways to welcome the sunshine into your life — literally or figuratively — and discover how life-lifting and life-transformative such a daily natural presence can be.

Petit plaisir Prepare a simple, comfort-food meal, elevated with a touch of French cuisine deliciousness. Let the red wine breathe, and situate your *mise en place* for a brioche burger and sweet-potato fries.

Explore further thesimplyluxuriouslife.com/january10 (recipe for brioche hamburger, complete with luxurious French delights: balsamic relish and garlic herbed butter)

January 11
Your One and Only Life

The universe wants to know what you want. Whether you call it the universe, God, the Divine, Goddess, or nothing at all, and while it may be assumed the universe can read your mind, here's some simple, but powerful advice: Even the universe does not know what you want unless you ask for it.

Not only do you need to ask for you it, you need to continue to ask for it by taking action, by how you live your life. Your action is your ask. Ask with sincerity and determination and persistence until the universe realizes you are not going to stop asking. From the goals you want to achieve and the life you wish to live to the boundaries you require in your life for healthy relationships, continue to ask (or in the case of boundaries, calmly, yet resolutely express them, and if they are not heeded, move on to people who will respect them), keep knocking on doors, keep picking up the phone, keep sending the e-mails, keep showing up in person.

If you have done the homework, if you have searched your soul and being and have taken the time to get to know yourself, you know that your requests are not empty wishes, but fruitful bundles of energy and vision waiting to burst forth and turn an idea into reality, if only you can find the help, the assistance, and/or the support you need. Keep asking. Keep being respectful, clear, and strong. But do keep asking.

You have one life. It is never a bad idea to repeatedly state this obvious reality. Understanding this truth will point you toward an infinite well of energy that will help you to push forward. Life is short, and your gifts are deeply needed — by those in your immediate world, by the world at large, and, most important, by you. You deserve to see what you can become when you realize your truest capabilities.

Do yourself this simple yet life-changing favor: Keep asking.

Petit plaisir Invest in hellebores. They should arrive in April and will begin blooming fully late next winter and each future winter against the last of the snow.

Explore further thesimplyluxuriouslife.com/january11 (inspiration for persevering and attaining your dreams)

January 12
Taking Risks

Finding our way requires each of us to take the helm of our ship's navigation system — in this case, our life — and steer with both hands and a sturdy stance. In other words, the only way to find our way is to courageously set our lives free, so that we do not just follow along and react to the world around us, letting it dictate which way we should go. Instead, we lead the way.

It may seem tempting at times to just "go with the flow," but if we do not steer through the waves (our own unique challenges), we will never know if we can make it through them. If instead we stay safely in the boat and just stay afloat, we will not drown, but we won't have a say in what shore we reach (or perhaps if we even reach shore).

No doubt you have read through the paragraph above and understand that risk taking and, more important, betting on yourself, is necessary if you are to discover what you really can do. No one has what you can give or share with the world. In this current time and place in history, you are unique. You may not know why, it may not yet make sense, but you do have something the world needs. Be courageous and take the helm, confidently navigating through the waves instead of letting the waves take you where they will, and be pleasantly delighted by what you discover you can do and why the world needs you once you decide to take charge.

How do you discover what you can uniquely give? It's simple: First, follow your curiosities, the ones that you never can seem to shake. Then read my second book, *Living the Simply Luxurious Life: Making Your Everydays Extraordinary and Discovering Your Best Self*, which offers chapter upon chapter of specific direction and ideas for unearthing your awesomeness and how to elevate it beyond what you may have thought possible.

Just when you think "it" may not come together, life will surprise you in wonderful ways. I experienced this in my own life when I founded TSLL blog and found Le Papillon and continue to experience it. It does not mean you will not face obstacles or frustration or sadness, but the surprises will buoy your spirits well beyond any days of doubt or despair and will reassure you that you have found the right path.

Ponder how you can take the helm and forge through your waves. You may never know in the moment what you are giving to the world, but in that moment, you do not need to know; you just need to give and be yourself. The fuel will magically seem infinite, and you will find it easier to remain present and enthralled in your efforts.

Petit plaisir Whenever you wake up early naturally, let your mind — thoughts not yet cluttered by the world — explore where they wish to go. Keep a journal by your bedside, jot down ideas, and let yourself explore possibility.

Explore further thesimplyluxuriouslife.com/january12 (discover your inner creative — a gift that resides within us all)

January 13
To Gain Perspective, Step Away from the Daily Routine

Sometimes we don't realize how much of a deep breath we need to take until we push ourselves to take it (even when we mistakenly think we don't have the time or resources to do so).

Every couple of months, I visit Portland for a day, and each time I venture to the Rose City, I quickly become aware how much I need to step outside of the daily routine that keeps my attention workweek after workweek — how much I simply need to gain perspective.

Sometimes we think we know what is best for us. We keep our head down and work until all is done, but when we do this, we can lose the ability to notice how refreshing, even necessary, it is to step back, take our foot off the gas, and catch our breath.

Letting ourselves explore what tickles our curiosity and letting ourselves not be constricted by a binding schedule — these moments enable us to breathe, let go, and remember all that truly matters and whether we need to spend any more time on the worries that put our mind in a tizzy.

While in Portland, I often step into Powell's Books to explore the new offerings, exchanging my consigned books for new volumes of interest. I zip into Zupan's to pick up my favorite French butter and take the boys for a walk around a favorite neighborhood. Each of these activities gives me time to breathe, to appreciate all that is going well, and to be thankful for the opportunity to step out of my everyday routine just for the day.

Returning home, I am more settled, giddy even, and glad to be back in Bend, yet grateful for the opportunity to have gained perspective.

Step out of your routine for a day, a half day, a few hours. Doing so does not mean your routine is bad or not working. Taking a breath often will allow you to acknowledge that the stresses you may be holding on to — created, for example, by the culture you work within — can be unnecessary. A breath can free us, remind us who is in the driver's seat, and strengthen our clarity about how we should proceed.

Petit plaisir Make a brown butter, lemon, and sugar crêpe dessert.

Explore further thesimplyluxuriouslife.com/january13 (recipe for brown butter, lemon, and sugar crêpes)

January 14
How to Attain True Contentment

Think about finding the right key to unlock a door. Navigating our way forward toward the life we desire works in much the same way. Often, if we force our way toward what we want — I will be married by a certain age, I will have 2.5 kids, I will make x amount of money, and then I will be perfectly happy — we end up more frustrated than fulfilled, more scarred than caressed by the amazing forces of life.

Often, we are confused about what we want. Often, rather than wanting specific things, what we really want is the *feeling* we believe those things will bring into our lives — contentment, fulfillment, love, happiness, etc. And as we become more familiar with ourselves, we discover that the path to happiness may be different than we imagined. The good news is that the life we are now creating is often far more fulfilling than what we thought we needed to bring us to the feeling we desired.

Ask yourself, what do I actual desire? Then ask, why do I desire the things, ideals, and outcomes that I have set in my mind? Once you realize that it is happiness and fulfillment you seek, continue to gravitate toward projects, habits, people, and routines that instill those feelings.

Petit plaisir Acknowledge personal growth with a celebration of quiet confidence and deepening peace of mind. Journal your observations in order to always remember such celebrations during times when you may temporarily forget.

Explore further thesimplyluxuriouslife.com/january14 (the power of journaling)

January 15
Opportunity

One morning, as I often did during the school year while teaching, I woke up around 5:00 o'clock, and learned that our school district was running on a two-hour delayed schedule. I had not looked at the weather forecast before going to bed and was shocked by the freezing rain that was wreaking havoc on the area's roadways, yet giddy at the opportunity that had just presented itself.

In that moment, I could have gone back to bed, but instead I was eager to take advantage of the two extra hours. Choosing to gobble up information about a project I was working on, I tuned into a couple of podcasts I had saved on my phone. With pen in hand, wide awake and not yet exhausted by a full day's work, I was ready to learn.

We all have such gifts, opportunities that we either make or that are thrust upon us. Some are small, such as the two extra hours I received that day, but others are large. Regardless of the size of an opportunity that briefly presents itself, if we continue to take these moments and apply them to the life we wish to live or use them to enhance the life we already are living, eventually the dream will become a reality.

When we are young, we can often miss opportunities because they may seem to be exhausting extra work when sleep may be beckoning. But as we learn as we mature, if we are willing to step into these opportunities, we may receive amazing and unexpected gifts. Before long, we have made gains without even realizing it, and in time, magic begins to happen.

Knowledge, information, and opportunities for growth exist all around you, no matter where you live, no matter how you live. Grab them, seek them out, and absorb these fleeting moments because who knows when they will come again?

Petit plaisir As you move about your day, listen to John Coltrane's "Giant Steps" from his fifth album of the same name. It contains all self-composed material and is a must-have for jazz lovers.

Explore further thesimplyluxuriouslife.com/january15 (opportunity's unexpected gift)

January 16
Obstacles and Your Journey

In the middle of a journey of change, we can run into a ditch — a deep, dark chasm of doubt and frustration. I have run into one more often than I would have preferred, but it is also true that, with time and self-growth, I more often also run into two other feelings: One reassures me I am indeed doing what I need to do and steadies my focus, propelling me forward despite the temporary uncertainty. The other feeling is a deep-rooted confidence in the journey I had chosen after much examination and contemplation.

In a segment that aired in January 2017 on "Afternoon Live" (KATU-Portland), I shared six ideas for sticking to the resolutions we make for the new year, and the last one revolved around the reminder that the universe will test you.

How will the universe test us? It has been my experience that, along the course of pursuing a dream or an idea, the universe will erect a roadblock that may seem permanent. (In reality, it is only temporary, but at the time, we do not understand this, and all we see is a halt in our progress.) Why does this happen?

To measure our desire. To determine — and really, this is a gift to you either way — if you truly do want what you say you do. When you run up against a roadblock, ignore your immediate response. Then, even while you are hurting, aching, or becoming more irate, never lose sight of what you are seeking. Keep striving forward.

Now, each time I strive toward a new goal and a moment of uncertainty or frustration arises, doubt always asks to dance, but I find it easier to dismiss it each time — and to do so more swiftly. My choice to keep stepping forward — determined to hold fast to the integrity of the project, objective, or outcome, but open to a better path forward — makes room for another amazing occurrence demonstrating that indeed the struggle is well worth it: I trust in myself and understand that I may need to polish my efforts along the way, but I am certain that my direction is correct.

I mention this inevitable, yet temporary emotional obstacle to remind you to not be stymied by the ditches you will run into. Just keep in the back of your mind the understanding that this is completely normal. What you need to assess in that moment is how you respond to the challenge.

Wade through your fears and come to understand how you feel about the direction you are traveling. Also explore logically why you are traveling the route you have chosen. Most likely, you will find you are making a journey that in the long run will take you somewhere you will be thankful for since you stayed the course.

Petit plaisir Cultivate a tranquil sleeping space. Consider soothing paint colors or wallpapering in a neutral, gentle print (all four walls).

Explore further thesimplyluxuriouslife.com/january16 (tour of my primary bedroom)

January 17
The Unknown and Debilitating Fear

As a child, did you have a favorite toy, blanket, or stuffed animal you would always take to bed with you? For some reason, sleep was easier to find, comfort easier to feel if your favorite blanket (no matter how tattered) was with you. In the *Peanuts* comic strip, Linus's blue blanket brought a feeling of security; it was a constant trusted entity, what he knew, and what brought him ease.

Our mind finds comfort with knowledge or known entities. The unknown freaks us out. Linus *knows* his blanket brings him comfort — it is a reminder of a safe, warm space, no matter where he is; even if the blanket itself actually does not provide the comfort, his mind rests in this belief. And even if we simply recognize a similarity (but know nothing else), our mind lurches toward what it recognizes. Humans hold tightly to cognitive biases unconsciously because we want to find certainty; that is where we find comfort. But superficial similarities can be akin to detrimental stereotypes that are based on one small coincidental shared trait and take into account nothing else.

By no means am I suggesting that, if you have gathered more information, you should not trust your intuition to flee or walk away. I am talking about the tickles of similarity that we often use as an excuse to stop seeking something better, stop seeking the potential for change, the change that will lead us to something we have been hoping for.

So instead of grasping for your "tattered blanket," thank it for easing your mind up until this point. Then put it down (perhaps washing it before you put it away in the linen closet) and go about the business of doing your homework: having patience with life and gradually exploring the new opportunity that has presented itself. I cannot promise that this will lead you to exceed your expectations, but I can guarantee that you will not find out if you don't at least give it try and let go of past fears.

Petit plaisir Listen to Mozart's Oboe Concerto in C major, K. 314, and lighten your mind's mood, letting the oboe's melody carry your confidence to a place of possibility.

Explore further thesimplyluxuriouslife.com/january17 (understanding the crucial importance of emotional intelligence and its ability to enhance work and life)

January 18
Go Beyond What You Think Is Possible

When we push what we think are the boundaries of our limitations, we open ourselves up to expanded options — opportunities or events that we previously perceived to be impossible but that we now consider viable.

The "scary" endeavor I, at long last, chose to pursue (incorporating my business) was in alignment with dreams I have always held and continue to strive for. And it is in such moments that Henry David Thoreau's quote from *Walden* rings true:

> I learned this, at least, by my experiment [staying in a small cabin in the woods near Walden Pond for two years]: that if one advances confidently in the direction of his dreams, and endeavors to live the life which he has imagined, he will meet with a success unexpected in common hours. He will put some things behind, will pass an invisible boundary; new, universal, and more liberal laws will begin to establish themselves around and within him; or the old laws be expanded, and interpreted in his favor in a more liberal sense, and he will live with the license of a higher order of beings. In proportion as he simplifies his life, the laws of the universe will appear less complex, and solitude will not be solitude, nor poverty poverty, nor weakness weakness. If you

have built castles in the air, your work need not be lost; that is where they should be. Now put the foundations under them.

Chasing our dreams comes with some unexpected and some expected "bills," but most are worth paying. Ultimately, the return on the investment we make regarding our dreams is unknown, but as I have experienced thus far in my life, beautiful, unexpected occurrences and opportunities continue to present themselves so long as I choose to believe in my journey.

And you should as well: Believe in what is speaking to you, what always occupies your heart and your mind, and keep striving forward.

The mid-point of January has come and gone, and we are now in the second half of the first month of the brand-new year. Why not take the time this month to invest in the foundation from which your dreams can spring?

Petit plaisir Take a midday nap after expending physical and/or mental energy on a task with which you are making progress.

Explore further thesimplyluxuriouslife.com/january18 (listening to your rhythms and understanding them)

January 19
Work Hard for Your Goals

Dreams that become realities arrive in unexpected ways, but none of our dreams come without excruciatingly hard work.

Time after time, my life has surprised me, shocked me, astounded me, and amazed me. Sometimes I know how I will proceed, and sometimes I do not, but each time, I have proceeded forward and figured out a path for myself. Sometimes I have models to follow and sometimes I do not. Relying on models assuages most, if not all, of my fears. Not having models is frightening, but I have found that only by moving forward is fear mastered.

What dreams do you have? What is holding you back? What is confounding you? I can assure you, if there is something that is perplexing you, there is a way to overcome it. There is a way to successfully navigate through it. In my heart of hearts, I do not think life presents us with something we cannot overcome. So long as you have made the best choices with the information you had at the time, you are where you need to be. The path may be unpredictable, but life can be the amazing experience we want if we live consciously.

January

Sometimes when we wish for something, we do not know the details achieving it will require, and so these unexpected events — good, bad, or seemingly out of the blue — are what would have been part of the plan in any case; we just didn't know these details existed when we had the dream. In fact, they will most likely be building blocks that will boost our confidence, improve our happiness, and open our eyes to perspectives that will help us appreciate the amazing life we get to lead all the more. So today I nudge you forward.

You *can* do what maybe, right now, you think you cannot. When you run up against life surprises, you can figure out a way to move forward, and you will be all the stronger and wiser for it. You can absolutely live the life of your dreams.

Petit plaisir Sow lettuce seeds — rocket/arugula and French mâche for fresh salad greens — and place them in pots on the garden porch by the end of February.

Explore further thesimplyluxuriouslife.com/january19 (how to sow your own seeds)

January 20
The Courage to Pursue Your Dreams

I will readily admit it: I am a dreamer. I can imagine, formulate, and curate ideas about projects, room décor, trips, outfits, how my days will unfold — all in my mind and without leaving the house. And while just exploring possibilities in my head makes for a lovely journey, I know that is not where life is lived. Life is lived based on the actions we take, on the courage we can muster, and the choices we say yes to versus those we pass up.

In a handful of instances, my life has reminded me of a lesson that Leonardo da Vinci summed up quite eloquently: "It had long since come to my attention that people of accomplishment rarely sat back and let things happen to them. They went out and happened to things."

I understand why many people sit back and behave passively, choosing to not ruffle feathers while patiently waiting for others to produce opportunities for them. It's safer, less risky, and reduces the chance of rejection. But it also increases the likelihood that your life will not be your own. After all, you are waiting for others to know what you need, want, and are capable of. But no one else truly knows what dances around in your mind as you daydream your far-fetched dreams. As actress Kerry Washington stated on *CBS Sunday Morning*, on October 7, 2018, "If

The Road to Le Papillon

I sit around and wait for other people to create magic in my life, then I will be waiting until the day I die."

But the exciting truth about life is that far-fetched dreams have a funny way of materializing when we have the courage to pursue them. The key? We must pursue them. We cannot sit back and hope they will eventually become our reality. We must be the advocate for our dreams.

Ask for what you want, seek out those who can help you live the life of your dreams, and along the way say yes to those who ask you for help or guidance. You will no doubt have something to offer them as they travel their own journey in search of their dreams.

Petit plaisir Enjoy a book set in the past, one that takes you to a beloved destination. For an Anglophile, I recommend the historical novel *The Mystery of Mrs. Christie*, by Marie Benedict; for the Francophile, there's Monty Don's memoir *A French Garden Journey: The Road to Le Tholonet*.

Explore further thesimplyluxuriouslife.com/january20 (how to live a courageous life)

January 21
Navigate without a Map, Seek Moments of Awe

The struggle to know which way to go as we navigate through life can be daunting and frustrating; at times, it may even feel futile as we think, analyze, and speculate upon what we should do. I can feel this way occasionally, and it has not stopped simply because I have found contentment in my life. However, when I find myself in this state, I am reminded of previous similar moments and am encouraged that somehow I found my way out and was fortunate enough to get on the right path.

So what is the lesson? How do we steer ourselves out of those moments of frustration? How do we ignore or bypass those early mornings when the sun has yet to come up and our mind is racing with worry and doubt?

For me, the first step is to merely get up and get busy doing something I love or working toward something I am passionate about. But beyond these two approaches, I am stimulated and enlivened when I intertwine time doing activities or spending time with people that leave me feeling inspired and loved. Interacting with amazing people, spending time at awe-inspiring events, or reading about people who do amazing things boost my positivity and remind me that I too am capable, that I will figure it out, and that life can be trusted.

January

In 2015, the *Wall Street Journal* ran an article titled "Researchers Study Awe and Find It Is Good for Relationships"; it revealed that experiencing awe has a profoundly positive effect on our way of viewing the world. What does a moment that may provoke the feeling of awe look like? It will be different for everyone. Perhaps you witness a beautiful scene in nature, or maybe an impressive athletic feat, or a euphoric moment at a concert, listening to your favorite artist. Or it may be something as simple as a moment with someone that was completely profound and unexpected.

The options really are endless, but the takeaway is to create and live a life that allows you regular opportunities to experience awe.

Petit plaisir Each week, peruse the Sunday papers, and keep up to date as monthly magazine issues arrive and/or become available. While you peruse, why not, nibble on a homemade croissant? (Find the recipe at https://thesimplyluxuriouslife.com/TSLLcroissantrecipe.)

Explore further thesimplyluxuriouslife.com/january21 (how to stay abreast of the news thoughtfully and healthily)

January 22
True Maturity and Retaining the Gifts of Being a Child

Oregon and the world lost one talented individual on January 22, 2018, when author Ursula K. Le Guin passed away in her home in Portland at the age of eighty-eight. A writer of fantasy and science fiction, Le Guin garnered top accolades during her career of more than fifty years. Her son said she continued writing until the end: "She was more or less never not writing."

During her lifetime, in her books and interviews, Le Guin shared many powerful insights about living well, women's equality, and other social and political issues, but one quote spoke to me: "I believe that maturity is not an outgrowing, but a growing up: that an adult is not a dead child, but a child who survived."

Another well-known and beloved author passed away four days before Le Guin: British ex-pat Peter Mayle, who lived and wrote about living in Provence since 1989. Mayle wrote about contentment: "I don't want to go anywhere else. I am happy where I am. That, I suppose, is contentment, and I shall always be thankful for the literary accident known as 'A Year in Provence' for helping me to achieve it."

Both authors have said that their success, while most certainly well earned, was not expected (Mayle) nor easy (Le Guin). But both did what they loved to do — write. Le Guin said repeatedly that a story must have something deep to offer readers, and Mayle remained resolute that a good story must be told with playfulness and a touch of whimsy to engage the reader. They both played with words, they both persevered in doing what they loved doing, and they both found an audience that gravitated to their sincerity, insight, wit, and talent. The fact that they wrote until the end of their lives is a testament to their passion for what they had the good fortunate to do for a living.

Not everyone wants to be a writer, but we do all have dreams of what an ideal career may be, and if we can mature as Le Guin says and be a child who survives and thus bring our most authentic selves to the world, well, that is true bravery.

Take care to not fall, lockstep, into what you are "supposed" to do. Rather, listen intently to what speaks to you, what intrigues you, and then pursue it without fail to see what it may become. That is indeed courageous living. And I have a feeling both Mayle and Le Guin would assure us that it is absolutely worth it.

Petit plaisir After awakening from a full night's sleep, enjoy a morning routine of ease, productivity, and enjoyment.

Explore further thesimplyluxuriouslife.com/january22 (the benefits of a good night's sleep)

January 23
Trust Your Journey

One thing that amazes and inspires me when I have been stuck at a crossroads in my life is how much I learn when reflecting back to a year earlier. Seeing where I was, what I was doing, who I was spending time with, what I believed was or was not possible never ceases to remind me that what I believe I can do and what I actually manage to do in such a short amount of time is nothing short of remarkable and would have likely seemed impossible to my former self.

Perhaps it is the same for you as well. Often when we are in the moment, submerged in our daily routine, we forget how quickly our lives can change. We forget how — with one unexpected introduction, captured opportunity, or risk taken — our world can change dramatically and in an instant.

So long as we place ourselves on the right track and begin to strive forward in the right direction, we are building momentum for the change we seek to occur. Accepting this logic is hard sometimes, but once we come to understand that there is much that is out of our control and instead take control of what we *can* maneuver, we set ourselves up for inspiring evolutions to reveal themselves.

You will undoubtedly have to confront unforeseen obstacles, but so long as you do address them and refuse to turn away, the path becomes clearer, and your dreams begin to become reality.

Petit plaisir Savor the weather outside at this very moment. Find something beautiful, awe-inspiring, and evanescent to celebrate. For me, during January, it is the gently falling snow, delighting in the birds flocking to their café at Le Papillon, and playing and walking in and shoveling the snow in pure enjoyment with my pups.

Explore further thesimplyluxuriouslife.com/january23 (encouragement to trust the timing of your life journey)

January 24
Less Complaining, More Trusting Your Journey

More confidence, less complaining.

I have decided recently to follow this motto. While superficially, such a statement would seem obvious in our efforts to attain success, it can be at times easier said than done. However, life has revealed that the more I complain, the less time I have to accomplish my goals. On the other hand, the more confidence and faith I have in myself to achieve what may initially appear to be difficult, the more likely I am to successfully attain what at first had seemed to be impossible.

After all, if you are complaining, you are not strategizing and problem solving. And you even miss out on the celebrations of what is actually going well (I promise, there is something!). On the flip side, if you focus on what you can do, you are using the limited energy you have in the most helpful way to attain your goals.

When we finally realize that our lives and our time are finite, we become more particular in scrutinizing how we spend our thoughts and our waking hours. Everyone has exactly the same amount of time every day. We can either choose to use the hours productively or waste them away, hoping a magical fairy godmother will arrive and rescue us. You would be correct to assume I am not putting much stock in the latter.

From this day forward, bank on yourself. Let go of the whining. Have confidence that what you are willing to work for, you will turn into your reality. Are you with me?

Petit plaisir Begin to build a community of trusted everyday acquaintances. Chat with neighbors as you tinker about, shoveling snow or running errands, taking walks, and enjoying the beautiful day.

Explore further thesimplyluxuriouslife.com/january24 (how to master the art of conversation)

January 25
Be Courageous

Twelve years. On December 26, 2021, twelve years had passed since TSLL blog began.

Courageous living does not mean we have to take down a bully (although it can). Often courageous living simply asks us to choose to live a life filled with joy and priceless everyday contentment. To the outside world, this approach may appear boring or odd, but the problem may be that it is something folks have not seen before (or seen that often); in many cases, it will not be something other people will initially understand or believe is possible.

I guess in a way, yes, courageous living does involve overcoming a bully, but as you continue to courageously live the life you love living, it does not feel as though you are engaging with an opponent at all; you expend little energy or worry about what others think and revel in the life you are living and growing. Bullies attempt to thwart or diminish someone; they believe that humiliating someone will help them appear superior — a state they believe the outside world must bestow. The reality is that insecurity riddles a bully's mind and life; when a bully observes someone who is at peace and content from within, instead of simply asking or exploring how it is possible, their weakness morphs into unconstructive behavior.

Throughout the twelve years of TSLL's growth and maturation, I have run into a few "bullies" along the way, though it happens less and less frequently. Or perhaps the frequency appears reduced because my courage has been strengthened from years of dedicating my time and curiosity to what I sincerely love doing — living simply luxuriously and sharing that it is indeed possible for each of us to find true contentment in our everydays. Even bullies want to find peace; they just may not know how to ask for it. And while I may not ever sit down with them directly, hopefully, the way I live my life will inspire their curiosity to one day explore and find the truth: We can all find true contentment because the skills to do so can be learned by each of us, and that learning will bring forth something unique that each of us has and that the world needs.

It takes courage to live a fulfilling and simply luxurious life, to live in a way the culture may not at first understand. But when you think outside the box, your bravery will be applauded by those secure enough in themselves to appreciate your quiet strength, and that applause will simply be the cherry on top of a life you have courageously built and love living each and every day.

Petit plaisir Snuggle into a favorite reading nook; if you have a pet who also likes to snuggle, welcome them into the space and read away.

Explore further thesimplyluxuriouslife.com/january25 (explore eighteen evening rituals to savor)

January 26
Exploring the Unknown During Times of Frustration

When a challenge presents itself in your life — the opportunity to learn something new, acquiring a skill you have never before attempted, resetting your routine — it is not easy at first. It can be tempting to throw up your hands and go back to the way you have always done things.

When we allow ourselves to be plunged into challenging circumstances — even with all of the uncertainty and moments of discomfort — we are doing ourselves a service. We are allowing growth to occur; we can see life in a new perspective and deepen our understanding about something more fully.

In our modern society, we are drowning in information, and while, in one way, it surprises me how we can cast such an abundance aside and go about with business as usual, at the same time, I understand. When we choose to bravely construct a life honoring our needs in order to bring our unique gifts to the world, choosing to continue with business as usual is more a choice of survival than of conscious disregard.

If you are having difficulty welcoming an opportunity, it may be due to the energy required to accept something new — it can be exhausting. Prior to welcoming these desired changes, choose to change one thing at a time. No matter how small, tiny changes in your habits eventually add up to a significant evolution.

When you are in the middle of trying something new and it becomes difficult, keep pushing — keep holding that yoga pose, keep

taking those dance lessons. Skill is not acquired overnight, but with patience, attention, and hard work, it gradually becomes part of you.

Petit plaisir Spend five minutes meditating or take your meditation app along on your morning or evening constitutional (if you have a pet who would like to join you, include them too).

Explore further thesimplyluxuriouslife.com/january26 (how to meditate and the benefits of meditation)

January 27
Navigating the Unknown

As an unknown and unwanted situation begins, our basic human reaction is fear. Some of us panic, while others stay measured and calm as we try to wrestle with the negative emotion that wants to grab our attention. As I walked Norman and Oscar one morning, I was reminded of how striving forward and winning the wrestling match with my fear can have a very good outcome. We wandered through innumerable pine trees, around and over the top of rock ledges, all just beside the Deschutes River, which runs through Bend.

Over the past five years, the boys (my dogs) and I have made this walk at least one hundred times. We love this route, where the soundtrack is the river running, sometimes whispering in the summer, sometimes with more volume in the spring, but it is always present and soothing. The trails run everywhere; many are not on any map.

The first time we walked these trails, I did so with more caution. I did not know where each would lead and could not see very far ahead or around me, as the forest was dense with lush, low shrubs and bushes and a multitude of pine trees — a beautiful aesthetic and setting for the mind to be present and decompress. However, on this first outing, Norman was beyond ecstatic, and he tore forward faster than I wished to go at a swift walking pace. Before long, I had lost track of him and became worried. Where did he go? I couldn't see beyond about 50 feet. I searched and searched, and asked passing walkers if they had seen a small red-and-white dog — no such luck. I went back to where we had already walked, but still no Norman. Then I heard a shout from a walker I had passed: "I found him!"

I ran forward along the trail where I had yet to walk — and found that Norman was searching for us. The helpful walker said, "He won't come to me, but he's looking for you!" He was looking for us but had followed the trail forward, because, *Why would I go backward, Mom?* (input Norman's voice in that question).

Norman learned one lesson during this heart-pounding (for me) situation. To this day, based, I assume, on that experience, if he gets far out ahead of me, he will stop and check to see if I am coming (I kid you not). The situation indeed scared us both.

This once scary, unknown terrain of twisting trails is an area we now know like the back of our hand (paw). Today, I no more fear Norman getting lost than I do falling out of love with France. We now know the area well, and know that if we each keep walking forward, we will meet each other — and we always do. Norman has never again gotten "lost," and I have never worried once since that first and only experience.

(Lesson 1) The unknown is scary when we are not prepared; acquiring credible knowledge calms us and eases the worry. (Lesson 2) Ask for information from those who know more than you do; my fellow dog walkers knew that area better than I did and helped to locate Norman quite quickly. (Lesson 3) Deeper appreciation and deeper awareness of what we value and care for increases quickly and in abundance when we are awakened to how fortunate we were to have it in our lives in the first place. (Lesson 4) Strive forward and do not dwell on the negative. I immediately began asking for help, but I did not go forward. That was my error: The only way to move through something is to strive forward.

(Some of you may wonder where Oscar was during all of this. He was trotting right alongside me the entire time. I never once worried about him as he is my shadow.)

The pandemic in which the world found itself in 2020/2021 offered many unknowns, but every day we had the opportunity to learn something new — when we trusted credible sources, when we did not overwhelm our minds so that we could think calmly and rationally and take care of ourselves mentally and physically. We made it through, and the only way through to a better outcome — to a better world that knows how to handle this situation should something similar emerge — is to strive forward and grow, and then apply the lesson.

Unknowns want to teach us something, but we have to choose to learn. What awaits us on the other side is knowledge of how to navigate unknown situations and lessen or squash our fear.

Petit plaisir Attend a yoga class or a fitness class of your preference. If you have the ability to do so near or surrounded by Mother Nature, all the better for the body and the mind.

Explore further thesimplyluxuriouslife.com/january27 (navigating the unknown)

January 28
Your Journey

What would you do if you knew you could live comfortably for the rest of your long life?

Often fear dictates how we live our lives rather than sincerity, passion, and true love for what we would do for free, whom we would love, where we would live, and the risks we would take. I have written many different posts, all inspired by the idea of shifting our motivator from fear to hope, to trust, to confidence in one's self, even when unknowns are knocking.

Having discovered that indeed it is wise to listen to my inner voice, I have learned to follow where it wants to lead me even if I have no true or concrete clue about where it is taking me.

An intelligent life unfolds gradually and is intertwined with struggles from time to time. But so long as we do not cower when confronted with unwanted events, we are capable of experiencing a life we did not previously imagine to be possible — a life of deep contentment, whether or not it follows "traditional" expectations. It may not make sense within the culture where you find yourself, but it may be realized in the future.

Consider why you have made the decisions you have made: Was it fear or a positive influence that prompted you to choose what you did? When you can honestly answer this question for each life decision that has led you to where you are today, you will begin to have peace as you go about your day, even if you run into naysayers. You know you are aligned with your truest self, and when you are deeply immersed in what you are doing, you do not notice other people scoffing at your decisions. You have met the opportunity, believed in and seized it, and love doing what you are doing.

Give a nod of welcome to your courage to honor those callings that relentlessly pursue you, and you will reach your full potential.

Petit plaisir   Enjoy a hot bubble bath, followed by snuggling into a comfy chair, listening to a classical music station (KUSC.org is my favorite) while reading a much-anticipated book or article.

Explore further   thesimplyluxuriouslife.com/january28 (how to simplify your entire life)

January 29
Perseverance: Don't Give Up

What if you walked away before it all came together? What if you were one more step, one more day, week, month, even one more year away from seeing your dreams materialize? But time has passed with no progress, you are frustrated, exhausted, and disheartened, and you decide to stop.

The tricky part is, we cannot know for certain how close or how far away we are at any given time, but we know more than we realize if we will only tune into our intuition. First, our intuition knows if we are sincerely passionate about something. Even if we cannot coherently explain our undying desires to someone else, we may have this innate pull, longing, or drive to do something; we know our energy levels and our capacity to have enough to endure long stretches of uncertainty. Second, while we may not know when we will "break through the wall," if you have been tuning into yourself and into the environment in which you are immersed, and if you have so far been heeding your instincts and they have told you that you are doing something right, you know more than you realize.

Check in with yourself regarding these two points, and if you were nodding your head, agreeing that both offer auspicious indications, then stick with it. The wall is about to break. Even on small things we are trying to figure out, it can sometimes seem we will never do them right up until . . . we do. Case in point:

I had been scratching my head, asking for help from a few people who knew the blog's intention and premise nearly as intimately as I did, to help me construct a more precise and accurate logo (one line descriptor). At one point, I thought I had it, but something still did not ring true. However, as I read a book about travels to France, a phrasing caught my eye and sparked a new turn of phrase: Cultivate true contentment, the art of living a life of quality over quantity.

I played around with it, and nearly immediately, I knew it was the tagline I had been looking for pretty much since the founding of the blog. Yes, the previous logo — "Refined living on an everyday income" — worked, but it was not entirely inclusive of the grander goal of living simply luxuriously.

If you are sticking to a resolution and just barely seeing results, keep doing what you are doing. Stick to that workout plan, stick to the daily habits that are making a positive difference. Perhaps your stick-to-itiveness pertains to a long-term goal you have been working on, and maybe the grand goal has not happened yet. Don't stop just yet.

Petit plaisir Brighten your living space by purchasing a bouquet of flowers for your home, and delight in their continued blossoming.

Explore further thesimplyluxuriouslife.com/january29 (how to arrange your own simple flower bouquet)

January 30
Resolutely Letting Go

Not knowing is vexing, perplexing and, yes, a gift.

I remain a planner in one form or another — for my future, for tomorrow, for the coming week — and I take great pleasure in clarifying an idea and have found that there are many benefits. But the truth is that we cannot know how events will precisely unfold, no matter how much precise planning we engage in.

I was reminded of this truth as I was taking the boys for a walk in the sunshine on a late-winter morning. As I walked, I was dreaming of long-held goals and wondering when or if such events might occur. But then I realized that such questions are not the ones to be asking. In fact, we need only ask ourselves two revealing questions, so long as we answer them honestly: *What am I doing now to bring me closer to a wished-for opportunity. And should it arrive, how do I plan to pounce upon it and turn my dream into a reality?*

As I asked myself these questions, I was doing what I could and needed to do. Following this realization, I reminded myself of all that I had to savor at that very moment, including the gift of relaxing and being present. At that moment with the dogs, taking in beautifully crisp, fresh air, gazing upon Mother Nature, I was indeed feeling quite fortunate.

We can frustrate ourselves unnecessarily at times and squash the many opportunities to find joy in the everyday when we worry about what will be instead of appreciating what is right now. While I regress from time to time and have anxieties about the future, it now happens far less often, and thus I have been enjoying everyday moments far more regularly. From working on my morning *New York Times* daily mini puzzle, to reading a book and losing all track of time, the beautiful moments are everywhere, and we do not want to miss them wondering about the future.

Take the time to determine a plan of action to follow to strive toward your goals and not be taken off track. Then live and enjoy the life you have the good fortune to build for yourself.

Petit plaisir Pay your monthly bills and celebrate each time you are able to do so with ease. Schedule time to talk with your financial adviser regularly — a six-month check-in or more often, depending upon your financial goals and chapter in life — to assess your investment for retirement.

Explore further thesimplyluxuriouslife.com/january30 (twelve steps for mastering your money)

January 31
Dreams and the Universe

Dreams can come true. Yes, they can.

And the only way I have found to experience extraordinary dreams coming to fruition is to take big risks. Do not get me wrong, I have taken big risks and fallen flat on my face many, many times. Ah, that time in my mid-twenties when I hopped on a plane to meet a close friend's brother — nope, that did not work out well at all — or that time I forgot to share with the movers that I would need them to pack up my rental as well as move it — yep, that made for an extremely long day (and night) in order to be moved out by the last day of the month. Yet it takes only one success to be motivated to never stop trying until what you seek materializes.

What have you taken a risk for lately? What are you hoping will materialize as you set your goals, refine your hopes, and dare to dream? I encourage you to stretch beyond what you think you are capable of and, if you have not already attained what you seek, to take that risk one more time. Why? Because whether it is with career dreams, travel dreams, romantic dreams, or personal, individualized dreams, the reality that can appear before your eyes can be something you never have imagined or perhaps have even brushed aside as impossible.

The good news is, your dreams can indeed come true. If the last few years of my life are any indication, dreams (no matter how small or large) do come true. But we have to have the courage to ask for them, be vulnerable, and listen to ourselves so that we know what it is we actually desire. Sometimes we dismiss what we discover; we think it could not be possible that the universe would say yes. But the funny truth — the beautiful and exhilarating and heart-warming truth — is that it does say yes. We just have to keep asking and investigating ourselves as we step nearer and nearer toward the truth of what is meant for each of us.

Maybe that sounds fantastical, but in all honesty, it all begins with you. I assure you: Beautiful, magnificent, extraordinary moments, individuals, and lives await.

Be honest with yourself. Fall in love with your own company. Fall in love with the life you have the opportunity to live each and every

day. Then have the courage to do what you want to do and be what you want to be.

Petit plaisir Check in on the lettuces you sowed two weeks ago. They might just be sprouting, and in about three to four weeks' time, you will be enjoying fresh greens in the middle of winter.

Explore further thesimplyluxuriouslife.com/january31 (potting table post and nine ideas for organizing an inviting indoor gardener work space)

February

Be Yourself Fully, but Stay Vulnerable

February

The final full month of winter, February also enjoys the unique distinction of being the shortest month. As a child, I always considered having my birthday in this month a special accident; after all, if one was going to be born in any month, the likelihood of being born in February was the slimmest. (Little did I know the odds had to do more with biology and the human gestation period, but still, even knowing the realities as an adult, I am a proud Februarian birthday baby.)

Hints of spring peek up every other year or so in the middle of February, just enough of an inconsistent occasion to remind us to delight in warmth that arrives, inexplicably, only to be followed, perhaps, by a storm of two feet of snow, as was the case in 2019 in Bend, Oregon. I reveled in this snowy surprise as we were given a week off from the classroom, to give households time to shovel snow so that we could make our way to the stores for basic necessities. In that particular year and during that particular week, I celebrated my fortieth birthday, and it was a delicious and wonderfully memorable occasion.

All of this is to say that any given month is as special or as mundane as we choose to see it. Turn your birthday month into something special, turn the shortest month of the year into something special, turn your life into something special — because you have within you the ability to leave a legacy that will outlast your time on earth. You have the ability to explore your childhood dreams — unlimited, vast, initially thought impossible or absurd. As we come to realize how short life is and how fortunate we are to be alive, those dreams are worth pursuing with all of our might and heart.

Devoting myself exclusively to being a writer and blogger is a childhood dream realized (the former more so than the latter, as blogging wasn't even a word in the 1980s, let alone a profession). My love of the written word — both expressed by my own hand and absorbed by my mind while reading great prose — drew me to teaching, and it was this love that helped me find the courage to conclude my twenty-year chapter of public school teaching and trust my inner compass to work entirely on my own.

Our childhood dreams and wonderings have much to offer. When we were children, our minds wandered wildly, freely, and creatively, without worry or limitation. As adults, we should cherish those ideas and activities we gravitated toward, dared to believe possible, and enjoyed doing in our own time, even if nobody else understood what captured our minds and attention. Our childhood dreams offer us a gold mine of *aha*'s awaiting our exploration.

February 1
Never Give Up Your Dreams

Recently, I was playing fetch with my dogs, and after one toss of the ball, Norman and I ended up looking fruitlessly for it after it took an interesting bounce. It seemed we had looked everywhere, in every possible corner, nook, or weird location it could have slipped into. We stopped our search momentarily, but later Norman and I returned to look for a ball that I refused to believe had just magically disappeared. In a most unlikely spot, we found it, and oh, was he overjoyed.

I began to think about how life often takes a similar course. Sometimes, even after carefully mapping out our steps and tirelessly checking all of the boxes, it may seem that what we seek disappears from our grasp. But sometimes we have not checked out all of the possibilities for how to make it happen. Sometimes we have been so focused on what we were told would happen if we approached our goal in a certain way that we ignore other ideas and methods and trajectories (such as the ball landing precisely in the elbow of two branches of the snowball shrub, nearly camouflaged from our searching eyes).

Don't think for one minute that what you desire cannot happen. Prior to moving to Bend, I had been on a multi-year journey, figuring out how to move to the place I now call home, a place that offers me opportunity for growth, proximity to Mother Nature, and intimacy in a community that I can connect with and become a part of with enthusiasm. Along the journey toward Bend, life threw some unexpected hurdles that initially left me doubtful that I could make it my reality, but then I reminded myself that the determined find a way, honing their patience and widening their open-mindedness along the way.

As Oscar looked on, Norman and I quickly went back to playing fetch, and the pleasure and joy on his face when he found what he thought was lost (it was, of course, his favorite ball) served as a simple reminder of the satisfaction and joy we can find when we help ourselves out by refusing to give up on what we truly feel drawn to bring into our lives. Dogs and their balls, people and their dreams: True contentment arrives when the two come together.

Because there is always a way forward as we seek what we want, know that it must be somewhere, and never stop looking, even when initially it doesn't materialize.

Petit plaisir Read *The Courage to Be Disliked*, by Ichiro Kishimi and Fumitake Koga.

Explore further thesimplyluxuriouslife.com/february1 (the courage to live fully and deeply: seven ideas to put into practice for a life of true contentment)

February 2
Be Your Unique Self

*Have you ever realized that when
people say you've changed
it's just because you've stopped
living your life . . . their way?*

Sometimes, we find ourselves frustrated because we cannot see our lives mirrored in the way others are living. After all, we are, to one degree or another, social creatures and want to feel included. Whether it be in grand or seemingly small ways — when we have attempted with great effort to be seen and to find others who understand us or are similar to us, but without success — it can be tempting to assimilate.

But to acquiesce to becoming something we are not is to be untrue to the light that is uniquely ours and that the world needs to see. The majority of people in the world or in our lives may not understand or agree with who we truly are and how we know our lives need to be for us to feel truly content, especially if we have not been completely honest in how we have presented ourselves. But we cannot let the majority's lack of understanding stop us. Given time, we can make great changes, but they may happen only inch by inch, and we can never inch toward the change we seek if we are not courageous enough to be who we truly are.

In the news as well as in my everyday life, I often see people being courageous enough to be who they are, abide by their core principles, and soldier forward, even if the majority doesn't follow. Perhaps you have your own examples that come to mind. Shedding the layers of societal expectations that do not align with our sincere selves lifts a burden whose true weight we did not understand until it was removed. In fact, as Martha Beck writes in *The Way of Integrity*, stepping into our integrity, being our true selves in our everydays, delivers more of the things we long for: "The closer we come to our integrity, the more 'magical' our lives become."

The foundation for a fulfilling, joy-filled life is set when you realign yourself with your true self. It will take courage, but what you are gathering up your courage for is one of the easiest capabilities you possess — being yourself.

Petit plaisir Enjoy a simple entrée: salmon rubbed in warm spices, placed on a bed of black rice, and topped with a fresh relish of avocado, tomatoes, corn, onion, and lime juice.

Explore further thesimplyluxuriouslife.com/february2 (recipe for spicy salmon rub with avocado and corn salsa)

February 3
Trust Your Intuition as You Plot Out Your Journey

Have you ever been in a situation and did not know what to do, but you knew you needed to do something?

As I am admittedly a searcher, I regularly assess and challenge myself to grow. I know I can always learn something new and will forever be a work in progress, but lately I have realized that some of my approaches (perhaps small and insignificant to the outside world, yet significant to me) have not been helping me progress toward certain goals I have set. So I sat down and did a little self-assessment.

As I went about my reflection, I came across two quotes. One by Tony Robbins, "Stay committed to your decisions, but stay flexible in your approach," and one from Bruce Lee, "Absorb what is useful, discard what is not, add what is uniquely your own." As I read these quotes a couple of times, to let them truly sink in, I realized there were a couple of habits that I routinely engaged in that, while enjoyable, were not helpful; they were, in fact, making me quite frustrated, as I was expecting certain results and not attaining them.

Doesn't the well-known adage state that insanity is continuing to do the same thing but expecting different results? Well, unbeknownst to me, that was exactly where I found myself. So a change was in order.

Let's take a close look at the quote by Bruce Lee, especially the last directive. Often we forget that we each have something unique to add to our efforts as we pursue our goals. We have something to offer that no one else does, and while we may look to others as mentors or for guidance, we truly do have something unique within us. It is imperative that we feed this gift and not drown it out because it doesn't make sense to others — or maybe, at first, even to ourselves.

Let go of habits that no longer assist you in proceeding toward your goals, yet remain resolute that you will indeed be successful in your journey. Listen and trust your intuition because when you let go of habits that are holding you back, your wings become more capable of carrying you where you intend to go.

Petit plaisir Watch *How to Catch a Thief*, with Cary Grant and Grace Kelly, set in the south of France.

Explore further thesimplyluxuriouslife.com/february3 (eight ways tiny habits will set the stage for the grand changes you seek)

February 4
Lose Yourself in Your Work and Revel in Every Minute

Whenever my schedule allows me to devote my sole attention to the blog and writing, I stop in to one of my favorite patisseries, bakeries, or cafés and type away. I am one of those camper-outers; I will find a table and chair and lose all track of time until I realize I should probably buy something else in order to pay the "rent" that's due on the space I am occupying.

I bring up this favorite pastime of mine because, on two separate days, I packed up my computer and set off to work, first in one favorite haunt and then a new one I wanted to explore. When I stated at one counter as I was ordering that I would be working away at my computer, the barista offered a conciliatory sigh, as if to say, "That's too bad." I was actually shocked by this because I had forgotten that too often we associate the word "work" with something negative. Why have we done this?

Well, it only makes sense that if we have to do something we don't want to do, this computes as drudgery. And at certain times, we all will have to be involved with work we don't necessarily enjoy (a summer during high school comes to mind when we students worked alongside the janitors to clean the building for the upcoming school year; the company of the custodial staff was great, the work extraordinarily hard), but it doesn't always have to be this way.

I feel beyond fortunate to find myself regularly losing track of time as I come up with ideas, writing and exploring for simply luxurious life projects and posts. Now that I have left teaching and stepped out on my own, my hope is that in the future I will have that opportunity more frequently. Either way, even if we only are able to do the work we love in our off time, what a gift, no?

The rewards, the sense of productivity and purpose, have a magical way of filling a void that in the past, when my self-awareness and mastery of my mind were less well-honed, have filled me with worry, angst, and unnecessary work.

I hope you continue to seek out work you can embrace fully. Fully embracing your work makes you better able to live in the moment, to be open to what unfolds, and to lose the dread that many have when they get up in the morning. Waking up without the alarm clock will become more common, as you wish to get the day started . . . Yes, it will happen, and as I finally had the opportunity to begin experiencing in July 2021, it is an amazing feeling.

Doing work you love will not necessarily mean your life will become a utopia, but it will be pretty close.

Petit plaisir Bookend your day with walks in your neighborhood.

Explore further thesimplyluxuriouslife.com/february4 (seventeen reasons to love your work)

February 5
Your Unique and Rich Life

When contemplating the definition of a truly rich life, and thinking about how to create it, I continue to come to the conclusion that any definition will be different and unique because the ingredients vary with each individual. With that in mind, I first want to list a few words that for me adequately describe a rich life: free, content, enduring, secure, peaceful, challenging, yet successful (on my own terms), healthy, regret-free, growing.

I am sure there are more, but the way I like to think of it is that to be able to hop on a plane to go anywhere my heart desires would encompass all of these descriptors. It does not mean I want to board the next flight to Paris (okay, bad example) because I genuinely love being at home, but it would be an amazing feeling to know that I *could*, if I wanted to, be my own boss and take the time to fly where I needed or wanted to be. (Of course, I would need to be in good health and financially secure in order to have such an ability.) In essence, this is the barometer by which I would measure my success on my path to creating a rich life.

How would you describe a rich life for yourself? What would it include? What would it look like and how would it feel?

Take some time to contemplate your idea of a truly rich life; perhaps even make a list of what comes to mind. You might be amazed at how truly rich you already are. After all, money can only get us so far; after getting your financial house in order, it is up to you to make the most out of this one life that you have.

Petit plaisir Sit down in the evening and melt with the help of Antonio Vivaldi's Concerto for Three Violins in F RV 551.

Explore further thesimplyluxuriouslife.com/february5 (three ways to design a life that works best for you)

February 6
Choose to Dance

Sometimes it is easier to be a spectator. Sometimes it seems better to sit and wait. Sometimes we tell ourselves that we are just lying low until . . . But really, what are you waiting for?

Recently, I came upon some news that prompted me to ask myself just this question — what was I waiting for? And secondly, why was I waiting at all?

Life truly does favor those who approach it with appreciation, not taking for granted that it will be here tomorrow. Whether it is to enroll in that tai chi class you have been hesitant to take, or to stand up for yourself the next time someone makes a joke at your expense, or maybe to start taking small steps toward a tremendous goal, start now. Start today. By deciding to make the effort now, you are already one step closer than you were a minute ago.

I must confess, the planner in me loves to put my entire dream life on paper and then list in detail the steps that will be necessary to create it, and while I highly suggest this process, the next step — putting those steps into action — can be intimidating. In fact, now that I am in my forties, I have greatly reduced the amount of time I spend planning. I keep it simple, listing no more than a handful of objectives or intended outcomes. I make a short list of three or four actionable items, and then I let them rest, to be read easily over the course of the next twelve to eighteen months. The fewer large goals I seek, the more successful I have found myself to be. I focus more easily on a short list and am far less distracted by other, less important items that may have made their way onto similar lists in the past.

Maybe you feel that now is not the perfect time to take that risk or to try something new, but ask yourself honestly, when will the time ever be perfect? Make the most of today, and who knows what opportunities you will create, people you will meet, or memories you will catalog when you step out of your comfort zone just a bit. Free up your mind to experience life, and let it surprise you. So long as you are pointed in the right direction, with eyes wide open and your energy prepped to take action, life will meet you at the dance in some form or fashion. Choose to dance.

Today, make a list of no more than five large, conceptual goals you are seeking. Below each item, note three or four actionable tasks you need to engage in to arrive at the desired destination. Do not be too strict about the timeline, but do regularly check in on your progress.

Petit plaisir Thin out your rocket and mâche starter lettuce plants and place them back under the growing lamp until they are strong enough to thrive outside.

Explore further thesimplyluxuriouslife.com/february6 (inspiration for taking a chance on your dreams)

February 7
Follow Your Inner Compass

On one episode of *The Oprah Winfrey Show*, Oprah interviewed writer and director Tom Shadyac, who said, "If we don't do what our heart wants us to do, it will destroy us." While this may seem to be an alarmist statement, it immediately resonated with me.

We all have innate abilities — many that take time and conscious effort to discover and nurture. We all have unquestionable passions — things we enjoy immersing ourselves in and can get lost in for hours without recognizing the passage of time. The beauty of following our heart, listening to our inner compass, is that they are very rarely wrong and become more and more accurate the more we choose to listen to them. And while following our passions may not initially lead to a steady paycheck, with patience, persistence, and a stubborn focus on the goal that refuses to blink, the ability to one day do what we love will materialize.

Often it feels as though we will never reach this point, but just as often, people stop just short of the finish-line tape. Complete the race. Go the full distance. You have come this far. Do not stop now. Keep toiling, keep working. The passion you have for what you are doing will continue, and once you reach your destination, you will be very glad that you pushed through the pain and questioning. After all, we are only allotted so much energy on any given day, so why not expend it on things we value?

My father asked me a question in the months leading up to my decision to retire early from teaching. He asked, "What does your gut tell you?" At first, I dismissed it: How could a response to such a simple question help with what felt like one of the most significant decisions in my life journey. A week or two later, I realized that, absolutely, such a simple question and an honest response to it can be very enlightening. Our "gut," or intuition, is honed over years of experience with ourselves and the world — if we are paying attention and are self-aware. Having made decisions or lived through experiences that were not right for our life journey, as well as experiencing when something is right for us, we know certain things at our core.

You know what your gut tells you. You just need to be brave enough to follow its sage advice.

Petit plaisir Invest in quality bedside table lamps. A gentle dimmer will allow them to cast a warm and functional light that makes for a beckoning sleeping space.

Explore further thesimplyluxuriouslife.com/february7 (explore intuition — when to trust it and when to ignore it)

February 8
A Strengthened Intuition Is a Wise Guide

To think we know what life has in store for us from day to day is to forget that while we may have control over our own actions, preparation, and thoughts, we do not have control over those around us.

When I was in my mid-thirties, someone from my past contacted me. It was someone I have not been in contact with for so long that I was completely shocked and stunned speechless for a moment. While it took me some time to understand why my past had reared its head, I came to the conclusion that I needed to be reminded of something I thought I had absorbed and learned: I had a tendency to lose confidence in myself when life became challenging.

What lesson had I learned from this phone call, you might be wondering? Trusting my intuition. Twenty-two years ago, I made the decision to walk away from a relationship — really more than that; I was engaged to be married. While I did not have concrete knowledge that it was not the right direction for the path I wanted my life to take, I sensed choosing to step into this marriage would be the wrong decision for the life I intuited was possible, and, more important, saying yes due to a feeling of obligation screamed, *Call it off if you care about either one of you.* After much thought and contemplation, even though all the arrangements had been made and "save the date" cards mailed, I gave him back the ring.

I have never regretted that decision, but there have been times when I doubted my gut in the face of other decisions — whether to chase certain dreams, take certain calculated risks, etc. If for only a moment, that phone call, and all it brought back, reminded me that indeed my intuition is very well-conditioned, and I need to trust it, especially in those situations when I have no way of acquiring all the information I might wish to have.

Our lives have a wonderfully powerful way of teaching us what we need in order to move forward to live contentedly. And while I am not one to linger in the past, there are instances when we need to pause and ask ourselves why a particular lesson keeps returning. How should I react? Most important, what is the lesson I need to learn in order to move forward?

If you can learn to trust your intuition, you will be richer than you ever were in the past, and a brighter future can begin to unfold for you. Your future can hold the brightest days of your life.

Petit plaisir Watch an episode of *The Secret of the British Garden*, hosted by Monty Don, on Acorn TV.

Explore further thesimplyluxuriouslife.com/february8 (twelve ways to learn the lesson)

February 9
Your Unique Journey

Consider an apple blossom or the blossom of any tree as spring returns. It is delicate, easily stripped away by a late-spring frost, yet, with careful nurturing, and with the last frost behind the gardener and an expansive, warm summer ahead, the fruit begins to emerge where once the blossom appeared. At that point, barring catastrophic weather, the basics are all that is needed as the fruit tree and Mother Nature provide them instinctively.

Our lives resemble the journey of fruit. While initially we are delicate, once we are standing on our own two feet — involved in our full life journey — we can be powerful in ways we may never realize unless we discover our innate gifts and nurture ourselves.

Recognizing this awesome gift often takes time. The moment we consciously acknowledge our hearts will not beat forever, there is often a shift — if we are brave enough to embrace the entirety of this truth, to hold it in our mind. Such a moment of awakening could be the loss of a friend or a loved one, or it could be an uplifting experience that opens our eyes to all that is possible. Whenever it happens, such an event changes us; some may say it awakens us. For me, when this happened, it was a recognition of the importance of soaking up the present moment as though it is gold that might never be seen again. In other words, oodles of snuggles and kisses with my pups each and every day, dancing for the simplest of reasons (for example, the roof over my head is still up: yeah! happy dance! or I just slept eight hours without waking up once: whoop, whoop!). It may sound silly to celebrate these types of moments, but doing so keeps us present, reduces stress, and improves the quality of our days.

Reading Eckhart Tolle's *A New Earth* was a profound learning experience for me; it was insightful, reassuring, and course-correcting in small, but significant ways. It was also helpful in offering insight into moments that are difficult or unwanted, but sometimes inevitable. Our lives may be finite, but how we choose to live our days determines their quality. In our everydays, we can elevate seemingly mundane, quotidian situations, as well as improve what once were unwanted situations into more tolerable moments that will quickly pass.

Immediately after reading Tolle's international bestseller, I read *Limitless*, by Laura Gesner Otting, which explores changing our understanding of what success is for each of us, carving our own path, and thus discovering our best life. Otting reaffirms the idea that we must live consciously in order to discover true success, bringing with us the knowledge of ourselves (or committing to getting to know ourselves until we do fully). The success we eventually discover will be something we cherish for ourselves, regardless of whether the outside world knows what we have accomplished. This is how we elevate our everydays, how we embrace the power of our lives, which we can share with the world in wonderful ways.

Initially delicate, you are full of potential to be quite awesome. You will never know where your life journey will take you, but if you will give your full attention and best self to each day, they will inevitably lead you on a memorable journey full of many wonderful experiences.

Petit plaisir Schedule a seasonal facial at a local spa. You will emerge refreshed and relaxed, and your skin will thank you.

Explore further thesimplyluxuriouslife.com/february9 (eight ways to create glowing skin)

February 10
Remain Flexible

Anyone who has experience with setting goals, imagining their future, and putting together a plan to achieve said future also knows that simply because we plan does not ensure that the journey along the way will go as expected.

Often detours will arise and realizations of what precisely is necessary will shift, and we get to know ourselves better during the journey. For example, at one point, I stretched myself a little bit, not knowing how I would be received. I had prepared for a couple of months for this opportunity, and thought I had covered all of my bases. The one thing I had not prepared for was my intuition stopping me in my tracks and blatantly telling me that I needed to alter my path in order to reach my desired destination.

Initially I was a wreck, wrought with a feeling of defeat, but then after hearing some trusted, encouraging words, and awakening from a much-needed full night's sleep, I realized my intuition had done me a monumental favor.

In this particular scenario, my intuition was finally able to grab my attention and put in front of me precisely what I thought I needed in order to navigate toward my goal. It also revealed to me that a few of the steps I thought I needed were not only unnecessary, they would also be detrimental in my quest to reach the long-term destination.

The takeaway lesson is this: As you carefully plan your path to achievement, remain flexible, ready to shift and adjust as you evolve along the journey, because you will, and that is a very good thing indeed.

Petit plaisir Layer an ivory V-neck cashmere sweater over an ivory silk camisole, paired with slim jeans tucked into cognac knee-high boots — the cozy and effortless approach.

Explore further thesimplyluxuriouslife.com/february10 (how to let yourself bloom)

February 11
Doing What You Love

Tenacity, perseverance, stick-to-itiveness — these are all admirable traits. After all, expertise with whatever we pursue comes with time, careful attention, and a sincere passion for what we are doing. It also helps to be surrounded by those who understand what and why we are doing what we are doing. However, when we strike out in a direction that is unfamiliar to those around us, it may take time for them to understand.

Of the four ingredients required for expertise — time, attention, passion, and support — the key to long-term success is passion. You must have a sincere, gut-level love for what you are pursuing as you spend time on it day in and day out, devote extra hours, working beyond any expectations, diving into and growing what you love.

While I have always been aware of it at some level, such a realization has become clearer to me lately, and I must say, it is enlightening. I have come to appreciate TSLL blog and community even more than I ever have in the past, if that is even possible. And I have come to realize that sometimes others may never understand what we are doing, and it is not our job to explain but simply to do what calls to us at the deepest level.

Sometimes it feels as though life is testing us, but if we look at the glass as half full, life is really opening our eyes to truths that, if we heed what we have seen, will lead us down the path that was meant to coincide with our gifts, our talents, and our passions.

You don't need to jump at this very moment, but begin to collect these realizations. If they continue to speak the same language, continue to send the same over-arching message, you will begin to figure them out and start putting your ducks in a row. Eventually, you will be able to strike out in a bold leap into your future.

Petit plaisir Read *The French Art of Not Trying Too Hard*, by Ollivier Pourriol. It is a lovely, leisurely philosophical read about approaching life by engaging with it, not expecting it to happen for you.

Explore further thesimplyluxuriouslife.com/february11 (ten ways to live with effortless ease: how to learn the French art of not trying too hard)

February 12
Everything Is Happening to Help You

I once posted on Instagram a quote from talk show host Trevor Noah: "Everything is helping you." After all, if the universe is indeed doing everything it does in an effort to help each and every one of us, all we need to do is allow it to do what it wants to do. In other words, all we need to do is let go of the assumption that the universe *isn't* helping us. In so doing, we free ourselves of unnecessary stress, angst, and fear, and avoid ruining things that have the potential to blossom into something splendid.

What if the event, the occurrence, the call, the invitation, the opportunity you wish would happen right now is taking its time because it needs you to fully appreciate it when it does? What if, on a day you needed rays of sunlight, the weather offers rain in order to slow you down, allowing your body and mind to rest? What if the job you have been doggedly pursuing continues to elude you because you need to realize your special talents that exist quietly under the surface? Had you attained what you thought you wanted, you might never have unearthed them.

On March 13, 2020, the pandemic sent all teachers and students in Oregon home. We taught from our homes for nearly a complete school year. During that time, the universe showed me — in plain, vivid, hands-on living — how much my everyday life was lacking in true peace, true contentment. If I wanted not only a more deeply contented and connected life regarding social relationships, but a healthy life as well, something had to change. I found more peace during the pandemic — if that wasn't a sign I needed to be brave in how I lived my life moving forward, I don't know what could be, and I didn't want to wait to find out.

I would like to accept Trevor Noah's motto. Why not? As we know, we can plan all day long, but ultimately, there are forces outside of our control. The true and ultimate experience is mastering what we are given and not sitting idly on the sidelines, waiting for life to happen. When we choose to partake, to be an active participant, our world opens wider and offers more brilliant opportunities than we ever imagined.

When you choose to see the world as working with you, you choose a life of extraordinary experience.

Petit plaisir Step into the kitchen with the French cozy mystery series *Magellan* playing in the background and make a recipe from *Plat du Jour*, by Susan Herrmann Loomis — a pear nutmeg crumble, to be savored after a sweet-potato gratin, a warm curly endive salad, and a sirloin steak.

Explore further thesimplyluxuriouslife.com/february12 (inspiration to remind you everything is working out for you — even when you don't think it is)

February 13
Internal Strength

Making lemonade when the universe gives you lemons can be taxing, heart-wrenching, and seemingly impossible to bear. The good news is that it is indeed possible.

In June 2018, I experienced one amazingly awesome high: the launching of the preordering of signed copies of TSLL's second book. I tried to fall asleep on that late Tuesday evening, but it was nearly impossible as preordering had begun. Once my brain turned off, I found just a couple hours of sleep before Wednesday began. That was the best night of non-sleep I have ever experienced, and I am so very grateful to TSLL readers. I cannot express the depth of my gratitude for their enthusiasm, their kind words, their time and interest. I was overwhelmed, and continue to be, by a wash of goodness and courage and determination to reach our fullest potential, as expressed in their comments and actions.

And while simultaneously a very negative (and unrelated) incident occurred in my life unexpectedly, I was forced to think about making lemonade. And I am equally thankful to have been able to do just that. How was I able to make the lemonade? It was because of the lovely people in my immediate personal circle. In fact, a few relationships were strengthened because of it. I have asked myself: If I had known the outcome (the lemonade) prior to the incident, would I have wanted the incident to happen? As someone who feels pain deeply (who doesn't?), honestly, I initially and perhaps still would say no. But I cannot change what happened, as it was outside my control, but I am focusing on the good that came out of it, and am thankful there was so much goodness that prevailed.

Knowing you can weather unexpected storms is an internal strength, a superpower of sorts that enables you to move confidently through your day. When you are not constantly afraid that something negative might happen, but rather are assured that, whatever happens, you will be able to handle it, your stress levels drop, and staying in the present moment is far simpler. My mind continues to go back to all of the goodness of that preordering Wednesday and the goodness that continues to be offered in my life.

Life can be funny and odd at times, but it always offers you an opportunity to grow and to be reminded of how strong you can be.

Petit plaisir After a productive exercise session or strenuous physical task, listen to Mozart's Piano Quintet in E-flat Major for Piano and Winds, K. 452, and let yourself melt. I first heard this piece after a morning of classic skiing with Norman.

Explore further thesimplyluxuriouslife.com/february13 (four healthy habits for continual self-growth)

February 14
To Find True North, Follow Your Instincts

A couple of years ago, after having settled into my life in Bend, I spent a few days in Portland, which is about a three hours' drive west. As I lay in bed typing in the City of Roses, the floor-to-ceiling windows overlooking downtown Portland, the buzz of nightlife below, and the serenity of settling into a cozy temporary sanctuary remind me of why I love the everydays I have created in Bend.

No matter how far away life takes us from what we define as our true home (physical or emotional), if we live consciously, if we are in tune with ourselves — our needs, our self-worth, and our die-hard dreams — coming home will feel like the most natural decision to make. Over time, we question such a decision less and less, and simply respect the idea that we know where our true north lies.

Along the journey of cultivating my own simply luxurious life and continuing to maintain and improve it, I have become more acutely aware when something is pulling me away from my "home." And a beautiful gift has come with this instinctive realization: The idea that it is easy to stand up, to speak up, to rise up and say, "No, I cannot walk any further from the destination that not only comforts me but lifts me up to help me reach my fullest potential."

Ask yourself, are you "at home," or is something (a demand, a job, a way of life) pulling you off course? The more you step forward on the journey of self-discovery and cultivation of the life that enlivens you and enables you to find true contentment, the less likely it is that you will be pulled away from your true "home." If you do get diverted, you won't be distracted for long before you put your foot down and say, nope, time to get back on track.

Petit plaisir Watch *The Intouchables* (2011), a French film starring Omar Sy and François Cluzet.

Explore further thesimplyluxuriouslife.com/february14 (discover twelve more French — or set in France — feel-good films from the past ten years)

February 15
Place a Bet on Yourself

When we push through difficult situations, we are rewarded in a way that confirms that our efforts were worth the temporary stress and, perhaps, the headache. Think about the pressure on the base runner as they round third and head for home or the basketball player who is given the ball to make the game-winning shot with seconds remaining; if either athlete lets up, becomes hesitant, or stops, success doesn't have an opportunity to materialize. The same acute stress appears for the actor on the stage, recalling page-long lines, or the interviewee sitting down for a chance at their dream job.

Even when a player misses a shot or a runner is tagged out at home plate or when an actor forgets a line or an employer hires someone else, valuable experience is gained that can be applied on the next go-round. Why would there be a next go-round, you may ask? Why would someone go through the angst and agony for something that may not work out? Quite simply, because if you truly want what you have set out to find, you will not give up, and you will discover that that hard-earned wisdom is a powerful asset.

While there is no telling what we will find when we invest in our dreams, what we *are* guaranteed is an opportunity to evolve into a person who is ever closer to their fullest potential. But if we do not choose to stretch ourselves, we can never live up to that potential.

In 2014, as I moved through the process of publishing my first book, after thoroughly investigating costs and benefits, I made a decision to bet on myself. The process was new to me, but no matter what happened, I was reassured, knowing I would gain valuable knowledge. Having a clear focus on the final product allowed me to make the decision without reservation.

When you take educated risks, when you choose to gather up the courage to believe in yourself and pair it with tireless work, life has a way of rewarding you. What risk are you contemplating?

Petit plaisir Enjoy a glass of champagne, sparkling wine, cava, or prosecco celebrating with a friend, partner, or spouse what you have achieved on a project that is important to you.

Explore further thesimplyluxuriouslife.com/february15 (knowing which risks to take)

February 16
Letting Go of the Wrong Dream

Sometimes life can shock us. It can reveal something unexpected. Even when we plan, work, and assure ourselves we know what we want, it may be that, once we attain it, we discover it was not what we wanted at all.

I am a hope-filled romantic. I have never liked the familiar phrase "hopeless romantic" due to the negative connotation. However, a romantic, defined as one who celebrates curiosity, spontaneity, and wonder, and is full of hope — yep, that would be me.

However, sometimes my hope leans too far over its skis, and one romantic relationship in my thirties ended without hesitation; however, in a moment of growth, rather than feeling like a fool, I felt that a burden had been lifted. And the only way I could have removed that burden was to ask myself — rather than a friend or family member — if ending the relationship was the right thing to do. The moment I asked the question, I knew the answer. I felt internally what I needed to realize rather than waiting to be told by an outside force.

Why did I need to learn this particular lesson firsthand? Because otherwise I would have always wondered and always had doubts. Also, because I knew that the people who may have given me genuine and heartfelt advice on these issues did not have the same vision for a fulfilling life as I did (one that was not better, merely different). And there is no reason they should necessarily understand this difference; my life path is not their responsibility.

In taking responsibility for my life, turning the page to begin a chapter I knew needed to begin but could not without my decision, I bolstered my self-trust and was able to strive forward, confident in my ability to navigate the unknown road before me.

Have you ever found yourself in a similar situation — standing still after having made the leap you have been dreaming of for ages, only to discover it was not what you needed or wanted? I am not talking about finding yourself in the middle of a change that is uncomfortable. All effective and necessary change is uncomfortable temporarily to one degree or another. I am talking about instantly knowing innately that something does not fit with your values, ideals, and life path.

The only way you can know what does not work is to know who you are. Which is why taking the time and having the patience to understand what makes your heart and soul sing is the greatest gift you can give yourself.

Petit plaisir Welcome a French bolster (a *traversin*) into your bedroom for ease of bedtime reading and (for me) sleeping.

Explore further thesimplyluxuriouslife.com/february16 (seventeen things to bid adieu)

February 17
Give What You Desire a Try

Say yes.

What question immediately pops into your mind that you long to say yes to? Be honest. Why do you want to say yes? Are you a little bit scared . . . but mainly over the moon in your yearning for the opportunity to say this simple, yet oh-so-powerful, and life-changing word?

Listen to what you want to say yes to. Over the past twelve years, opportunities arrived in TSLL's inbox, and I have said yes. Most of them were opportunities I had been wanting to say yes to if only the chance would present itself. All of the opportunities I stepped forward and said yes to stretched me, pushed me a bit (if not a lot) out of my comfort zone, and revealed something I had not seen, known, or understood.

One of the opportunities was an interview with the woman who was my guest on the podcast on Monday, May 29, 2017 (listen to episode #157 of *The Simple Sophisticate* podcast). I cannot speak more highly of her. Born in France, Elizabeth Bougerol, jazz musician and singer for the Hot Sardines, was born in France, with lineage from Toronto; she now primarily lives in Brooklyn, with the occasional trip to Normandy to visit family. We talked life, we talked jazz, and we talked about the differences in approaches to living between France and America; we talked about stepping into shoes that appear too big and not feeling ready to wear them, but recognizing there may never be a perfect time.

When opportunities arise, whether you think you are ready or not, step toward them with courage and do not shrink away in fear.

Petit plaisir Play Ella Fitzgerald's album *The Lost Berlin Tapes*. Let it fill the house, and let yourself dance without inhibition.

Explore further thesimplyluxuriouslife.com/february17 (a listener-favorite episode of the podcast, discussing passion projects and living in the moment with jazz musician Elizabeth Bougerol of the Hot Sardines)

February 18
Gaining Clarity

One of the most powerful gifts we can give ourselves is clarity, knowing precisely what we are striving toward and, generally and gradually more specifically, how to attain it. Upon becoming clear about what we want, knowing why we want it, and then knowing how to attain it, a deep sigh of relief immediately washes over us. Although we should not relax entirely, as we still have a lot of work to complete, we should savor what that moment — when we tap into the clarity that may have been long elusive — feels like for our mind and our body. That feeling is the reward, and that feeling will help keep you grounded and on track.

During the spring of 2017, I began reassessing my priorities. At times, what I discovered or recognized shocked me, and in other moments of discovery, it seemed hands-down obvious. One of the mini-gifts clarity gives us is the ability to let go quite easily of anything impeding our path to reach our destination.

I took some time to edit my budget as I began to recognize that a few items — monthly, seasonal, and so forth — were not serving me any longer. A few that I let go surprised me, but upon contemplation, I realized that holding on did not make any sense. A quote I came across recently summed it up quite simply, "Keep in mind that letting go isn't the end of the world, it's the beginning of a new life." And while merely editing my budget may not create a tidal wave of change, it is a small step in the right direction to the change I seek. And those small steps add up if we keep walking.

Do you have clarity? Do you know where you're going and why? And if so, was it easier upon reaching that destination to let go of what no longer served you? I do believe we hang on to habits, people, hopes, anything that doesn't serve us because we don't know what we want. The attainment of clarity simplifies and offers the courage we need to let go of what we should have relinquished some time ago.

Petit plaisir Share a dark chocolate and hazelnut tart with your neighbors just because.

Explore further thesimplyluxuriouslife.com/february18 (recipe for a double-chocolate hazelnut tart)

February 19
Act on Your Instincts

One of my favorite books is *The Alchemist*, by Paulo Coelho. A reader gave it to me as a gift, and for a handful of years, I passed it along to high school graduates. From time to time, I reflect on one of the many beautiful lessons the book provides:

February

Before a dream is realized, the Soul of the World tests everything that was learned along the way. It does this not because it is evil, but so that we can, in addition to realizing our dreams, master the lessons we've learned as we've moved forward toward that dream.

Often it seems that we find words of *aha* when we need them. Perhaps it is simply because we are looking and the words of revelation have been there all along. But either way, upon seeing these words again, I find reassurance within myself to continue to pursue a life journey many may not understand, but one that brings much inner calm and thus everyday contentment.

After enduring all of the lessons and being presented with the final lesson — the one that is the key to reaching the finish line — we may be exhausted, dubious as to whether to trust our instincts because of the pain we endured along the way. However, the difference between knocking at the door of success and making the wrong decision (not knocking) is that choosing to take on the final challenge will instinctively be the right decision to make. The catch is that your instincts will not be confirmed until you act. But almost immediately, when you do act, when you choose to tackle that final challenge, you will see the door open, and the confirmation that you did indeed learn the many lessons that were thrust upon you will bring a huge sigh of relief and exhilaration.

Trust yourself. Apply the lessons. Life is trying to show you what and where you should go, but you must pay attention and not be afraid to act.

Petit plaisir Read Paulo Coelho's book *The Alchemist*, an allegorical tale about the journey and finding our way "home."

Explore further thesimplyluxuriouslife.com/february19 (discover how to trust, how to be trustworthy and how understanding both will transform your entire life)

February 20
Just Be You

This year, now nearing the end of its second month, is ours to make what we desire, dream, and hope it can be. What exactly do you want it to be?

Recently, I was thinking about the concepts of "becoming" versus "being." We are always evolving, growing, and moving forward in life, consciously or unconsciously, and that, in essence, is "becoming." At the same time, if we are always in the mindset of attempting to "become" something, we are not "being" present. Keeping this observation in mind, I did my best to self-assess.

I have spent many years intentionally trying to "become" something, but I cannot honestly say I have intentionally directed myself to just "be." Perhaps that is part of the culture, part of my upbringing, or simply who I am, but the more I get to know myself, the more I know that this has been taught to me and I have accepted it, for the most part, because of the practical benefits of striving to "become" my best self.

However, at this moment, I am intentionally putting forth the energy to shift from becoming my best self, from becoming the Shannon that I desire to be, to just being who I am, to just be Shannon.

I have intentionally put forth the energy, curiosity, plans, and courage to become my best self. After all, my journey is what inspired my second book (its subtitle urges you to discover "your best self"), and because of what I learned and how my life has evolved, I have eagerly shared what I have discovered.

Once "becoming" has taken place in your life, you need to trust that you are on the right path. Knowing that you are doing your best, sometimes you need to just let yourself "be."

Petit plaisir Listen to cellist Gretchen Yanover's "Blossom and Cadence."

Explore further thesimplyluxuriouslife.com/february20 (inspiration for finding the courage to be yourself)

February 21
Confronting What Others Think

I have heard it said many times that anyone who chooses to spend their time sharing what they love doing with the world needs to grow a very thick skin. While I have always accepted this as largely sage advice, actually preventing harsh words from penetrating the boundaries we create is easier said than done.

Fortunately, throughout the duration of TSLL, the blog's readers have been very supportive and kind not only with their praise, but also with their critiques. I have received many helpful e-mails with suggestions, ideas, and edits I might want to make. I digest each one wholeheartedly, for, as I readily admit, the blog and all aspects of my efforts will always be works in progress. For the graciousness and gentleness of my readers, I will always be thankful.

February

From time to time, most of us, if not all, will eventually come in for harsh criticism, most certainly so if we pursue a path, take a new action that is beyond the norm of our culture or different from the way we have lived in the past. Not all criticism deserves our attention; after all, it's worth remembering Teddy Roosevelt's words regarding the man in the arena — "It's not the critic who counts, but the man in the arena . . . who does actually strive to do the deeds" (I encourage you to read the entire quote titled "The Man in the Arena"). When we face such criticism, we appreciate more fully the support, guidance, and encouragement we have received along the way.

As I look over the designers' collections each September and February as the models make their way down the runways, I imagine what it might feel like to send all of your hard work down a catwalk for everyone to see. After all of the energy, hours, and perspiration, and then the anticipation, it can seem that essentially the public's reception of your work is left in the hands of the observers. Or is it?

Often we do not rightfully appreciate and congratulate ourselves for a job well done; instead, we can be consumed with how others will receive it. While, to some extent, reviews do matter, we must not be at the complete mercy of others' critiques.

Critics don't always get it right: The *New York Times Book Review* has acknowledged that they have made a few errors in too harshly criticizing several titles that have become classics: L. M. Montgomery's *Anne of Green Gables* — "The author's probable intention was to exhibit a unique development in this little asylum waif, but there is no real difference between the girl at the end of the story and the one at the beginning of it" (1908); "*Catch-22* has much passion, comic and fervent, but it gasps for want of craft and sensibility" (1961); and "Bad news is best blurted out at once: *Tender Is the Night* is a disappointment" (1934).

When we do any job, complete any project, or mount any performance, the only thing we can control is that we give 100 percent of ourselves, our abilities, and our time. While the rest in some ways is left up to the sometimes fickle opinions of critics, our attitude and how we handle what follows also determines where we will land in the future. Our world, our destiny, truly is in our own hands. Everything may not go exactly as we have planned, but we can find the life, the dream we crave if we temper our pride and keep striving forward, no matter what others may say.

As you pursue your dreams and goals, as you put yourself out there in any capacity — how you raise your children, how you do your work with the public, how you dress, the words you speak, the optimism you exude when it is easier to be cynical — there will always be critics. So long as you know you are doing your best, accepting that perfection is impossible, keep doing what you love.

  Keep putting more hope, goodness, and inspiration out into the world. By doing this, you not only will live without regret, but you will also inspire others to find the courage to do the same.

  Petit plaisir   Delight in the Globemaster and Gladiator alliums beginning to emerge from the earth.

  Explore further   thesimplyluxuriouslife.com/february21 (inspiration for letting go of seeking others' approval)

February 22
Enjoy Your Own Company

One unexpected treat after my first book was released involved perusing readers' initial comments. What I appreciate most is readers' honesty, and while most reviews have been very positive, one comment offered a piece of constructive criticism regarding my statement about embracing the life I had created and enjoying being single. To her, she said, it was redundant. "We get it," she said, "you enjoy your life, and you're happy being single."

  But as no doubt other readers have discovered, the book is not about being single; in fact, I directly state that I would love to share my life with a partner, but as I cannot control when or if I will meet that special person, I am delighting in the life and details I do have control over. I am open to a relationship, but to adhere to such a prescriptive and parochial definition of contentment is foolhardy and life-limiting.

  I bring up my reader's comment not to praise or dismiss the idea of being single. I am ever more convinced that in order to enjoy our lives with a companion, we must become wholly comfortable with our own company, understand how to fill our lives with our own hobbies, passions, and interests, and become clear about what is worth speaking up for and what is mere idle chatter and can be tweaked and changed.

  When we know how to bring peace and comfort into our lives, we are not seeking someone else to do it for us; rather, the person we welcome into our lives can enjoy it with us, and we enjoy their pastimes even more fully because we have communicated our preferences clearly. We can judge if we mesh based on knowing such important details about ourselves, and we can know what we can wiggle on and what we cannot.

  And that is often when the magic happens. When we pursue our own passions, curiosities, etc., we step into a world of our own authenticity. We are not trying to be someone to please the outside world; we are rather trying to enjoy life based on our intuitions and tastes. When we let go of *trying to be*, and instead just *be*, we free ourselves, and that is attractive.

Go forward and live a life that speaks to you. Take that tae kwon do class, organize that dinner or cocktail party you want to throw, and live your life without worrying whether it meets the approval of the outside world. Who knows whom you will meet or what opportunities will present themselves? Perhaps it will be a new friend; perhaps a new door will open further in an area you are interested in; perhaps a new connection will appear in your work life; and, yes, perhaps, someone who tickles your heart will walk into your life.

Petit plaisir Stock up on French butter; my favorite is Isigny Sainte-Mère. Purchase as much as your budget will allow, and notice the difference in your baking (croissants!) and cooking (beurre blanc sauce).

Explore further thesimplyluxuriouslife.com/february22 (explore a butter tasting, and my favorite French butter)

February 23
Be Yourself

On one of my walks, as I listened to a podcast that included an interview with Marianne Williamson, the conversation turned to the shadow effect. While the definition of this concept is a bit ambiguous, I like to refer to it as a side of ourselves that we are fearful of or have not accepted. Some people never accept all that they are and thus cause themselves preventable problems. I am not talking about strong versus weak aspects of ourselves that we must accept, but rather what is easy to project out into the world versus what is often viewed as odd or out of the ordinary; it is something many try to suppress.

When we choose to embrace all that we are, we often discover what we were meant to become or pursue. Often we discover that we possess unique gifts. So many people would rather become sheep-like in order to be accepted when the grander, more fulfilling life lies in tapping into what makes us each unique, allowing us to offer our gifts and our unique being to the world. Many friends, family members, and associates may not initially know how to respond; they may even shun us because we are a reminder of what they dare not investigate about themselves (even though they wouldn't understand this to be the reason), but we owe it to ourselves to embrace all that we are.

Perhaps it is your sensitive, introverted nature or your ability to dance or hear a rhythm that no one else can understand. Or maybe you have an eye for composition that comes naturally, while others look at the same thing and are unable to see the magic you immediately home in on.

Whatever your uniqueness, whatever your fear, embrace it. Then, as long as you do not impede on anyone else's rights, hug it with all your might.

Petit plaisir Gaze and gawk and be awed by a full rainbow in the middle of an afternoon rain shower.

Explore further thesimplyluxuriouslife.com/february23 (inspiration for owning your uniqueness)

February 24
Trusting Your Journey

Each of us contains within ourselves the answers we seek; however, somewhat paradoxically, we must look outside ourselves to gain the tools needed to excavate the knowledge from within. The key is to look in the right direction, walk down the right path, and let go of what has led us astray in the past.

I had just this *aha* related to a matter I have been working through for some time. Upon reflection, I realized I did not have the right resources around me. I had been reaching out in the wrong direction and hoping for a different result. But then I realized there never would be one so long as I was headed in the wrong direction.

A couple of years ago, I visited Seattle for a blog project. It was a day trip — I would arrive in the early morning and return during the afternoon rush hour. Upon completing my mission, I began to make my way from downtown to the airport. As I hustled along, looking for the train to Sea-Tac, I came upon the station I needed. In a moment of flurry (Hurry, make a decision!), I thought the train that was arriving was the one I needed, so I hopped on . . . and quickly realized I was headed in the wrong direction.

Here is the lesson regarding life and the advice we seek to improve our lives: If we look to the wrong source, if the expertise we consult is far from what we need, the only way to head in the right direction is to get off the wrong train and find the right one. Which is exactly what I did. Actually, I called a taxi so that I could be delivered directly to the airport. In the nick of time — thirty seconds later and they would have left me at the terminal — I made my flight.

The first step is often the most difficult: to recognize that you are heading down the wrong path. Such a recognition is hard because often we look to people who sincerely have our best interests at heart but may not be experts about what we seek. The good news about detecting the wrong direction is that it becomes easier with each experience because it begins with trusting yourself.

Once you find the right direction and the right experts, you will notice the quality of your life elevate to what you had hoped and perhaps beyond. When you find them, it will feel like sliding into a seat that was made especially for you — much like Goldilocks, just right. Folk singer Joan Baez is credited with coining the maxim "As long as one keeps searching, the answers come." Don't stop. It is as simple as that. Eventually, the answers you seek, the answers you need to open up the world that you know is possible, will come.

Petit plaisir As inspiration to find the courage and step onto your own path, listen to Mozart's Violin Sonata no. 21 in E Major, K. 304, his first major work after striking out on his own, away from his father, following his mother's passing in Paris.

Explore further thesimplyluxuriouslife.com/february24 (seven signs you're moving in the right direction)

February 25
Dreams

Dreams can come true; they honestly can. The key is knowing what you want and then being willing to put in the hard work until you arrive at your goal.

The hard part is knowing what to do when you have arrived. Once you reach that goal, your life will take on a new feel, pace, and outlook. At first, it may even feel uncomfortable — like a new shoe — but if it really is what you were hoping for, have confidence that, after a few strolls around the block, you will feel at home in your new, if somewhat unfamiliar world.

Achieving your dream may force you to eliminate things you once thought important. It may force you to realize that you don't need what you once thought you needed to live a full life. And it may force you to grow into a better person than you thought you could be.

Currently, I find myself in such a situation: I am leaving one world where I was only dreaming and entering another in which my dreams are evolving into something real. I am having to adjust my life, and while it is a significant shift, my exhilaration to have this opportunity is high, and my depth of gratitude extends fathoms deep.

I continue to fine-tune and tailor my schedule to the person I know more fully and honestly than ever before. I am witnessing drastic improvements in my quality of life, which strengthens my trust in my intuition, grounding me in a firm foundation of listening and honoring what I know about myself. With that said, I am being patient, and am welcoming space to feel my way through what works best for me.

Always keep in mind all the hard work — the days, months, and years that you have invested — and refuse to let your achievements slip through your fingers. Not everyone turns their dreams into reality because not everyone is willing to put forth the necessary effort. You are, you have, and you deserve to make this new life work for you. Savor it, revel in it, and never take it for granted.

Petit plaisir Pair apricot-hued lilies with a matte green/turquoise Poirot-esque vase (in other words, a beloved vase that tickles you; I adore Agatha Christie's Hercule Poirot, and this vase is rotund in all its glory). Place the arrangement on the side table in your reading nook.

Explore further thesimplyluxuriouslife.com/february25 (eleven things to do to create the life of your dreams)

February 26
Taking Risks

How do you know? How do you know when it is time to take the leap, to take that risk you have been daydreaming about for years? How do you know when it is time to move on, to try something new, to take the chance that will most certainly change your life but in ways you are not quite certain of?

The answer is that nobody knows with 100 percent certainty when to take their life in a new direction, but there are clues.

The clues can come in many different forms, but here are a few: the life goals you had once set in front of yourself have all been achieved, and you are ready to begin chasing new challenges and experience new opportunities that your previous goals prepared you to now tackle; you have come to understand your true abilities and passions and are more certain of what you can and cannot live without; you have given everything and are looking to grow even more; your priorities have changed; you have a self-confidence and an inner courage that you did not have before; you have too many valid reasons not to and would regret not taking the chance.

Everyone's scenario is different. One person may be contemplating letting go of a relationship, while another is pondering a move across the country to start a new life. Whatever your scenario is, listen to that voice in your head that cannot be silenced. It is one thing if you hear it by chance and never again, but it is quite another if you find yourself mesmerized by its hypnotic possibilities incessantly.

Begin by investigating and exploring in the comfort of your current life, make a few temporary changes or go visit the city, state, or country you have had your eye on, and get a feel for what your intuition has to say while you stroll about.

Most important, listen and don't ignore what your subconscious is hinting at. Indulge it ever so slightly, possibly by just picking up a book on the idea of the change you have been considering. But do yourself a favor: Never ignore the idea of letting go and moving on to a greater possibility.

Petit plaisir Light an Un Soir à L'Opéra candle on a small table next to your reading chair. Snuggle in.

Explore further thesimplyluxuriouslife.com/february26 (seven French candles I recommend)

February 27
Chasing Your Dreams

When Steve Jobs announced in 2011 that he was stepping down from Apple, it was impossible not to notice all the reverence that sprang up from people from all different walks of life. I reflected on his 2005 commencement address to Stanford's graduating class, and I was inspired yet again by his insights and lessons about life.

It is not news to anyone that we will all cease to live at some point, and such a concrete understanding should propel each of us to make life into our own unique work of art. Once we understand how fleeting chances, opportunities, and even youth can be, we should not hesitate to seek out what stirs our souls, cast aside doubts and naysayers who are unable to understand our dreams, and simply go for it.

Jobs's legacy is profound. His life is a testament to doing what you love, never giving up, and never letting people who don't understand you hold you back.

It is easy to wonder, in the present moment, how the actions we engage in will pay off in the future. One of my favorite quotes from the 2005 speech is about how having confidence is its own sort of reward; Jobs reassures us that as long as we stay true to our passions, the dots will connect themselves. "You can't connect the dots looking forward; you can only connect them looking backward."

The key in all of this is *knowing* what you love, understanding what intrigues you, and believing in yourself. One of the best and simplest pieces of advice I try to remember when I am having doubts is, "You must first believe in yourself in order for others to see a reason to believe in you as well."

You cannot always know where life is going to lead you, but you can at least decide on the amount and type of energy you will put in to get to where you would like to go. That is some very powerful fuel, if used wisely and judiciously.

Petit plaisir Host a small dinner party for a group of neighbors. Start with sparkling wine for an aperitif, followed by smoked salmon rillettes on fresh, thinly sliced English cucumbers.

Explore further thesimplyluxuriouslife.com/february27 (confidence: how to gain it and why it is important)

February 28
Understanding Where Your Creativity Flows

I sometimes wonder why I am able to work without watching the clock when I surround myself with nature, and I also remember a conversation I had with an author about the idea of finding inspiration to work without prompting. She explained that the buzz and energy of New York City spur her muse and poke her creativity. But for me, the sound of a flowing creek, the chirping of birds, and a soft breeze, with my dogs nestled nearby (Norman usually snoring, Oscar silently sleeping), seem to make time disappear. The point is that we are nurtured to be at our best and produce our most loved work in different environments.

These are the sanctuaries we must create or find and then spend time enjoying. These are the destinations that will nurture our best selves and reveal our authentic talents and gifts.

Set aside the idea of where you are most creative and instead contemplate where can you sit with a book, with no noise and distraction, and just immerse yourself? More likely than not, this is a place where you could be most at peace doing just about anything.

Often we become so busy and consumed with our schedules that we forget that we need to slow down, to consider our surroundings and how we respond to them. Are we helping or hurting ourselves? When we can answer this question honestly, we need to respect the revelation and work to include more time cultivating the preferred sanctuary that brings us the most peace.

Consider for a moment where you are most at peace — calm in your mind, shoulders relaxed, and breath slowed. Where are you when you don't care what time it is or would feel at ease even if you knew?

Petit plaisir Prepare for the upcoming spring growth by cutting back grasses in your garden (I have more than a few Karl Foersters, which have been beautiful through the cold, snowy winter). Consider adding similar grasses to your landscaping, no matter how small, as they provide a wonderful natural structure through the fall and winter months.

Explore further thesimplyluxuriouslife.com/february28 (explore eight benefits of banishing busy)

February 29
Remain Resolute in Your Journey

I tend not to believe in fate or destiny, mainly because unless we do the work, life cannot offer us what we are capable of attaining. But what I have begun to realize is that the more we become in tune with our innate talents, our sincere passions and preferences, the more we appreciate our temperament and allow it to thrive, certain paths will feel most comfortable and others will not.

That recognition grows in strength as our talents, passions, and preferences become second nature, and we begin to sit well within our own skin. We begin to rely less on what others would do or recommend. And while we gather feedback from experts, we trust that once we have all the necessary information, only we can make the best decisions for ourselves because only we know what we can endure and what would be unsettling.

I have found that the true gift of reaching this point in life — and I can only imagine and hope that the benefit increases over time — is that we recognize when life is speaking to us and pick up on opportunities to choose a more fortuitous and more fulfilling path. Those who do not know themselves — who do not trust themselves, who are not aware of what they can contribute to the world and what they need in their lives to do

The Road to Le Papillon

that — will ignore such opportunities. For them, the lesson must, and will, reappear until they learn it.

The first step and the best gift we can give ourselves and thus the quality of our lives is to get to know ourselves, enjoy and revel in what we discover, and then keep our eyes open. Life will speak to us when we least expect it.

Petit plaisir An extra bouquet for the extra day of the year. A simple trumpet vase with white freesias on the nightstand in the bedroom.

Explore further thesimplyluxuriouslife.com/february29 (twenty ways to be prepared for opportunity)

March

Embrace Patience, Healing, and Growth

March

Gardening is a step to your future life because if you are planting things, you have to be there to care for them. Gardening is something that takes you forward.
—*Gardeners' World*

When I began to garden in earnest, the entire day became a joy for me. For as long as I can remember, morning has been my magic moment of the day. Fresh with energy, bursting with ideas and optimism, I wait for the sun to wake up during three of the seasons (in summer, it beats me in rising, but just barely). With the arrival of evening, I snuggle in after a full day of play or work, feeling productive and exhausted and eager to slow my pace, sip some tea, watch a favorite cosy mystery, or read. But afternoons? Nope. For nearly forty years, we could not find chemistry.

Spring 2020. The pandemic demands that we all stay home. Since I enjoy the rejuvenation of my sanctuary and am a writer and lover of nature, I gladly oblige.

I adhered to a regular schedule of writing and teaching in the morning, so the afternoons became my time outside to tinker in the dirt. First, the daffodils greeted me, then the tulips, and then I began planting my annuals, herbs, and vegetables, if not on the weekends, during the afternoon after my creative mind was done. When my ideas and cognitive synapses were tired, I welcomed a robotic exercise in which nothing too taxing is required; I needed to unwind and soothe my being. I planted, I strategized, I weeded, I dead-headed, and I quickly came to look forward to my afternoons.

I have deduced that part of the reason I formerly did not connect with afternoons was my weakened willpower and lessened ability to be the master of my mind. My worries would arise more frequently in the afternoon, just as they can in the early morning when I wake faaaaar too early. My exhaustion from activities and tasks earlier in the day would muddle my ability to create and be as jovial as I would have liked. It was no wonder I generally did not look forward to my afternoons.

My mother is a gardener, and while I appreciated the natural beauty she cultivated in my childhood home's landscape and garden, for some reason, gardening never clicked with me. When I purchased Le Papillon and had the opportunity to engage with my garden, I found I had become curious about how to best tend to it. The BBC's *Gardeners' World* became my classroom. Monty Don and Adam Frost and the rest of the BBC gardening team became my instructors, and I became a student, waiting with great anticipation for the latest weekly episode to discover what else I could learn and apply to my own garden.

Gardening has the potential to teach us about our own life journey, to teach us how to live well. When we give plants the proper nutrients, enough sun, and enough water, the necessary climate in which to thrive, and practice patience, they do thrive, and so can we. As well, gardening teaches us to be fully present, to savor, not squander; to appreciate what is and not ask for more.

Impermanence is part of the gardening journey. While life ends, there is a cycle of growth and renewal, and when we acknowledge and embrace this truth, we more readily and fully seize the opportunities to grow and celebrate each day. British horticulturist Gertrude Jekyll (1843–1932) put it nicely: "Each new step becomes a little surer, and each new grasp a little firmer, till, little by little, comes the power of intelligent combination, the nearest thing we can know to the mighty force of creation."

Growing a thriving garden has a lot of similarities to knowing how to live and love well. The same is true of our pursuit and perseverance with a passion or caring for a pet. When we show kindness and dependability and build trust, our pets, those involved with our passions, and, yes, even our gardens feel safe to grow, to reach their full potential, and connect and share themselves with us. Such a connection to other entities reminds us to let go and act not with expectation, but rather because we truly wish to give of our time, attention, and expertise.

The awakening of my love for gardening taught me the depth and breadth of my capabilities. I never thought I could sow seeds. But now I too can grow a seed into a plant, into a flower or an herb, and enjoy its beauty and gifts in my own garden. Of course, not every seed will germinate, but more will than not, so long as I provide what they need. This is the lesson the gardener learns — nurture yourself, care for yourself so that you can love this amazing life, and share it well with others.

March 1
Spring Changes

The birds are delighting me. As I type, two are congenially nibbling on an afternoon snack, and earlier today I sat not 10 feet from them while working on my porch, and they continued with their feasting.

Maintaining a feeder with food consistently is key, especially during the migration seasons (spring and fall); once the traveling birds come to know your "café" will be open, they will depend upon it, flying in regularly to dine. I am trying to do my part, and I smile giddily as I observe them. (*Birding tip*: Black oil sunflower seeds are the most recommended feed for birds.)

A sense of community, like the one we can create in our gardens with the birds, blossomed in my neighborhood and town during the uncertain time of the pandemic. While I took my afternoon or evening neighborhood stroll with the boys during the time of lockdown and isolating at home, residents were on their porches or sitting a healthy distance from neighbors on chairs they had brought out onto the sidewalk so they could chat in the warm spring sunshine. Other neighbors had company who drove to see them from across town; they sat on the sidewalk in folding chairs to catch up with their friends. All of this conveyed the determination to connect in healthy ways, and I smiled and waved as I passed each conversation (from the middle of the street, mind you).

The pandemic was temporary, but it prompted a dramatic shift, and the reality hit each of us differently. One positive part of the upheaval, however, is that we went through it together. Each of us did the best we could to navigate the unknown, which seemed to shift with each day. Saying hello to neighbors, maybe some we had never met, we offered a boost that reminded us we were strong and resilient and would make it through the crisis, and in so doing, exemplified thoughtfulness, respect, and gratitude for sharing our common space in Bend.

Meanwhile, the trees are beginning to bud up, getting ready to leaf out here in Bend, and I am excited to get outside this weekend and weed. I have ordered some mulch to be delivered later in the month and will need to spread it on my boulevard (the area of ground between the sidewalk and the street). I cannot wait to see leaves on my trees again, to see green, lush foliage. What a gift Mother Nature gives us, what a reminder that beauty comes from struggle as well as rest.

Yes, we may struggle, but we are also able to rest. So let's do both, and then, let's spring forth. Will you join me? I do hope so. I will admit, I sometimes have had some moments of angst during the pandemic, but staying in touch with my friends, my parents, TSLL readers, my students, and my neighbors has helped, and then I do what I love: I listen and adhere to what works for me, and that is a priceless practice.

Seek out such knowledge, and you will give yourself a wonderful treasure.

Petit plaisir Sow tomato seeds and begin the germination process using grow lamps.

Explore further thesimplyluxuriouslife.com/march1 (explore a list of tasks and ideas to be prepared for the coming of spring)

March 2
Life's Journey

My garden, though it is full of limitations . . . enables me here and there to point out something that is worth doing, and to lay stress on the fact that the things worth

doing are worth taking trouble about . . . but it is a curious thing that many people . . . when I show them something fairly successful . . . refuse to believe that any pains have been taken about it. They will ascribe it to chance, to the goodness of my soil . . . to anything rather than to the plain fact that I love it well enough to give it plenty of care and labour.
— British horticulturalist Gertrude Jekyll on cultivating one's garden

During the fall season, planting bulbs that will bloom in spring serves as a gift to ourselves: something to look forward to after winter's chill and challenge.

Like a bulb tucked safely underground, waiting for the temperatures to be gentle and nurturing enough, our life will blossom and bloom once we have given it the care, knowledge, and patience it needs to offer its fullest beauty.

Admittedly, there have been times, as we reflect upon history, when justice has been denied, but with time and perseverance, we have still seen progress. Whether it is waiting to walk across the graduation stage or waiting for justice to prevail, in small and large ways, life amazes us, reassures us, and empowers us to keep our face turned forward.

Sometimes you can forget that there is a journey to the life you wish to see come into fruition, but with the proper attention, learning, and application of the skill of letting go — rather than forcing what you want to happen when you want it — life has an amazing way of surprising you with awesome dreams coming true.

Petit plaisir Bring out the pillows and rug for the front porch. Get ready to watch spring's arrival.

Explore further thesimplyluxuriouslife.com/march2 (take a tour of my front porch)

March 3
Keep Searching

Recently, an ominous thundercloud hovered overhead and quickly, and unrelentingly, let its rain fall, free and fast, upon us pedestrians, who were sent scurrying to find our vehicles or the nearest place of refuge. However, within ten minutes, the sun was shining on glimmering pavement that had been doused with moisture.

Such scenes are common during the throes of spring's fickleness, but they make me ponder how quickly the status of our outlook and the lives we live can change, similar to the rhythm of spring showers and subsequent sunshine.

I don't know about you, but I am constantly reflecting, analyzing, and planning how to improve, elevate, and learn. There are times when it seems that there is not an answer in sight, but just as quickly as the downpour began and ended, so too could our questioning result in answers in our lives.

The key to making sure that this quick turnaround has a chance to occur is to never stop looking.

Petit plaisir Listen to Gustav Holst's "Jupiter, the Bringer of Jollity," from *The Planets*, op. 32: IV. Spring is near, bringing an end to a long winter.

Explore further thesimplyluxuriouslife.com/march3 (understanding how awareness and being present leads to deep contentment and peace of mind)

March 4
Mother Nature

I find myself frequently taking in all that Mother Nature allows us to witness during this beautiful time of year — jewel-like blossoms appearing magically on the fruit and deciduous trees, daffodils resolutely arising from the barely thawed soil, the melodious symphony of birdsong as males seek mates, and the fragrant, intoxicating scent of cool rain hitting the warming earth.

There is such a comfort in being in Nature's presence, and at the same time, a humbling effect on us earthlings. Our lives wouldn't be possible without Mother Earth. I am reminded that if I do not care for something, it perishes. On the flip side, if I offer time, attention, and effort to take care of something in the way it needs, beautiful things can reveal themselves.

Renowned horticulturist Gertrude Jekyll once wrote, "The grand way to learn, in gardening as in all things else, is to wish to learn, and to be determined to find out — not to think that any one person can wave a wand and give the power and knowledge." The same can be said for humans — our dreams, our structures, our loved ones, and our communities.

Appreciating the elements that provide such a wonderful life is an act of responsibility. Being willing to put forth effort to maintain, strengthen, or improve what we want to see continued is a sign of love, but often we become complacent and forget the basic laws of nature. An important one: That which we actively attend to multiplies, and that which is ignored strays out of our control.

Look around you today — at the beauty, the people, the jobs, the home, your way of life — and be thankful. Then get busy maintaining and strengthening what you would like to continue to see in your life. You must play an active part in preserving the beauty you love and treasure if you want to be assured of its permanence.

Petit plaisir Sow snapdragon seeds. They take about a hundred days to reach maturation (tiny little peeps, but oh they rebloom and rebloom all summer — wonderful for cuttings).

Explore further thesimplyluxuriouslife.com/march4 (sixteen ways to get out of your own way)

March 5
Celebrating Change

Spring is peeking at us from around the corner, and the need to remove a layer or two when I head outside has arrived. And while sometimes change in general can be a daunting concept, the change of the seasons is something I quite enjoy. Perhaps it is because the change is one in which we know what to expect as it happens every twelve months. If only all types of change were so simple and comforting.

But if the unknown gift of change was not available to us, we would not have the opportunity to grow, to evolve, and to become our best selves. While yes, the opportunity to become tripped up is possible as well, as soon as we realize we have more input into how it works out, based on the attitude we bring with us, the change that is bound to happen feels more exhilarating than frightening.

If you as well enjoy the change of seasons, why not try to become more comfortable with other types of changes you may be contemplating? As you approach them, consider your thoughts and your attitude. After all, they have more power in determining the outcome prompted by the change than you may realize.

Petit plaisir Take a nap as you begin to listen to Unico Wilhelm van Wassenaer's *Concerti Armonici*.

Explore further thesimplyluxuriouslife.com/march5 (reasons to slow down and how to do it)

March 6
Seasons

Mother Nature often sprinkles days of spring throughout February or early March, as if to give us a taste of what is to come and to encourage us to hang in there as, rest assured, winter will conclude soon. At this point in the year, I eagerly await spending time on my front porch and garden porch; often I will bundle up and sway back and forth on my porch swing, taking in the brilliant burst of yellow blooms from the forsythia, the first color seen in months.

If you live in a region where the seasons change, you will periodically celebrate their arrival and mourn their temporary ebb. Recently, I was reminded of an idea we should make sure to always incorporate in our day-to-day lives: the simple decision to celebrate that which you wish to see more of. If you are going to miss spring terribly, celebrate every day of the three months, and if you are like me and are quite thrilled to see warmer temperatures arrive when winter ends, celebrate the commencement of a grand time of year. Celebrate something good, something that infuses your life *with* life.

How to celebrate, you may be wondering? There are endless ways, depending upon what is enjoyable and most pleasurable for you. If you are a fan of winter, and want to wish it its proper adieu, perhaps a final homemade *chocolat chaud*, sipped and savored while you are bundled up, sitting on your porch while the temperatures are still chilly. Or make time to snuggle up inside in your favorite cozy attire; make a lovely French onion soup paired with crusty bread and watch the snow or inclement weather pass by your window while watching a favorite classic film.

For those eager for spring, why not begin planning your garden — what will go where for a successional display of color from April to October. Or plan your first trip to the nursery when it finally reopens for the new season. Or to epitomize spring, make something with rhubarb (rhubarb and frangipane tart is a favorite of mine) or asparagus paired with prosciutto and a poached egg with hollandaise sauce — yum!

Whether it is the changing seasons you wish to celebrate or some completed small steps along your way to a desired goal, celebrate these significant moments. By doing so, you tell those around you what matters most to you; it is a way of communicating with the world in a

manner that helps your life become a magnet for more of what you wish to see.

Petit plaisir At dinner tonight, enjoy a cheese course paired with a fresh salad tossed with a homemade vinaigrette. Try a classic English Stilton and be delighted. Have small slices of artisan bread ready for sampling with the cheese, and sip wine to complete the course.

Explore further thesimplyluxuriouslife.com/march6 (inspiration for celebrating small, yet significant private-life moments)

March 7
The Magic of Time

For those of us who want our dreams to materialize now, it can often seem that nothing happens quickly enough, and we can begin to feel that what we want will never happen. But the magic of time can either work with us or against us.

During the first spring of the pandemic (2020), I sowed seeds for my first herb garden. I chose seeds for plants that are hard to find as starter plants in nurseries — sorrel, chervil, and bush basil. It took three weeks for the seeds to sprout and another couple of months for transplanting, so that the plants could mature indoors before it was safe to plant outside (after the last frost), but the reward for my patience was enjoying fresh chervil on my morning omelet and julienning two cups of sorrel for my new favorite chicken recipe, inspired by a trip to France.

Growing plants from seed is much like aging: The way we nurture ourselves along the journey will determine our strength, our energy, our soundness of mind, and our ability to contribute well long into our later years.

So much of what society perceives as inevitable as we age is actually avoidable. Rather, what yields the effects so many equate with old age is our failure to take care of our bodies and our minds, and to build a life that is full of substance, joy, productivity, and play. Yes, someone may be older, and yes, time may have compounded the effects of the passing years, but often it is how one has lived that has caused the negative effects. I am by no means saying one can live forever, but the quality of our lives can be increased and may even surpass what we may define as a full and amazing life as the years pass by.

Likewise, achieving real success is not a short-term venture. It takes time. However, because we are impatient, we can spend the interim between now and potentially achieving our dream whining, worrying, or giving up, which will never lead us to where we want to go.

Real success can happen when you give your effort time to mature and strengthen, as well as time to determine if indeed what you seek is what you truly desire. Then, so long as you stay the course, almost like magic, the success will materialize, just as we see green sprouts rise from the soil. And while the materialization may occur years down the road, so long as it is a journey you wish to be on, your life will be filled with everyday joyful and pleasurable moments.

Today, let the angst that impatience is causing roll off your back, and be assured that you will meet with success when your journey is meant to meet with success. Simply by understanding such a truth, you are already successful, as you have brought back to your being more energy, more contentment, and less worry. At some unexpected moment — just like that — it will happen, and it may not be a surprise, as it will feel as though it was meant to be.

Petit plaisir Ease into the day listening to Erik Satie's *Gymnopédies*.

Explore further thesimplyluxuriouslife.com/march7 (where true success resides)

March 8
Are You Ready?

Hearing the first birdsong of the new year fills me with hope — hope that far more will be possible than we may have imagined in the depths of winter. In a way, the first birdsong of the year wakes us up like a morning alarm clock, albeit far more beautifully, nudging us to rise to a fresh start, an opportunity for a new beginning, a reminder that if we are lucky, we will have eighty or more springs in our lifetime. In my case, I have already lived through half of them, so what am I waiting for? What are you or I waiting for to take this one turn we have to live our lives?

I had been over the moon when I was hired six years earlier, but in March 2020, I turned my resignation letter into my administration at the public school where I taught. I knew, with grounded clarity and exhilaration, that a new chapter needed to begin if only I would find and exercise the courage to open the new door after gently and respectfully closing the previous one. My twenty-year teaching career would end. My solo entrepreneurial career, writing and blogging, begun twelve years earlier, would be my sole focus. It was time. I chose to not sit on the sidelines and simply dream and wonder.

Spring's arrival is powerful, and it comes every year, but only once a year. Are you ready? What are you longing to explore, to try, to clean out, to change, to redo, to experience?

When we sit with ourselves, letting the birdsong drift through open windows, the melodies settle us, but just as quickly, the birds' conversations cease and the performance is complete for the day, the morning, the afternoon. Just like that, it's done. Our lives too are fleeting, so what will you do? How will you live? What will you try? What is worth the risk? What is worth changing for a moment or even months of discomfort if that effort results in an improved quality of living?

When you are strong enough to know that, while you are grateful for a certain experience, it is time to let go, go ahead and take action. Turn in your resignation letter on that habit, that task, that career, that relationship — whatever it might be that is no longer meant to remain if your life is to move forward.

Petit plaisir Sow more arugula seeds (do it every two months), and prepare your lawn — rake, thatch, aerate. Take a hot bath afterward to soothe your sore muscles; they have earned it.

Explore further thesimplyluxuriouslife.com/march8 (letting go and hanging on: what falls where?)

March 9
Enjoying the "Now"

Spring will soon arrive with the snowdrops, English bluebells, daffodils, tulips, muscari, hyacinths, and fruit tree blossoms. Having planted our bulbs in the garden or our indoor pots last fall, we know we will have to wait to witness these perennial spring blooms. But we wait, because it is worth it.

Perspective is a powerful gift we can give ourselves for a wide range of scenarios in our lives. Studies have shown that the honeymoon phase of anything new will subside in time. For marriage, it might be two years; for a change regarding lifestyle (location, job, etc.), it might be six months. The length of time will vary from person to person, but the blissful stage diminishes as we become acclimated to our new way of living.

Certainly, becoming comfortable with our way of life is a good state to be in. It conveys that we feel secure to some degree and stable, knowing what to expect and how to get along. But what is always needed is the ability to have perspective.

A quote I saw somewhere said, more or less, "Appreciate what you have now, for it was once what you had hoped for." Because we become acclimated, because we become comfortable, we can unconsciously forget what we fought and worked so hard for in order to arrive at the place we are now. Perhaps it is a degree, perhaps it is a particular income or level of intimacy we share with a loved one. Whatever it is, the overall reminder is that we have a tremendous amount to appreciate.

We must remind ourselves that dreams do not materialize with a snap of the fingers. They cannot transpire just because we want them to. Why? Because it takes time, and because life is wise. Why would life give us what we asked for if it wasn't sure we truly wanted it? We must demonstrate that we have thought through what we seek and then show that we are willing to sacrifice and prioritize our lives so that we might attain it. Life is patient, and it asks that we build patience too. After all, "Patience is not the ability to wait, but how you act while you are waiting."

The time between setting forth your desires and the moment you acquire what you have wished for is what will determine your success. What are you doing while you are you being patient? Are you whining or are you working? Are you savoring or are you worrying? The contentment we experience is determined by the quality of our everydays.

Petit plaisir Read Norma Kamali's part memoir, part self-esteem book *I Am Invincible*, and listen to episode 303 of *The Simple Sophisticate* podcast, which extrapolates key points that speak to living simply luxuriously.

Explore further thesimplyluxuriouslife.com/march9 (why the journey might just be more significant than the destination)

March 10
Mother Nature and Her Temperatures

I woke up yesterday morning — as I do each morning, ready to take my early-morning walk with my dogs — to rain falling from the sky and the corners of my mouth rising in glee. Upon checking the temperature outside to see if I needed my earmuffs and gloves, I realized that the temperature had increased ten degrees from where it had been the previous day. I was surprised, and pleasantly so.

Mother Nature never tells us when spring has begun and winter's chills are officially over; it seems that it just happens, almost without warning. And while there will be cold spells every so often for the next few months, it feels as though winter has decided to retire until next year.

The events that occur in our lives to change or improve the course we are on often reveal themselves in much the same way. As we go about our daily routines, doing our best, all of a sudden the veil seems to drop, revealing something that had not previously been there. However, the reality is that we were making progress the entire time, little by little.

Small steps made as you progress toward your intended destination will eventually place you at the finish line. You may not know when you will arrive, but so long as you keep going, focused on today and refusing to be distracted, beautiful revelations will occur. Today, remind yourself that the grand reveal will eventually happen so long as you keep your head down and do what is necessary to reach your goal.

Petit plaisir Welcome a vintage tea table into your living room or a cozy corner.

Explore further thesimplyluxuriouslife.com/march10 (tea tables, a British décor detail for your sanctuary)

March 11
How to Establish a Clear Direction

Gardens have to do with sensuality. All of our senses are involved. They play a very important role in one's reaction to a garden. And so the breeze in the leaves, you hear the leaves shaking, and you smell the fragrance of the flowers, and you get turned on by all these things happening. So, think, you can't go wrong if you emphasize the sensual elements in your garden when you make it.
—Frank Cabot, gardener of Les Jardins de Quatre-Vents (La Malbaie, Quebec)

During the summer of 2018, I arrived at the Jardins de Villandry, in the Loire Valley, pretty much by accident. I had been traveling around France for just over two weeks, was staying in a nearby château converted to a bed-and-breakfast, and was seeking a place of calm, somewhere to wander about without the clutter of tourists.

I entered "nearby gardens" into my GPS, and Villandry popped up. While the destination also included a historic château, it was the gardens that I sought with eager anticipation.

March

Arriving mid-week within twenty minutes of the garden's opening, I had the grounds seemingly to myself (which, I later heard from a local, is rare). I immediately lost track of time, let myself and my mind wander, and began to feel refueled. Wandering about the Jardins de Villandry gave my mind the time to breathe, savor, appreciate, and garner great inspiration, for we can learn a lot when we choose to garden, and in return we are given much.

Alice Sebold was correct when she wrote, "I like gardening. It's a place where I find myself when I need to lose myself." I would add that even visitors to a garden are able to experience this paradoxical gardening truth. And again I must quote British gardener extraordinaire Gertrude Jekyll: "A garden is a grand teacher. It teaches patience and careful watchfulness; it teaches industry and thrift; above all it teaches entire trust."

In a garden, order and perhaps symmetry are paired with natural splendor, and for me, that helps bring clarity and calm. There is a power in balancing order with natural gifts and temperaments, and while it is not easy (gardens take an immense amount of regular work), when we take the time to establish a direction that aligns with our truest selves, the journey becomes easier to travel. Not because it is obstacle-free, but because we know which obstacles to face and which are not worth our time.

Examine your daily, weekly, or monthly routine. Does anything bring you stress without fail — a particular person, a particular responsibility, a destination you have to visit? First, if you are able, eliminate the interaction or the task from your routines. If you cannot eliminate it, combine it with an activity that immediately reduces your blood pressure. For me, being outdoors, amid Mother Nature's beauty, is where I turn without hesitation. Where will you turn?

Petit plaisir A pair of swans that call Les Jardins de Villandry home swim gracefully about the ornamental pond at the center of the *boulingrin* (a sunken garden, formally known as the Water Garden), designed in the form of a Louis XV mirror (see them in the video link below). It only seems fitting to listen to Camille **Saint-Saens's "The Swan"** ("Le Cygne") from *Carnival of the Animals*, R. 125: XIII, and drift away from the day, if only for a moment.

Explore further thesimplyluxuriouslife.com/march11 (enjoy a tour of the Jardins de Villandry)

March 12
Growth

Certain quotes and aphorisms finally resonate with me as my life experience builds. In fact, I could not fathom some of these quotes that I happened upon when I was younger. How could what they were stating possibly be true or even a good thing?

As I was driving home one recent day, this quote came to mind: "Life doesn't get easier. You just get better at being able to handle it." Years ago, I saw this quote as an absolutely dreary proposition for getting older and advancing in life. But now I took a moment to look at my life and the things that I had chosen to put on my plate (and some that I had not), and I realized I was handling it all quite well (not perfectly, mind you, but better than I would have twenty, even ten years ago).

This quote no longer appeared dispiriting to me. Rather, my current response to it was a reminder that I have learned from past life lessons, learned to trust myself and my ability to respond and deal effectively with whatever crosses my path. I came to appreciate the quote; it was a reminder that I was maturing. I was no longer the young, naïve girl who worried at the drop of the hat. I no longer needed everything to be perfect. Knowing I was no longer that person was liberating and exhilarating.

Knowing we can be our best advocate, knowing we can remain strong and calm even when we wish that what we have to deal with would just get fixed — would just happen, would just hurry up — is a tip of the hat to our ability to incorporate calm habits into our lives and learn from the many lessons presented to us along the way. Instilling calm habits into our daily lives can make a tremendous difference in the quality of the life we live, no matter what happens outside of our control.

Today, take a moment to ponder how you have evolved, how you have matured. Because I have a feeling you have grown in enormous ways that sometimes you forget and need to be reminded you now possess. Embracing and celebrating that you are a work in progress requires a conscious choice to refuse to remain stagnant, and if you are living consciously, it is easier for your mind to remain open and for the growth you seek to occur.

Petit plaisir Delight in the birdsong on your morning walk, and be reminded to put your bravery into practice. The future is not written; that is the gift.

Explore further thesimplyluxuriouslife.com/march12 (how to be brave)

March 13
Observe Nature's Pace

Birdsong gently awakens me in the spring and summer months. Because I can rely on my feathered friends to begin singing around five in the morning, I leave the windows open, preferring a natural alarm clock to begin my day. Gradually, the night's dreams and unrealities dissipate, and a fresh twenty-four hours begins.

The mornings of days filled with daylight are a treasured time. The pots of annuals and herbs that I cultivate need refreshment, and I do some tending to the garden as I stroll through the boulevard and along the borders. The boys trot along nearby, letting curiosity lead them off the quickest route to where we are going. Eventually we make our way back to the front porch swing. Tea is steeped, shoes are off, and time stalls for a moment, if only in my fantasy world. The birds continue to sing. A few feathered visitors stop by the garden's bird cafés, and still others swoop about, getting their daily exercise. Perhaps that is my reminder to partake in my own workout, but I stay put: Delighting in the birds' morning routines is a ritual I treasure.

Lessons from nature are infinite, and savoring what is, without holding on, is wisdom we ought to practice and polish. Fortunately, the seasons are cyclical and will return, but it will take a long while, and to drink up all that spring, then summer and fall, and even winter have to offer is to be dazzled by the cinematic magic provided by Mother Nature.

Petit plaisir Delight in the emergence of the snowdrops and daffodils.

Explore further thesimplyluxuriouslife.com/march13 (journey at the pace of nature)

March 14
Being Present

Eckhart Tolle's book *The New Earth* talks about the shift from doing to being and how it can elevate our everyday lives, enabling us to fully appreciate the present.

The concept seems simple enough, but after listening one day to someone in a nearby conversation talk about how she feels guilty if she is not doing something (for example, taking a nap would be impossible for her as her guilt would be immense), I began to ponder the root of feeling guilty for not "doing."

Unfortunately, I don't think this woman is alone in her thinking. For much of my twenties, I too felt this conflict, and perhaps it was guilt for not being constantly on task, focused on a project, a job, or a chore during my waking hours. However, at the same time, I also was not comfortable with this approach to living; constantly "doing" did not feel right, yet the culture seemed to encourage it obsessively — from the media, to the books I was reading, to the people I was around at the time. But constantly running from being did not sit well with me, and gradually, I began to question this need to do, to always be busy.

What I discovered was the foundation of living simply luxuriously; a life well lived is not full of *more* and constant "doing," but instead is quality, thoughtful living. And not all living needs us to be physically in motion. Yes, we do need to exercise regularly, and yes, there will be regular chores to attend to, but sitting down and relaxing regularly, and taking time for self-care in any one of the many activities that enables us to rejuvenate, are just as crucial to our well-being. And there's that word again: being.

Being exhibits a calm and clarity about ourselves, and in order to become comfortable with being fully present in the moment, we have to stop busying our mind by busying our feet or our hands. Sometimes we stay busy doing so that we will not have to confront what needs our attention in order to grow, in order to understand, or in order to find peace. And when we find each of these (growth, understanding, peace) and work through the challenges to attain them, we can find more comfort in being because we are at peace with ourselves and where we find ourselves, and can then take in all that is around us at this very moment.

Petit plaisir Explore the warmth and potential of wallpaper in your most personal spaces — the bedroom, the office (if you work from home), your bathroom. Purchase quality paper, and be amazed by its grand transformation and mood-lifting, comforting power.

Explore further thesimplyluxuriouslife.com/march14 (discover how to wallpaper by yourself — yes, you can!)

March 15
Love Yourself

Peonies in early summer. Planning for the garden begins well before such beauties can dazzle, but it has always been a dream of mine to have a bevy of peonies in front of my house to greet guests in June and July, so I placed my orders, some as early as the previous fall and wait patiently for my favorite varietals to arrive for planting.

Coral Charm, Sarah Bernhardt, Hermione, Bowl of Cream. Each of these and many other varietals dazzle onlookers (especially myself) when I see them in gardens, freshly cut at the market, or in my imagination growing in my own yard, as I wait for my peony plants to mature.

I love peonies because they are evanescent. They do not re-bloom repeatedly, only once each year. We cannot make them something they are not. We love them all the more because of their singular offering, but what a magnificent offering it is. The herbaceous plant gradually begins to emerge from the soil seemingly out of nowhere in early spring, finally reaching its full maturity in June, and then offers its dazzling gems. We cannot rush them. We cannot change them. We must love peonies for what they are.

And, after all, that is the love we desire — a love for exactly who we are — not because we force ourselves to be something or someone else, not because we change our color, the amount of our petals, or the length of our growing season. No, real love is loving someone for who they are fully.

Often we feel a lack of love because we feel misunderstood or unseen. Such a feeling prompts a deep ache and a depletion of emotional elation to go about our days well. When we can identify why we feel this way, we find strength in valuing ourselves and refusing to conform. We achieve strength when we find the courage to be who we are and to free ourselves from the burden of conforming and thus diminishing our unique light — one that the world needs and wants to see.

Real love of any kind celebrates your sincere self. Begin celebrating your strengths, acknowledge your imperfections, and gradually work to learn and strengthen what you do not know. "Get off your back," as my friend once said to me, and refrain from being so hard on yourself. You are enough. You are amazing. You have something the world needs. Love yourself, give yourself permission to be yourself in the world. The real love you seek will be present in you, and thus you will attract it from others.

Petit plaisir Watch the Danish series *Seaside Hotel* and be swept away to the coast of the North Sea.

The Road to Le Papillon

Explore further thesimplyluxuriouslife.com/march15 (the benefits of self-compassion, and how to have it)

March 16
Unfruitful Attempts Can Lead to a Bountiful Harvest

With spring's arrival in 2012, I took a risk and began renting an apartment in Portland's Pearl District as a way to find out where I wanted to live, as I knew Pendleton would not be my forever hometown. Spring brings with it buoyant new energy, inspiring a bounce in one's step, an extra boost of hope, and a renewed sense of determination.

While we can play it safe and choose an unobstructed path, following what works — sticking to the same routine day in and day out, waiting for the monthly paycheck to arrive, clocking in and out of work five days a week — blindly choosing a routine often leaves us wondering what might have been. What were we really capable of?

Of course, it is true that doing what one needs to do to put money in the bank for basic necessities and caring for loved ones is paramount, but once those needs are covered, why not . . . take a risk?

I was incredibly excited to explore living with my two dogs (my eighteen months of living on Portland's NW 23rd pre-dated Oscar's arrival) in the city I used to love living in and calling home. However, with this leap, I took a risk. I admitted then that there was a hint of uncertainty dancing around somewhere in my head at the time. But based on how my mind works, that small dose of fear is what gave me the confidence to make something wonderful out of a bit of uncertainty, and in hindsight, it was a great decision.

For nearly my entire life, it has been my experience that taking a risk on something that captures your mind, heart, and imagination is well worth a little temporary timidity . . . even if it does not quite work out in the way you initially imagined.

Fast-forward three months. Spending my weekends in Portland had not turned out the way I had imagined, and I slowly saw my hard-earned extra money being spent on something other than the opportunity to purchase a ticket to travel to Paris or eventually England. As well, and most important, my boys needed the outdoors, not the city, and I did not want to waste their time, when I did have two days off, on elevators and in the car commuting.

So I reclaimed my deposit, moved out, and spent the money on my first solo trip to Paris since college. What I gained was clarity about where I would eventually call my forever home. It would not be Portland because I had changed since I last lived there, and loved it, in my early twenties, and while it offered culture and the arts, it lacked easy access from my back door to the outdoors, which I had found was essential for not only my boys' health and happiness, but mine as well.

Today consider taking your own leap. And keep in mind that even if it doesn't turn out as you initially hope it will, it may reveal insights, previously unknown, that will lead you ever closer and more confidently in the direction of your true contentment.

Petit plaisir Make molten lava cakes for dessert. It takes only fifteen minutes to create scrumptious chocolate deliciousness.

Explore further thesimplyluxuriouslife.com/march16 (recipe for Molten Lava Cakes)

March 17
Motivation and Discipline

Sometimes we place deadlines on ourselves, and sometimes people and institutions place them upon us. Either way, deadlines can be a positive concept to welcome into our lives.

Deadlines impose an expectation. If we are expected to produce or complete something, we must be proactive; something must be produced, and sitting and doing nothing is not an option. If the deadline does not involve us taking action but rather is asking us to be patient so that someone else can do something by a particular time, then arguably, that is easier.

Either way, deadlines can teach us something about ourselves. During the journey leading up to the deadline, we discover what we are truly capable of if we apply ourselves, and we also discover our ability to be patient, have faith, and give time to people, projects, etc. that may be on a different time schedule than we are. During this waiting process, we also come to learn what sparks our passion. In other words, what are we willing to wait for? With reference to the former, what are we willing to sacrifice?

The tricky part about setting deadlines yourself is that you have to have the discipline to establish either consequences or rewards for your progress (or lack thereof). Too often we take for granted that we met the deadline and completed the necessary task, and forget to reward ourselves for the success.

I encourage you — as I need to continue to remind myself — to reward yourself. Perhaps it will be a day off. Or maybe give yourself

that "luxury item" you have had your eye on. Our confidence is built gradually, and finding the willpower to motivate ourselves when nobody else is checking in is a powerful skill. Setting significant goals reminds you how capable you are.

Petit plaisir Clean and reorganize the office or any work spaces in your home in order to start fresh and clear in the upcoming new season.

Explore further thesimplyluxuriouslife.com/march17 (ideas for creating a productive office space and desk)

March 18
Curiosity

First, it was the rhubarb. Then, the strawberries. And then the cherries.

The spring and summer of 2020 provided the opportunity for the residents of my new, small Bend neighborhood to become better acquainted. We worked in our gardens, weeded our boulevards, monitored small children as they played in the cul-de-sac, spent time on our front porches, brought back our pups when they wandered to say hello to the neighbor next door and encouraged us to do the same. These outdoor activities strengthened the neighborhood's common appreciation for a safe, kind, and peaceful community.

Two of my neighbors across the street — a brother and sister, ages five and seven, respectively — became my companions for a few minutes at a time this summer. To be honest, the boys (my dogs) were the residents of Le Papillon that the two siblings wanted to see when they stopped by, and then there was the fruit.

I offered a stalk of rhubarb to the boy when he pointed out the large leaves, and his glee prompted him to run to his bike and pedal across the road and back into his house to show his mom; I didn't see him again until a few days later. Then the two children, who always asked permission to enter my yard, found the strawberries that grow in the borders edging my lawn. Realizing the loot of red jewels was more than their small hands could hold, they returned home briefly to find a small bowl. Quickly, the picking resumed, and the strawberry patches were prepped for the second harvest to arrive.

Months later, the cherries, which the two youngsters had first observed as green camouflaged fruit hanging among the leaves, finally got their red shine of ripeness. The girl tucked cherries into her overall's back pockets, and I think the young boy ate his straightaway; he didn't have any pockets.

When you keep your eyes open, what is new, different, and ever-changing will catch your eye if you remember to be present. Young children remind us to stay in the moment, as each one can bring a wonderful discovery.

Petit plaisir Pour a favorite cuppa while delighting your senses with sounds and sights and smells to make you smile. Using your personal stationery, write a thank-you to someone who brought a smile to your face or ease to your day.

Explore further thesimplyluxuriouslife.com/march18 (nine benefits of being enthusiastic)

March 19
Savoring the Present Moment

I recently had a conversation about preparing for the next season. My friend suggested that to fully enjoy the arrival of the new season — any season — preparations are in order well before the season begins. For example, if you are a skier, make sure your skis are waxed and ready to go for the first snow; if you are a paddleboarder, have your board and the rack on your car set up so you can take advantage of the first warm day. I can absolutely see the benefit of such preparation.

There is nothing like the first time doing something when you have been unable to partake for an entire year, but I must say, there is as well something about savoring the last days of each season. For example, these weekends in March are still chilly in the morning and evening, so much so that the furnace comes on, and when I return home after a long walk, it is so nice to feel the warmth of the house as I walk across the threshold.

Perhaps what I am suggesting is to strike a balance. Perhaps we should not wish the current season away too quickly because when it is over, we will not see it for quite some time, but at the same time, we can do a few things here and there that allow the next season to begin with celebration and the ability to fully appreciate it. For example, spring cleaning — I love the feeling when the floors get a deep cleaning, closets get reorganized, and the big jobs such as cleaning out the refrigerator or editing the garage are complete.

But at the same time, why not savor those mornings when, still in your favorite pajamas, you snuggle in to your favorite chair with a cup of *chocolat chaud*. Such moments are quite sweet as well.

Petit plaisir Tune in to a new season of *Gardeners' World* on BBC Two and slip away to the countryside of England.

Explore further thesimplyluxuriouslife.com/march19 (seven reasons to watch *Gardeners' World* — whether you are a gardener or not)

March 20
The Simple Pleasure of Spring Rain

There is something serene about the rain in spring. Perhaps it appears more tranquil following an extended winter, but when the rain began steadily falling one recent morning and continued into the afternoon, it seemed fitting to turn on Count Basie's "April in Paris," throw on my raincoat, and take Norman for a walk. (He loves the rain, while Oscar prefers the comfort of our home when the wet weather arrives.)

Since I know that these spring rains are few and far between here in Bend, Oregon, I try to savor them whenever they arise. For me, the rain is a simple pleasure that costs nothing but my time, and upon returning home, I always feel refreshed and more at ease than when I walked out the door.

The beauty of incorporating simple pleasures into your life is that it requires very little expense, and only asks that you be conscious and fully present. For when you are present, appreciating the comfort, calm, and sincere joy of a situation, you can often put other things into perspective as you go about the rest of your days.

Petit plaisir Listen to birdsong as a new spring season begins, along with Vivaldi's Flute Concerto *Il Gardellino* (The Goldfinch) in D, RV428, Allegro.

Explore further thesimplyluxuriouslife.com/march20 (inspiration for reveling in simple pleasures)

March 21
The Beginning of Spring

If you want to be active for life, create a garden.
—Luigi Valducci, renowned grower of brugmansias

Dancing into spring, yes indeed!

Knowing that spring would bloom into being this week, I picked up a bunch of daffodils at Trader Joe's. They bloomed on cue and offered a weeklong burst of sunshine in my bedroom. I found myself smiling each time I walked past this bouquet that cost fewer than $10.

When we welcome simple, thoughtful touches or restorative rituals into our lives throughout the year, they can be more elevating than we may expect. Whether it is buying a seasonal bouquet, engaging in an activity that brings us joy and deepens our appreciation, or planning a short seasonal getaway to freshen our minds and routines, tending to our everyday and seasonal needs, along with regular self-care, makes a positive difference in the quality of our lives.

One such seasonal activity I have regularly talked about on the blog is going through my closet. Twice a year, I try to go through and edit, noting what I need and what I need to fix, and figuring out what no longer is part of my style. Upon finishing this seasonal task, I have more clarity about the outfits that I have already prepared and that are ready to wear for the new season, and I am better able to shop for the items I truly need as the new collections arrive in stores.

Such activities offer clarity and can save money in the long run as well. And while not all of our seasonal rituals or activities may be simple or free, the goal is to ultimately elevate the quality of our lives. Spring is one of my favorite seasons. The opportunity to start fresh is an amazing gift, allowing us to make the most of what it offers.

When you finish your wardrobe edit, plan your getaway, or purchase a bouquet of flowers, you feel lighter, more eager for the new season to unfold and better able to savor and appreciate the new spring season.

Petit plaisir Try a new outdoor activity. I gave snowshoeing a try for the first time in 2021, paddleboarding in my thirties, and yoga, in my twenties.

Explore further thesimplyluxuriouslife.com/march21 (eight ideas for making spring truly bloom)

March 22
Persistence

All of a sudden, the weather warms up, daffodils begin to bloom, and evenings become longer. Even though the cold, dreary days that winter brings seem to drag on a bit long as March reminds us it is primarily a winter month, spring does come. March 22 does arrive. The persistence of the perennial flowers that eventually emerge from the thawing ground reminds me of the amazing talents we can discover that we have when we are confronted with difficult obstacles.

"Adversity has the effect of eliciting talents, which in prosperous circumstances would have lain dormant." I particularly like this quote from the ancient Roman poet Horace, as so much truth exists in his claim. Too often we do not test our abilities until we are forced to. Ideally, we would figure out these revelations in gentler, safer ways, but thankfully, one way or another, life places a mirror in front of us to show us of what we are truly capable.

Take the time to assess what you have discovered about yourself during the winter. What are your resolutions? What are your dreams and wishes? Do not become so soothed and complacent with the warming weather that you stop striving toward what you wish to create. After all, another winter will come, and don't you want to welcome it as a better version of yourself?

Petit plaisir Watch anything that features British actor and presenter Penelope Keith for a good, smart laugh and a moment of lighthearted escape. *Penelope Keith's Hidden Coastal Villages* is a lovely introduction and great way to travel without purchasing the airfare. Her earlier *To the Manor Born* and *Good Neighbors* are also wonderful series to view.

Explore further thesimplyluxuriouslife.com/march22 (the importance of continuing to knock)

March 23
Personal Growth and Growing Pains

Spring has arrived, but it seems to be having a tough time making up its mind if it is really ready to spend time with us and send winter packing. Yesterday morning, I woke up to see my neighborhood dusted with snow and large, wet snowflakes effortlessly falling from the sky. Personally, I found this quite serene, but I know that for many, it was not as welcome.

Personal growth can be much like March, when the weather tends to be a bit uncertain. When we begin to seek to change something within ourselves — whether it is how we handle money, how we take care of our bodies, how we use our words, or whether we believe in ourselves — we can feel uncertain. We may first wonder if the uncomfortable feeling is how we are supposed to feel, or we may be tempted to step back into our old ways.

Even if we progress, we may still run up against frustrating situations and again question whether it was a good idea to seek such dramatic change. However, these are simply growing pains. Much like physical growing pains, they are uncomfortable, and while we are in the middle of this process, we are not exactly sure how it could possibly be a positive thing.

Seeking change within yourself is a sign that you respect yourself, that you know yourself well enough to understand that you can do more to fulfill your potential and that you want to live your best life. The path to fulfillment will not always be crystal-clear and blissful. Yes, many moments will be, and reaching your destination will be worth the struggle, but making permanent changes in how you think and behave will be difficult at times. But just as March has an end, so too does the pain you feel when you choose to change how you live.

Petit plaisir Remove from your bedroom all technology that enables you to check your e-mail or social media or to scroll through the internet.

Explore further thesimplyluxuriouslife.com/march23 (why growing pains are a very good sign)

March 24
We Are the Source of Our Happiness

One of the best ways to make yourself happy is to make other people happy. One of the best ways to make other people happy is to be happy yourself.
—Gretchen Rubin

As I was scrolling through Instagram, I came across this quote from the Happiness Project founder, and the beauty of its truth made me smile. Indeed, if those around us sincerely want to be happy, they will want us to be ourselves, engrossed in what makes us happy; just as we want them to feel such contentment, they want the same for us. After all, seeing those we love happy is a wonderful gift.

But our contentment is entirely dependent upon ourselves. This means that we must be the curators of our contentment, rather than rely upon others to offer it to us. Those outside "life measurements" (being in a relationship, having children, reaching a particular point in your career, buying a house), once reached, are not a guarantee that you will instantly become "happy" if you were not already. We must know how to be content all on our own, so that when we experience these occasions of happiness, we can appreciate them all the more.

Often, the reason we perceive ourselves to be not happy is that we are focusing on circumstances beyond ourselves, and not focusing on our own behaviors and thought patterns as the path to contentment.

When others no longer have to do something to make us happy, because it is contentment we seek and happiness we celebrate when it dances through our lives, our steady contentment will become infectious. In other words, when others realize that we are at peace with ourselves, they will also realize that they must be clear about how to gain their own peace of mind. Ultimately, we make this discovery through a personal journey to get to know ourselves. It will lead to security within ourselves, as well as increased self-respect as we become aware of what we can and cannot tolerate.

True contentment allows us to live peacefully in our everydays, no matter what the day's events, our emotions (negative or positive), or world news. Cultivating contentment provides stability for the mind as we engage with love, openness, presence, and kindness to others and ourselves.

As for the first point of Gretchen Rubin's statement, when we do something in an attempt to help, ease, or brighten someone's day, the gesture is the gift; the giver seeks nothing more than to bring joy into someone else's life. And so it is a balance, but one that ultimately involves awareness on both sides: being aware of oneself (self-awareness) and being aware of what will help the individuals one loves (emotional intelligence). When we discover these truths, the decisions in life become easier, the choices fewer, and the outcomes extraordinary.

Sometimes you can be lulled into a routine and forget to be present, appreciative, curious, and explorative when opportunities present themselves. Consider approaching your everyday life as you approach these once-in-a-lifetime moments, and I am confident your life's overall quality will increase beyond your expectation.

Petit plaisir Read Jay Shetty's book *Think Like a Monk*, and then recommend it to someone you love who might appreciate it.

Explore further thesimplyluxuriouslife.com/march24 (explore nine ways to think like a monk)

March 25
Appreciating Life's Surprises

The climate of Portland, Oregon, differs from that of Bend, a three-and-a-half-hour ride away. When I drive over the mountains to visit the Willamette Valley (where Portland is located), I often pop into the local nurseries. The spring plants — the lupins, the salvias, the nepetas — are in full bloom. Excited, I will purchase a few of my favorites to build up my boulevard. When I return to Bend, while I may want to place them in the ground, our climate is not at the stage to properly nurture the delicate blooms, so they remain indoors to be nurtured a bit longer until the temperatures improve.

Sometimes life unfolds so beautifully that we forget to appreciate how amazing such occurrences are, until nothing seems to be going as planned — the love life, the career path, the daily routine, the flowers not blooming as early as we thought they might or not reaching their full potential as they are placed in the wrong environment. No matter what you attempt, destiny seems to keep stopping you from getting what you think you need to be content.

It's funny how life follows contours and unknown side roads we did not even know existed and often introduces us to a secret garden of abundance we would never have known was available to us if our initial plans had worked out or if we had simply had more patience or done more research.

Sometimes when we are presented with what we wish for, what we thought we wanted seems, surprisingly, to be a consolation prize in the life we have now begun to live (maybe, in the beginning reluctantly, but without realizing it, and now with resolute passion and joie de vivre). And isn't that the breaking news we never could have imagined?

Life has a magnificent power of surprising us in wondrous ways. That should be reason enough to give something we are unfamiliar with a shot. Here is another way of thinking about this: "If life can remove someone you never dreamed of losing, it can replace them with someone you never dreamt of having."

During the throes of the pandemic, amid the lockdown and isolating in our homes, I met my neighbor, a man similar in age, who lived on his own in his house 10 feet away from Le Papillon. I had lived in the neighborhood for nearly six months, and until March 2020, I had never spoken to him; we had never happened to cross paths. Forced to remain home, I often stepped into my garden to weed, to plan, to mulch, to just be, and he too would be outside working in his yard. Our occasional conversations over the fence at a safe distance provided in-person contact I greatly appreciated; we would talk about current events, sports, gardening, house projects, life, and everything in between. Very little was off limits. A year later, he sold his house and moved, but his unexpected friendship during an unexpected time in our collective history serves as a reminder of life's surprises.

This idea of life having more breathtaking plans for us than we could imagine has been giving me pause for the past few months. And while I still do not have the slightest idea what life has in store for me, it has already taken me down a path that I could not have imagined regarding the gift that is TSLL. I have a feeling you too have something in your life that is grander than you could have predicted.

If, right now, you are in a quandary, perhaps what life is asking you to do is take a deep breath, do the things you love doing on a daily basis, and be present to discover the opportunities that present themselves. Who knows, the gift of your life may be just around the corner so long as you do not force the bud to bloom before it is ready.

Petit plaisir Cut or buy a small handful of daffodils and welcome them inside. Double Repletes look like a beautiful, fresh-poached egg and dazzle on the south side of my house, the first to roar up bravely from the ground in Le Papillon's garden.

Explore further thesimplyluxuriouslife.com/march25 (five things to do to build healthy relationships and four things to let go)

March 26
Continue to Have Courage

When spring arrives, it comes with many different unique, exciting, and long-anticipated events. While this is true with each of the seasons, spring for me has always offered moments to shift, grow, progress, and shed the ill-fitting past.

Sometimes what needs to be shed are clothes that no longer fit my signature style or fit as well as they should. Sometimes a way of life needs to change: a location, job, or relationship; sometimes a way of thinking needs to change. The self-talk that runs through our minds each day we are going about the life we have chosen to live is what will be the soundtrack of our lives. If we are humming a cheerful, sunny song, such as the Beatles "Here Comes the Sun," we may see events through a filter that glosses over the minor hiccups and reminds us of how fortunate we are. If we are humming Sarah McLachlan's "Fallen," it can be more difficult to see through a fog that has been self-made (don't get me wrong,

March

I adore Sarah's music, but there are a few songs that are ideal for wallowing, which sometimes we need to do before we can move on).

 Whatever needs to be revamped, have the courage to get your hands dirty and do it. While time will need to pass once you make the decision, eventually, if you stick to the change you have pinpointed as necessary, the life you have imagined will begin to unfold and gradually become your reality. As you consider your mental soundtrack, I will leave you with Monty Python's "Always Look on the Bright Side of Life" (played at soccer games as well as funerals in the United Kingdom). After all, how can you listen to this song and not add a skip to your step?

 Petit plaisir Begin reading the first cosy British novel in D. E. Stevenson's four-book series set in a small English village in the 1930s: *Miss Buncle's Book*.

 Explore further thesimplyluxuriouslife.com/march26 (how to live a courageous life)

March 27
Everyday Moments

I fell asleep earlier this week to the pattering of steady rain on the roof and the porch and through the branches of the trees in my yard. I think I fell asleep smiling. Such beautiful little moments, which are created beyond the grasp of our preferences or control and make living life well priceless, do not happen every day.

 I enjoyed a phone conversation with a dear friend who I speak to regularly just to catch up, and our conversation made me feel so very fortunate. I walked along the river with my boys one afternoon this week, and seeing them walk with happy steps made me giddy to be able to share my life with such lovely companions.

 It can be easy to rush, to hustle and think we cannot slow down. I too have these moments, but then I remind myself that when I hustle I cannot be fully present. Yes, we do need to be respectful of others' time and try to not be late, but slowing down will help our moods and thus the quality of our overall lives because all we have is the present moment.

 What moments did you savor this week as you went about your everyday routine? Even if it takes a moment, it is in remembering that we are reminded ever more why we need to savor and be fully present in our lives.

Petit plaisir Transplant snapdragons once they reach an inch in height, and they will grow far more successfully into their full maturation.

Explore further thesimplyluxuriouslife.com/march27 (learn how to truly savor everyday moments and watch it elevate your life)

March 28
Trust Your Journey

Yellow, they say, is the color of the positive, leading us forward into the new season with joy and gaiety.
—Carol Klein (from *Gardeners' World*)

When I saw Le Papillon for the first time, I had not been intending to buy a house for myself. Do not get me wrong, I had been *wanting* to buy a house in Bend for four years but had stopped aggressively searching, somewhat exhausted by trying and not wanting to dash all hope with one more thwarted go-see. I happened upon Le Papillon by chance, but when I saw her, I knew. It was the rhubarb.

The house intentionally was placed on the market in early July, and now I know why — the garden looks magnificent in July when the majority of the perennials and vegetables and fruit trees are in full maturity. Had I visited Le Papillon in March, I would not have known that the rhubarb situated to the left of the front porch Craftsman column, perched up on the landscaped rock terrace, would exhibit such massive stalks and leaves.

I say it was the rhubarb because I had attempted to grow rhubarb at my rental for the past four years, and it had yet to offer a stalk to bake. Even at my previous home, after more than a few years, the rhubarb plant was still quite small in comparison to Le Papillon's single and mighty plant. I was in awe, and I continue to be.

Perhaps when we look for something, we can find it, or pretend to find it, anywhere, but if my happening upon Le Papillon in 2019 taught me anything, it was that perhaps that is not quite true. So long as we are striving forward, remaining in tune with our inner calling, events unfold as they should. We may not understand this at the time, but eventually we do. The key is to continually put yourself out there. Engage with life, and offer opportunity the chance to present itself.

Sometimes the opportunity can seem to be a roadblock, a frustrating one that even the most tenacious of us cannot overcome. But even in these instances, as time passes, I have found that these so-called "roadblocks" happen for a reason, as though life takes the wheel for a moment and says, "No, trust me. I have a better route for you to travel. It won't make sense now, but it will eventually. Go with it."

And the brilliance, as we later appreciate, is that when future events occur, we are even more certain of what we want and what we don't want. It is as if the passage of time fine-tunes our decision-making process. If there is any gift I can give or wish I had possessed earlier in life, it would be this superpower: the ability to make the best decision for myself, at a moment's notice, without wasting any unnecessary time.

In prior years, I may have thought such a capability was a superpower, but the truth is, we can learn the skill of making the best decision for ourselves without lengthy delay. So while it can seem a difficult, nearly impossible wisdom to possess, in fact, when we choose to be the student of ourselves and do the necessary, uncomfortable, and undesirable work, we can possess this superpower. It is not elusive. It will arrive once you have continued to slog through the uncomfortable moments, stood up against what did not feel right, taken the time to get to know yourself, and faced your question marks. It is a journey, without question, but the bucket of gold coins on the other side is absolutely worth it.

But back to spring. The closure of winter that occurs when spring begins is much like ending a book. It is a fresh start. But in order to have a fresh start, we must shut the door, finish the book, and move forward. Period.

If spring is any indication, the book that was winter is worth closing. It no doubt taught some invaluable lessons, but now you need to go forward, apply them, and be the better you that you are.

Petit plaisir Sow seeds for tomatoes, herbs (chervil, sorrel, bush basil, anything you cannot find in local nurseries in plant form), Bells of Ireland (after freezing the seeds for a week), Prairie Sun, Cup and Saucer vines, and broccoli, and always more lettuce — this time more French mâche (aka lamb's lettuce).

Explore further thesimplyluxuriouslife.com/march28 (the first post introducing Le Papillon to readers of the blog in 2019)

March 29
Slow Down and Take Care of Yourself

Each of us is the gardener of our own inner landscape. The plants we give most attention to are the ones that flourish. When we complain, we water the weeds. Gratitude waters the flowers.
—adapted from *Awaken the Happy You*, by Richard Paterson

The sunshine garden, the garden porch, the front cottage garden.

When I saw them, prior to making them my own, each of these areas around the exterior of Le Papillon tugged at my need to settle and just be. It was almost as if this one-level house, ideal for one or two people, knew the humans who inhabit it need regular time to be still; the design of the house evokes an honoring of tranquility and self-care. Now that I have lived in my home for just over two years, these places invite me to slow down, pick up a book or a cuppa and a nibble, and just be. I do so more and more regularly with each passing month and year as I become accustomed to letting my home nurture me.

Finding time to unwind does so much good for our psyche, relationships, mood, and creative process. While knowing this life-truth and practicing it can sometimes be two different things, if we each make a regular appointment with ourselves to say no to obligations, refuse to multi-task when we take time for ourselves, and respect ourselves enough to realize it is okay to regularly put ourselves first for an hour, an afternoon, or even a weekend, we will be amazed at the improvement in our lives.

Not only will we feel better, but we will also be in a better frame of mind when spending time with those we love and work with. And for anyone who works in a creative field or is trying to come up with unique ideas for décor, garden design, travel plans, outfits, a child's birthday party, or sweet somethings for a partner, the ability to think creatively will soar when we take time to just relax and unwind on a regular basis.

It may sound absurd initially, but when we let our minds temper their speed and come to a neutral place of no stress and silenced stimulation, they begin to restore themselves, much like our bodies restore themselves during sleep.

Taking time for ourselves is a necessary practice to incorporate into our daily lives. Sometimes it is hard for people to be comfortable with their own company, but speaking as someone who, while introverted, had to transition into becoming comfortable with myself when no one else was around, I have discovered it is the best gift we can give ourselves, and it only asks of each of one necessity: time . . . time to put ourselves first, time to respect who we uniquely are, and time to be with our thoughts, hopes, and dreams without outside interference or persuasion.

Be proactive. Take care of yourself first, so that you can give fully of yourself and live beyond just trying to get by. Consider it an investment in yourself, your peace of mind, and your legacy when you value the necessity to unwind, relax, and do so regularly. After all, if you are not willing to look out for yourself and invest in your own peace of mind, why would you expect someone else to do so?

Petit plaisir Sleep on linen pillowcases and surround yourself with French or Belgium linen sheets.

Explore further thesimplyluxuriouslife.com/march29 (French linen: the fields, the history, and why it is truly luxurious fabric)

March 30
Consistent, Steady Effort

Life has a way of surprising us, teaching us, reminding us, leading us. I am always reminded of this fact when spring is in full bloom, and I am humbled by the dependability that results in success: cultivating patience, working hard, trusting oneself, and pushing forward gradually, yet steadily, in our day-to-day lives.

In the previous house I owned prior to moving to Bend, one such reminder came as I toodled around in my yard, taking care of the hostas as they revealed their full, luscious leaves and as a young magnolia tree's blossoms finally burst with brilliant yellow color. None of these plants had been planted during the same year or were around before I moved into my home. But I had lived and cared for the grounds of my home for the previous five years, and the beautiful spring perennials and trees had sprung up in a display of foliage that at one time was not there.

Therein lies the lesson. Consistent, steady effort that may seem to go unnoticed or unappreciated, and that yields little, if any, immediate results, will in its own time shower us with unexpected treasures and surprises. The surprises might not be things. They may be a realization of a newfound confidence or strength, or an ability to let go of something we once tightly grasped. If we set into motion an effort toward a goal and are willing to back it up with our time, sweat, and tears, amazing outcomes await.

Once your destination is certain, stop fixating on the end result and instead place your attention on the daily effort that is required.

With this approach, you will conserve energy that you had been wasting with worrying and fretting, instead of gaining ground as you progress toward your intended goal.

Petit plaisir Refresh your eye makeup. Brighten your eyes by using less black and choosing eye shadow that complements your natural skin tone.

Explore further thesimplyluxuriouslife.com/march30 (thirteen instances in which slow and steady is the best approach)

March 31
When Our Lives Burst Open

You need enthusiasm and determination, and knowledge follows later on.
—gardener of Breezy Knees, in York, England (shared on *Gardeners' World*)

The rain came down one recent afternoon, and it came down ferociously hard. It did not ask for approval. It did not check to see if the sidewalks and streets had been swept so the drains would not be clogged. It did not even hint that we wouldn't need to water our lawns for the day, saving on the water bill. It came because the clouds burst and the circumstances were ideal for gully washers to have their way with the town of Bend. It came because it was time.

Just as spring storm clouds burst, dousing the ground, our lives can burst as well: with fantastical, amazing experiences, as well as some of the not-so-wanted variety. A buildup occurs, a stress point can no longer endure the pressure, and a release is needed. There are many ways to avoid negative bursts: be proactive, find balance, know your limits, understand your feelings, and be strong enough to know how to deal with them even when it is uncomfortable.

We sometimes forget that eventually a cloud needs to burst. And if we keep showing the universe that we are sincere about our direction and passion, windows will gradually open, and then doors. And then we are crossing the threshold and sitting down at the dinner table. Life is full of energy, and it has to go somewhere. We each might as well make it work in our favor.

You can help stack the odds in your favor, to make it likely that something wonderful will occur. You can fine-tune your discipline, have clear goals, be a person you want to be around, find your voice,

March

and practice patience. You have so much more control over the life you wish to cultivate than you realize. Mastering your mind, check. Understanding your emotions, check. Refusing to be stopped by frustration, check. Finding the courage to push forward, check.

Petit plaisir Does your computer need more memory, not more storage? Tech tools that hum along efficiently make the necessary tasks and the pleasurable ones all the more enjoyable. Know what you need, and invest in quality.

Explore further thesimplyluxuriouslife.com/march31 (ten truths of successful people)

April

Speak Up, Communicate Well, Set Boundaries

April

> *We set ourselves up for long-term trust when we let it evolve naturally.*
> —Jay Shetty, *Think Like a Monk*

My child-mind governed my approach to relationships, of all types, for far longer than I want to admit over these past twenty years. But beginning in my early forties, my monk-mind, as Jay Shetty calls it, or my Inner Sage, as Due Quach names it in her book *Calm Clarity*, began to receive regular exercise consciously. I regret not having learned how to use my brain better earlier in life, but I am choosing to use all of my experiences to remind myself why the child-mind is an unhelpful place for experiencing true contentment.

Trust is essential in relationships of all kinds, and the truth about trust is that it takes time, and only very few can embody all four types of trust (Consistency, Care, Character, and Competence) as laid out by Jay Shetty. Not only is it hard to find someone who embodies all four basic traits of trust, it is hard to *be* someone who embodies all four as well. Keeping this life-truth in mind reminds us how difficult it can be to reach such a high bar and to be more self-forgiving. In a reminder that we must take responsibility for our lives, the deeper truth is that we must get to know ourselves, choose to continually grow, and follow where our curiosity leads us.

Here's more of Shetty's wisdom: "When we learn to love and understand ourselves and have true compassion for ourselves, then we can truly love and understand another person . . . Once we've unpacked [our] own bag and healed [ourselves] (mostly), then [we will] come to a relationship ready to give. You won't be looking to them to solve your problems or fill a hole. You don't have to be perfect, but you have to come to a place of giving. Instead of draining anyone else, you're nourishing them."

The goal is not to find only people who embody the four types of trust. We would be missing out on wonderful, loving relationships if we were that rigid. Think about your parents or a beloved sibling or friend. Likely, you hold them close, even throughout your adult life, because they embody the Care type of trust — "they care about your well-being and what's best for you, not your success." But they may not offer the Competence trust component — "the person has the right skills to solve your issue. They're an expert or author in their area." Perhaps they are an expert in their field, but your issues may not be in that field. You are still going to want to build a meaningful relationship with them.

As with Consistency, in your local community, when heavy snowfall happens each winter season, as it does here in Bend, Oregon, we feel an increase in trust when it is removed in a timely fashion; however, you are not going reach out to your local officials for Care on an intimate level. Character, as well, may be a core component of the trust you have in your life partner or spouse, along with Care, but you may not be Consistent with the small details of life, not out of malice but due to circumstances out of your control. Yet trust strengthens, and the relationship deepens because the quality of Character remains ever-present.

As a general approach, after coming to understand the four trust components, if someone over time demonstrates an embodiment of two of the components, I feel gratitude for the opportunity to connect with them.

Demanding that others be trustworthy in any or all four areas, expecting that they will give us what we need (something we should first give ourselves) is letting the child-mind direct our lives and is a recipe for hurt, pain, and a dissolving of our ability to trust others. While the child-mind is impatient, the monk-mind tends to "look for meaning (practices awareness) and absorb what you need to move forward instead of getting locked in judgment (good or bad) . . . when you apply filters like the four C's [of trust], we can see if our network of compassion is broad enough to guide us through the complexity and chaos of life."

My relationship with Veronique, now a dear friend, began as an exchange between a customer and interior design expert over five years ago. First, Veronique introduced me to French and other European brands and companies that make items for the home, and with each purchase, my trust in her strengthened as the quality of each product was superb. When I purchased Le Papillon, as I began to explore creating a primary bedroom that married comfort and signature style, including layers of quality linens and a wallpaper to echo my appreciation for Mother Nature while maintaining warmth and tranquility, I turned to Veronique.

Each and every time, her expertise exceeded my hopes, and with each bill paid on my part, each detail brought to fruition on hers, our interactions built upon themselves. When I had first introduced myself in 2016 upon walking into her boutique in Bend, Veronique did not know me, but I quickly came to appreciate her expertise and confidence with textile and design issues. When she opened Studio Vero in Bend a couple years later, I regularly visited, purchased small items for my home and shared what I loved with readers on Instagram and my blog. I conveyed my trust not through my words to her directly necessarily, but through my actions.

Our conversations and planning for the décor of my bedroom began in April 2020, and one year later, my trust was so deeply rooted that I left the room in her hands, with my boys as her hosts as she came in to install my curtain rod and window treatments as well as arrange the linens on my bed while I was at work. Our first project together, my satisfaction beyond met and all bills paid (trust components: Consistency and Care), built upon the trust we already had begun to build.

April

  I sought Veronique out for more upholstery projects throughout Le Papillon, for which I needed her expertise (trust component: Competence). She knows I am serious when I share my ideas, and she goes out of her way to provide small extras I had not expected but am deeply grateful for (trust component: Character). While our relationship began as a business exchange, it organically evolved into a friendship as over time, all four components of trust (Competency, Consistency, Character, Care) had played a role, and the way we handled our exchanges built a trust stronger than I could have imagined. But it is important to underscore the importance of time, and therefore patience, equally paired with two individuals secure enough in themselves to speak honestly, saying not what the other person wanted to hear, but what the truth was (what they knew, wanted, understood, didn't understand, preferred, etc.), but always in a respectful manner and always with the intention to figure out how to make it work for both parties involved.

  Patience, observation, awareness, and honest communication of needs: these are also components of trust. Others cannot connect with us (if they want to, and some will not) if we do not share with them what we need to feel — loved, seen, heard — and we cannot connect meaningfully with others if we do not listen and observe what they in turn share with us.

  Our mind can be an amazing student if we remember that it is a student and that we can be its teacher so long as we have constructive tools (experts, teachers, books, neurologists). Be patient with yourself as you learn how your mind works. I was put at ease when Due Quach shared, in *Calm Clarity*, that her mind is not forever locked in her Inner Sage. There will be times, often regular ones, when our minds regress or we wake up in the child-mind. Awareness is key so that we can bring it back to a higher state of thinking, observing, and engaging healthily with others.

  When it comes to relationships and building trust, we must not forget to build trust in ourselves as this is a necessary skill to exercise in order to deem accurately whom to trust and for which of the four C's. After all, as Shetty sagely reminds, "only you can be your everything." In other words, knowing who to reach out to (Care), who to rely on (Consistency), who to look up to (Character), and who to trust (Competence) is a daily exercise, a vital part of our decision making and mental mastery. As I move forward, fewer unnecessary stressors appear in my days, and navigating external headaches becomes easier as I know what I can do well and who can do well in areas in which I am not the expert.

  While my child-mind attempts to grab control from time to time, I am now aware, for the first time, of its attempt and more quickly shift back to my "monk" or "inner sage" mind. As a result, my trust in myself has strengthened, enabling me to build healthier relationships in all arenas of my life without rushing, without expecting, only observing, acknowledging, and trusting I will know the best next step forward.

April 1
Choosing a Career You Love

Recently, I listened to a podcast that discussed Nobel prize-winning author Albert Camus's essay "The Myth of Sisyphus" in relation to today's worker. The focal point of the discussion was the concept of choosing a job one enjoys.

So many people have a *job* — something they do that pays the bills, puts food on the table, and provides economic stability. Yet many long to work somewhere else. Modern-day philosophers have applied the lesson Camus taught in his essay by suggesting that it is our responsibility to bring meaning to our work, rather than to expect the work to provide meaning.

In other words, we are responsible for our own contentment or state of boredom. We are responsible for adding spice or taking on challenges at our place of work. We are ultimately the one who decides to take risks, to try doing something differently or learning something new.

When you recognize that your approach to life is the greatest predictor of your state of happiness, you can stop searching outside yourself and start stirring the creativity that already exists within.

Petit plaisir Begin the day with a hot cuppa green tea — to soothe the mind and boost your health. Try Mariage Frères' Vert Provence with mellow rose and lavender.

Explore further thesimplyluxuriouslife.com/april1 (ten health benefits of drinking tea)

April 2
The Role of Role Models

But nothing important, or meaningful, or beautiful, or interesting, or great ever came out of imitations. The thing that is really hard, and really amazing, is giving up on being perfect and beginning the work of becoming yourself.
—Anna Quindlen

April

Role models are meant to inspire us and show us what is possible. Mentors are meant to lead us and guide us. And while it is wonderful good fortune to have such people to look up to, it is important that we realize our own uniqueness.

As students in elementary school, we are given breaks throughout the day for recess; designated play periods paired alongside blocks of time for learning. We become conditioned to a certain schedule, and the routine provides its own sort of comfort, whether we thoroughly enjoy ourselves or not.

As adults, we are given expectations and parameters as well from society. And while these societal "rules" can provide comfort to some extent for most and ideal contentment for a handful, they can be absolutely wrenching for others. As Anna Quindlen suggests in today's quote, we should not try to be exactly as everyone thinks we should be, following the trail that someone else has left for us. Instead, we should follow our own path.

We can use a trail provided by our role models and mentors as a starting point or as a checkpoint, but we must be brave enough to charge out on our own, let our hair down, and be our authentic selves. Ironically enough, it is easier to precisely follow the path that someone else suggests we travel than it is to find the courage within ourselves to simply be our best selves.

When you follow the "rules," you can blame someone else if a situation doesn't feel right, or you can feel a false sense of calm when you do what is needed in order to be accepted. Do not resort to either behavior. Instead, accept who you are, and do not apologize for finding contentment in a life that others may not understand.

Petit plaisir Occasionally, stay up well into the early morning hours reading (and finishing) a book that has smitten you, then gift yourself with a leisurely morning of sleeping in from utter exhaustion after delighting in how all was resolved.

Explore further thesimplyluxuriouslife.com/april2 (how to be brave: follow your "this" to live the life you have dreamed about)

April 3
The Journey: Slow and Fast

Progress and plateaus. I have been thinking about how life progresses after speaking with blogger and author Sharon Santoni during her first visit to my podcast (2016). She mentioned that her blogging venture, several years old, has had a progression of movement and then plateaus. After much contemplation, I came to grasp this life-truth more fully and found great comfort.

Simply because we are not progressing at the speed or pace we would like does not mean we are not making movement forward toward our goals; however, what tends to happen if we allow our mind to control our thoughts is that we compare our turtle pace to that of bursts we have experienced previously. Understandably, those bursts were thrilling, wondrous, and adrenaline-racing experiences, but when we do slow down, and our minds are not sparking as quickly as we would like, it does not mean they won't again in the future.

So long as we keep trying out new ideas, gaining new information and ultimately stimulating our minds and challenging ourselves, the quick, heart-pumping pace and creative bursts will come again. To know this life-truth is to give ourselves comfort and reassurance.

If we are in a slow period, our minds are resting up before the next big game, the next big performance. After all, for an athlete, musician, or actor, the night before a game, concert, or performance is not the time to expend energy. Rather, it is a time to rest, to become focused, and to become clear about what will occur the next day. Like the progression of the seasons, life is cyclical; the only difference is that we get to carry our newfound knowledge and life experience with us to the next big peak, which further enhances the experience.

May the new month of April find you being gentle with yourself. Whether you are resting on a plateau for a moment or peaking, trust that even the smallest steps forward will keep the momentum going in the right direction for when the wind picks up yet again, as it inevitably will.

Petit plaisir Plant shallot bulbs now for harvesting in late July. Each bulb can produce twelve shallots, and they store wonderfully through the winter months.

Explore further thesimplyluxuriouslife.com/april3 (your unique journey and how to navigate it successfully)

April 4
Personal Values and Standing Strong

It is easy to say that our values soundly support a life we will be proud to have lived, upon reflection, when we surround ourselves with people who agree with us. However, when we go about our daily lives, meet new people, and keep our minds open to other ways of thinking, the values we say we have can be tested and examined to determine our sincere understanding — whether we believe what we say we do or are simply following what others believe.

After all, it is much easier to be swayed by someone else's values when we have been told what we should believe and have not truly come to know why we believe what we do. However, when confronted with situations that make you uncomfortable, explore the reason why. When you have had time to step away from the situation, explore why you felt uneasy. In time, it will become clear. Yet again, we need to trust ourselves, trust our instincts, but then be willing to do the work of understanding why we feel the way we do.

Recently, I was unexpectedly confronted with a situation that tested what I valued. My immediate response was one of discomfort and distress because I had an inkling I was the only one in the vicinity that felt as I did, but I could not bring myself to go along with the group. After assessing the situation the next day, I came to realize that while others may try to explain why such a situation was acceptable and attempt to belittle my reasoning, I needed to stand my ground. It was not easy, as I lost the friendship of someone I had come to care about, but I slept with a sound conscience that night, knowing I had adhered to what I valued.

I am a strong proponent of keeping an open mind and listening to all sides of an issue; in order to be at peace with ourselves, we must know where we stand. And we must know when bending our principles would discredit our integrity or weaken the life we wish to live. We must know what we believe and thus live by if we wish to respect ourselves and gain respect from others.

There is a catch: It is not easy, as I can attest to firsthand. Once you know what you most value, you will be tested, prodded, pushed, and at times cleverly manipulated when others try to sway you to go along. After all, it is easier when the flock aimlessly follows the lead sheep and no one strays.

In order to live the life you wish to live, you must be free to make the decisions that will create such a life. In order to be free, you must have courage, and courage begins by knowing what you value and being willing to stand by what you believe. While it often seems that

we have control over very little, there is actually much we do have control over that we often forget about.

Petit plaisir Watch *Murdoch Mysteries* for a dose of history, mystery, science, and characters who you will become quite fond of over the course of fifteen seasons.

Explore further thesimplyluxuriouslife.com/april4 (eighteen red flags to pay attention to in relationships)

April 5
Try What Scares You

Conquering what scares us can provide an amazing boost in our belief in ourselves.

When we are faced with challenges or attempt to do something we have never done but have always been curious about, we have the opportunity to take another step toward our full potential. Initially gathering up the courage to try a new venture can be unnerving. But consider giving podcasting a try, teaching a new course with high expectations from the school and academic community, daring to explore the French countryside on my own in a rental car, or driving on the left side of the road in Britain for the first time — each of these instances from my own life remind me that when we choose to put forth our best efforts and complete a task, we often surprise ourselves and stir up a reminder that we are capable of so much more than we realize.

Perhaps, as you look forward to the coming summer, you will see some free time ahead. Why not attempt something you have always wanted to do but that perhaps intimidated you a bit? I am confident you can do it, and simply completing the first attempt can fill you with more than enough confidence to try it again the next time and with even more success.

Petit plaisir Begin the day by listening to Johann Sebastian Bach's Oboe Concerto in F Major.

Explore further thesimplyluxuriouslife.com/april5 (your fear is speaking)

April 6
Determine What Is Worth the Wait

At some point, you have no doubt waited in line for something — whether queuing at the grocery store, waiting at a red light, waiting for the workday to come to an end, or waiting in line for a performance or speaker. While these seem like simple ways to wait in line, I would like to take this concept a step further.

There are outcomes in life that we have to wait for whether we want to or not — our paycheck, our turn to check out at the grocery store, notification of acceptance to a program, school, or club — but there are things in life that are worth waiting for, and thereby we choose to do so.

Those things in life that are worth waiting for are what I would like us all to think about today. In 1962, after being exiled for nearly half a century from his mother country, Russian composer Igor Fyodorovich Stravinsky was invited back to conduct a concert in Leningrad, inspiring people to wait in line for a full year, to see an event that prompted Olga Grushin to write the historical novel *The Line*.

After learning of such dedication and willingness to wait for something, I could not help but wonder what in my own life would be worth waiting such an extraordinarily long time for. But then I began to realize that I, like so many people, am waiting for so many things already. Some of these things are goals we have set for ourselves (personal, retirement, family, love, peace, etc.). Waiting in line is essentially putting our priorities in order: What is worth working and striving for and what is not?

Hopefully, you have long ago determined what is worthy of your time, hopes, and dreams and are able to clearly ignore deterrents that grasp at your attention but have no role to play in fulfilling your heart and life. Such a distinction is easy to discern when you know what your priorities are. Whether it is waiting for the opportunity to live in the town you have dreamed about, investing in the foundations of a garden that will take at least five years to reach its full beauty, or bearing the heat to see the future president of the United States speak only 50 feet in front of you, you will know what is worth your time when you listen to your inner voice.

Petit plaisir The daffodils around Le Papillon put on a show at different times throughout the spring, depending upon where in the garden they are planted. While I leave most on display in the garden, I will snip a couple or three and bring them in for a simple bouquet.

Whether you grow your own or simply love daffodils, find a bundle and add a touch of spring to your home.

Explore further thesimplyluxuriouslife.com/april6 (discovering what is worth the wait)

April 7
Exercise the Mind and Expand Its Capabilities

Life is full of moments, people, and situations that are out of our control. However, the things we do have control over are our perceptions, beliefs, assumptions, expectations, and feelings, as I was reminded after being introduced to Deepak Chopra's *The Healing Self*.

Any time heartbreak or pain occur in our lives, especially when it comes from a source beyond ourselves, the survival instinct to self-protect emerges. We may wrongly label and oversimplify any subsequent interaction or person with similar traits to avoid future hurt. The boyfriend who belittles us in public becomes "All men are unkind." The girlfriend who becomes jealous of our interactions with other people becomes "All women are insecure." The boss who dismisses our ideas becomes "I don't have anything worth contributing." Unhelpful assumptions, beliefs, and feelings based on our experience can give rise to generalized false truths, when, in fact, they can only be true for that particular incident, person, or relationship. Our job is to grow in awareness of why we hold each of the perceptions, beliefs, assumptions, expectations, and feelings that stand in the way of true contentment.

Mastering our perceptions, beliefs, assumptions, expectations, and feelings, instead of letting them master us, takes a conscious and constant effort, and I will honestly admit, I am still a work in progress. However, when we face obstacles we believe are insurmountable, instead of adjusting our perceptions, beliefs, feelings, expectations, or assumptions, we can instead come to realize that the solution is within our grasp, and we are able to flow with the events that occur in our lives instead of constantly struggling against them, thus reducing our stress and anxiety and increasing our happiness and joy for life.

Based on our past experiences, we can quickly jump to a conclusion and assume the worst, but if we remember and trust the decision making that has put us in this present moment, we can trust ourselves. We can look for our purpose in being placed in such a situation and rise to the occasion to make the most of it, instead of freezing and making the situation worse.

April

A mind shift is not easy, but the more you practice it, the more it will become a habit, and the more contentment and subsequent happiness you will experience in your life.

Petit plaisir Consider naming different areas of your exterior space and even the rooms in your home, especially if, as with Le Papillon, you have rooms that open to each other with no dividing walls. When it comes to my garden, even though it is quite petite, I have a kitchen garden, a woodland area, a rockery, a sunshine garden, and a cottage garden. Doing this imparts purpose and helps guide planting and décor decisions (and you can always change the name as you better familiarize yourself with the space).

Explore further thesimplyluxuriouslife.com/april7 (twenty-four ways to live beyond labels)

April 8
Journaling Through Feelings and Unwanted Events

The therapeutic powers of journal writing are often forgotten as the world around us clips along at a frantic pace. The initial thought may be to dismiss this exercise as unnecessary, especially when time is of the essence. However, I have been reminded of this habit that I sorely need to make myself dive into, especially during moments of emotional turmoil or stress.

The act of putting pen to paper is a healthy way to vent, to sort through your thoughts and make sense of what exactly it is you are feeling — and, more important, what caused you to feel this way. When we take a time-out to open our journals, we don't jump to conclusions; we help eliminate the possibility of blowing things out of proportion and saying things aloud we may not truly want to say.

If this is something you have been wanting to try but are having a hard time incorporating in your daily routine (it doesn't need to be daily but can be used as relief during times of stress and questioning), turn it into a simply luxurious ritual. Buy a beautiful journal. Purchase a pen that begs to be used. When you are able to find some time to yourself, pour yourself a cup of tea and sit in your favorite spot. Before you know it, you will long for this time, and you will also notice many positive results in your mind, your emotions, and your day-to-day routines.

Petit plaisir Schedule a day for yourself. Call it a good health day. Plan ahead just enough so that you look forward to it and can plan what would enhance it effectively — perhaps a facial, or attending a particular favorite event. Savor this special time without worrying about responsibilities, and pay no mind to the clock.

Explore further thesimplyluxuriouslife.com/april8 (six reasons to journal)

April 9
At Least Try ... Give It a Good Swing

As spring begins, so does the baseball season, complete with the smell of freshly cut grass, the traditional pace — slow and drawn-out to blend the appreciation of the sport with the time spent with fellow fans — noshing on hot dogs between innings, and paying attention, if only not to be hit by a foul ball.

I began to think about the sport of baseball recently — specifically, that the only way a player will ever earn extra bases is if they swing, swing well, and swing hard. Sure, they may get on base with a walk or being hit by a pitch, but neither will take them farther than first base. The only way to go farther, arrive closer to making it across home plate, is for the batter to step into a pitch and watch the ball meet the bat.

A savvy pitcher can maneuver a ball around even the most talented hitter, but eventually, if a batter keeps swinging, keeps practicing, keeps their eye on the ball, they will connect. And that eventual connection will feel ever so sweet.

In 2012, Aaron Sorkin, writer of *The West Wing*, *The Social Network*, and *The Newsroom*, said, in a commencement address at Syracuse, "Baseball players say they don't have to look to see if they hit a home run; they can feel it." I think the same can be said for life: Sometimes you just know when it feels right; you just know, when an opportunity presents itself and you have decided to swing, that the outcome will be something amazing. But here's the catch . . .

You have to put yourself in the batter's box. You have to know when to swing, and you have to have the confidence to swing fully in order for the ball to sail over the back fence. That is the hard part. Because until it lands on the other side of the fence, bouncing down the city sidewalk, you are taking a risk. Your swing may result in just another fly-out, but it could also be the walk-off home run that wins the game.

You do not know where the economy will be in three years, you will not know if consumers will like what you have to offer, you will never know if he/she will say I love you back, but you will never find out unless you put yourself out there and try. Keep on trying until you understand what will work and what won't, what is worth investing in and what is not.

The key ingredients to making your dreams become your reality include being married with practice, being engaged with courage, and being grounded with confidence in yourself.

Petit plaisir Sow nasturtiums. They will pop up out of the soil before you know it. They are beautiful flowering plants for edging the garden or filling and draping down pots — Claude Monet's Giverny is awash with shades of orange nasturtiums — and they are edible!

Explore further thesimplyluxuriouslife.com/april9 (welcome serenity into your life with these fourteen key ideas and practices)

April 10
Spring as a Classroom

If there was ever a season that caused me to become twitterpated, it would be spring. With the lush green grass nurtured solely by Mother Nature's watering can, magenta, blush, and white blossoms that flirt with passersby, and showers that sing me to sleep and often wake me the next morning, I find myself wishing that spring occurred throughout all twelve months of the year.

As much as I dream that this magical scene could present itself each day, I am aware that I might not relish it as much if it occurred constantly. And when wonderful, exuberant moments and good news we have been hoping and wishing for finally arrive, the waiting and anticipation make them much sweeter and far more appreciated.

The waiting process is not easy, but it does allow us time to make the most of the moments in between, to not squander these opportunities, and to use such time to help create what it is we are hoping for, as we fine-tune our efforts, learn more, and apply the new knowledge we receive. Every day, there is something to learn — about ourselves, about life, and about others.

Petit plaisir Read Bryan Kozlowski's *Long Live the Queen: 23 Rules for Living from Britain's Longest-Reigning Monarch*, for insights and worthwhile approaches to living well from Queen Elizabeth II; for example, one suggests refraining from venting to reduce your own stress, as well as considering the well-being of others.

Explore further thesimplyluxuriouslife.com/april10 (six thoughts on reasons to savor the seasons)

April 11
Goals

Have you ever experienced a time in your life when you felt as though you were following all of the necessary and correct advice to help you achieve your goals, and have been doing so for quite some time, yet you have come to a point where you have to ask, What else do I need to do, because my goal has not been achieved yet?

During such moments, it can seem as though you are never going to reach your dreams. You can begin to question your approach and your carefully laid plans. You may even reconsider giving any more effort because you are not sure it is worth it. I have been there, and if you have been there as well, you know it can be extremely frustrating and often mentally taxing.

Keep following your plan. Keep sticking to the strategy you so carefully researched, planned, and laid out for yourself because you will arrive where you had imagined; it just may not be on the time schedule you had hoped for.

Some years ago, I was reminded of this advice when, after carefully researching how to write an ideal query letter for prospective publishers and agents, an agent finally asked to see my work. This did not necessarily mean anything for certain, but it was a step in the right direction, and it demonstrated that I was doing something right. Before this happened, I was questioning myself repeatedly, running doubts around in my mind, asking myself what I needed to change or abandon, as it seemed nothing was working. After many rejections, I just kept my head down, kept polishing my query letter, and continued to believe in my product. Yes, those days of frustration happened periodically, but they passed, and I got busy again.

Having a clear plan, being knowledgeable about the process you have chosen, and being willing to learn constantly as the process unfolds will eventually result in good things materializing for you.

Petit plaisir Design and decorate a workspace — whether at home or at the office — that invites you to do your best work. Shop on consignment sites such as Chairish or 1stdibs and brick-and-mortar second-hand and vintage shops for signature items to enhance the space.

Explore further thesimplyluxuriouslife.com/april11 (ten steps to help you begin to customize your home)

April 12
Invest in Your Dreams. Invest in Yourself

Investment: the act of buying or paying for something that is seen as having value and that will continue to increase in value into the future.

I cannot think of many investments that are more valuable than ourselves. And whenever I sit down to set goals for the future or plan where I want to use my hard-earned money, at the top of my priority list lies what I value the most. Where do my investments go? To my retirement, to property, to business building, and anything else that will provide growth, an even better life, and security for my future.

In addition to the traditional avenues of investment mentioned above, I include investing in education, the value of which is often debated, but in my opinion it is worth pursuing if you have a vision and exercise patience and persistence as you pursue your dream. Perhaps your dream is a new small business, perhaps it is publishing a book or creating a website centered on your area of expertise, or perhaps you wish to open a catering or styling company. Whatever you dream, why not invest in it? After all, if it is what you feel you are destined to do or if you would regret it if you never made the attempt, why not?

So long as you do your research ahead of time, have a little cushion saved up to get you started, and are willing to work hard, why not invest in that dream you have had running around in your mind? Why not take the risk, make the leap, and continue to strive toward what you have dreamed would become your reality?

Petit plaisir Add one or two more investment pieces to your capsule wardrobe. Shirtdresses and wrap-dresses are a go-to item in my wardrobe — linen or cotton — for spring/summer.

Explore further thesimplyluxuriouslife.com/april12 (six reasons to invest in education)

April 13
Friendships

Genuine friendship is a rare thing. At least it has been for me as I have navigated through the past twenty-plus years of adulthood. I have found that distance, age, or life experience make no difference in cultivating a friendship; rather, it is the content of one's character that determines one's sincerity, compassion, and compatibility. Our life circumstances will prompt us to connect with others more readily during certain times in our lives, but some life events reveal one to be a forever companion or a fair-weather friend or foul-weather friend.

A friend worth having meets our magnificent news with overjoyed excitement, just as they greet an unforeseen heartbreaking moment with tenderness and encouragement. Strong friendships in many ways resemble healthy romantic relationships in that they require two secure individuals who see no need to compete, but merely agree to support, encourage, and respect the understood space that each needs to be their best selves.

During times when we do not have strong friends in our lives, it can be tempting to wander back to people who continue to keep us down, who gravitate toward us only when we are suffering, and who run from us when we are soaring. I have learned that such second attempts are not worth the emotional angst. We must find the strength within ourselves to weather the loneliness, by first befriending ourselves wholly and then by putting ourselves out there to meet new people and build a different social circle. So long as you present yourself with self-assuredness, humility, respect, and clear boundaries, you will find people who are secure in their own lives and who will appreciate your courage, healthy sense of self, and authenticity.

The saying turns out to be true: Good friends are hard to find, but when you do find them, especially if you have experienced the contrary, you will realize that no matter how far apart you travel, no matter what the age difference, these are people who are worth the effort.

Today, whether you have one solid, quality friendship or five, be thankful and remember to continue to invest in small, everyday ways.

Petit plaisir Celebrate the serendipitous moments that brighten your days. They don't happen each day, but when they do — you hit all green lights, the much anticipated phone call rings with good news, the line is absent at your favorite takeout restaurant after a long day at work — acknowledge them and pay gratitude, and such a practice will amazingly bring more to your attention in future days.

Explore further thesimplyluxuriouslife.com/april13 (quality friendships = a quality life: ten benefits of cultivating healthy bonds)

April 14
Choose Relationships Wisely, and Be Patient

Among the life-truths I have learned along life's journey, two stand out regarding relationships: The strength and talent of those around you will either help you soar or help you sink. And cynicism will never be a component of a fulfilling and amazing life.

On the latter point: It can be risky to have high hopes, as they can be dashed, but eventually we find what we look for, and personally, I would rather find what I am hoping for than what I am fearful of. As I go forward, I am hopeful, and if this something does not work out, I know I will be alright, but I sure hope it does.

As for the former statement: It is worth investing in relationships with those who are wiser and have more expertise. Time is money, and if they can save you a headache or open your mind to potentialities that avoid pitfalls and navigate you onto a straighter path toward building stronger relationships in either work or your personal life, in the end you are in a neutral or better state than you would be with the alternative.

Both truths ultimately rest on where you want your life to eventually go and how you want the journey to materialize. Disregard the short term. Yes, you may have your heart broken because you had your hopes up, or you may have to pay a bit more up front, but in the long run, you will be far better off.

We live in an impatient culture, and too often we make decisions with limited foresight, choosing the cheap decision to protect our wallet or the safe decision that protects our heart. Hearts expand and strengthen even after loss, and savvy investments may pay off beyond our imagination, but each take time to yield their results.

Have patience with your life, choose wisely, and move forward with confidence. It is my hope that by doing so, you won't have to learn every life lesson from experience.

Petit plaisir Make primavera risotto. Pair with a crisp glass of chardonnay, turn on your favorite tunes, podcast, or show while you cook, and dance a bit while the arborio rice simmers to al dente perfection.

Explore further thesimplyluxuriouslife.com/april14 (a truth to understand about healthy, long-lasting romantic relationships)

April 15
Become Your Own Cheerleader

In the midst of amazing progress, we may find ourselves doubting, wondering if indeed our efforts are fruitful and on track, whether they are aiding us in achieving the goals we have longed dreamed about. Even the most confident of goal seekers have moments when they lose their footing. A loose, thoughtless comment from a family member, friend, or colleague, an article that prompts questioning of our likelihood for success, or a temporary setback — such events, if they arrive at a moment of weakness, can render us doubtful.

As fallible creatures, we can become exhausted, we make mistakes, we forget how hard we have worked and sometimes that we need to trust ourselves more. As a result, we often need cheerleaders to remind us of our goodness and our potential when we cannot seem to see it for ourselves.

I admit to feeling such pangs of doubt from time to time, often when I have been exhausting myself in the pursuit of a desired outcome. In the past during these moments, I would reach out to my cheerleaders (my closest confidants) to be refueled and reassured. If they can see the potential and the possibilities in my effort, then maybe I am missing something. Maybe I am short-changing myself.

We all need at least one cheerleader in our lives who is in our corner, who recognizes when we need unbridled optimism and refuses to let us give up. We need reassurance because we are human.

However, interestingly enough, if we rely solely on seeking reassurance outside of ourselves, we actually get the opposite result — perpetual anxiety and depression. Why? Because we reveal again and again a lack of trust in ourselves.

As you grow along your journey of navigating toward your true self, you will discover you must become your own and most vocal cheerleader for yourself. In fact, one of the most valuable pieces of life advice I received throughout my journey, guided by my counselor, was to become grounded in trusting myself and being able to recognize when I became unsettled.

In such moments, which are human to have, I was to hold myself in the present, gather up my fears, and be as objective as possible, acknowledging that the fear stemmed from not knowing, a feeling of something new occurring in my life that did not have an outcome I had experienced in my life yet. Grounded in my knowledge of myself, I learned to talk honestly, compassionately and clearly to my worried self, reassuring myself that even though nothing can be known regarding the future, what is known is how I will handle myself moving forward.

While providing and receiving reassurance for and from those we love is an act of kindness, the truth is that you *can* give yourself what you need in such situations of worry. Nobody knows what tomorrow will bring, and the only person who knows whether you will meet what you discover with a determined mind and a sure heart is you.

Speak lovingly to yourself the next time a moment of uncertainty arises and you are about to pick up the phone to ask someone else to tell you what you already know you are capable of, and remind those who reach out to you for reassurance to trust in themselves as well. Build the strength that already exists within and is simply waiting to be nurtured.

Petit plaisir Today is tax day in the states, and universities and college prep classes are nearing their final exams. Play Joseph Haydn's Symphony no. 22 in E-flat Major, *The Philosopher*, to remind yourself of your preparedness and wisdom.

Explore further thesimplyluxuriouslife.com/april15 (the components of a healthy social circle)

April 16
Fear and Taking Risks

Springtime was dependably speech time in my classroom for nearly twenty years, and I always enjoyed perusing the web, especially TED Talks, to discover new and inspiring speeches to share with my class for analysis. One speech I came across was given by Larry Smith. It was titled "Why You Will Fail to Have a Great Career," and before you assume any negativity about the speech, listen to his message. It all comes back to conquering fear and the amazing revelations that determination can bring into our lives.

Why not seek a great career, the speaker asks again and again. He offers a couple of reasons, but primarily, it comes down to fear of the unknown, and preferring what we know.

Living our best lives undoubtedly takes courage. Choosing to conclude my teaching career well before I had planned required more courage than I thought I possessed, but I found out that I do possess the necessary amount, and so do you. Your yearnings regarding your career path, your life track — because they are not currently a part of your life and are positively life changing — require much more than you may think you have, but I assure you, it is within you because the yearning came from you as well.

Take a moment to honor the yearnings that never seem to entirely leave your heart, and begin to explore them in earnest. You will never know how deep your contentment can be until you have dared to be brave.

Petit plaisir When you are able to take walks in the morning before the workday begins, choose to do so, especially during the spring. The blossoms and soft, sweet spring air will set a calm tone for your day.

Explore further thesimplyluxuriouslife.com/april16 (once you have made a leap, a significant change, how to move forward successfully into your new life)

April 17
Unwanted but Necessary

When my school district, prompted by the pandemic in 2020, set up remote teaching for the first time, we also rolled out an entirely new online communication system for collecting and assigning work and staying in contact with students. Had an unexpected, life-routine-changing event not happened to require such a tool, we might not have appreciated all that it can do as a way of staying in close contact with our students during uncertain times.

I was most appreciative for this new platform as it solved most, if not all, of my concerns for teaching, assessing, etc.; however, sometimes we do not know how insufficient or limiting our current way of doing something is until we are forced to try a different approach. Yes, it is true: Necessity is the mother of invention. But necessity could also be said to be the mother of progress.

Often we are getting by with what works adequately for now and do not realize we would be better off if we tried doing something differently. The known is comfortable. Exhaustion and mind fatigue are normal when we have to do something new, but such exhaustion is only temporary; it lasts only until the change is habituated in our minds, thereby freeing up space and energy to move fluidly through the new routine and to use our minds in additional ways.

Longtime and beloved TSLL reader Sue shared with me this quote: "In the rush to return to normal, use this time to consider which parts of normal are worth rushing back to." The originator of the quote, life and business coach Dave Hollis, makes a point that is important to ponder: With all that we are being forced to do, what is it making us realize about what we *were* doing? What was *actually* working? And not only working so-so, but, most important, what was working well? Why not return only to what was working significantly above average, but also take a look at what was working mundanely and, in the latter case, try something new?

There was a real opportunity in the state of crisis brought on by the pandemic. It began with reflection and raw honesty about how we wanted to live the rest of our lives. One small, but perhaps significant detail to examine in my own life was taking a close look at my online habits and how they might be unconsciously influencing certain decisions and unhealthy life habits that were not helpful to my goals. How could I reduce stress? How could I better manage my time when it came to my use of technology?

From choosing to no longer welcome technology into my bedroom in order to give my mind time to fully relax and fall asleep swiftly, to delaying when I open my e-mail for the first time in the morning routine in order to set a better tone for the day, to tailoring how I communicate with readers, stepping back from using social media to instead engage with readers more intimately on TSLL blog — each action is seemingly simple, yet all significantly have improved the quality of my days and interactions and connections with others.

Take advantage of this opportunity to get some key aspects of your life right, or at least to improve upon what was already more amazing than we fully appreciated before everything changed.

Petit plaisir Ensure a restful night's sleep — welcome a humidifier into your bedroom, choose a beautiful goblet for a refreshing glass of water, and find nourishing lavender hand lotion as well as a favorite foot cream to apply before slipping under the covers.

Explore further thesimplyluxuriouslife.com/april17 (how to transition into a better, more fulfilling "normal")

April 18
Opportunity

When opportunity knocks, it usually doesn't ask if now is a good time. It usually arrives unannounced and requires you to determine how badly you want what it has to offer. Recently, a few opportunities in both my professional and personal lives presented themselves, and after letting the ideas and the potential ways they could change my life roll around in my head for a while, two major points occurred to me: First, the opportunity is not guaranteed to be in your area again. Second, it is knocking and you were insightful enough to notice, and that is something to not brush aside lightly.

Sometimes we forget how fortunate we are when opportunities pop up unexpectedly. Sometimes when an opportunity reveals itself, we become a little cocky, assuming that if it happened once, it most surely will happen again. While sometimes that may be true, depending upon what is being offered, most of the time, a subsequent opportunity will find you at an entirely different place in your life, and you might not revel in the gifts offered as much as you would have initially.

Ultimately, what it comes down to for each of us is how an opportunity fits within our priorities. How does it match up with what we deem most important in our lives? And are we making the decision for ourselves or for somebody or something else? When we are honest with ourselves, it will be that much easier to respond.

I hope that many an opportunity comes your way, no matter what stage you have reached in your life, but, more important, I wish for you to always receive such opportunities with an attitude of gratitude, so when you find yourself in such a position, you will always feel rich and be able to make the best decision.

Petit plaisir Give your roses their first food of the year for full and happy blooms come late spring and early summer.

Explore further thesimplyluxuriouslife.com/april18 (twenty ways to be prepared for opportunity)

April 19
Where to Seek Advice

Where do you seek advice? From whom do you seek it? A particular person? Books? Seminars? Research? The list of available sources is potentially endless.

One of the significant life lessons I learned as I moved through my thirties was to seek advice from an expert in that particular subject matter. I know, it sounds moronic to have to be reminded of this, but sometimes we want advice and suggestions on what to do so badly that we will seek anybody who will lend us their thoughts on the topic. And that isn't always a wise move.

On the flip side, when we do take the time to seek out an expert who has succeeded in the field we are inquiring about, the resulting peace of mind is priceless.

Case in point: In my new house, I have the gift of a landscape and yard that has an immense amount of potential, but it needs some serious love and attention. I had been contemplating what to do but also didn't know exactly how to do it. And so, with a visit this past weekend from my mom, I now feel confident of the direction I wish to travel.

However, I did not merely seek her input because she was my mom. No, no, no. You see, my mom is an unofficial master gardener. Her vast yard, which she has been tending for decades, is an outdoor escape I thoroughly enjoy stepping into as the weather becomes warmer. There's the plethora of daffodils that burst in the spring and her moonlight garden and, of course, her vegetable garden, which is her own little farmers market. Oh, and do not forget her peonies, which she occasionally takes to the farmers market in the late spring, but usually to friends' homes. In short, my mom is an expert in the field of gardening, plants, and working her magic with Mother Nature. And I look forward to seeing what can become of my garden at Le Papillon with her advice.

Often when we impatiently seek out advice from anyone who will listen, we are revealing more about what we want to hear. More often than not, we seek out the person based on what we think they will tell us. In other cases, we want what we think we should or want to pursue to be validated by someone, even if it should not be validated.

The advice that will bring true peace of mind is advice grounded in expertise. Such advice may challenge us or provide constructive criticism, but ultimately it will teach us who is worth seeking information from about issues that are important to us. When this is our experience, the bright side is that we can trust the source.

Whether it is gardening advice, relationship advice, money, or any other topic, seek out the expert who knows of what they speak and can be trusted to give you an honest answer.

Petit plaisir Speaking of advice, gardeners, watch Carol Klein's *Life in a Cottage Garden* on BritBox, a series of six episodes to take you through the seasons.

Explore further thesimplyluxuriouslife.com/april19 (a wise investment: understanding yourself by taking off the blindfold)

April 20
Surviving the Unknown

It is okay not to know, and it is okay to just make it through.

A major home appliance goes on the fritz at the most inopportune time, an unexpected bill arrives in the mail, or your dog or cat or child wakes up under the weather — because we did not plan for these events and do not know when they will be resolved, such moments can seem to flip our lives upside-down. In the back of my mind, I know that everything will be okay, but when foundational pieces of your everyday life are not running as you would like them to or as they used to, or when a relationship is shifting and the change is out of your hands, the ride of life can feel unsettling.

The first thing I remind myself to do is to take a deep breath. I then take a look around and remind myself of all that is going wonderfully well, and then I just put one foot in front of the other, making sure that today is a great day, or the best that I can possibly make it for myself or for others.

When such unexpected "boat rocking" (but not "boat tipping over") moments enter our lives, focusing on the present and remaining in the moment is even more important. And then I am reminded to make such a practice even more of a priority when all is going smoothly.

So I have been soaking in the details of my everydays that I love: the sunshine, the moments with my dogs, my garden and the plants that are flourishing there, and so much that I know I am fortunate to have in my life.

The truth is that we cannot always predict these unsettling moments; in fact, we rarely can. They just happen, and we have to learn to engage with them in a constructive fashion. Sometimes that comes after a bit of reaction and befuddlement, but then we gather our composure and do what needs to be done, and yes, we make it through.

When we come out on the other side of these events, there is the option to change and thus improve the quality of our lives. We have been given the opportunity to deepen our awareness and appreciation for all that we have and are able to do. And if we are able to do that, that is when we need to say thank you. Yes, thank you.

Even those events in your life that perhaps right now are not making you happy or at peace are, in fact, wonderful gifts that will add to the quality of your life once you make your way through them.

Petit plaisir Now is a wonderful time to purchase cashmere staples for next fall/winter, as often retailers are making space for spring/summer collections.

Explore further thesimplyluxuriouslife.com/april20 (ten things people who have found contentment understand about uncertainty)

April 21
The Need to Adjust

Adjustments are necessary. Regularly.

From adjusting our perspective so that it is broader about the world we live in, to adjusting our eating habits after a long, lovely holiday, or adjusting how and what we are doing on any given day, when we adjust, we give ourselves the opportunity to experience more contentment, more fulfillment, and more appreciation, and we deepen our understanding of whatever happens in our lives.

Adjusting was a means to welcome more enjoyment into my daily routine in 2018 when, after three weeks of a colleague urging me to watch *The Marvelous Mrs. Maisel*, insisting that I would absolutely enjoy it (Mrs. Maisel reminded him of me), I finally sat down after the show won eight Emmys (including best comedy and best actress, supporting actress, and writing) and began devouring the series. I am still not sure which part of Mrs. Maisel's personality made my colleague think of me, but at this point, I am just glad he suggested it because I am absolutely enthralled.

When we choose to adjust our lives, even the smallest details, we are choosing to continue to learn and explore, and consider that we may not have everything figured out. And that is a choice — to forever remain a student of life. Because, after all, the fountain of youth can be found in the choice to forever remain curious.

If you remain curious about how to improve your contentment, how to improve the everyday routines you include in your life, how to

improve the quality of your relationships at work and in your personal life, and how to improve the world you live in, your life will never become stagnant, and you will continually find moments of delight, even if it is something as simple as a thought-provoking show to enjoy in the evenings.

Petit plaisir Create an alternative work area outdoors or away from home at a favorite coffee shop or library that quiets your mind in order to motivate it to work well. The porch swing on the front of my house becomes a favorite place during spring as I am surrounded by birdsong, ideal temps, and fresh air.

Explore further thesimplyluxuriouslife.com/april21 (one small adjustment away from contentment)

April 22
Apply the Lesson

While living in the present is necessary on a daily basis in order to live a truly contented life, sometimes, reflecting upon our past can be a source of fuel to enable us to fly into the future we desire. Years may pass before we find the time and the insight that our past has been waiting patiently for us to mine and unearth, and then finally express gratitude for the discovery.

It can be easy to fall into ways of living that get us by, that do not ruffle any feathers, but when something is against our true nature, when it asks us to be less, we shrink ourselves and unconsciously withhold what we can uniquely contribute from the world.

Defaults are easier to fall into than we may first think, especially if we are applauded for going along, for not going against the crowd, which would force people to consider new ideas, to see things differently. And they may make it easier to sleep at night . . . for a while. Then we begin to remember what we are truly capable of, what we have done in the past, who we were in the past, and what we refused to accept in the past.

The past that matters will differ for each of us. For some, it may only be last year, while for others, important events took place decades ago. The timing need not matter. What matters is that we remembered. And it is even more important that we not dismiss or continue to forget, but instead apply what we know is true to who we are and what we are capable of.

In the early spring of 2012, twelve years since I had last visited Paris, the opportunity to return was presented to me. It was not until I realized that indeed I would actually be boarding a plane and making the trip to Paris, nibbling on croissants, seeing the Seine with my own eyes, that I felt a surge of previously ignored unabashed exuberance. It was as though a hibernating life force awoke from its slumber and a piece of me, of Shannon, returned. The wake-up call awoke me to an essential curiosity and passion not found anywhere else, and as it had been so long since I felt aligned with something I could not quite explain, I vowed to never let this realization slip away again.

When we feel stuck or uncertain, we simply need to leave gaps or moments during our days to catch our breath, to set aside moments for our minds to wander, because that is how a new idea can enter. And when it speaks to us, when it lights us up, then we can recognize a "before" and an "after."

Recognize the awesomeness of the past that is asking to be part of your present. Use it for fuel. Use it to power your wings as you leave the ground, and fly as you were meant to, if only you had not forgotten how. But now you know, so fly, and soar, and enjoy.

Petit plaisir Consider adding delphiniums to your garden's perennials collection. They have the potential to bloom twice each blooming season, and their wonderful tall blooms can add height to a border.

Explore further thesimplyluxuriouslife.com/april22 (doubt the default: choose to live with intention)

April 23
Love

I am a big believer in new beginnings, starting fresh, and making the most of a clean slate. When an artist gazes at an empty canvas, anything is possible: a mediocre watercolor, a mistaken, yet temporarily magical color combination, and yes, even a grand masterpiece.

I went on a journey of the heart in my thirties with hopes and excitement, and dove into the unknown for the first time in a very long time. I let go of fears I have had, and for over eighteen months, the experience, the dancing with the unknown, made me understand something about life that I did not fully grasp until now: Love is magnificent, powerful, and absolutely worth the risk. But remember: Love can occur with someone special, but the journey through life is all the sweeter if we love the life we build for ourselves because that is the company we will always have to keep.

The eighteen-month romance ended unexpectedly, and while I will keep the details private, the transition back to the life I have lived on my own was a lovely place to return to because it was sincere love that brought me to where I am in Bend, Oregon — a sincere love for my life journey and my relationship with myself that provided the strength to protect it and thus walk away from what no longer provided nourishment.

Part of me felt guilty, while another part felt gratitude — deep, visceral gratitude — as I had experienced ending a relationship before. When previous relationships had ended, part of what made that much more difficult was my insecurity in my own life and with myself. When, after a relationship ends, you return to a life that is not a dream come true but is one marked by uncertainty and lack of self-trust, it is far more difficult to settle into your own company and routine. In fact, you may (unwisely) want to return to the relationship, only because you neglected to create for yourself a life you enjoy living. Currently, I am tickled to be where I have the good fortune to be at this very moment in my life, and my hope for a future healthy, loving, and supportive relationship is but icing on a scrumptious cake.

I am now walking forward on my own with more confidence than I might ever have expected. It turns out that I do have the wherewithal to love another, and as one good friend told me following the end of the relationship, "It's just part of the process [of finding the real love we hope to find]." I cannot think of a better way to look at it.

Loving the life we build for ourselves is a process, one in which we should be kind to ourselves and to others, being honest about what we can and cannot waiver on. And along the way, we grow, discovering new things about ourselves: hurts, joys, dreams, and fears.

So long as you are honest with yourself, are willing to learn lessons but also stand behind what you know, regardless of someone trying to convince you of something else (always consider the source!), the process will continue to unfold and reveal to you where your arrival gate will be located.

Petit plaisir Cherry trees are beginning to be bejeweled with blossoms. If you don't have a cherry tree nearby, seek one out in your town and walk or drive by it at various times during the day (white blooms under a clear sky and moonlight are quite magical).

Explore further thesimplyluxuriouslife.com/april23 (the most important ingredient for a healthy relationship)

April 24
Dealing with Insecurity

When we are presented with uncertainty, we may experience a natural, understandable urge to seek reassurance. On its face, reassurance can be seen as a positive response from one person to another. Reassurance is often positive, supportive, and uplifting of one's confidence, and thus we may pursue it because it carries a positive connotation.

For children or for neophytes in anything, reassurance from someone who is an expert can be, I would argue, beneficial. After all, in order to know what we should be doing or how we should do something in order to be successful, reassurance from someone who has succeeded in the field or life arena we seek to improve is an appreciated gesture.

However, a novice seeking reassurance from an expert is an acknowledgment of inferiority. The benefits of receiving reassurance can be completely understandable and expected in a learning situation such as the one described above, but when we wish to be seen as an equal, seeking reassurance reveals our insecurity.

When it comes to business relationships, romantic relationships, and even friendships, when one party regularly seeks reassurance, they reveal their insecurity and awareness of themselves and what they have to offer. And here is an irony that, when I discovered it, stopped me in my tracks. When we seek and receive reassurance from a partner or a friend, it can feel like a drug: We want more. Why? Because reassurance from beyond ourselves actually provides the opposite of what we seek. Our anxiety is strengthened, our self-doubt increases, and we weaken our trust in ourselves.

Ironically, we think that when we get the reassurance we seek, we will be satisfied, but the opposite is true. Why? Life happens, and relationships are dynamic, moving, and ever-evolving. Once our mind is eased about one unknown, another will arise that we could not have predicted, and we will again seek reassurance. Often the additional reassurance will need to be greater and more complex. And unless we realize the damage our insecurity is causing in a relationship, ever so slightly and gradually, we will exhaust the other individual because we have not found peace within ourselves.

If you find yourself routinely seeking reassurance in a job or a relationship, take a moment to look within. More often than not, you will find that your insecurity stems from a past experience when something out of your control threw you off course and caught you by surprise, leaving you to assume you must have done something wrong, if only you had known what so you could have fixed it. But the truth is — and here is the good news I want you to absorb, understand, and apply as you move forward — the loss, the debacle, the heartbreak was going to happen one way or another. You could not have stopped it.

And so as you move forward, and when you think you need reassurance, look within. Ask yourself, why am I fearful? If the answer is doubt, why do I have it? What is my intuition trying to alert me to? Know that part of having doubt, which is different from fear, is our intuition recognizing something that does not ring true based on past experience. Good news also comes with this realization: one, you have found something that speaks to you, that sings your unique tune; and two, you now have to allow yourself to trust and step forward with hope, letting go of expectations.

The last part is scary, but accepting that you cannot control everything as you move forward should also be a reason to breathe a sigh of relief. Think of what you can remove from your worry list or your to-do list, so that you can just enjoy the life you have created right now, in the present moment. When you do that, you become the person you are capable of being: a person who enjoys their life, a person who creates a bit of mystery because they do not have to share or reveal all.

Confidence is attractive. It creates desire, while reassurance, when we seek it constantly, squelches both confidence and attractiveness. Recognize when the need for reassurance arises, and then step beyond it. You will be okay. You are okay. You are more than okay. You are absolutely amazing.

Petit plaisir Take a book on your next walk. Midway through, find a bench or a comfortable seat, ignore your watch, and just read.

Explore further thesimplyluxuriouslife.com/april24 (twenty-one lessons learned in my forty-second year — see #2 on the list)

April 25
Unexpected Help Along the Way

Lessons for living well can reveal themselves in the most unexpected manner, but at one point in my thirties, I found myself running into (gladly so) more than just a few as I went about my weekly routines.

A TEDx Talk offered beautiful insight about life and trusting your journey, and then I received unexpected help to complete a project from my web designer. Both reminded me that kindness, offering help just because you can, is a lovely gift. As well, there were other moments of kindness from colleagues and neighbors that would buoy anyone's spirits, but certainly put more of a bounce in my step.

One of the grander lessons I was reminded of was a simple one, but one I often forget when I am in the middle of a project that requires much time and steady persistence: It is how we handle the journey, even when we have to work to iron things out, that draws others to us, inspires them to continue to work with us, and ultimately reveals the desired result.

We had been transferring my second book into the template for publishing it, and eventually we made it through the process, which was detailed and somewhat complex. And while along the way there were times I did not know what the answer would be, I kept trusting we would find the answer (after all, we had found it with the previous book). Unknowns can cause our nerves to rattle, but often they rattle before we give ourselves a chance to put everything into perspective.

Hindsight is a beautiful gift and teacher of humility, reminding us to take a breath along our journey, wherever it may be heading, and to just take the steps we can each day. Eventually, we will arrive, even though there may be times when we do not know how.

When the week begins and you see Friday so very far down the way, you know it will arrive. It is how you travel through the week that will determine how it ends. Hopefully, you will travel it well, no matter what the world tosses your way, and if perhaps there will be moments you will want to forget, just remember that you have next week. You are only human, and you need good weeks to balance out the frustrating ones, to remind you to savor those that end so very sweetly.

Petit plaisir Cut a fresh slice of crusty, artisan bread from a favorite local bakery. Toast it. Smear it with mashed avocado mixed with lemon juice and sea salt (add a smidge of red-hot pepper flakes for a little heat).

Explore further thesimplyluxuriouslife.com/april25 (a simple, flavorful avocado toast recipe)

April 26
Opportunities for Growth

Springtime during the school year can often be angst-ridden as budgets are announced and teaching positions rearranged; unspoken uncertainty lingers in the air. During my second year of teaching in Bend, over the course of approximately eighteen hours, a series of events played out that revealed to me and those involved the true colors of the people I had worked with at my final teaching post. Once we came out on the other side, I was humbled by the community, the support, and the sense of being on a team in my workplace.

It was not a life-or-death situation, but it was an unexpected event that a handful of us did not see coming. The good news is we are all more than fine, and one individual raised the bar and reminded us all how to live selflessly, so long as we take care of ourselves first.

I share a glimpse of that experience in order to offer a reminder that often, when we are going through times of uncertainty and fear, we see truths about others and ourselves that we had not known previously. We may have seen hints or had inklings, but when the rubber hits the road and the show is live, it is only then that we know for sure. Don't get me wrong: I do not want to have to go through stressful situation after stressful situation to find out the deeper truths about those in my life, let alone about myself, but we do get the opportunity in such moments to see with our eyes quite wide open, so long as we choose to look. And then we grow from the experience.

There was much to process over the course of the eighteen hours, but one thing I know is that it was my good fortune to teach with my colleagues in Bend. As well, I learned a few things about myself that I did not expect to ever have to put into practice, and that too is worthwhile information to hold on to and apply moving forward.

Whether it is to grow in the relationships you share or to grow as an individual, such unexpected, unwanted times honestly do offer much goodness.

Petit plaisir Watch *Last Love*, starring Michael Caine and Clémence Poésy, and set in Paris.

Explore further thesimplyluxuriouslife.com/april26 (the gift of discontentment — yep, that's no typo!)

April 27
Knowing What We Truly Want and Need

I have discovered two ways in which we can come to understand what we want in life: First, we may get a momentary taste of what we want, but then have to go back to a life that does not include it. Second, we may have it and cannot imagine living any differently.

April

In each case, I may begin to feel doubt and worry that what I hoped to attain or maintain would be hard, if not impossible, to achieve. However, I have eventually come to realize that I have such doubts because of my intense desire for and clarity about the life I wish for or enjoy living. Often our fears stem from not yet having gained sought-for information that will clarify why we are unsettled. But the mere fact that we are unsettled indicates that we are searching and that what we are searching for will eventually be found.

Reflect for a moment upon how it felt before you either did not know what you wanted or had not experienced the feeling of being "at home" in your life. Throughout my twenties, I felt rudderless and deeply unfulfilled. First, I thought that my lack of a long-term relationship was the problem, so I tried to be the "perfect" girlfriend. Then, I assumed it was the town I lived in, and I moved to live closer to my family roots, only to discover, when I finally found my true calling (writing, blogging, indulging an affinity for the French and British cultures), that I needed to fly on my own. Knowing I could soar without assistance — all the while acknowledging the family ethos instilled within me of trusting myself and having the courage to give something new and unknown a try — made the discovery possible.

Coming to a point when you know the direction you want to travel, where you wish to put down roots, is something grand to celebrate. It is something to cheer about because it is not easy to find.

When we shift from fear to appreciation, we cultivate positive energy and let go of the negative energy that scares more goodness away. Being appreciative does not mean we will not have to work hard to either attain or maintain what we have discovered, but it makes our lives far more enjoyable, and it is more likely that we will create more positive energy around us, which brings more of what we want.

Consider shifting the way you handle the knowledge you now have about your life and what you would like it to be (regarding your personal life, career, legacy, etc.). While you do not know what the future will bring, the type of energy you bring to each day will determine your life, so make it celebratory, hopeful, and determined.

Petit plaisir Read one or both of Mason Curry's books *Daily Rituals: How Artists Work* and *Daily Rituals: Women at Work* to explore how to finesse your daily work routine.

Explore further thesimplyluxuriouslife.com/april27 (thirty-four inspiring daily rituals to ignite your creativity)

April 28
Dive In and Hold On to the Unknown

Much of life boils down to this question: What do you want? Some people choose the path of least resistance: fewer worries, less struggle. I understand the motivation, and in some avenues of my life, as I reflect upon my past, I no doubt took the least-difficult route, but if it involved something I was passionate about or something that would hold great significance or value in my life, I did not choose the easy path, as my mom will tell you. Nope. And I have a feeling you have not either.

I didn't refrain from the facile path because I enjoy undue stress. Absolutely not. Sometimes I wish my conscience preferred the easy path. I continue to choose what seems to the outside world to be the more challenging path because it aligns with what is right for me.

I have a feeling that you too have chosen what others (and maybe you yourself) may describe as the more difficult journey, but in so doing, you know it is the best choice for you. Because we have to enjoy the journey, and when it leads us to where we wish to go, the memories we made along the way are easier to appreciate and savor as they lead us in the right direction.

Ask yourself: Am I merely heading down the path I am traveling because the wind is at my back, or is this the direction I would choose to go anyway? My hope for you is the latter, and even when you do choose a journey that pits you against the wind, rest assured that the many lessons you will learn, the strength you will build along the way, will prepare you for a most awesome outcome.

Petit plaisir To strengthen your awareness of your finite energy in order to construct your days well, read David H. Pink's *When: The Scientific Secrets of Perfect Timing*.

Explore further thesimplyluxuriouslife.com/april28 (enjoying your uniquely chosen life journey)

April 29
Dynamic Balance

Recently, as I began to make progress toward more of my goals and my excitement accelerated, I found that my schedule was becoming a bit more demanding, which required me to take a closer look at exactly what helps propel me toward my goals and what does not. And one of the most precious resources throughout all of this schedule analysis was the realization that my energy level is key to doing anything at a high level of quality.

Acknowledging that any gathering of people, no matter how much I enjoy their company, depletes my energy reserves rather than fueling me has taught me to buffer such events with a slower or less demanding schedule the next day. Conversely, give me an afternoon with no *have-to*'s but lots of time just to potter about in my house and garden, and I am more than ready to go for an evening out.

With that said, knowing myself — what activities to involve myself in, which to politely say no to, which battles to engage in and which to walk away from — plays a crucial role in being able to successfully complete the goals I am striving toward.

So how exactly do we discern which activities to involve ourselves in and which battles to throw ourselves into? As for the former: Only engage in or commit yourself to activities that take you further toward your goals or bring you joy, pleasure, or contentment without detracting from the progress you have already made. And for the latter: Only engage in arguments or battles that will improve a relationship or require you to stand up for your reputation should it be damaged if you do not. In other words, keep your ego in check and realize that sometimes not saying something is just as powerful as speaking your mind; it can demonstrate self-restraint and avoid bringing you down to what may be an insecure and petty level.

Being aware of how you are spending your energy will allow you to be better able to save your finite energy for projects that matter and that bring more value and fulfillment into your life.

Petit plaisir Prepare to be inspired to travel and to eat well while doing so. Watch the *Moveable Feast with Fine Cooking* series.

Explore further thesimplyluxuriouslife.com/april29 (a powerful skill to possess: willpower)

April 30
Transition with Ease

Up my feet go to rest on an antique hassock that doesn't match the buttery yellow print of the modern wingback chairs in front of my fireplace. The story behind its arrival at Le Papillon, as well as its ideal height and "cush" for the heels, make me anticipate and savor the resting of my feet. I have just enjoyed an especially warm and lovely visit with houseguests, and the hours since the suitcases were packed and the goodbyes exchanged found me with my feet up on my beloved hassock, wearing a cozy oversized sweater *sans* bra — oh, and the feet are bare, of course.

The fresh bouquets placed around the house still express their full beauty; the clean house asks not to be touched, and I oblige without hesitation. Oscar and Norman accompany me near the fire, curled up in my chair's partner, and I pull out a journal to capture the memories before the daily schedule of life begins anew.

Relationships lie at the foundation of a life to savor, with their ebbs and flows and exhilarations and unexpected awesomeness. The strength of any relationship rests in each individual's ability to nurture their relationship with themselves and to give each other the space and ability to tend to themselves as necessary without judgment.

For me, the time immediately after a visit with friends or family or a partner is all sweet and no bitter. I revel in my own company all the more after bouts of honest conversation, good food, good laughs, and time spent on projects have deepened the quality of my relationships even further into the realm of the irreplaceable.

Today, decide to cultivate rituals to engage in when your favorite company says goodbye, concluding a wonderful visit. By taking the time to imagine what you will do, you create a transition of ease and peace of mind, permitting you to not long for more but savor what was.

Petit plaisir Read Alain de Botton's *The Course of Love* to deepen your understanding of loving relationships.

Explore further thesimplyluxuriouslife.com/april30 (the importance of minding everyday transitions)

May

Love Mother Nature

May

Sometimes "coming home" leads you to another country. Walking upon the sloped, bramble-covered, stone-framed fields in North Devon, looking out onto the Bristol Channel — at such moments during each of the four days of my visit in 2017, I was reminded of my love for slower living, with Mother Nature at my doorstep. I felt entirely at home.

The more rain the better. Let it blow sideways for hours. Mother Nature's symphony only improved as I snuggled in with a hot cuppa, soaked in the tub, and whiled away my vacation, leaving only for sustenance from the local farmers market or to walk along the beach at nearby Woolacoombe. Never before had I found such absolute comfort in a country, a house, a land not my own.

The start of *The Simply Luxurious Kitchen* cooking series began in this Devon cottage, and I am grateful for my mother's suggestion to pack my video camera just in case a moment struck me. A moment indeed struck, and it helped bring me to this place, doing something I had been searching for.

As the saying goes, if you keep searching, you finally find the answers, even if you don't know exactly what you are looking for. Truth be told, if you knew what you were looking for, the searching would not be needed. In America, you would just go buy it. (I joke, but only a little.) No one country is perfect. Some harmonize with our predilections more beautifully than others, and the English countryside was the symphony I did not know I had been looking for nearly my entire life.

Tradition has a place only if it serves a better future. Tradition for tradition's sake can be a recipe for stagnation and limitation and exclusion. No thank you. I studied British history and literature in college, taught Shakespeare to high school students, and appreciated Jane Austen's short but prolific writing career. Agatha Christie's Hercule Poirot holds a tender spot in my heart, and I have explored Linda Lear's biography of Beatrix Potter and all that Potter did for the Lake District. My fascination and appreciation for Britain is rooted deep. Add my introduction in 2020 to *Gardeners' World*, which I enjoyed every weekend beginning in March and running through October, and, well, plant me in England, if only for the ability to have a lush garden for far longer than a resident of Bend, Oregon, could ever hope for.

Britain speaks to a significant part of how I enjoy constructing my days and living my life. We can draw inspiration from new-to-us cultures when we cross paths with a way of life that speaks to something innately within us. When such an opportunity occurs, listening and heeding what we witness can benefit us greatly.

Thankfully I listened.

From the simple everyday rituals, such as enjoying a cuppa, to gardening as a "pride of place" hobby to soothe the mind and spirit, the British countryside specifically reminded me of the comfort I enjoyed as a child growing up on Alder Slope, with 20 acres of wide-open land to explore. Dogs off their leashes, horses to ride, sheep and cows to care for, and a donkey to give regular head rubs to with love. My mom in her garden and Dad tinkering in his shop; in late June, sitting on the wide-open back outdoor patio, next to the brook cascading through my mother's hostas under the cherry tree and next to the peonies, all while gazing up at Ruby Peak's magnificent natural beauty.

I continue to enjoy such moments when I visit my parents, and that grounding inspired me to create a home at Le Papillon where I can while away the days tinkering in my garden, chatting randomly with my neighbors, resting on my garden porch in the evening, welcoming family and friends from time to time to enjoy a cuppa or an apéritif, snuggling up in my down-filled Poirot armchair to read, all the while feeling incredibly grateful to have spent time in Britain. A haven with its fondness for pups, gardening, the sea, and tea.

May 1
Seizing Your Dreams

Where to start. First and most important, with gratitude.

As I returned from the morning market near Ilfracombe, I stood alongside a winding country road to take a photo of rolling green fields divided by stone walls. I gave thanks for more than I ever imagined I would experience: exceedingly beautiful and idyllic countryside and people, readers, listeners, and friends who came along with me virtually as I made my way on this journey, however simple it may be or how short, and brought my excitement about the Devon countryside into their lives, no matter where they called home.

I was grateful for the time to be able to be open so that inspiration might strike, for the ability to seize it, for having conquered unknowns that were daunting until I stepped forward and dared rather than doubted, and for the peace of mind that, while I miss my two spaniels terribly (there are spaniels everywhere in England, which made it all the more apparent that this is their native home!), I know that they are well cared for, walked daily, and pampered.

From the moment I stepped into my cab to head to the airport to the last walk I took along Devon's shore, my awe was captured, and I am forever grateful that I found the courage to finally see the countryside of England (a nearly lifelong dream of mine) and to forge ahead on a more recent dream that has been dancing about in my head for some time.

Life is about living, not dreaming, not wondering, not worrying. As I read recently, "The goal at the end of one's life is to have

memories rather than dreams." You are asked to dare, to be a little uncomfortable from time to time, as you don't always know how things will work out, but to step forward anyway toward your dreams.

Petit plaisir Let yourself dance about in the garden or a favorite space in your home as you listen to Vivaldi's Concerto for Two Guitars in G Major, RV 534, Allegro.

Explore further thesimplyluxuriouslife.com/may1 (ideas for creating a beckoning sanctuary that reflects your journey)

May 2
Savoring May

As the days stretch wonderfully longer, and the neighborhood birds sing more and more melodies as they nest and mate, I must say, May is a delightful month to savor.

    I chose to cultivate at Le Papillon a cottage garden inspired by the British approach, which invites less formality, more mixing of flowers and herbs, vegetables and berries, different colors that seem haphazardly planned yet are intentionally mixed and matched. The first spring (2020) was a year to learn the garden's rhythms, discover where the sun landed and for how long, as well as how the plants would work with the nearby large pine tree and fences. Especially important was learning when the last frost typically occurs, and well, I made a few mistakes in my first year when I attempted to guess.

    During the first week of May, I tended to some plant deaths as the frost took a few of my more delicate annuals that I had neglected to bring inside. I learned, later in the year, that an unfortunately timed frost nixed any fruit for the year from my peach trees, though the magenta blossoms were beautiful.

    Having an outdoor living space is a luxury indeed, especially since I did not have a backyard in my last owned house, which was tucked away from the street, and at my rental prior to owning Le Papillon, towering pine trees allowed little sunshine to reach the earth.

    May is a lovely month — warm, but not too warm, with an occasional rainy day. The grass and trails are green and lush, the birds return and gently nudge us to start the day, and the peonies, tulips, and daffodils are fresh and blooming for their limited, but gloriously beautiful moment in the sunshine.

Each season and each month in the climate zone where your sanctuary is situated presents evanescent beauty. Take a moment to exercise your senses: observe, listen, smell, brush your hand along the petals, and catalog in your mind the gifts shared. Savor them now and look forward to them again next year when May returns.

Petit plaisir Purchase a special varietal of blooms for a bouquet in your home, just because. Parrot tulips are always a welcome treat.

Explore further thesimplyluxuriouslife.com/may2 (video tutorial sharing ideas for arranging a simple, yet stunning, flower bouquet)

May 3
Be Present: *Aha* Moments in the Everyday

The sun had just broken through the clouds. A stream of sunlight washed over a portion of my front garden as I sat down to type. And that was the precise feeling I felt that weekend — an *aha*, an appreciation, a reminder to be present and savor.

I spent the entire long weekend at home, in Bend. No getaway weekend, no quick flight to somewhere enticing and new. Nope, I just stayed in my hometown. And doing so was lovely.

Maybe too lovely, I will admit, because it made it hard to return to school knowing how close the summer holiday was, but that moment reminded me of the joyful days and weeks that were ahead.

What helped make the weekend a true joy to luxuriate in: books, flowers, an abundance of rain, time without a clock, a smartphone that no longer worked, food in the kitchen for tinkering around with new recipes, a wonderful new-to-me film and series, my boys (*bien sûr!*), a beckoning, cozy bed, and a quiet neighborhood.

Listening to what brings us joy makes it easier to celebrate and support the joy others find, even if it may be different from our own. So long as all parties are respectful and supportive of what others have found to be most enjoyable, our world can be elevated, our relationships can be elevated, and thus we discover the power of getting to know ourselves.

As I dug in the dirt, tending to some weeding after a lovely spring rain made the soil malleable and the weeds easy to remove, Norman moseyed about, and Oscar watched from the porch, keeping guard. I could not imagine a more lovely moment. At such times, as we listen to ourselves, we are able to separate ourselves from the *shoulds* and see our everyday lives elevate.

May

Your moments will be different, your *aha*'s will be unique to you, but a similar discovery will bring you to an inner calm and a deep sense of liberation.

Petit plaisir Read Paul DeWitt's *The French Exit*, and then watch the movie starring Michelle Pfeiffer.

Explore further thesimplyluxuriouslife.com/may3 (ideas for welcoming more joy into your life)

May 4
Letting Go

I have discovered that there are three components to successfully finding what I am looking for in life. Whether it is the perfectly cut blouse for my broad shoulders or something intangible, such as compatibility and trust in a relationship, the three components are clarity, resisting the firm grip of time restraints, and trust in our ability to seize opportunities when we find them.

Let me explain. (1) Clarity is knowing just what we are looking for and accurately understanding what would be the best fit, which can take time to discern properly. (2) Not being constrained by time means acknowledging that our timetable does not necessarily match the timetable of others or the world at large. (3) Once we have carefully and thoughtfully tended to component 1, we must trust that when we come across what we have been looking for, we will have the courage to say yes.

For example, each spring I look for annuals suited for the shade to place in the pots on my front porch. One year, I knew I would eventually find what I needed (I just didn't know when), and I wanted to pay a reasonable price. I looked for two weeks and had not found a begonia in a color that would complement the perennials surrounding the front stoop, but as I did my market shopping, I spotted exactly the style, flower, and price I wanted. So I brought it home. Front-porch pots complete!

On a grander level, when a job you love becomes available or the job you love might be shifted away from you, knowing what you love, knowing where you shine and bring forth your best skills and passions is the automatic fuel to demonstrate you are the best person for the job. Whether it is knocking the interview out of the park or communicating convincingly that you are the best person for the job, based on what you have done thus far, the courage to take either stance exemplifies component 3.

Taking action becomes far simpler when you have done your due diligence with component 1. Part of the reason you may be hesitant to act on what presents itself is that you don't know for sure what you want. This feeling is a sign to step back and do the homework, something you can spend years on or just days. But the act of tending to component 1 can ease your mind immensely, especially when you are making big decisions.

Petit plaisir If you have trees in blossom that are becoming overgrown, trim as necessary and bring the branches inside for a seasonal bouquet.

Explore further thesimplyluxuriouslife.com/may4 (inspiration for finding the courage to say "yes")

May 5
Trust Your Journey

Each of us has the answers within us that will assuage our fears, steer us in the right direction, and calm our worried minds. What stands between us and this truth we seek is a lack of trust that it is possible, others who try to answer the questions for us when no person or institution can do such a thing, and the errant belief that the answer could not possibly be so simple to find.

But the good news is that it is that simple, which is what makes it so complicated.

Since I was a young adult, I have always yearned to travel and visit the countryside of England. I cannot tell you why precisely, but the yearning to visit has never abated. It was just a matter of opportunity and having the financial means. This is just one of many instances in my life when the answers may not have been spoken in a language I understood, but I began to trust with more and more fidelity that my intuition was speaking. I simply needed to continue to be the student of myself.

Being the student of ourselves, coming to understand what pushes and pulls us, takes time, for some more than for others, as some of us are more resistant or distrustful, while others come to trust what they feel more readily. Now, when I say "feel," I don't mean the fleeting emotions we all have throughout our days. No. When I say "trusting what we feel," I mean something more grounded, more raw and authentic. Something that speaks to us from our core. Sure, we can be fearful in a moment about something, but often that is due to lack of knowledge. Rather, a feeling that comes from the core arises from the acquisition of knowledge that we may not fully be able to appreciate . . . yet.

So long as you keep listening, quieting yourself more often, and trusting — even when you do not know why or where that trust will lead — and taking small steps until you are more assured, you will become fluent in your own unique language of self.

Petit plaisir The farmers market is sure to have rhubarb, or maybe you have some growing in your garden. When harvesting, remember to run your hand to the ground, where the stalk meets the dirt, and twist, pulling it loose, not tearing it or cutting it. Enjoy it steamed with orange zest and juice, served over yogurt, or paired with strawberries in a tart.

Explore further thesimplyluxuriouslife.com/may5 (recipe for rustic frangipane rhubarb tart)

May 6
Trusting the Unexplained Yearnings

We have all a better guide in ourselves, if we would attend to it, than any other person can be.
— Fanny, in Jane Austen's *Mansfield Park*

At the end of November 2017, before I ventured to England — first to London and then on to the Devon countryside, I came across this quote from Jane Austen. Unbeknownst to me, my trip would unfold very much as though Austen's quote was a prediction of what was to come.

I cannot recall when I first dreamed of visiting the English countryside. And while I have since studied abroad in Angers, France, and become, as well, a Francophile, the Anglophile in me has been steady, reserved, but always present, if only in the background.

When the Great Western Railroad train emerged from London and into the green, rolling hills of southwest England, I saw what I had doubted was real until I saw it with my own eyes: peaceful grandeur and simple vignettes of a quieter life.

After I acquired my rental car and drove for the first time on my own in a foreign country, I saw even more intimately the farms, quaint towns of two or three thousand residents, and stone-lined roads and fields. What I discovered about the countryside and about myself surpassed my expectations and gave (and still is giving) me great pause.

Sometimes we do not know what will speak to us until we see it with our own eyes, but clairvoyant as it may sound, for some time, decades even, I had been drawn to the English countryside. Perhaps I had watched too many *Midsomer Murders* or Miss Marple episodes or maybe too many hilarious antics on *Agatha Raisin*, or perhaps too many images from *The Vicar of Dibley*'s fictitious English country town had imprinted on my mind . . . but I had been right even before I arrived.

Trust your compass and listen to the tugs and curiosities that catch your eye. Never ignore your dreams and what captures your attention as you meander along the journey of your life. When we heed these helpful happenings, we create the magic to cultivate the contentment we long for.

Petit plaisir Find a blanket for your bedroom that not only works with your décor but that can be a cover when you take a nap (a lovely necessity). I found mine at Coyuchi and had two small throws sown together to create a queen-size blanket — the perfect size.

Explore further thesimplyluxuriouslife.com/may6 (trusting passion to be your guide)

May 7
Where True Love Resides

As I planned my first visit to the English countryside, I sought a rental that had a soaking bathtub and space to roam. With some searching, including a focus on North Devon, I found a completely remodeled guest cottage overlooking the Bristol Channel. Called The Linney (long ago, as the name reveals, the building was a cow shelter), it gave me the ability each morning to wave hello to Wales across the water, and the 180-degree views of the ocean captured my attention. I made my reservation immediately.

The Linney was located on a family farm, below the owners' house and out of sight. There were many pastures in which to wander, as well as walking paths down to the ocean along trails that I took advantage of each day. And yes, there was a grand soaking tub, which I indulged in each evening, after having walked about on the slopping hillsides and along the coast in intermittent rain.

While staying in The Linney, I taped the pilot episode of *The Simply Luxurious Kitchen*. I finally had the courage to put myself in front of the camera doing something I love — cooking and sharing what I've made.

Perhaps there is something in your life that you enjoy doing and wish that you could have more time to focus on, or that you wish you simply had the courage to do. It may be a new business idea, a different career pursuit, a hobby, or a new skill. Whatever it is, first be thankful that you have found something you love so deeply. That, in and of itself, is not something everyone discovers.

Once you have found such a love, even just spending time when you can makes a difference. You may only be able to spend a little time for a while, but if you are serious, if you find the willpower to make time for it, the love will gradually grow and develop. It may gradually become something significant, and with time, your skills will become more fine-tuned so that you will begin to open doors for yourself that initially seemed closed.

When it comes to your loves, your passions, you can strengthen your technique, your abilities, your business, your knowledge, by honoring the calling from within to pursue what piques your curiosity and by daring to trust that the future, while it won't reveal its hand, tends to favor the brave when they align themselves with their true self. While it would be easier not to, to follow the crowd, to tire of exploring your path and just let go, our lives elevate only when we take a leap. When you strengthen your courage through taking leaps, your life becomes easier, your path becomes clearer, and you come closer to your dreams being a reality.

Petit plaisir Become smitten with oboes while listening to Sinfonia for Two Oboes in G Major, composed by Tomaso Giovanni Albinoni.

Explore further thesimplyluxuriouslife.com/may7 (watch the pilot episode of *The Simply Luxurious Kitchen*, recorded in North Devon)

May 8
Have Patience

One of the biggest lessons life has taught me — and it continues to check back in to make sure I have not forgotten — is to have patience, especially when it comes to something worth waiting for.

When I am introduced to something I am eager to welcome into my life, I have to remind myself to take a breath. Good things indeed take time — four years to find Le Papillon, twenty years to be able to be a full-time writer, thirty-seven years to travel to Britain.

While it may seem that other people experience overnight successes and out-of-the-blue wonders, often if you look behind the curtain, you will discover there has been an immense amount of planning and prepping, followed by patiently waiting for the opportune moment to present itself. In other words, be assured that your efforts will pay off in the end.

However, taking a breath does not mean doing zilch. Absolutely not. In fact, in order to make tranquility part of your state of mind while you wait patiently, you must do everything in your control to the best of your ability: Educate yourself so you can make the best decisions. Eat well to fuel your body. Educate, prepare, and/or save up so that when the opportunity you have been waiting for appears, you can pounce.

Petit plaisir Explore purchasing a Burleigh teacup and saucer, maybe even a teapot. (Arden Blue was the featured tea set giveaway in TSLL's 2020 British Week — be sure to stop by the blog every third week in May — and is the design that inspired the illustration you see next to each listed *petit plaisir* throughout the book.)

Explore further thesimplyluxuriouslife.com/may8 (while you exercise patience, master the skill of tranquility — thirty ideas for finding tranquility in your everyday)

May 9
Dealing with Unknowns: Everyday Routines

Often the solutions we seek are the simplest. However, we may doubt ourselves and first seek the more difficult solution until we eventually are led back to what was right in front of us.

The best solution to dealing with unknowns and aspects of life that are out of our control is to luxuriate in the life we have created for ourselves. Revel in what we do have control over, cultivating celebratory, much-anticipated everyday moments that enable us to be truly present. In other words, build an everyday life that brings contentment, sprinkled with daily, weekly rituals that remind us of all that we must not take for granted. Whether it is the hobbies we enjoy, the exercise we engage in, the time spent with friends and loved ones, the moments we spend cooking meals, or even the moments just before we fall asleep, as well as before we get out of bed, we must live in a way that is truly conscious, rather than allowing ourselves to go through the motions until the next big, exciting moment arrives. As we know, big exciting moments are not all that frequent. However, the seemingly small everyday moments can become big amazing moments to treasure.

Some individuals always do as they are told, to their detriment. It is perhaps not conscious, and perhaps they are not being influenced by any one individual. In fact, these people may even think they are living an independent, conscious life. But as I see them complaining about everyday events, people, and the ways of life they have chosen, I wonder why they stay in situations they regularly complain about. Everyone's life is a journey, and we learn as we go, applying the lessons and doing our best as we move forward.

The good news is that sometimes we personally do not have to make the mistakes. Sometimes we can observe and learn from others. The most significant life lesson I have learned is to make sure the decisions I make, the life I am building, is one that fits well with me, my temperament, my strengths, my passions, etc. I don't follow what I "should do." When we unconsciously live the life the zeitgeist expects, we end up doing a lot of complaining, wondering, and whining. When, instead, we choose more wisely, have more patience, and trust our internal compass, we will be reveling and not yearning to escape the everyday lives we are living.

As I reflect on my weeks, the everyday routine moments that fill me with joy are simple: tending to my weekly grocery shopping at Trader Joe's and picking out the week's flowers (the first peonies of the season!), walking my dogs at the off-leash dog park and seeing them frolic, smile, and venture about until flopping, exhausted, into the car for the ride home, enjoying my first outdoor picnic of the year with new friends, carving out one day during the weekend to peruse the shelves in my favorite local bookshop, taking my computer to work at the neighborhood bakery, viewing a matinee, and playing in the kitchen with a handful of new recipes.

I have a feeling you too have many everyday routines you could make even more worthwhile than they already are. Why not continue to invest and build an everyday life that sings, that leaves you excited to wake up in the morning and delighted when you go to bed because you had the opportunity to experience it and will be doing so again the next day? I don't know about you, but knowing that the everyday is so grand makes the extra-special moments all the sweeter and easy to return home from without lingering.

What you have the opportunity to return home to can be very sweet indeed. It is the simple everyday life we live that can be the solution we have been seeking all along to a deeper, more fulfilling way of living.

Petit plaisir   Savor an everyday black tea from Britain. Twinings is my daily workday favorite from the United Kingdom.

Explore further   thesimplyluxuriouslife.com/may9 (inspiration for everyday routines to elevate your life)

May 10
Savoring the Simple

Make this a day to leisurely step into a month to awaken to. Become excited, thinking about all of the beauty and goodness that lies before you, waiting to be enjoyed, savored, and appreciated.

Often, when I take walks with the boys, something seemingly inconsequential will take place or be found — a new trail, a conversation with a fellow dog walker, spying a nest of hatchlings perched high upon a tree, pristine skies, or picturesque mountain views. Each time, I cannot help but stop for a moment and just be grateful, letting myself become lost in the moment, savoring each and every detail that is entirely out of my control to create.

Embracing these moments, and simply basking in the beauty of the present, thankful for both the natural beauty but also the gift of where I am and how I arrived is a learned skill and one that costs not a penny. Have you ever had these moments in your daily life? They are truly sweet, no? Nothing from the outsiders' perspective would hint at anything extraordinary or a reason to celebrate, but such moments give me reason to celebrate and do a happy dance.

Life really is about the simple things, the everyday moments that bring us immeasurable joy and pleasure all mixed into one. I do hope you have many of these moments, and if you do not, know that you can. It truly is all within your power.

Petit plaisir   Keep a gardening journal for each gardening year. Not only will it inform you and create a record of what you have planted and what worked; it will also remind you of the cycle of the seasons, and to have patience, as you have so much you have been able to savor and share.

Explore further   thesimplyluxuriouslife.com/may10 (discover how to invite the skill of savoring into your life)

May 11
Life's Timing

The idea of timing is often important in our lives, and as we know, there is much that is out of our control. Often we cannot know why, at the time, things did not happen the way we had hoped or imagined. But sometimes, if we are lucky, hindsight allows us the vision to understand and hopefully pass along this advice: We must trust the timing of our lives.

Thankfully we always have the opportunity to grow, evolve, and reach ever-more-impressive versions of who we were yesterday and are today. We cannot know what skills we need until an opportunity presents itself and we find that we are either lacking or sufficiently prepared. When it is the former, sometimes we try to keep pushing, try to force an unpolished us into a hole that was designed for the finished version. And to prove its point, the universe will sometimes give us what we thought we wanted, only to show us, "Nope, you weren't ready."

The mystery of timing is perplexing and frustrating, but simply knowing it exists within each of our lives should give us some comfort. What else can we learn? How else can we grow? What mini journeys and adventures can we embark on while the future we thought we wanted tells us, "Not yet"?

If we choose to see timing, something that is out of our control, as a gift, we can see the extra time we did not know we had as being to our advantage. Simply because something has not occurred does not mean it won't. The onion that is our life has many layers, and often we have no idea what lies beneath the next one we pull back.

Revel in the time when you become a person you never thought you could be but now have the opportunity to become. When what you wished for does occur, you will begin to see why it had to play out the way it did.

Petit plaisir As you head out on a walk, into your workday, or maybe home from work, or into the garden, listen to George Frideric Handel's "The Arrival of the Queen of Sheba."

Explore further thesimplyluxuriouslife.com/may11 (thoughts about "yet")

May 12
Keep Trying

During the summer of 2012, a childhood dream of mine came true: the opportunity to travel to the Olympics while the games were taking place *and* to a city I had longed to visit. The London Olympics officially began on July 27, 2012, for an unprecedented third time in the capital of Great Britain, or, as many label it, the cultural capital of the world. Whether you are a sports fan or not, the Olympics offers an opportunity to see the world (205 countries were participating, and for the first time, each country had women and men participants) come together in peace for the common goal of sportsmanlike competition and athletes excelling to attain their full potential in athleticism and mental strength.

I watched Oprah's interview with ten iconic American Olympians, and gold medal winner Bart Conner made an observation about the Olympics. He stated that they were the great leveling field of life; to explain what he meant, he said, "There's only one way to the top of the podium, and that's hard work, focus and determination."

While not all of us will have the privilege of being an Olympian, we all can find the inspiration the Olympics provides and use it to motivate ourselves to continue to be focused, determined, and willing to work hard for what we want our life to become. Money cannot create fulfillment if we do not appreciate the effort it took to acquire it. Good looks may garner attention but not always respect if we do not behave in a respectable manner and continue to expand our intellect.

At the Olympics, the medalists who stand atop the podiums certainly deserve applause, but also look for the stories of athletes who earned the title of Olympian and simply did their best, no matter the results. Those are people to be inspired by as well.

You may not always live up to the expectations you set for yourself on the first or second attempt, but you can always choose to learn and apply the lessons the next time around. You are never truly defeated unless you throw in the towel.

Petit plaisir Stroll through a neighborhood awash in spring blooms and blossoms.

Explore further thesimplyluxuriouslife.com/may12 (the characteristics of a high achiever)

May 13
Lessons Take Time to Present Themselves

I am always amazed by the melody of our lives. One week can be truly cacophonous and confusing and the next full of window-opening moments that offer clarity and more certainty, and thus calm.

Whenever I travel, upon returning home, I take a good amount of time (partly to let the jet lag wear off) to ponder lessons I learned. Sometimes the *aha*'s are immediate, and sometimes they take weeks, months, and even years to understand. By beginning the initial exploration of pondering, you turn the gears in your mind to begin the search for discoveries.

One lesson travel has taught me is the power and importance of patience with ourselves. As a dear friend said recently, the most beautiful conundrum to discern is the one in which a dream of a trip takes place and you are left to figure out why it happened.

I will take that challenge indeed, and perhaps when you look at your life, instead of seeing the problems or the obstacles, you will be thankful for the events, the people, the world that enabled them to *be* choices in your life. What if we did not have the choice to change, adjust, or improve our lives? What if we were stuck exactly as we are today? Initially, to some this may sound appealing, but with each day, new information is presented to us, new concepts that we could not have fathomed yesterday are brought to light, and in these revelations, we see more of what we can become, of what the world can become.

Consider where you are right now in your life. What is perplexing you? Can you shift your perspective on that conundrum? Can you see the good fortune? Let your "little grey cells" (to quote Agatha Christie's Hercule Poirot) do what they do best so that you can see the good the conundrum is revealing to you, and then be patient with yourself. The answers come, so long as you let go and remain open to what crosses your path.

Petit plaisir Figure out the few nights when the cherry trees are in bloom and the moon is full, cross your fingers for a clear night, walk or drive to the trees, if you don't have them in your neighborhood, and savor a magical spectacle, courtesy of Mother Nature and our solar system.

Explore further thesimplyluxuriouslife.com/may13 (the power of a new perspective)

May 14
The Rambling Rose

A cottage is not a proper English cottage without a rose or two or many (but that might just reveal that I have watched and read far too many British cosy stories). When I decided to cultivate the aesthetic of a cottage, especially in my garden, I knew I wanted to welcome roses into it. From shrub to climbing to . . . Were there more varietals? Where should they go? Lovely dilemmas and quandaries to ponder.

And then I learned about the rambling rose. It grows taller/longer than a climbing rose (a climber grows 7 to 10 feet high, while a rambler can grow 12 to 15 feet), producing an abundance of blossoms, and it is often wonderfully fragrant, lovely not only for us humans but also for the pollinators. At one time, rambling roses would produce many roses on one stem but only once a year; however, now some rambling rose varietals will produce roses continually throughout the summer.

Perfect for the front of a house, over a pergola, along and around the porch, or any space you want to cover with roses, compared to their cousin, the climber, rambling roses have more malleable branches that you can bend and twist to where you need or want them to go, and they also often produce an abundance of wonderful rosehips. You can also mix them with other climbing vines, such as clematis.

The rambling rose grows well. It produces rosebuds on new growth each year. Consequently, in early spring, you will want to remove the stems that are not needed or that are growing where you do not want them. When you plant them, the new stems will sprout and then produce roses in the coming summer.

I have welcomed David Austin's rambler, the Albrighton, to the front of my home, where I have a pergola-esque design that will hopefully enable it to easily climb above the porch and frame the front stoop. I am dreaming of the multiple blooms that this rambler varietal can produce throughout the summer. Hopefully, in a few short years, the front porch will resemble even more an English cottage (albeit in Bend).

What "rambling rose" detail can you add to your sanctuary? Whether you live in an apartment oodles of stories up into the sky or a stand-alone house, what garden or décor detail is worth waiting for as it matures into its fullest beauty to create a space uniquely yours? Mine your past for moments during travel or visiting others' homes — what details aesthetically caught your eye, strengthened your peace, and beckoned you to stay?

Petit plaisir Dare to customize details in your home and/or your wardrobe. The time and investment will be well worth it. My fireplace, while small, is framed with Delft-inspired tiles hand-painted in England from Douglas Watson Studio. Each tile captures an image of my life journey — a pup chasing a butterfly, cherries (Le Papillon's garden has two cherry trees), a soufflé to represent my love of French cooking, and a handful more.

Explore further thesimplyluxuriouslife.com/may14 (join me for December 2021's A Cuppa Moments w/Shannon video chat where I sit with Norman by the fireplace)

May 15
English Gardening Essentials

Let's stay in the garden, shall we? Perhaps you too have noticed that gardens are ever so subtly present, almost as background characters, in many British films and TV shows. The plot finds its way to a garden, and the person is holding a wooden basket, perhaps full of freshly cut flowers or just-picked vegetables. This basket is the Sussex trug.

Trugs, as we know them, evolved out of what in Anglo-Saxon times was called a trog: "a wooden vessel carved out of solid wood in a round form, which archaeologists believe probably had handles carved underneath." As they were solid baskets, trogs would be used for carrying any number of farm commodities, including liquids such as milk.

Enter Thomas Smith, who in the mid-19th century created a much lighter version of the trog and called it a trug. Queen Victoria came across the trug at the Great Exhibition held in 1851 in London's Hyde Park, where the trug was awarded the Gold Medal and Certificate of Merit First Class; those awards forever changed the future of the trug and of those gardening in England. After visiting the show on the first day, Victoria ordered several gifts for members of the Royal Household. The legend is that Smith himself made all of the trugs she ordered; he and his brother walked the 60 miles to Buckingham Palace to deliver them in person.

Thomas Smith's trugs continued to gain attention throughout Great Britain and across the European Continent.

The classic Thomas Smith's trug (aka the Royal Sussex Trug) is made of sweet chestnut wood (handle) and willow wood (body). To clean a trug, simply wash it with soapy water. Use it in the garden for everything from dead-heading blooms to picking berries, fruit, and vegetables. You can let a trug get dirty as it is made to be used.

Originally, trug sizes were given as, for example, "pint" or "bushel"; however, Smith changed the sizes to numerals. They are given a number, ranging between 1 and 8, that indicates length and width. You will see this number when you are deciding which size to buy.

I love many things about my garden trug (no. 4), and I look forward to acquiring one more in a larger size for larger produce and pruning:

- The "feet" on the bottom enable the basket to sit just about anywhere.
- The basket is light, but not flimsy.
- Small details, such as copper nails, add a thoughtful touch of quality to a functional product that will last for decades (not all trugs are made with copper, but many are, and all Sussex trugs are).
- The handle is soft in the palm.

Whether you choose a large or small trug, for a classic garden or a small patch of flowers, one made in Sussex or one made in Oregon from myrtle wood — once you have a trug, you will use it often and for many years to come. As well, you no doubt will be able to quickly spot them in your favorite British programs. Here's wishing you many happy and fruitful years of gardening.

Petit plaisir Welcome a traditional Sussex trug into your life for gardening, home décor, or just because (there are many sizes to fit your lifestyle and preference).

Explore further thesimplyluxuriouslife.com/may15 (discover where to find your own traditional trug)

May 16
A Private Garden for Writing

I had just a few more days in London and didn't want to waste a minute. Tonight a play in *Trafalgar Square*, a morning Tube ride to the Olympic Park, and an afternoon stopping into Manolo Blahnik's flagship store in Chelsea, then perhaps a bit of shopping and choosing a lovely teacup to take home.

With a quiet private garden behind the flat to escape to for writing in my daily journal and a winding staircase to the third floor, where I gladly put my feet up at the end of each day, I was feeling rather spoiled. Nearby pubs — the Warrington and the Prince Alfred — were a treat in the evenings; I could grab a pint of beer or a lovely white wine while the Olympics were live and being thoroughly enjoyed by all patrons.

During my first trip to the United Kingdom, the space that gave me much respite and deepened my appreciation for all that London revealed was a private garden surrounded by 20 or 30 flats; the tenants had keys to an exclusive gated entry. It was similar to a garden I saw while watching *Rosemary & Thyme* a couple years later, and I wondered if perhaps the same garden I had once sat in nearly each day of my week in London appeared in the cosy mystery series. I later learned that many neighborhoods offer such a gated, private space for residents, a special, really priceless benefit.

I took inspiration from that trip. At home, my sunshine garden during the warm months of the year, protected from most peering eyes by the full cherry trees and a slight elevation from the sidewalk, contains an Adirondack chair and a footstool, which provides a wonderful place to sit, rest, read, or write, and to always enjoy the birds dining at their café no more than eight feet from where I sit.

Travel surprises us with gifts we were not expecting. Two trips to the UK have influenced how I live in my everyday life — enjoying tea throughout the day, a love for print wallpaper and upholstered furniture, mixing and matching seemingly dissimilar patterns and colors, only to be surprised at how they work for the eye, learning how to garden and to savor the *doing* of gardening, not just the end result.

When you bring home ideas and inspiration from your travels, you deepen not only the pleasure you get from your everyday experience, as they evoke memories of your travels and also reinforce your contentment. Travel reveals what it is that speaks to you, and like an uninhibited child, you respond without editing. When you return, with new rituals and new ideas, your home becomes your sanctuary, encouraging you to simply be yourself.

Petit plaisir Plant sunflower seeds, even if the last frost has not happened yet. The end of July and August will make you smile when their beauty is revealed.

Explore further thesimplyluxuriouslife.com/may16 (explore thirty-four ways to add more "cozy" to your everyday)

May 17
Look for What You Seek

The English cottage garden has fascinated and enthralled me for most of my life. It began with Peter Rabbit's adventures, which my parents read to me as a child, and continued through endless *Midsomer Murders* episodes in which the characters often potter in their gardens, trug in hand. I finally understood what a true cottage garden is when I read Monty Don's *Down to Earth* and watched him in his garden in Longmeadow, a portion of which is designed as his cottage garden.

Le Papillon incorporates the potential for a cottage garden to be cultivated without being too much for one person to tend to, which is partially what drew me to the property. Vegetables and berries are dispersed throughout the garden, not in a single plot, and the herbaceous plants — along with the lavender and roses and fruit trees — are intended to look unplanned in their placement, offering a variety of color and seasonal beauty that shifts as the spring, summer and fall months unfold.

Roses have become a fundamental part of Le Papillon's garden, with a David Austen rambling Albrighton framing the front porch, and a Kiftsgait rose beginning to run along my garden fence. I have planted David Austen buttercup shrub roses in my boulevard to complement the lavender and the soft red shrub roses, part of the original landscaping, that greet you as you make your way up the walk to the front door.

Not only do most of these roses bloom all summer, so long as I deadhead regularly, I also purchased them with the intention of creating a pollinator's garden that would be especially attractive to butterflies. And so it was with utter delight, on the first day of my kitchen customization project, that, on my morning neighborhood walk with the boys, I found a swallowtail butterfly resting among the red roses. Its large black-and-yellow wings splayed entirely open to present its impressive wingspan, it was easing into its day and gave me time to capture a photo. I took this discovery as an auspicious sign that this day was a positive first step toward a new chapter.

While my take on what I found may sound absurd, silly, or illogical, we find what we seek. If we are looking for validation, if we are looking for reasons to pursue a particular path, we will eventually find them or the people that will support our journey. If we doubt ourselves, if we believe we cannot possibly do something, we will likewise find naysayers who will support this belief. There is immense power in the thoughts we entertain and accept. Set it as your objective to stride forward and eventually be able to bring forth what you wish for. It is possible.

I did not know for sure that my choice to invest in a kitchen customization was a wise investment, but I knew I loved spending time in my kitchen, and that it brought me and others great joy. I stepped forward toward the ability to do something I knew I loved; that was my fuel.

There are endless unknowns in your world, but you can know yourself, if you will take the time. Let that be your guide, and also let yourself be stretched by what you hope for but may not think possible.

I have no doubt that you will find a butterfly on the first day of your journey, if you will look for it.

Petit plaisir Tend to that simple thing that is causing you a headache in your everydays, yet you put up with it because "it is not that bad." Maybe it is a squeaky garage door, or a favorite coat's button that has become loose, or a too-full inbox that needs organizing, or a quick purge of one particular cupboard or drawer in your home.

Explore further thesimplyluxuriouslife.com/may17 (how to step through and embrace the change you seek)

May 18
The Garden as a Teacher for Living Well

There is nothing quite like gardening. We work with nature to create something unique. In the process of planting seeds, caring for plants, adapting to seasons and weather, and the physical work, we find something greater within us. Gardening calms. Encourages. Uplifts. Invigorates.
— Monty Don, during a talk in Sweden in 2017

Each of us has our preferred garden style that our eyes gravitate toward and treasure. We may or may not be able to grow the types of plants we love, but that does not mean we cannot appreciate differing styles and see the beauty, the unique aesthetic qualities, in each. Whether it is our own garden or another's, there are powerful health and well-being benefits to be had from gardening, and I will share below ten of what are no doubt many more.

What I appreciate immensely about Monty Don is his approach to gardening. He casts aside perfection, instead seeking to learn and explore; in so doing, he becomes our teacher, someone who not only has done the research and homework, but through his easy, calming manner, inspires us to give it a try, whatever that "it" may be.

Ten reasons to give gardening a try:

- In life, we each need to find the soil that works best for us to grow and live to our fullest potential.
- Cultivating the skill of patience welcomes the best growth and reward.
- Healthy, well-maintained borders create respected and appreciated boundaries.
- Weeding is work but offers great reward.

- Differences make a beautiful, much-appreciated difference.
- Good nutrients and good support make a strong and beautiful plant.
- We do not all have to speak the same language to respect one another and see the humanity in each other.
- Each "oops" is an opportunity to learn and apply forward for greater success.
- Being present provides peace.
- Gardening is the gift of a life in motion.

The British surely know how to garden well. Maybe it is only me, but before I had the opportunity to take my first train ride into the Devon countryside, all I could imagine were the rolling green hills, the plentiful, seemingly easy-to-grow blooms and gardens as the regular rains encouraged abundance. When the opportunity came to finally see and witness it with my own eyes, the reality did not disappoint. Yep, rolling green hills, blooms even in November, and oodles of rain.

Mother Nature and Britain have been dancing beautifully together to offer the gifts of gardening for centuries, and oh my goodness, do I have so much to learn. However, along the way, I am confident my days will be all the better for welcoming this pastime into my life, and I know the same can be true for you as well, however you wish to do so. Here's wishing you may happy days, seasons and years of gardening.

Depending upon where your ideas about gardening originated, you can see gardening from many perspectives. When you see a garden as a showcase, a molding of Mother Nature into a perfect, pristine, static state, your blood pressure may immediately rise, but if you instead see gardening as more than a finished "look" or a way to impress others, you can welcome a natural stress reducer and, yes, improve your well-being and create a more fulfilling, well-lived life.

Petit plaisir Visit a nursery to shop for herbs for a mini herb garden.

Explore further thesimplyluxuriouslife.com/may18 (how to grow your own herb garden)

May 19
Understanding What You Yearn For

The truth is that one experience taken to heart will satisfy our hunger to be loved by everyone.
— Mark Nepo

When we give to ourselves what we long for the outside world to give, we actually draw to us opportunities for healthy connection. In loving ourselves, we will create a separation from those who do not agree with our choices or dislike the boundaries we set in place, but in so doing we are actually protecting ourselves from pain and propelling ourselves toward more kindness, love, and acceptance.

When we allow ourselves the freedom to pursue our deepest needs, values, and wishes, we begin to show ourselves love, and even if the entire world or even the majority of the world applauds, when we hear applause, when we gain acceptance, it is merely icing on the cake, because we have already given these accolades to ourselves.

Begin giving yourself the five A's author David Richo describes as necessary as one part in a healthy relationship: attention, acceptance, appreciation, affection, and allowing. Equally, give these five A's to those with whom you are intimately involved and discover how the quality of your connections and time in your own company improves.

Petit plaisir Welcome peonies into your home for simple or grand bouquets or bud vase displays.

Explore further thesimplyluxuriouslife.com/may19 (five key components to building healthy relationships)

May 20
Life's Wonderful Surprises

A simple event — a glimpse of a new idea, an unexpected smile from a stranger, a phone call or text from someone you have not heard from in a while, a rare weather occurrence, an introduction to someone who ends up playing a pivotal role in your life journey — can change our lives in drastic ways.

Just as Mother Nature can wreak havoc in the blink of an eye, so too can an idea that sparks across our minds, after we read or hear a particular phrase or unique way of thinking, provoke unimaginable change and evolution in our lives.

Whenever I think of such powerful forces, I immediately notice my thoughts shifting and my ideas becoming much more realistic and concrete, and at the same time hopeful and determined. I have a hop in my step as I move about the day.

Isn't it wonderful to think that life, no matter how much we plan, can still offer us wonderful surprises? Knowing that this is possible is one of the many reasons I am fascinated with the journey. So long as we feed this magic and do our best to place as many variables in our favor as possible, the surprises can far outweigh the tragedies and disappointments.

Even if you find yourself not precisely where you want to be, remember that events outside of your control may just have something tremendously magnificent coming your way, if only you will continue striving forward.

Petit plaisir Be inspired by Claude Monet's garden in Giverny and plant the nasturtiums you sowed on April 10. Plant them after the last frost, and enjoy watching them spread swiftly in the summer's heat. (Both leaves and flowers are edible).

Explore further thesimplyluxuriouslife.com/may20 (enjoy a video tour of Claude Monet's garden and home at Giverny)

May 21
A Celebration of All Things British

Since 2019, during the full third week of May I have hosted on my blog, *The Simply Luxurious Life*, an annual British Week. I have meant for it to coincide as closely as possible with the annual Chelsea Garden Show, as well as the anniversary of the wedding of the Duke and Duchess of Sussex. And, if I am being honest, I also chose May as it is a month when there are typically equal days of rain and sun — something Britain offers in spades. When I think of Britain, I think of oodles of rain and lush, green, and brilliant gardens. What better time of year to step into the garden than May?

I decided the celebratory week would be a wonderful fit for the blog's content as I noticed — while I spent my first weeklong holiday on my own in London and the countryside in North Devon, engaging with readers along the way — that TSLL community had an affection for Britain. Whether readers lived in Britain or abroad and dreamed of visiting or returning, the positive response to my posts made it clear that not only is TSLL a Francophile destination, it may just also be an Anglophile destination.

So British Week began in earnest, and it has quickly become the second most popular week of the year on TSLL blog.

Not a day goes by that I do not boil water on the stove top and pour myself a cuppa. Twinings' English Breakfast has become one of my top two teas of choice (the other is a French black tea from Palais des Thés). Armed with a brown betty (cobalt, in my case) teapot and tea cozy, the end — or middle or start — of the day cannot be any sweeter.

Celebrate aspects of a culture that speak to a passion you hold dear. Whether it is British culture that tickles your toes, as it does mine, and makes you smile, or any other culture and its way of life, intentionally create space on the calendar to do something special each year. Reveling in what makes it special to you elevates your appreciation and brightens that particular time on the calendar, creating our own "holiday" to look forward to each year.

Petit plaisir Stop by TSLL blog for the annual British Week, full of multiple British-inspired posts each day, multiple giveaways, and an opportunity to "travel" to the land of Jane Austen, brollies, and clotted cream.

Explore further thesimplyluxuriouslife.com/may21 (are you an Anglophile? check out this list of thirty signs you just might be)

May 22
Speaking of Enjoying a Cuppa

But indeed I would rather have nothing but tea.
—Jane Austen

Just saying the informal word *cuppa* brings an upturn to the corners of my mouth. Understood to mean "a cup of tea," the phrase originated in Britain and always refers to tea, not coffee (unless someone explicitly states "a cuppa Joe"). Hinting at comfort, warmth, a deep breath of reassurance, and good ol' gumption to persevere, to indulge in a *cuppa* is to enjoy the everyday all the more.

While there is some debate about when the word *cuppa* was coined (Merriam-Webster claims 1934, and thank you, TSLL reader Susanne, for this), in New Zealand novelist Edith Ngaio Marsh's mystery *A Man*

The Road to Le Papillon

Lay Dead (published that year), *cuppa* is used for a cup of tea. Whenever it came to be, it has remained and with good reason.

Tea is the oldest beverage in the world, second only to water, and is enjoyed around the globe. Americans have not quite caught on to enjoying a warm cup of tea as a daily ritual. While we drink 1.42 million pounds of tea a day (as reported by the United States Tea Association in 2010), 85 percent of that is iced tea, which is not what the British are seeking for their cuppa.

An interesting idea to ponder is that the primary reason Americans may not have been quick to adopt hot tea is because it runs counter to our culture's habit of hustling, not sitting still, and trying to not waste a minute. In 2019, food writer Max Falkowitz wrote, "It's no coincidence that many of tea's fundamental attributes — inherent slowness, its tendency to gather people, its relative subtlety — stand in opposition to the American patterns of consumption that have allowed coffee to thrive, and historically acted as impediments to tea gaining a greater cultural foothold." However, I have a strong inkling that this cannot be said for the Americans who are a part of TSLL community, as I know many of you savor your cuppa on a regular basis, just as I do.

As I shared in the pilot episode of *The Simply Luxurious Kitchen*, I was introduced to tea when, in my twenties, I traveled to Victoria, Canada, with my mother, well before I began the blog, and enjoyed high tea at the Victoria Hotel. It was a celebratory and grand occasion, complete with a triple-tier cake stand full of afternoon tea sandwiches, biscuits, and cakes, served by a dapper and welcoming waitstaff. I never looked back. Tea became my hot drink of choice and my frequent multi-cup per day choice.

On average, the British enjoy 165 million cups of tea every day (as reported in 2017) or approximately 60 billion cups a year. The historically designated afternoon tea time was begun by Anna, Duchess of Bedford (1788–1861), who first began enjoying her tea, with scones, at 4:00 p.m., in what soon became an English tradition. Whether you enjoy your tea then or at any other time, simply taking a pause from the day, sitting still and savoring the moment, is an everyday ritual to welcome into your life.

Petit plaisir Search consignment and vintage shops and online sites for a tea table.

Explore further thesimplyluxuriouslife.com/may22 (eighteen ideas for enjoying a good cuppa)

May 23
Taking Décor Inspiration from the English

The transformation of a home into a sanctuary begins with the courage to understand what is needed to rejuvenate and restore us when we return from the outside world, when we emerge from our deep slumber each morning, and what we need as we potter around the house, resting and creating and enjoying our time within our four walls.

The first room I wanted to decorate and furnish in Le Papillon was the first room I see when I enter into my home and the last room I see when I leave, the mudroom. The goal for redecorating this space was to create a room that enables ease of entry and exit each time, and that offers organizational systems and locations for the everyday items I use but that can also create clutter if not stored properly.

My aesthetic preferences were to create a mudroom that included my English country predilections — my love for rain (there must be a place to put my umbrella) and covering the walls in a classic English wallpaper print — as well as incorporating my love of France, as I wanted to showcase my French market totes, but also make them readily available for use. From when I began, perusing the possibilities for wallpaper, which would determine the color scheme, to finding the necessary details that married function with aesthetics — a large storage basket for newspaper recyclables and canvas market totes for everyday grocery shopping — until the bench cushion was reupholstered with an Anna French small print to complement rather than compete with the wallpaper, it took twenty months to locate materials, have them shipped, and finally complete the room.

I looked at offerings from a handful of English wallpaper companies, but when I came across Little Greene's Grosvenor's Primrose print (there are four additional colorways), I knew it was the one. Wallpapering is a décor idea that will significantly change any room in a most wonderful way. As one TSLL reader describes it, wallpaper gives the room and therefore the home "a personal, friendly hug" (thank you, Sheryl M.!). I have since brought more wallpaper into my home (five more rooms to be exact), and after completing this room, I was even more confident I could indeed do it by myself.

Completing that first room, the first stage in a journey of customization, reminds me of the power of simple changes that each of us can manage without a contractor or extra help. We just need to know where to begin.

Petit plaisir Grow three or four strawberry plants in frost-free pots. You will have strawberries all summer, with no need to do anything through the winter; next spring, they will revive and grow new blossoms and berries again. I have six — three on each side of my garden porch — to frame the pillars as they "soften" the edges and offer great nibbling.

Explore further thesimplyluxuriouslife.com/may23 (take a tour of the mudroom with Little Greene's Grosvenor's Primrose print wallpaper)

May 24
The Art of the Cosy British Mystery

Whether in written or video format, a cosy (British spelling) mystery has specific "rules" it abides by so that the reader/viewer is not shocked or pained. What are those rules? Have a look below:

- Those who are murdered are not characters who are beloved or well-developed; sometimes they are not even introduced before we learn of their death.
- Animals are always left alone and remain safe, and may even help solve the murder (see, for example, "The Dumb Witness" episode of *Poirot*).
- The sleuth is an amateur of some sort, not officially part of the local police department, or if they are (as in *Midsomer Murders* or *Inspector Morse*), they no longer live in the big city (that is, London), a circumstance initially seen as a demotion to the countryside.
- The setting is an everyday town or village of some sort, with all its "goings-on."
- Glimpses into the sleuth's life humanize the main character and playfully reveal unique talents/gifts as well as "flaws."
- Often the sleuth has a sidekick who "fills in the gaps" and has a likable personality, sometimes complementing the main character; in other cases, the two act as a team, as in *Rosemary & Thyme*.

   While Britain has long produced mystery novels and television series, from Sir Arthur Conan Doyle to Agatha Christie to Gladys Mitchell (the *Mrs. Bradley Mysteries*) to, more recently, Caroline Graham (creator of Chief Barnaby of the *Midsomer Murders*) and M. C. Benton (*Agatha Raisin*), it is the *cosy* mystery that has captured so many viewers around the world.

   Embrace your inner Anglophile, and create a ritual of savoring what you love about the British culture. The next evening when rain is steadily falling, enjoy an hour or two watching a favorite cosy mystery, while savoring your favorite British simple luxuries — I'm thinking a hot cuppa paired with a favorite biscuit for nibbling; Walkers are my go-to — and look for all the details that lead to a satisfying closure when all is solved just prior to the credits rolling.

Petit plaisir Watch any Hercule Poirot episode starring David Suchet (BritBox and Acorn TV offer all episodes).

Explore further thesimplyluxuriouslife.com/may24 (explore sixteen British cosy mysteries I recommend)

May 25
An Afternoon Tea to Savor

Afternoon tea needn't stand on ceremony. Anything that becomes more important than sweet fellowship, whether lace or linen or the china itself, is pretense. How much more we enjoy life when the pretenses are discarded!
— Paul F. Kortepeter

As a young girl, maybe eight years of age, for my birthday party with a gaggle of my friends, girls and boys, we dressed up with gowns and dapper attire, complete with hats and heels from my "dress-up box," as well as other accoutrements. We then went into the sunroom in my childhood home and devoured the birthday cake. And while we did not have tea, the idea was a tea party of sorts. The details are fuzzy (Mom, if you are reading this, I can see the pictures of the occasion in my mind's eye!), but I remember that dress-up box vividly and the dresses that were my favorites.

While some may find the idea of dressing up and tending to a thoughtful tablescape too pretentious, any pretentiousness I find is only present when there is an expectation that the guests must engage in a certain way. Ultimately, the goal is to enjoy oneself, to relax from the rest of the world, and to be present, eating delightfully delicious morsels of food (many of them small bites), all the while drinking something deeply comforting and spending time with others or just oneself.

And that is one of the important details to remember when it comes to afternoon tea: Focus on the scrumptiousness and let go of the precision. Some may debate with me on this point, but when we are too concerned with how to behave, we lose the joy and peace the moment is meant to cultivate and restore.

Below are seven ideas for your next afternoon tea, if you are thinking you may indulge in one, whether you share it with one friend or many or simply in your own company. We can all benefit from an afternoon tea —

to remind us to pause, take a breath, and settle ourselves, regardless of what is going on around us.

- Serve a scrumptious tea that you love.
- Include savory and sweet items.
- A full, matching tea set is not necessary — use what you have.
- Add flowers.
- Use the platters you have and a tablecloth that brightens the space.
- Serve lemon curd.

The ritual of an afternoon tea can vary in its scale and scope. Whether you organize a tea for a special occasion with a gathering of friends or family, or enjoy it on your own, to calm the day down and compose your thoughts and restore your energy, or with a partner or dear friend, to simply be in each other's company — welcoming this simple, yet truly luxurious routine into our daily lives indeed elevates the everyday.

Petit plaisir Make a simple lemon and orange pound cake (don't forget the crème fraîche!). Recipe included in the link below.

Explore further thesimplyluxuriouslife.com/may25 (explore both savory and sweet recipes for an afternoon tea)

May 26
My Discoveries in the Devon Countryside

Each time a trip abroad concludes, I board the plane for the transatlantic flight, returning to Oregon filled with both melancholy and exhilaration. Sad to leave, grateful for all I have experienced.

To assuage the sadness, I tap into the gratitude, and over the course of the ten-plus hours of the flight, I make a list of all I learned during my time away from home in a country I longed to visit and return to.

I spent Thanksgiving 2017 in my own company for four days, tucked away in the North Devon countryside, savoring views of the Bristol Channel, walks upon the green, rain-drenched rolling hills in my wellies, and loving every single minute. Below is my list of life lessons, which I have vowed to apply, garnered from my time in Devon. Each is applicable wherever I find myself in the world — at home in Bend, Oregon, or traveling to beloved destinations.

- Choose a place in the world you would want to call home, no matter how often you venture from your nest and explore.
- Slow down and pack your wellies.
- Make the journey comfortable: Choose first-class rail tickets in advance.
- Give yourself as many tools to be successful as possible in unknown situations.
- Let go of time.
- Be a traveler rather than a tourist.
- Give yourself time to absorb everything.
- Listen to your inner yearnings.
- Seek out details or items to take home with you that speak to your experience.
- Visit local markets.
- Converse with the local residents.
- Listen to what speaks to you, and follow your inspiration's direction.

Until life's journey reveals more of her answers, I will trust in Jane Austen's words from *Persuasion*: "Time will explain." If the past is any indication, it most certainly will, so long as you stay attentive and observant and revel in the journey as you travel along.

Petit plaisir Pick up a bouquet of sweet peas (or plant and grow your own!) and enjoy their subtle fragrance.

Explore further thesimplyluxuriouslife.com/may26 (seven ways to build a wealth of contentment during tough and good times)

May 27
My First Visit to London

In 2012, I finally saw London with my own eyes.

My first few days in London were surreal and magical. While there was a drizzle of rain every once in a while, the sun finally kept the clouds at bay. With temperatures in the upper seventies, the perfect weather unfolded for endless sightseeing and soaking in the international energy of the Olympics.

The Tube was a tremendous help in getting around ("Mind the Gap!"), and with an Oyster card in hand, I was able to get to many places I wanted to see. Amazingly enough, even with rides from one Tube station to the next, I would say that I easily walked five miles each day. Which means that I devoured an impressive plate of fish and chips one evening at Pembroke Pub, while watching the women's 200m and the men's 110m hurdles, with thorough enjoyment and not an ounce of guilt.

For whatever reason, my childhood dream of visiting England, as well as visiting the host city during the Olympics, had shrunk as a possibility that would ever happen in my life, but when the off-chance opportunity presented itself to experience both simultaneously, I figured out a way to make it happen.

What dream have you quietly let go, but only did so due to lack of trust that it could be possible? Breathe life back into that dream. It resides within you for a reason.

Petit plaisir Plant tomatoes you have grown from seed or pick up favorite varietals at the nursery for ripe, flavorful harvesting in August and September.

Explore further thesimplyluxuriouslife.com/may27 (explore the twelve characteristics of being a late bloomer, and the benefits of embracing this gift)

May 28
The Garden as Teacher

> *You can't believe the way that the garden has changed in the last few weeks. When [March and April began], everything was bare and bleak. You really felt some days a sense of disillusionment, like nothing was going to grow, but now look at it! What's next, May! My favorite time. It's froth time in the garden. You know, [March and April is] the time of sort of hope and growth and everything getting going, and May is the time to just celebrate.*
> —Carol Klein, British garden expert, on her Devon garden

Gardening arrived in my life with full force during the 2020 pandemic, but the seed of gardening and its gifts were planted in my childhood. My parents' house and garden (theirs for more than forty years now) demonstrate how magnificent tending a garden can be with vision, curiosity, patience, and the ability to let go, learn, and try again.

British gardener and television host Carol Klein and her husband's garden was also established more than forty years ago. In her *Life in a Cottage Garden* series (2013), she shares her genuine love and tenacity for getting into the dirt and gardening year-round. Gardens that bloom beautifully throughout the seasons bring into focus the cyclical nature of life.

Life leads us through times in which seemingly nothing appears to be working, even after we have invested endless hours of planning and sweat to bring a dream to life. The same can be true of cultivating a garden. Early in the year, as we step outside after a long winter to start sowing, transplanting, planning, and pruning, everything seems bleak, and even after a couple of months of effort, nothing much happens. But one morning, we wake up, wander out into the garden holding a hot cuppa to greet the day and keep our hands warm, and blossoms have burst beautifully from limbs, tulips twist in the breeze, and the bees and butterflies have returned. Just like that, the garden awakens.

So too will your dreams be realized. You do not know when exactly, and you often do not know exactly how they will present themselves, but they do arrive if you don't lose hope in what is possible. Keep putting in the effort; keep taking one small step after another. Keep watering your dreams, nurturing the soil, and just as Thoreau teaches, you "will meet with a success unexpected in common hours."

Petit plaisir Save up for a Haws outdoor watering can (the 1- or 2-gallon size). They will last your lifetime and then some.

Explore further thesimplyluxuriouslife.com/may28 (eleven gifts of a garden and yard when the yard is small or the time is short)

May 29
Cultivating Comfort

From classic favorites, such as Agatha Christie's Hercule Poirot, to contemporary comedic approaches, such as M. C. Beaton's Agatha Raisin, British cosy mysteries played most often in my house during the pandemic. Why would murder solving be soothing during a period of tremendous loss? From the feeling of closure and resolution, I would be transported, in under two hours, to likable, reliable characters who made me feel at home, welcomed, and virtually social when I could not be with people outside of my home.

However, cosy mysteries were a favorite genre of mine before Covid-19 hit. Dogs and English gardens, cottages and oodles of rain. Each connotes comfort, immense amounts of comfort. Include all of them in an episode of *Midsomer Murders* and I am hooked. Cultivating real comfort in our lives is to live simply luxuriously. When we have taken the time to understand what brings us comfort and why, when we understand that true luxury marries living intelligently, thoughtfully, and sincerely, when we finally invite and invest in such comfort and everyday living, our contentment elevates, and we appreciate it and are far less likely to take it for granted.

My dogs, Oscar and Norman, to whom I dedicated my second book and whom I describe as my muses in the introduction to my first book, bring me incredible comfort, and not for a moment do I take them for granted; they provided a variety of lessons in my early adult life. True comfort includes appreciation and a full understanding of what was missing prior to enjoying it.

Comfort is different than a crutch. An often-shared quote states: "Everything you want in the world is just right outside your comfort zone. Everything you could possibly want." What you need, however, is different than what you want. We can have our comforts, ones that provide a safe place to rest, rejuvenate, and find our calm in order to gain clarity about how we want to live when we step back outside our comfort zone, but so long as we remember to step outside our comfort zone regularly, the comforts themselves are a way to refuel and reenergize. The process is much like returning home to our sanctuary at the end of a long day. We cross the threshold and feel a flood of peace, calm, and understanding, so that tomorrow, we can step out into a world, a day, full of uncertainty, with strength and confidence.

Today, and until you become clear about what brings you comfort, listen to yourself, observe your responses to different stimuli, events, people, choices, etc. Why do you feel the way you do? Is it a healthy comfort? Or destructive? Why do you choose it? At what times of the day or in what emotional states do you turn to it? What does it give you that is otherwise missing? Does it last? How do you feel after you have taken the time to enjoy it? Being honest with yourself will help you to intentionally invest in the comforts that are worth keeping in our lives, and not feel guilty for doing so. Our comforts need not cost money, but when they do, it is an investment in our well-being.

Invest in your well-being, take the time to explore what your investment will be, and discover a deeper peace as you navigate through your days knowing you have your comforts to enjoy.

Petit plaisir Watch Dawn French in just about anything, but I highly recommend *The Vicar of Dibley* and *The Trouble with Maggie Cole*.

Explore further thesimplyluxuriouslife.com/may29 (four core components of a home to nurture your well-being)

May 30
Getting Out of Your Own Way

I was looking for peace and discovered I stood in my own way.

I often enjoy novels set in the English countryside, but there was a point at which I began to acknowledge that considering the murder at the center of each episode of Poirot's capers was not doing my overnight dreams any favors. Tending to our minds includes what we feed it, even if the story is called "cosy." Thus I was happy to stumble upon D. E. Stevenson's Miss Buncle series (four books in total), the first two set in pre–World War II England; they are void of murder but include all the other elements of a cosy. Eureka!

The journey of self-discovery never ceases. As we gain one insight, others needing our attention hold their place in line, ready to be explored and better understood when we are ready to be the student. Reading a well-written novel, but one that lacks upsetting drama, just before I turn off the bedside lamp each night helps me to calm my mind and end the day free of unconscious negativity.

I explore weightier nonfiction and fiction titles, just not right before I turn in. Intentionally designing our days, aware of our emotions and the impact of outside factors on our thoughts, sleep, and peace, is yet another tool worth cultivating and utilizing in your everyday life. An evening routine designed to calm the mind frees you of unnecessary restlessness and worry, ensuring a long, deep sleep.

For my bedroom, I have chosen wallpaper printed with soft white and beige vines, which enhance the natural light bouncing around the room from my north-facing windows, linen sheets, a French bolster, and bedside lamps with dimmers so that I can enjoy just the right amount of light. I keep a glass of cool water on a small tray next to my bed, along with a lavender-scented candle, a candle striker, and a place for my books. I begin my evening bedtime ritual by journaling a few thoughts, and then I begin the reading I have looked forward to all day. When my eyes can barely stay open, I place my bookmark and turn the lights off for sleep.

Design a restful sleeping space for yourself, as well as an evening bedtime routine. Consider what you feed your mind just as you go to bed, and be mindful of even the subtlest negative or frightening influences. Read something delightful (such as a Miss Buncle book), calming (a gardening book such as Monty Don's *The Road to Le Tholonet*), or delicious (why not a cookbook! Nigel Slater's *Notes from the Larder* is a favorite of my mine, as is *Kitchen Diaries*, and most recently his *A Cook's Book*). Observe how far more restful your dreams become.

Petit plaisir Thoughtfully construct daily transitions. For your return home from work, consider listening to music that sweeps you away while you commute. Upon arriving at your sanctuary, transition into an activity you love (in May, for me it is gardening, as it swiftly removes my mind from work and holds me in the present moment).

Explore further thesimplyluxuriouslife.com/may30 (thirty-six bedtime daily rituals and essential details to ensure a restful slumber)

May 31
First Nurture Well, Then Soar and Explore

"Root to rise." It is a common phrase from yoga class, and one that applies to living well in all the arenas of our lives. Year after year, the month of May reveals how, once we root well, the rising, while slow, is indeed strong, serene, and filled with an abundance of contentment to savor.

Le Papillon, TSLL's house, has had much of my attention as of late. Some may say it was a helpful distraction as I wrapped up my career as a teacher. While admittedly it does help to focus on something that will be with me as I transition into a new year-round schedule of solely writing for the blog and my latest book, I am also far more clear-eyed than I have ever been about the necessity to root well.

The pandemic gave us the opportunity to look around our sanctuaries — not only the people we live with and our relationships, but the homes we sleep in, eat in, dream in, and return to after work and travel. The impact of our homes, the places where we spend the most time, on the quality of our lives is incredibly powerful. I have delayed my first post-Covid-19 plane trip, and likely won't fly until 2022, maybe later, because I want to root well — translation: tend to my "nest" that is Le Papillon.

As I begin to plant many of the seedlings I grew from minuscule specks (such petite seeds!), I am reminded of the importance of quality soil, and the care each seed needs to develop its awesomeness once it is placed outside in the elements.

We too need to be nurtured when we are in our sanctuaries because when we step outside into the elements of the world — the crowds, the customers, the students, the masses, whatever it is that you immerse yourself in regularly and have little control over — we need to be grounded in what we know to be true, our ways of navigating the new and unknown, as well as in the ways we enable ourselves to grow and thrive in this ever-changing world.

For me, it is my physical sanctuary, and from that space, what I am able to spend time doing that involves my mind. With a mind that is at peace, regularly able to calm down and be still, be present, when I step outside into the "elements," each moment, each interaction, goes far more smoothly and productively. Last summer, fall, and into December of 2021, I put my bathrooms through the customization process that my mudroom and kitchen had also received. Yes, it was an investment, but an investment in comfort for me and for my guests, and it is an investment in grounding and rooting well.

Clarity and patience. When you can marry these two powerful abilities, you can look forward to amazing real-world outcomes that nurture a truly simply luxurious life.

Petit plaisir Watch an Australian cosy mystery series, *Mr. & Mrs. Murder*. The couple's dynamics — "nontraditional gender roles," as described by the Mister — had me giggling and watching just one more episode, then just one more.

Explore further thesimplyluxuriouslife.com/may31 (four ways to gain clarity)

June

Let Your Curiosity Expand the Everyday and Open Your Mind

June

Travel is fatal to prejudice, bigotry, and narrow-mindedness, and many of our people need it sorely on these accounts. Broad, wholesome, charitable views of men and things cannot be acquired by vegetating in one little corner of the earth all one's lifetime.

—Mark Twain, *The Innocents Abroad*

A tourist sobbing in a phone booth. It was not something I observed; it was me. In the summer of 2000, a twenty-one-year-old college student, I had been studying abroad in Angers, a mid-size city about 200 miles southwest of Paris. My first three weeks of coursework completed, I headed to much-dreamed-about Paris for a week of exploration, and on day two, I was in tears in a phone booth, ready to board a plane and return to Oregon. I am grateful that my mom gently, but unwaveringly, did not jump through hoops to "save" her daughter who found herself "stuck" in Paris.

In the throes of the Paris Syndrome? Perhaps. Mental exhaustion and fatigue? More likely. It was my first venture traveling alone — and to France, where I barely grasped the basics of politely asking for food and where the bathrooms were (the two questions my professor had ensured I knew, even though she also knew I comprehended very little else).

France broke me open. For the first three weeks in Angers, I observed fellow students from European countries engage and explore and socialize with aplomb, while more than a few Americans floundered — why wasn't the country catering to us? Determined not to be one of "those Americans," I supported one or two of my floundering compatriots, listened to their homesickness tales, but vowed to myself *not* to be one of them. I held out for three weeks, and then the phone booth incident.

The paradox revealed by this anecdote demonstrates the power of traveling and exploring new cultures. I no more disliked France than I dislike dogs. *J'adore* them both immensely, and a piece of what makes me who I am would be gone without them. The long communal lunches and dinners at school, enjoying a glass of red wine, the slower pace of life, the encouragement to walk nearly everywhere within the town — all make it possible for a visitor to find herself, against a background of a bucolic countryside and a long, rich history, not to mention the *fromage*! As a student in awe of the culture, I did not hesitate to visit. What turned on the faucet of tears was my inability to engage with it.

Because of my lack of confidence as a young woman told by media and society that I was never "enough" of anything and accepting such messages as true, and held back by my weak French speaking skills, not once did I sit down on a *terrasse* and order a meal or enjoy the crowds and people of Paris during my first visit to a country I so loved. But I longed to, intensely.

The Road to Le Papillon

Travel reveals a fundamental truth about the human condition: We dislike what we do not know and seek security by hewing to the known. For most of us, this impulse is unconscious, but its existence becomes vividly clear when we observe Americans as well as visitors from other countries bringing their expectations and language into a country and culture and expecting the local citizens to understand how to "work with them." I excuse such behavior only because these folks do not know that their fear is on display in vivid technicolor. And then I apologize profusely for the Americans who do our best to speak clearly, however broken our French, and extend respect to the culture we have chosen to visit.

Feeling uncomfortable irritates the ego because it either has to humble itself and step back and learn something new to engage with or walk away from something it may have greatly desired. The ego does not like to lose, and if we do not have awareness of its modus operandi, belittling, complaining, and stereotyping can ensue.

When our awareness is strong, we acknowledge the ego's behavior, put it in its place, and successfully stop sowing the seeds of "prejudice, bigotry, and narrow-mindedness." Instead, we plant stronger and deeper roots of acceptance, open-mindedness, and curiosity.

June 1
The Joys of Travel

What rejuvenates and inspires you? After a recent day to trip to Portland, I realized almost immediately a difference in my mood and my ideas. I felt refreshed. I felt invigorated.

Why, you might ask. It is not as though I had never been to Portland before. After all, I lived there for three years in my late twenties, but it had been about four months since the last time I visited; even in that short amount of time, I had become in need of a reboot.

For me, taking in the seasonal natural scenery as I walk down the streets, partaking with presence in each interaction with the people I meet, popping into shops I love but infrequently visit, and enjoying the conversations that stimulate or reenergize something lying dormant within me — each alone perks up my senses, and together they often shake ideas loose.

If you are feeling that the same old routine you have been obediently following is not doing anything for you, or if you have begun to question yourself, take an opportunity to change up the scenery — even if just for a day. It is amazing how, with only twelve hours in a different town, state, country, or routine, you can quickly see things you had never seen before, appreciate what was working that you may have become blindly accustomed to, and come back to the drawing board the next day with a clearer, more energized mind.

Whether it is choosing to see a movie you have been curious about, dining out at a restaurant that serves cuisine you don't normally try, or hopping in the car or on the train and visiting a town that has a completely different vibe than yours, make an appointment with yourself to reboot — sooner rather than later (and write it in ink in your planner).

Petit plaisir Read *The Untethered Soul: The Journey Beyond Yourself*, by Michael A. Singer.

Explore further thesimplyluxuriouslife.com/june1 (live differently for one month)

June 2
Self-Growth

June begins with sunshine and warmth. Rain falls to nurture and calm, and natural beauty abounds around us.

Growth within ourselves occurs in similar scenarios: Something occurs that opens a window or a door of illumination, and we are encouraged to step forward because the opportunity for something better is presented — more contentment, stronger relationships, a healthier world, etc. Then we are often encouraged to nurture what we seek with new knowledge and experiences, which allow growth to occur and be noticeable.

As the school year wound down in 2019, the last unit I presented to my students grappled with the issue of implicit (unconscious) bias in our media and American culture. I had recently read *The Person You Mean to Be*, by Dolly Chugh, where I found answers I had been seeking for some time: how to identify implicit bias within myself, how to embrace a growth mindset, how to navigate and communicate effectively with others at various stages of implicit bias understanding, and how to reduce any implicit bias I found. But it took until I was forty years old for me to find these answers.

It was not that I was not looking for the answers until I picked up this book; rather, I did not know what I was looking for, and when I finally did understand, I was not sure where or how to find the answers I sought. Growth, especially self-growth, requires patience but, at the same time, persistence. The answers will come, growth can happen, but we have to keep searching — whether that is to keep trying, but doing so in a different way, reading another book by another expert to gather a different perspective on the same topic, or exposing ourselves to new experiences while letting go of our assumptions of what should happen and instead letting our awareness unfold.

It can be hard to see our own growth, especially regarding events in the recent past. I have found that reading past entries in my journals — one, two, five years ago — is often therapeutic; as I read, I can hear a slightly different voice and know that, yes, growth has occurred.

Sometimes we recognize our growth when we return to a place or visit a person we have not seen lately; we see things through a different lens; we understand what we are experiencing differently, and in that moment, we know we have grown.

Understanding that you have the potential to grow and be different and better than you are today or were yesterday is certainly something to acknowledge and, perhaps most important, celebrate. Make what may initially seem small but is actually quite significant a reason to cheer and elevate the everyday.

Petit plaisir After a long hot day, sit on a porch swing and watch the rain pour down while enjoying the scent and feel of the fresh, clean air. Snuggle in with a good book, a loved one, or a beloved pet, and just savor, savor, savor.

Explore further thesimplyluxuriouslife.com/june2 (little by little, grand things are achieved)

June 3
Embark on an Excursion for a Spark of Inspiration

Getting away from the regular routine and your daily environment can lead to interesting and unexpected *aha* moments.

Upon visiting San Francisco in June 2019, I began to recognize a shift in priorities for myself concerning where I want to spend my time — a shift that I made when I stepped fully into writing and focusing on TSLL blog and online destination in the summer of 2021. At the time of my visit, I had not precisely laid my finger on what I would be changing in my life. Most likely, I imagined the changes would only be significantly noticeable to me and involve how I go about my daily routine, but isn't that yet another beauty, or should I say gift, of travel?

Travel has a way of awakening parts of ourselves we have left alone, ignored, or not even known existed. Travel's unique mechanism is the new experiences it brings into our lives. The ways we interact, how we engage, what is sparked within us — that is the gift. Some of what we discover may be a joy to receive, and other discoveries may be fuzzy and confusing, as we may not yet be clear about what we are supposed to understand. However, with the latter, which is where I sometimes find myself, we just need to give ourselves time to process. For me, it will be time alone, in solitude; when the firm, clear *aha* is ready to reveal itself, it will. Often it seems to happen on my daily walks in the outdoors. We simply need to remain open and consider all that comes forth.

Travel that sparks *aha* moments need not be to a new place or to a place where we spend a lot of time. We can visit a city we have visited many times before, but because *we* are changed, we see and experience what takes place in a different way. A new discovery reveals itself — a moment of realization, one of self-discovery; in other words, an *aha* moment. Such was the case when I flew down to San Francisco for two nights to explore the city again with my mother. Each of us had spent time in the City by the Bay years ago, but this visit was different. This visit provided perspective on strengths I loosely knew I had but had not concretely trusted; helped by further reflection, I began to develop trust in myself to take risks I had dreamed about taking for some time.

Your travel excursions need not be far and wide or new to offer you moments of discovery. All that is needed is choosing to travel.

Petit plaisir Welcome into your home new, vintage, consigned, or antique side tables in different styles to pair with each chair that you sit in for leisure. On each table, allow space for a beverage and proximity to flattering light.

Explore further thesimplyluxuriouslife.com/june3 (simple tips to follow for being your own interior designer

June 4
Finding Your Travel Equilibrium

Upon arriving home after a journey to South Korea in 2017 in which I crossed more than a few time zones, I found that sleep had become a precious commodity. I could not seem to get enough of it.

After we fly across continents and an ocean or two, the body and the mind, including our emotions, need time to get back into sync. Knowing this will be the case is the first and most powerful step in not overreacting or saying or doing something not in alignment with your true character when you are experiencing jet lag. The jet lag was eased on both ends of my journey to South Korea, first by the person I had flown to visit and then by my mom and niece when I arrived home in Bend. The boys also eased my mental and physical malaise, and I tried to make sure I did my best to communicate to these people and pups what I needed without getting my grump on.

After a handful of days, the jet lag subsided, and I savored my trip all the more. Yes, it was very hard to leave, but one of the sweetest realities was knowing I was quite content where I had traveled to but also had a home to return to that I loved. That is a significant accomplishment: to find and nurture a sanctuary, a space that provides grounding and security that enables the inhabitants to spring freely, widely, and as often as desired, exploring without abandon because the peace of mind exists that a home awaits when they return

I admit, some of my earlier attempts at travel did not succeed on either front. Sometimes the home that I returned to did not feel right; at other times, the destination I had traveled to did not live up to my unrealistic, heightened expectations. With experience, time, and patience as I vowed to better understand myself, I made my sanctuary to return home to in Bend, Oregon, a place suited for growth, outdoor exploration, and cozying in on a daily basis. Likewise, I tasked myself to be open and present during each trip while letting go of expectations of others I may be traveling with or the experience I am choosing to embark upon.

Admittedly, while I have not perfected this life skill, each trip has become more memorable, even life-awakening, more so than I could ever have planned. Finding this equilibrium between reveling in my travels and savoring returning to Le Papillon is something I celebrate.

How do you feel when you travel? Are you as comfortable traveling as you are when you return? And if not, what might you want to tweak, change, or add? Whether it is the travel situation that could be tweaked or the everyday routine that needs improving, the key is, first, to get to know yourself better. The second step is to speak up and take action in a manner you are proud of. Courageously and respectfully, acknowledge what is needed for you to have a wonderful experience, whatever it may be. Your getaways should be designed to elevate your life and fuel how you move through your everydays upon returning home to your sanctuary.

Petit plaisir Sow directly into the soil squash, *courgette* (zucchini), and pumpkin seeds now for a bountiful fall crop to harvest. As well, sow foxgloves from seed to be planted in the fall and enjoyed in the garden next summer (they are biennials).

Explore further thesimplyluxuriouslife.com/june4 (twenty-one life lessons learned in South Korea)

June 5
Leap, Just Do It

On this day in 2018, Benoît Lecomte dove into the Pacific Ocean off the coast of eastern Japan to begin a six-month, 5,500-mile swim to San Francisco. While, after swimming 1,700 miles, his attempt was thwarted by heavy winds, his attempt was not a failure. No, he did not set a record, becoming the first to ever swim across the largest ocean (in 1998, he swam across the Atlantic, just shy of 4,000 miles, in a non-contiguous swim), but he successfully brought the world's attention, in even more intimate detail, to the pollution of our oceans, as his swim was recorded for a documentary, released in 2021, titled *Swim*.

    At some point, we too just need to dive in. Even when we are not certain how it will work out, and when no one before has completed or attained what we hope to accomplish, we need to find the courage deep within ourselves, trusting in our preparations (Lecomte spent seven years gearing up for his mega swim) and knowing in our heart that we will do all that is in our power to make it a reality.

    This is a frightening directive to give ourselves: Just dive in! Even Lecomte, upon arriving on the shores of Normandy after his Atlantic crossing, said, "Never again." That reminded me that the difference between tasks that we love and seek and those we are capable of based on our skill set are not always the same. The difference is the internal navigation for those tasks we love that, like a magnet, pull us toward a particular destination, dream, task, or outcome, even when we do not fully understand why. What we do know is that our dream is ours to pursue, and we want to pursue it. When we are doing so, our fuel reserves seem to be infinite, and we become capable of pursuing what to outsiders would appear to be an exhausting or impossible goal. Nonetheless, we strive on.

    For some reason, while the struggles are hard, in time, the rejections turn into acceptances, opportunities become accomplishments, and unforeseen positive outcomes begin to materialize as we pinch ourselves in disbelief at how far we have come and how much we have grown.

    There comes a time when students, players, patients, and mentees need to discover they can navigate without their teachers, coaches, counselors, and mentors. The guides are not gone forever, but they need to be out of arm's reach; at times, we need to go about our journey on our own to see what we have learned, apply it, observe the growth, and honestly face what we still need to work on. We must learn to navigate on our own, as that is when we build confidence and deepen our understanding of ourselves — our needs, our limits, the skills we are missing but that we can add to our toolbox. In other words, we need to travel beyond our comfort zones.

While Lecomte swam each day for eight hours during the 1,700 miles he completed, despite not attaining the initial goal he had set, each evening, when he climbed onto the yacht for meals with his team and sleep, he had the opportunity to visit with his coach and other motivators. But he still swam on his own, and we must continue on as well, so that we can come to trust that we have learned the lessons and see them as worth our choice to change and come ever closer to our fullest potential.

Your fullest potential resides within you, waiting to be discovered, unearthed, revealed, and then strengthened to its fullest capability in ways you cannot fully predict when you initially dive in, following what unceasingly tugs at your curiosity. Dive in anyway.

Petit plaisir Watch fledgling birds as they grow and mature. I lose track of time regularly watching them outside my dining room window as I enjoy my breakfast.

Explore further thesimplyluxuriouslife.com/june5 (how to use failures as guideposts to success)

June 6
Be a Discerning Traveler

"When you leave a place, evaluate the experience. Trust your instinct. This is your journey." Upon hearing this quote from the film *The Hundred-Foot Journey*, starring Helen Mirren, I immediately catalogued it my mind.

What we encounter and experience when we travel gives us the opportunity to change, to grow, to realize, to recognize, to wake up, to evolve more surely into our best selves. However, this growth must be a conscious choice. Traveling and returning home do not magically transform us into better people with more clarity about the direction of our lives, but we can be transformed if we evaluate all that has been presented to us.

Perhaps it was a play you saw that caught your attention, or the person you struck up a conversation with while on a tour, or maybe it was simply how people in an unfamiliar destination went about their days — their priorities, behavior, routines — and you recognize what you wish to be or what you need to refrain from doing.

Each time I step on a plane for my return flight, I begin doing what I suggested above. With my journal out, I will try to make sense of all that made an impression on me (and oh yes, each trip presents so much wonderful material) and assess how I felt in each situation and why. In so doing, I may not discover all the answers to my questions, but I have no doubt, based on past experience, that I will learn something I did not already know when I arrived.

Whatever it is, upon returning home from your next journey, sit back, relive your trip as you reflect on the memories, and discern what was presented to you . . . because something always is.

Petit plaisir Place one peony in a bud vase on your desk. That's it. One is all that is needed.

Explore further thesimplyluxuriouslife.com/june6 (twenty-five life lessons learned in New York City)

June 7
Step into the Unknown

One summer while I was living in Pendleton, Oregon, I had the opportunity to do something I had wanted to do for quite some time. I had learned that, on an upcoming evening, I and a few of my neighbors on our quiet street all planned to be at home, and I grabbed the chance to invite them over for a mid-week dinner party.

Doing my best to follow my own advice for a successfully hosted event (cooking itinerary made: check; background music prepped: check; glass of wine thirty minutes prior to help the host relax: check, check), I welcomed these neighbors, whom I felt fortunate to live among, into my home, and the evening exceeded my expectations. I am not exactly patting myself on the back as my dogs were overly friendly and one dish did not live up to my expectations, despite a few test runs, to name just a couple of *oopses*. What I most enjoyed was the conversation.

It was absolutely delightful to step away four hours later from a dinner table where I had learned about history, books to read, shops to visit, places to travel to, and so much more, all void of gossip and discussions of safe or nosy topics. And I owe it all to my guests. I found myself sitting back in my cozy dining room chair, sipping my glass of wine, and soaking it all in.

One of life's realities was confirmed for me as the evening unfolded: The people we surround ourselves with can drain us, or they can uplift and inspire us. That particular evening was most certainly the latter. I was able to spend time with people who, regardless of age or circumstance, have an insatiable love of and curiosity for life, and in acting on that love and curiosity, they elevate the quality of their lives and the lives of those around them.

Each of our one and only lives will unfold according to the attitude, preparation, and tenacity we are willing to invest. Life is not out to hurt or destroy us, but neither does it give us everything we want, and certainly not a road map. Life is what we make it — clichéd, but true. Here is how Ichiro Kishimi and Fumitake Koga put it in *The Courage to Be Disliked*: "We determine our own lives according to the meaning we give to those past experiences. Your life is not something that someone gives you, but something you choose yourself, and you are the one who decides how you live."

You can fall prey to the cacophony of voices that remind you what life will be when you are thirty, fifty, eighty, and so on, or you can rewrite the rules. By doing your homework, by finding the courage to step into the unknown from time to time, you can create a magnificent life tailored to your tastes each and every day, and contribute something positive to the world along your journey.

Petit plaisir Watch Barbra Streisand in *The Mirror Has Two Faces* (1996), adapted from a 1950s French film that she directed and co-starred in with Jeff Bridges. Be sure to watch the credits roll — the cherry on top of a wonderfully uplifting film. Lauren Bacall won a Golden Globe and a SAG award for her supporting role and was nominated for an Oscar. The song "I Finally Found Someone," co-written by Streisand and sung with Bryan Adams, was also nominated for an Oscar.

Explore further thesimplyluxuriouslife.com/june/ (ten ideas gleaned and confirmed from a recent dinner party)

June 8
The Benefits of Being Still

I usually head out for my first paddle outing of the year within a week or so of Memorial Day. In 2020, Norman and I took the stand-up paddleboard out for our annual inaugural outing, and it happened to fall on Memorial Day itself — Monday, May 31.

Should we take the time to indulge in it, stillness gives us the ability to reflect and give thanks as we let our minds wander into the past. Most important, being still focuses our full attention on the present.

June

The sun rose at 5:26 a.m., and we were on the water by 6:30 — on top of our board, I paddle in hand, Norman in his life jacket.

To begin, we set our direction, enjoying an easy drift downstream, a gaggle of geese and many goslings our sole companions. Before engaging in a workout when we turned around and headed back upriver, I sat down on the board, staying quiet and calm and giving Norman enough space that he was not flustered or bothered. My little pup stood still, taking it all in, with seemingly no impulse to move, just being still. (View the "A Cuppa Moments" video from June 2021 to see this moment.)

Prior to leaving my house that morning, I could not have dreamed of such a surreal and peaceful moment. While it was fleeting, it remains in my memory, to savor upon each reflection. Being still allows us to see, to observe, to witness, to not be distracted by pulls from the future, the past, or others' desires.

Being still initially can be excruciatingly uncomfortable if we do not regularly spend time in our own company. In fact, it might even feel "wrong," but in actuality it is precisely what provides clarity, appreciation, and grounding. We can know true contentment only when we are consciously living our everydays fully. Being still is the way.

Of course, you are not going to be still throughout your entire day, but regular, intentionally chosen stillness — whether in meditation, sitting in a favorite chair, standing in mountain pose on your yoga mat, or leisurely sitting on a board while paddling — is like lubricating a squeaky hinge. It improves your entire everyday experience as you choose better, honor necessary boundaries of yourself and others, and appreciate both the small and grand moments you witness.

Petit plaisir Read Margaret Roach's *And I Shall Have Some Peace There*.

Explore further thesimplyluxuriouslife.com/june8 (seven components to cultivating a great start to the day)

June 9
Create Memories

Worthwhile occurrences, relationships, and milestones take time. At the age of eighty-one, Eleanor Coppola directed, wrote, and produced her first narrative feature film. After she decided on the project, it took her six years to raise the money, but once she did, she created a feast for the eyes and the mind in *Paris Can Wait*, starring Diane Lane.

I viewed the film in a small, quaint, and comfortable (as well as very affordable) boutique theater in Bend, which enhanced the overall experience. It was yet another lesson about life to contemplate and integrate into my everydays moving forward: We must create moments that ask us to be fully present — and then we need to oblige, because yes, reaching the destination is a triumphant occasion, but the journey is quite sweet as well, even with all its unknowns.

A life truly well lived is a life you can enjoy in the moment and then again as you look back. As a mentor of mine has suggested to me more than once, "Create memories, Shannon." Engage in activities and events that are so delicious that, when you reflect upon them, you are reminded of why the person you created them with was so sweet and special. In that reflection, you can share the moment again, and thus savor it twice. The same can be said for creating memories even if you are the only one experiencing them, as I did when I viewed *Paris Can Wait*.

The key to being able to create such memories is to live sincerely. This was a crucial *aha* for me as I evolved and grew up in my teens and twenties. If I was not able to be myself — if I felt stymied or limited or knew, based on past experience, that I would be laughed at, shut down, or denied when I was being myself — I could not be fully present to create memories I wished to remember. When I was in my thirties, I finally began to change and to build a life I loved living, a life that set me free and brought into my world people whom I could relax with. I learned as well to let go or step away from those who could not bear to see who I was. I began to step toward what was authentic to who I was and wanted to become, and that has made all the difference. This change and evolution has taken time. Good, worthwhile things usually do, and sometimes we have to remind ourselves of this truth.

Be open to life, and communicate gently, yet without expectation, your curiosity about people, the world, and everything in between, whatever that may sincerely be for you. When you open a window (it need not be a door, metaphorically speaking, if you are not comfortable doing so), you allow *opportunity* to say hello to you. Reach out to people you would like to hear from or connect with, even if it happens weeks, months, or even years down the road; convey your sincere interest, and be open while consciously staying in the present moment. Explore what piques your curiosity and go forward to experience it in your own company to see what you discover.

Petit plaisir Let people know you appreciate them and why. Write cards to colleagues you greatly appreciate working alongside.

Explore further thesimplyluxuriouslife.com/june9 (explore Diane Lane's timeless wardrobe in *Paris Can Wait*)

June 10
Releasing the Pressure

It was the second day of ninety-plus-degree weather in early June 2021. The clouds darkened, gathered, settled, and a bolt of piercing white lightning sliced through the sky above my Bend neighborhood. The thunder rattled after a few seconds. Minutes later, the rain fell in buckets, rapidly, and created two rainbows just above the roofline of my house. Sitting on my front porch swing, I gawked, gazed, smiled in awe, and watched it rain. For forty minutes, it poured.

Whether it is steam, stress, suppression of emotions begging to be explored, or anticipation of something long waited for — built-up pressure eventually bursts, and all that is held within is expressed. Today's gulley-washer, as some in Bend call it, brought nourishment to the garden, freshened the air, and created rainbows to top it all off, as if placing a bow on the gift Mother Nature had given a thirsty central Oregon town.

Concentrating our efforts and attention creates energy. Our time, our knowledge about a subject, our savings for an expenditure — whatever we give our concentration to strengthens. Built-up pressure is often presented as something negative, but let's consider the instances when it works in our favor.

When you focus your energy, clarify your direction, and home in on what you know, you create momentum. You show the universe, the world, your loved ones, your boss, the community what you sincerely care about, and if it is indeed sincere, eventually something breaks forward in your favor. You will not know when. You will not know what the positive outcome or revelation may be, but it will happen. Just make sure you hang in there long enough to experience the flood of rainbows and raindrops.

Petit plaisir Pour a cup of something quenching or comforting, then close your eyes and take a deep breath while you listen to J. S. Bach's Orchestral Suite no. 3: Air on the G String, BWV 1068.

Explore further thesimplyluxuriouslife.com/june10 (how to live a life with less stress and why it is vital for good health)

June 11
Traveling with Rose-colored Glasses

People use the term *rose-colored glasses* to describe seeing something in a more positive light than it otherwise appears in reality, and I have discovered something on my travels: Sometimes the removal of rose-colored glasses is the best gift we can give ourselves. In some ways, it is quite liberating, offering a deeply calming breath of fresh air. It is a gift that enables us to deepen our experience and increase the quality of our everydays, no matter where we find ourselves in the world.

Sometimes we can dress something up in our minds so that it seems far better and more "perfect" than it actually is. And it may not be the fault of whatever or whomever we may have projected this idea upon. Rather, it may be a reflection of the person making the assumption — ourselves. Often, it is a revelation of something we are seeking that feels out of our control or that we do not know how to solve or correct or improve. So in order to attain what we seek, we think it must reside someplace else.

Paris and France have been and continue to be dream destinations for many, offering a supposed alluring way of life for people around the world; I include myself in accepting this alleged truth or romanticized myth. Please do not get me wrong, France is fascinating, inspiring, magnificent, and a deliciously lovely place (pun intended), but context is deeply important.

The more I converse with people who live there, including expats who have lived in France for decades and would not consider leaving, I begin to understand more about the ways of the culture, the ways that drew me to this magnetic destination, and the history of such a desirable place.

However, I also know marketers love using any reference to France or Paris to draw more eyeballs, collect more sales, and create an excuse to raise their prices. They do so because they can — because it works. It does not mean the wine and cheese aren't top of their class. They are. It does not mean that we can't find historical destinations somewhere else in the world comparable to the Musée D'Orsay and the Palais-Royale. We cannot, as each historical destination is unique unto itself.

But what I am finally discovering for myself, based on nearly twenty years of visiting France, are the lessons the country has been trying to teach me. I am discovering that we cannot escape to any place around the world and make the assumption that life is so much better there when we have not come to terms with why we have placed this destination on such a pedestal without truly understanding its rich and lengthy history, nor our true reason for seeking it out.

Every destination offers beauty of some sort, and every destination has its flaws, some more than others. But no matter where we find ourselves on Planet Earth, it is possible to find contentment. It is possible because we are our own constant companion, and we must find peace within ourselves, the strength to be strong with our life choices and to not follow where the crowd says we should go, or not to like what the masses prefer or not to live in a traditional way if it suffocates our beauty and truest being.

Part of the gift you give yourself is doing the homework of figuring out why you think "someplace else" must be better than where you are making your life currently. You can enjoy your getaways and *vacances* far more fully when you are not asking them to be something that they never can be. A place cannot bring us contentment. Rather, it is a contented person who finds contentment in any place.

Petit plaisir Watch *Lupin*, a caper story of a gentleman thief, in a series set in France, starring Omar Sy.

Explore further thesimplyluxuriouslife.com/june11 (the cure for the Paris syndrome)

June 12
Celebrate Your Journey

Symbolic activities, signifiers, rituals completed to commemorate a significant task that has been completed — I had been thinking about such things after a colleague asked me how I transition from the end of the school year into my summer. As he shared his annual most-anticipated activities, I realized I wanted to come up with something as well.

Symbolic activities, whatever their size, are worth taking the time to cultivate, much like celebratory gatherings after we overcome big hurdles, and even the rituals we incorporate into our daily lives to set the tone for the day or signal to our brain that it is time to unwind.

Maybe it is that trip down the slopes after the first snow of the season; as you journey to the mountain, you indulge in a special cup of hot chocolate, sing your favorite song, and make sure your skis are properly waxed. Or maybe when the first daffodils come up in the spring, whether in your own garden or at the market, you pull out your favorite vase, dust it off, and cut a bundle or splurge on a beautiful, exquisite bouquet to place on your dining room table that would make even *House & Garden* envious.

The Road to Le Papillon

Often when a school year ends, families and teachers alike may acknowledge the close of the year and all of its highs, lows, and in-betweens by traveling or changing up their daily routine. Such closure, however you choose to recognize it, enables you to celebrate completion and pat yourself on the back for pushing through the exhaustion and perhaps confusion and wobbliness of it all. Whatever task or job or responsibility you have taken on, perhaps you too have a symbolic way of celebrating its completion: something to look forward to, something to enjoy, and something that you don't do regularly but allow yourself to indulge in without apology.

In a past issue of *The English Home*, the "Mrs. Minerva Writes . . ." column offered a simple observation about country dogs. They eat well "because it is understood that a well-fed dog is a generally a well-behaved dog." And perhaps we need to think like this in terms of humans also. When we take care of ourselves, when we recognize that we need special care after arduous tasks or jobs well done, perhaps we need to create and enjoy symbolic moments or events.

Allowing ourselves to indulge from time to time makes it easier and more natural to then return to being moderate and appreciating those special times when we simultaneously savor our everydays. We no longer feel deprived, but rather are satisfied. Instead of jumping from one busy schedule to the next without a symbolic shift that is luxurious or a treat, why not welcome into our lives symbolic opportunities to be still, savor, and celebrate what was before moving forward toward what is to be so we have the energy, the renewed spirit, to step forward with enthusiasm into whatever else we must do?

Contemplate situations that may be deserving of a symbolic indulgence. Then be sure to put them on your calendar so that you can look forward to them.

Petit plaisir Turn your dream of growing wisteria into a reality. Hardy up to zone 3, Summer Cascade Wisteria is the varietal I now grow in my garden, and after one year, it offered a few gorgeous blooms, followed by a growth spurt of 6 feet. This vine teaches the value of patience, as it grows more robustly with each year, sharing an abundance of purple flowers in late spring. Dare to grow this beautiful flowering vine — and oh, the scent! Even Norman agrees (see IG pic on June 12, 2021).

Explore further thesimplyluxuriouslife.com/june12 (why not . . . celebrate the ordinary?)

June 13
Travel and Its Lessons

Travel offers an abundance of life lessons so long as we listen, take a step back, and understand that there is a rich opportunity to be absorbed should we want to do so.

In early July 2018, I found myself in the Loire Valley, having arrived by train after spending two weeks in Provence. I had called several beautiful places throughout France home during the past fourteen days. Then, in the "valley of châteaus," I did extensive driving about, enjoying a few touristic explorations, experiencing many moments of absolute joy and a few moments of frustration. In those moments, I tried to take a step back, to keep myself from reacting undesirably upon reflection, and tried to figure out the real source of my exasperation. I needed to reset, take note of what worked and what didn't, and move past it.

Case in point: After two days in the Loire Valley, staying at a beautiful château's bed and breakfast inn, an accommodation with vast acreage and gorgeous gardens to wander about, I needed to find some "me time" (which may sound absurd, as I was traveling on my own), but I did. Indirectly, the owners made known that they preferred their guests to leave the premises during the day and only return for meals and to sleep. No lingering about was encouraged. Unable to fully rest at the château and its gardens, I set out to find a place where I could find respite and stumbled upon the gardens of nearby Château Villandry. This medicine, which I did not know I would need but drank up fully, alleviated all angst held during my time at the bed and breakfast château, and thus will forever hold a special place in my memory.

Upon even more reflection and a few more days removed, I became aware that this was a learning opportunity. The refuge I found at Villandry provided a lesson for me to observe and apply to my life.

Sometimes we see something in others that reveals how we may appear if we were to embody such behavior. When we recognize what it feels like to be in this type of presence or energy, we can learn a lesson: that we never want to be or act that way, as we do not want people to feel the way we felt. And while we do not need to be traveling to learn such a lesson, in this case, it was magnified as I did not have an escape; I was traveling and thus had to work through it as healthily as I could.

Take a look at unwanted moments in your life. What followed? Examine closely what *aha* moment was made available for you to learn and apply moving forward for a deeper appreciation of living and how to do so even better than before. "Everything in your life journey is happening for you rather than 'to' you." The sagacity of author Byron Katie's words rang true for me in the above shared quandary. Hold

onto her words when the next unwanted moment occurs. Take a breath, making sure you respond rather than react, and redirect your course to learn the lesson and move forward well.

Petit plaisir In the Northern Hemisphere, spring is nearly over. As we step into the final week of the season, savor it while listening to Ludovico Einaudi's *Primavera*.

Explore further thesimplyluxuriouslife.com/june13 (ten healthy coping skills to learn and habituate for better living in tough times — and all times)

June 14
The Joy of Returning Home

Planning my return home before I have even left the house for a trip has become a delicious ritual to enhance the memories created while I'm away.

Not only is the house cleaned, but the fridge is stocked with just enough and just the right ingredients for a favorite comfort-food meal that I can enjoy without further forethought when I cross the threshold of home exhausted, loaded down with more luggage than what I left with, yet feeling deeply grateful for the journey. (If I have been traveling for an extended period of time, I leave extra money with my house sitter to purchase the necessary fresh grocery items to make the meal.)

As Le Papillon becomes ever more my personal sanctuary, I rely on my beloved daily routines less for stability and almost solely to elevate the quality of my everydays. Keeping this truth in mind when I travel, I loosen my approach to each day, while keeping what I know grounds me in the present and nurtures my health and peace of mind.

While traveling, knowing the necessary routines to take with me to maintain my physical and mental good health cultivates a greater appreciation for the everyday routines I have created at home. I am grounded in an inner calm whether at home or away. None of my routines strangle me; instead, they are tailored to help me to be more fully present wherever I am.

It is important for our stability, peace of mind, and well-being to have certain routines that largely remove the need to actually think about certain tasks so that we can focus on things that need our full attention. Likewise, it is a wise idea to include a shake-up of your schedule once in a while in order to broaden your perspective, heighten your appreciation, and stimulate your creativity.

To live the same life day in and day out is to waste the gift that life gives you. When you step out of your comfort zone, you step into areas that may pique your curiosity, helping you to build an even richer and more fulfilling life.

Petit plaisir Visit a local nursery and bring home vegetable plants ready to plant in the garden to complement the ones you have successfully grown from seed.

Explore further thesimplyluxuriouslife.com/june14 (the important detail to not forget when making travel plans)

June 15
Traveling in Comfort

Traveling well is a skill that takes time to acquire. At least that has been true for me. I have always admired those individuals who gracefully go through the security line without tugging along a pile of items that seem to shift at the most inopportune times, or they nonchalantly board the plane without worrying that there won't be space in the overhead compartment. Their attire is effortlessly chic, their travel tote neatly organized, well-stocked but not overstuffed, and they seem to comfortably enjoy the flight right up to arrival time.

Being such a person has always been my goal because I enjoy traveling, which provides time to think, dream, read, and plan. However, it can be a stressful experience if we are not properly prepared.

Thankfully, with practice and much experience, I think I have figured it out. It all begins with awareness.

Here is how Andy Puddicombe, mindfulness teacher and co-founder of Headspace, which offers meditation training, puts it: "Awareness is clarity. And clarity is light. When we rest in awareness, we see more clearly . . . If we bring awareness [with us into our lives], the skill we've learned, we can start to experience a healthier, happier life and hopefully a more harmonious experience with the world around us."

And so it is with knowing how to travel well through life. Instead of being solely focused on the destination, when we realize that, beyond our arrival, how we travel elevates or diminishes our entire trip, we begin to give it our attention fully. I pack and schedule what I know I need for comfort, tailored to my temperament, but remain open, leaving air in my itinerary and life journey to move with the day's and life's events as they unfold.

The Road to Le Papillon

How I have begun to customize Le Papillon, even the choice of purchasing Le Papillon, are parts of the exercise of clarity gained through awareness. When I have a sanctuary to rejuvenate me, I step out into the world open to experience whatever the day may bring.

Back to packing for the flight: I ensure the basics are packed (tickets and boarding passes in order, cash or traveler's checks in hand, passport and visas in place), decide how much I can pack in my carry-on, choose what I will wear to make it through security without too much undressing, and stock my tote to include my simple personal luxuries (Mariage Frères Vert Provence tea, slumber mask, and cashmere scarf). With these kinds of preparations, travel has become a more pleasurable experience for me, and not just something to be endured as I make my way to my desired destination.

Strengthen your awareness of the truths of you. To gain more objectivity, schedule a session with a counselor, as often it can be hard to see how we present ourselves to the world. Once your awareness is strong, you can gain clarity, bolstering the foundation from which your contentment will spring. Your openness to possibility will now be easier than ever before.

Petit plaisir Make a simple salmon salad with avocado and cucumber dressed with a basil-lime vinaigrette.

Explore further thesimplyluxuriouslife.com/june15 (fifteen ideas for traveling well)

June 16
Travel and the Pull of Home

We do not achieve beautiful, dream-come true moments without perseverance, maneuvering around obstacles, and support.

I love traveling to France, and start looking forward to my next trip soon after I return home. But while traveling, I also have moments of longing for something from home. Usually, it has been the company of my dogs, but on a recent trip that was a dream come true in so many ways, it became my life in Bend. Never before I have had yearnings for home quite like I do now, no matter how spectacular the trip, and I have come to recognize this as a very good thing because it means that I have cultivated a life I love living each and every day. This is something we can all do for ourselves.

June

Will it be easy to cultivated a love for home that persists even while you are traveling? Not necessarily. Will it take time? It usually does. But with careful self-examination, courageous exploration, and determined patience, and as you navigate through the questions and answers presented during your unique life journey, you will find a beautiful place in this world to call home.

When you travel to distant or near lands, no matter how much they may surpass your expectations, you can return, incorporate what you can that you loved and admired, and curate a life that is unique and truly, simply luxuriously right where we feel at peace.

Petit plaisir Enjoy an aperitif with friends or family — coupes of prosecco paired with salmon rillettes on slices of cucumber.

Explore further thesimplyluxuriouslife.com/june16 (eleven tips for settling back in after traveling to a beloved destination)

June 17
Travel Can Be Grounding

When someone is properly grounded in life, they shouldn't have to look outside of themselves for approval.
— Epictetus

The more I travel to destinations outside of my everyday world, even if I return to a place more than once, I am reminded how many different ways there are to live life well. Especially when I have had the opportunity to travel outside the United States — to France, Great Britain, South Korea, and Canada (not too varied, but still quite different from life in the States) — I see more clearly that our way of living is actually only one of many ways to live well.

Such a discovery is liberating, but it also can make life when we return to our everyday routine a bit more challenging if we are choosing to push back from what we have unconsciously accepted as the norm. Each time I return home from traveling abroad, I push back. Whether it is resisting my own unconscious beliefs or other people's expectations, with each trip it becomes easier to change, evolve, improve, and thus find more contentment.

Upon returning from our travels, no matter how much we love our everyday life and no matter how memorable the trip was, it is not always easy to get back into the rhythm of everyday living. The brain fog of jet lag is real, but it can be eased. Part of the brain fog is navigating the *aha*'s

The Road to Le Papillon

I discovered, making sure I don't forget anything, and making sense of how I want to apply them to my life.

Whether we travel often or infrequently, the gifts of travel are available to us all. And better understanding what is truly necessary and what is no longer worth our energy or time is one of the best gifts travel offers. It is never easy to say goodbye temporarily to a home, a routine, and, most important, the pups that I love, but I know I am doing myself and the life I love living a favor.

Ironic as it sounds, travel has a grounding effect as it can awaken us to what should be stripped away, what can be relinquished, perhaps what *should* be relinquished to live our fullest life. In this way, travel reveals more truths about who we are, what we are capable of, and what speaks to us if we truly listen.

When you see so many different people living life in so many varied ways, it becomes clear: Approval from society is not necessary and, in fact, can be stifling and stunt your growth. When you understand this, you begin to trust yourself more, and living begins to be more enjoyable and far less stressful. May your next trip or the most recent trip you have returned from lighten your burden of *should*s that are ill-fit to your true self and enlighten your way forward.

Petit plaisir Seek out and visit a local farmers market in your area. Purchase at least one produce item that is hard to find and only available for a short time. For me, finding morel mushrooms is a boon, and I delight in bringing home one small basket to pair with eggs in the morning.

Explore further thesimplyluxuriouslife.com/june17 (the gift received upon letting go of the word *should*)

June 18
Tackling Our Fears

It is in our nature as humans to become comfortable with what we know. When asked or forced to try something new, our hackles go up ever so slightly (sometimes more immediately and more protectively), and our fear steps into a void created by what we do not know.

In 2013, I had the opportunity to learn how to stand-up-paddle on the frigid, yet crisp and beautiful waters of glacially carved Wallowa Lake. As I knew how cold the water was and was not sure how difficult it would be to learn this new skill, I was a bit anxious.

The demonstration began with three other women in attendance, with ages ranging from nineteen to sixty-five. None of us had ever surfed, and only two of us had the somewhat relatable (in a fourth-cousin sort of way) experience with boogie boarding.

While we were all excited to learn, each of us seemed certain we would make a mistake at some point and fall into the water. After all, we were novices and had no clue what to expect. However, to our collective delight, standing up was much simpler than anticipated; even more shocking was that no one even came close to falling into the morning-chilled waters of the lake. Tranquility and the ease of the moment soon replaced our doubts and fears, and I became a convert, ready to buy my own board (to use on what body of water, I was not quite sure as it wasn't until 2015 that I moved to Bend).

Much like attempting to learn to stand up and paddle when I had never done it before, when we don't know how exactly something will go in life, or what a travel experience will offer or reveal, we tend to exacerbate our sense of worry, blowing completely out of proportion what might actually happen.

After all, in order to change, grow, and evolve, we must be willing to look self-imposed fear in the face and stare it down; we must eliminate its power. This will be most difficult the first few times, but once you can discern what self-inflicted fear looks like and invalidate it, you will find yourself less frozen in fear and more consumed with the curiosity to try.

Look at situations in your life at this moment that you have dismissed because they are new or foreign and you are not sure how they will work out should you attempt them. Then evaluate whether or not, if the feat were to be successful, it would add value to your life. If the answer is yes, then resolve to get out of your own way and give it your best shot.

Petit plaisir Listen to Bach's Brandenburg Concerto no. 2 in F Major, BWV 1047, and let the trumpet's triumphant energy carry you through the final days of spring into summer.

Explore further thesimplyluxuriouslife.com/june18 (how fear can be an opportunity for amazing life changes)

June 19
Celebrate Your Own Special Moments

Summer is nearly officially here, while unofficially it arrives on the last June day with students in the classroom. There is something similar to New Year's that occurs in the middle of June each year. Understandably this is likely because I was a teacher for twenty years, but it makes me want to prompt each of us to consider when a "new chapter" or "new page" turns in our yearly schedule.

What is it that takes place to make us feel renewed, excited, and even more eager for the next day to begin? When we find these moments in our lives, we have the opportunity to celebrate and elevate. And even if nobody recognizes the dates you select as significant, if you do, you can plan, design, and revel in your own way, one that you will look forward to each year.

Choosing to find our own everyday moments to celebrate has an amazing power of increasing our love of the life we are living. For a couple of recent summers, shortly after my last day in the classroom, I had hopped on a plane to somewhere I was curious to see. As well, a few years ago, I hosted a dinner party at my home near the summer solstice, and in 2019, I decided to do the same as a good friend was coming to town, and I couldn't think of a better reason to gather a few more good friends — old and new — and enjoy a meal and an evening without a clock.

There are simple ways you can choose to live that will improve what once you may have thought of as mundane and humdrum. You are living your life now, and it frequently offers opportunities to savor, celebrate, and appreciate all that you have the opportunity to experience. I wish for you many moments to celebrate, and even more that you may find upon contemplation.

Petit plaisir Watch the documentary *The Truffle Hunters* and slip away to the Piedmonte region of Italy.

Explore further thesimplyluxuriouslife.com/june19 (how to flourish rather than languish in your one and only life)

June 20
Hope at the First Light of the Day

One of my most beloved parts of the day takes place the moment the sun's first hello of the morning streams through windows, yet with only a sliver

June

of daylight illuminating the horizon. In Bend in mid-June, that would make it about 4:30 a.m. As I lie in bed, witnessing this gradual, yet inevitable shift of time prompts the hope inside me to swell, without fail. Why? Perhaps it is because, after so much darkness, the light is always around the corner — a new start, a fresh beginning, a brand-new day to enjoy and appreciate, one in which we may shift into the gear we need in order to steer more intentionally toward the life of our dreams.

Isn't it wonderful to know that this daily event will always occur? While it is a humbling truth, it is also a reassuring one, and I felt it especially as my final year of teaching came to a close. The final paycheck from the school district had arrived, my work-related e-mail account had been closed, and my files were transferred. I was officially moving on, and moving forward.

I have felt a bevy of emotions around this shift in my life, some I probably do not know how to accurately label. In fact, at times I have been at the brim of bawling, and the irony is that it was a decision I have been wanting to make for years — and without question still do — but still . . . tears?

In Mitch Albom's book *Tuesdays with Morrie*, Morrie Schwartz advises, "By throwing yourself into these emotions, by allowing yourself to dive in, all the way, over your head even, you experience them fully and completely" and then detach. But detachment does not mean you don't let the experience penetrate you. On the contrary, you let it penetrate you fully. That is how you are able to leave it. I let myself feel each of these emotions, ebbing and flowing with them instead of fighting them. And for that advice alone, I am thankful because today, now, each morning, is a new day. A fresh start.

We each get this opportunity every day. What we do with it is entirely up to each one of us. Are you looking for or wanting to make a leap? Do you simply want to make a simple change that, if adhered to with persistence, could make a tremendous difference in your life? Today is the day. Do something that will edge you toward the goal you are seeking, the life you want to live, and the person you know you are capable of becoming.

So much time can pass without realizing how much is behind you. Do not waste a moment. Live, experiment, try, fall down, get up, stop and savor, and then strive forward. At some point along the way, you will be glad you did.

Petit plaisir Watch *Destination Wedding*, a well-written, witty, dialogue-forward film starring Winona Ryder and Keanu Reeves.

Explore further thesimplyluxuriouslife.com/june20 (nine ideas for savoring everyday routines)

June 21
The Limbo of Travel

Happy first full day of summer (winter for TSLL Southern Hemisphere readers)!

During the summer of 2018, with the arrival of the longest day of the year, TSLL arrived in Paris on a jet plane, and the immense amount of daylight and beautiful weather made for a wonderful first day in the City of Light.

I began thinking about the time travelers spend as they wait at the garage, airport, or station, ride in the car, plane, or train, wait to collect their luggage — all moments in which we become temporarily acquainted with strangers who share a similar moment of uncertainty. Sometimes this uncertainty is riddled with fear. At other moments, it is bubbling with hopefulness. These two feelings can occur within the same person, even on the same trip.

There are so many uncertainties — will we arrive safely, locate our luggage, be fed food we enjoy when we are hungry, be able to sleep or tolerate our seat partner? When the stars align and all goes well, I am reminded to celebrate in some small way — perhaps champagne upon arrival or a generous tip to a busboy or taxi driver who embellished a trip's memory in a beautiful way (simply by connecting the dots smoothly).

Even when details don't work out as we had hoped, we can still open the door to other wonderful memories of growth and discovery. It may be something as simple as the car you scheduled to pick you up not arriving, so you are left to find a taxi — something most of us can do without a hitch — or your luggage not arriving; when this happens, my mother says, go to retail or consignment shops at your destination, pick up clothing that works, keeping what you love and consigning or donating the rest before you leave. When things don't work out as planned, look for the treasures; they are there to be found.

Back to the uncertainty of the traveler who is moving from point A to point B — basically in a moment of limbo. I felt moments of angst even on that trip in 2018 (probably more out of habit because everything went very well). But isn't that a significant part of growth — feeling the angst, the sense of being in limbo, and saying yes anyway? When we say yes, we move forward; we choose the opportunity for growth. We may not know what we are growing into, but we nonetheless open the door and introduce ourselves.

Travel and dance with what life would like to share with you, as it often is a wonderful invitation to accept, no matter where you travel or whom you travel with. Acknowledging the amazing gift that such an opportunity has presented is reason enough to seriously consider exploring what it may teach you.

Petit plaisir A new season, a new chapter. Add a bounce of intention with Johann Heinichen's Concerto in F, SBL 234.

Explore further thesimplyluxuriouslife.com/june21 (the difference between a traveler and a tourist)

June 22
True Happiness

The first week of summer has begun, and with it, ample time to read more books of our own choosing and extra daylight hours to luxuriate in when we want to read outside. In *Happiness by Design*, by Paul Dolan, a book centered on the topic of happiness and what it truly means to be happy, the author makes an interesting observation: Many happiness-centered books do not provide a definition of happiness. Isn't that odd? We blindly go forward, assuming we know what happiness is. But as Don Miguel Ruiz's best-selling book *The Four Agreements* reminds us, we should make no assumptions in order to attain personal freedom.

Ruiz defines happiness as soon as his book begins: "Happiness is experiences of pleasure and purpose over time." It is vitally important, and many of us make the mistake of seeking and paying "attention more to what we think should make us happy rather than focusing on what actually does." In order to abandon this futile pilgrimage, we need to instead seek a balance that aligns with our personality traits and welcomes both pleasure and purpose.

Too often, in the search for what will bring us happiness (we have talked about it many times on TSLL blog), we assume that bigger is better, more is better, when, in truth, we determine our happiness not by the quantity but by the quality of life we create when we make purchases and invest our time.

Evaluate what truly makes you content, and eliminate what you think "should" make you happy. The key really is to live consciously. We all make decisions or choices that we will eventually realize were not in alignment with our values and priorities. The key is to adjust and move forward, rather than dwelling. Cultivating contentment in each and every day of your life is a journey toward understanding yourself, and if you choose to live consciously, which is what living simply luxuriously is all about, you will certainly attain everyday contentment.

Petit plaisir In early summer, I have a ritual: Whenever it rains, I pour a small pot of tea, select a biscuit or chocolate truffle from my tea cupboard, snuggle into my porch swing with the boys, and watch the rain (and perhaps thunder and lightning) for however long it may last. Create such a ritual that spontaneously happens only when a particular unplanned event takes place.

Explore further thesimplyluxuriouslife.com/june22 (the importance of finding contentment)

June 23
Living Luxuriously No Matter Where

One of the things I enjoy when I travel to Paris and London is spending time in one of the cities' many *jardins* and parks. Small or large, it doesn't matter; all I look for is a quiet respite away from the city's hustle to savor a slice of Mother Nature.

Two places I have enjoyed spending time in were the Jardin du Palais Royal, in Paris, and a private, residents-only garden in the Maida Vale neighborhood in London. Both were remarkably quiet, and I would sit or stroll for some time, simply get lost in a journal entry, leisurely eat lunch, or even take a nap.

Part of living a simply luxurious life is having the ability and the wherewithal to seek out similar moments, no matter where we reside.

In the summer of 2021, for the first time in three years, I will not be jetting over the Atlantic to wander the streets of Paris or toodle about on a French country road. And, curiously, I have paid this pandemic-related hiatus no mind. Why? For two reasons: One, I am confident that I will return again, and, two, I have found ways to bring a little bit of what I love about Paris, for example, into my daily routine, no matter where I might be.

Before I moved to Bend, I had a few empty hours one summer and headed to the exquisite, long-established Pioneer Park in Walla Walla, Washington, where large, nearly century-old deciduous trees dot the neatly manicured green areas. With my dogs in tow, a blanket, a book, and a journal, two hours quickly passed. With the soft breeze, chirping birds, and beautifully landscaped grounds, I was able to create a Parisian moment that I could never have appreciated in the City of Light. Why? Because my dogs were at my side.

Part of knowing why you love what you love regarding Paris or any other beloved location is seeking similar moments of simple luxury in your day-to-day life. This magical, yet simple formula is one of the primary keys to creating your simply luxurious life, no matter where you call home.

Petit plaisir Visit a local farmers market and beeline to a flower stand to pick up a bouquet.

Explore further thesimplyluxuriouslife.com/june23 (ten ways to set up your home like a luxury travel accommodation)

June 24
Step into Another World

One of travel's most powerful gifts, especially if the travel involves boarding a plane and crossing time zones, is somewhat prompted by physiology; low air pressure reduces the oxygen in our blood, which can affect our decision making and emotions. As well, low air pressure can result in dehydration, causing fatigue or mood disturbances we may not otherwise encounter when our feet are on the ground.

Following my two-week trip to London and Paris in August 2012 with an ex-boyfriend (yep, we were exes traveling together, but we had planned the trip while we were together, and we each saw it as a unique opportunity to see the world). Needless to say, many emotions ebbed and flowed during the two weeks, and while it was a lovely, most memorable trip, we deplaned at the end of our travels as amicable exes, confirmed we had made the right decisions — taking the trip, but also moving forward in our separate directions.

Heightened emotions — prompted by not only plane travel, but simply being away from your regular routine and in a different culture — are a test for the mind in awareness. Emotions, dutifully kept in check while going about your everyday routine at home, may have a better chance of coming forth as your willpower is lower due to less habituation and the change of routine.

However, the new world you step into, prompted by traveling, can be revealing. This is not to say you have to reveal all that you are suddenly feeling to someone, but acknowledging what rises to the surface can provide insights you had unconsciously been seeking. (Another reason to always remember to pack a journal.) Why am I uneasy in this relationship? What do I long to express about myself? Why do I feel such peace in this environment — one I have never stepped foot in — prior to this trip?

Shortly after arriving home from London and Paris, I resolved to make sure the lessons from the many *aha* moments — the floods of tears as I realized truths I was not able to see before, giddiness about what was now possible — were not wasted, and I was overcome with a feeling I can only describe as life awakening. I was full of awe because I could have never predicted the power of stepping away from my day-to-day life to travel with someone in a way I would not have chosen.

That trip to London and Paris woke me up after a twelve-year hiatus during which I thought I would never be able to return to Europe, and it infused the blog and what has become my full-time job creating TSLL with a clarity of focus that now seems too obvious . . . but it was not. I had to shake up my life a bit, in a way I could not have planned and did not initially want to happen (the traveling with an ex, not the traveling to London and Paris).

The trick — and what I want to share with you today — is to allow yourself to step away from the life you have created. Step into another world for a day, a weekend, two weeks, or more, and absorb all of the newness. Let it wash over you, and see what captures your attention, what warms your soul and tickles your curiosity. With as much objectivity as possible, observe what you are feeling. What prompts such feelings? Don't act on your response or judge it; just observe it, write down your thoughts in your journal, and then keep on traveling.

These opportunities only come when you are strong enough to do something outside your regular routine. Your perspective will be widened, your mind will be more open and understanding; your certainty of what you want will often be more cemented, but sometimes, for your benefit, it may be crushed as you realize you want something entirely different. All of these are good things. Each of these discoveries will help lead you to your most fulfilling life, but it will take strength. It will take courage. There will be moments of tears, frustration, and question, but I urge you to dare to expose yourself to new ideas and ways of doing things. You may not like everything, you may not like much, but I guarantee you will return changed for the better.

Initially, these negatives may feel like deterrents, but they are actually signs of growth, signs that you want something different, something more, and that you are finally realizing you are capable of making it happen. One other difficulty is that, at the moment, you are relying primarily on what you currently feel, on what sits well with you. Sometimes you can explain this, sometimes you cannot; either way, explore where your curiosity leads.

You may be hesitant to act on what you are feeling immediately, but take the time to investigate what your instincts are telling you. More often than not, they are speaking words of wisdom. Be courageous enough to travel this unknown path to see what you discover. After all, you are coming back home, and that is where you can contemplate why it was presented to you in the first place.

Petit plaisir Listen to Joseph Haydn's Symphony in D (*London*), no. 104, and feel a spring in your step as you jaunt off to a much-anticipated getaway.

Explore further thesimplyluxuriouslife.com/june24 (give yourself permission to be awkward)

June 25
Travel, Love, and Taking Risks

"There is no remedy for love but to love more." Henry David Thoreau wrote many of my favorite quotes about how to proceed through life, as did Ralph Waldo Emerson, his mentor in many ways. These two men capture the beauty of life and remind readers of how simple it really is to be full of joy and find our way in the world with satisfaction and appreciation.

When encountering the above quote, many people instantly jump to the idea of romantic love, but if we could step back from that notion for a moment and look at the idea of love in general, we would be amazed by how rich our everyday lives could become if we just loved more in every interaction and moment we find ourselves.

Love for our neighbors, love for strangers, love for our community, for nature, and for ourselves. There may be moments or longer periods in our lives when we feel that love is not present, that we are lacking. But while we cannot control others' reactions or behavior, we can control our own. We may have to let go of certain people, places, or ideas in order to discover a life full of more love, but we will never reap more love by holding it back.

One of the many gifts of traveling alone is strengthening the ability to take risks, and that includes taking risks when it comes to love. While we will be presented with opportunities to connect with people intimately —

whether romantically or platonically — the opportunities are not infinite, just as the opportunities presented while we are traveling will not wait around for us to give them a go later. There will always be unknowns, and you can jump an inch or a mile, but I encourage you to jump just a little bit out of your comfort zone to see what might be possible.

The idea of being vulnerable might spring to mind, and that is precisely what we must do — wisely and confidently, knowing that we are capable of sharing love and why we are sharing it. When we share in an honest manner, with our roots firmly planted, yet being flexible where we know we can be, we open the door for more love to enter our lives.

Whether it is taking a risk and stepping out on your own at an event or getting to know new friends and colleagues, when you extend kindness and thoughtfulness, gradually and without expectation, you become filled with more joy. And if something more, a friendship, a sense of trust as a loyal customer, or perhaps even the hope of romance happens to occur, well, that's wonderful too. But even if it doesn't, your life will abound with joy because you are engaging joyfully in each moment. So, yes, you are responsible for the amount of love you have in your life.

Petit plaisir   Enjoy the first season of the Parisian reality series *L'Agence*.

Explore further   thesimplyluxuriouslife.com/june25 (a powerful couple: boundaries and vulnerability)

June 26
The Power of Dreams

Each of us has an ultimate dream or fantasy that, for many, was born during childhood. Some of our dreams change, some are forgotten or silenced; yet for others, the dream remains ardently clear, never going out of focus and always demanding attention. The latter of these instances seems to be the situation I find myself in.

While some may dream of their wedding day, others wish to travel the world or aspire to open their own business. I have only wanted to become a published writer — in other words, as someone once clarified, an author. From as far back as my pre-teen years, I wrote in journals, attempting to create my own magazines and imagining the life of being able to write for a living. What bliss! To hold in my hands a book with my name on the cover would be proof that my time on the planet produced something of substance. As many longtime TSLL readers know, the dream became a reality in 2014 with the publication of my first book, and in 2021, I took the risk of focusing fully on being a writer.

The whispers grew louder, the yearning never left, and as hard as I tried to continue in a profession I highly regard and feel privileged to have contributed to, writing and exploring and sharing and continuing to learn and then sharing some more through my own writing increased their volume.

Traveling, whether to France or Britain or simply taking my first getaway in-state to the Oregon coast with the boys in 2012 — the first one I could afford, something that turned into a ritual every year — kept breathing life into my dreams because I gave myself time to set my mind free. And when I set my mind free to wander, I allowed the volume on my dream of being a writer to be turned up. And as the volume rose, I began to understand what it confidently knew I should do (though I didn't do it yet).

Marry your dreams with your excursions, no matter how far away or nearby you wander. Give your dreams of the life you want to live the breadth to dance about and see what they are trying to say. If the whisper remains, the time traveling will likely increase its volume and clarify a yearning worth exploring.

Petit plaisir Blossoming sweet peas at the market, with their subtle scent, make a welcome bouquet to bring home. Purchase one bundle, and place it somewhere in your home that will light up your day each time you see or smell it.

Explore further thesimplyluxuriouslife.com/june26 (investing in your dreams and how to do it)

June 27
Letting Go to Move Forward

I remember going to the playground as a kid. Swings, teeter-totters, and slides were usually options, but monkey bars were also usually available. The goal was to swing, grip by grip, from one end to the other without falling.

While it takes a certain amount of arm and shoulder strength, navigating monkey bars also takes momentum, courage, and a touch of acceptance of uncertainty. In order to move forward, you must let go with one hand and hang a bit awkwardly until you grasp the new bar. So long as you hang on with both hands — one in the past, one in the present — you can make no forward progress. What makes the progress easier is building up momentum, using a steady swing of your body.

Progress in life is somewhat similar. We cannot know with absolute certainty what will happen in the future, but we will never find out if we continue to live in the past, mulling it over, over-analyzing, and letting it hold us back. We may assume that because particular events played out as they did, they or similar events must always follow the same course. Such a mindset can be caused by not letting go of the past, and it is death to progress.

The perilous part is letting go of what you know, of what you thought would work but didn't; or maybe something worked but didn't have the effect you had imagined. Instead of brooding unnecessarily on the past, let it go. Learn the lesson, and find a wave of inspiration to propel you into the future.

Progress can only happen if you let go of what you thought would work but didn't. You must be brave enough to let go of what was and swing toward something that could be, even if you aren't quite sure how it will materialize. So long as you have one hand in the present and are clear about your focus and your direction, something amazing will occur when you swing toward your future.

Petit plaisir Plant nasturtiums grown from seed this past spring. They have been protected indoors and are now ready to be outside, to edge a border or fill and spill over the edges of pots placed about the garden or on the porch.

Explore further thesimplyluxuriouslife.com/june27 (growth is a choice. eleven ways to grow up)

June 28
Be Vulnerable as You Pursue Your Dreams

If you are going to doubt anything in life, doubt your own limitations.
—Dan Brule

One of the most frustrating parts about letting yourself be vulnerable — in your career, in a romantic relationship, with friends, or among a new culture — is when, having mustered all of your gumption, strength, and courage, you find that, for whatever reason, it has not worked out.

June

Case in point: During my first visit to France in 2000, I knew next to nothing of the language (that's why I was going to French school during the study-abroad program). After the summer-long program concluded, followed by a week in Paris on my own, I returned home (remember my phone booth incident from this chapter's intro?) feeling unsuccessful in my attempt to explore the culture and successfully grasp the language.

For twelve years, my love of France sat in idle gear in the back of my being, but it did not die. My initial pursuit of a sincere dream was not for naught. That first trip as a twenty-one-year-old ignited a truth about something I needed to continue to explore, I just didn't have the muscles to do so at that point (nor the funds), even if I had wanted to.

You may feel like a fool. You may feel embarrassed. You may even begin to believe that being vulnerable is a bad idea. But I implore you to continue to be open to what life has to offer. Continue to be a little vulnerable in life, in love, in where the path of your journey may take you. Do not shut down. Keep searching for the answers, no matter how frustrating the process may be. Even though it seems that all you have is a list of endless questions, the answers will eventually present themselves — if you keep searching for them.

Dan Brule's quote holds wisdom and truth. In moments of doubt, keep putting one foot in front of another. Keep seeking, and you will eventually be pleased with where you are going and where you end up. While sometimes it may not work out as you have planned, eventually it will work out — maybe even better than you expected.

Petit plaisir Unwind at the end of the day, while maintaining a reserved bit of energy and listen to Georg Telemann's Viola Concerto in G Major.

Explore further thesimplyluxuriouslife.com/june28 (how maturity and making dreams a reality go hand in hand)

June 29
Getting Away from the Tech and Bustle

Turning off our technology while we travel may, to some, seem an absurd thing to do. How will I navigate? Translate? Share my experience on social media? But doing so may just be the best detail to add to your trip to ensure it is memorable.

Technology takes many forms — yes, our smartphones and computers, but television as well. Give yourself permission to lose track of time, let your body catch up on sleep, mosey to the market or the local restaurant when you are hungry, and become comfortable with the present moment. Become grounded in the pleasure of your own company. Mindfully keep yourself in this unique moment, free from the everyday tugs and pulls when you are at home or at work, and let this skill of being present strengthen itself.

The more such strengthening becomes commonplace in your being, the easier it will be to find contentment in your everydays, whether you are traveling or simply going about your life, and then maybe, just maybe, your travel plans won't have to be made to escape, but to expand.

Be honest with yourself about your motivations for getaways, vacations, and travel plans. When your time away from home becomes about expanding your world rather than escaping your world, you have done the hard and conscious work of building a life you love living. Celebrate. True contentment is yours.

Petit plaisir Listen to Mozart's Clarinet Quintet in A, K. 581 – 4. Allegretto con variazioni. If you find yourself smiling spontaneously with eyes closed, the composition has worked its magic.

Explore further thesimplyluxuriouslife.com/june29 (the power of solitude)

June 30
Get Away to Return Well Rested

One sign of a restful holiday is our pace when we return home, especially if we love the home to which we are returning.

The pace I found myself keeping as I left for a holiday to Portland and then to the Oregon coast, while not harried, was quick and time-conscious. Not necessarily because I was late, although I did have a scheduled rendezvous with a friend, but more so because the momentum of my daily schedule had not yet slowed down.

Conversely, when I stepped into my car for the return home, after an hour-long walk on the beach with the boys and popping into the local bakery to purchase a hot tea and almond croissant, I felt no sense of hurry in my being; instead, I enjoyed a soft smile and a calm mind behind the wheel. The cruise control was set comfortably, but on the slow side; cars passed me from time to time, but with new episodes of my favorite podcasts as well as my classical music playlist, I was in my own little blissful, relaxed bubble, and adhered to my steady speed.

The significant difference in my pace as I drove home, as opposed to when I had left, did not occur to me until I was about three hours into my drive with another ninety minutes to go, and I realized that this shift was a very good sign.

While we can never predict how our holidays will unfold, we can be thoughtful about the choices we make and the schedules we set up, as well as keeping in mind previous trips and what worked and what did not to calm our minds and beings.

In the past, it had been extremely hard for me to return home from trips, as where I was returning home to never felt truly as though it was my home. That has changed with my move to Bend, so it means even more to me when I am in no rush to get home, even though I love pulling into my driveway.

However you design your getaways, give yourself buffers, especially at the end, but in the beginning as well — a few days of rest at home before you have to return to your regular work schedule or a few days before you leave to prep your home so you can return to a clean and welcoming abode. Travel when you know you will be rested and alert, and prepare the accoutrements that make you comfortable. If you are traveling by car, clean it thoroughly before the long trip, and treat yourself to something lovely to do or eat before you leave.

Finally, be sure you can have a delicious meal when you arrive; either have the grocery items in the fridge waiting for you, pick up a few things on your way home, or pick up a favorite to-go order to bring home so you can fully relax after unpacking.

Whether you too are in the middle or wrapping up a getaway or looking forward to enjoying one in the near future, my wish for you is that your pace upon returning is leisurely and that you are smiling.

Petit plaisir Savor the final day of the month of June by listening to Bach's Cello Suite Gigue 6.6, arranged by Peter Gregson.

Explore further thesimplyluxuriouslife.com/june30 (the priceless gifts from the ocean: solitude and comfort)

July

The Gifts of France: Awakening, Savoring, and Being True to Oneself

July

Take your time. Don't try and control everything. That's usually how destiny reveals itself.
— Ben to Mathilde, in the TV series *Blood of the Vine* (*Le Sang de la Vigne*)

I remember the first time I stepped foot in France. A dream of a lifetime had finally materialized (okay, my lifetime at that point was only twenty-one years, but still), and for a mere moment it felt surreal . . . and then I had to find the correct train to take me to Angers. As I did not know much French (okay, truthfully, next to nothing), my face must have revealed my panic, uncertainty, and utter confusion. Somehow good fortune guided me onto the train to take me west (where I needed to go), but it would be another forty-eight hours before I would feel at ease as jet lag introduced itself to this neophyte international traveler.

A state of perplexity, uncertainty, and doubt can often occupy the same space in which our dreams arrive. Disbelief and astonishment provide a temporary rush of adrenaline, assisting us in forging ahead through feelings that may, without the exhilaration of realizing a dream come true, otherwise halt us.

Perhaps that is exactly why we need to dream beyond our self-imposed limitations. As for a pole-vaulter, the bar may be high (our dream), but the pole works as the adrenaline to provide us with the necessary oomph to reach the heights we dare to sprint and leap toward.

As I shared in my first book, *Choosing the Simply Luxurious Life*, my inaugural trip to France came about after taking what felt at the time to be a risk of a lifetime — calling off a wedding to my college sweetheart. After ending the relationship, with the dream of visiting France dancing about within me, I catapulted myself into just enough college work to meet the requirements to study abroad.

At the time, in the summer of 2000, a dream came true for a young woman (*moi*) who knew not a personal soul in her family who had traveled to Europe, let alone France. Yet after giving back the ring, I charged ahead without hesitation and, in five months, was on a plane headed to France to make one of the most far-fetched dreams in my world come true.

Similarly, in 2015 and 2021, I picked up my "pole" and vaulted into two dreams I had long held as seemingly impossible. But for some reason, I chose to unconsciously trust that indeed each was possible. (After all, the word itself states, "I'm possible," *non*?)

In 2015, I secured, after two years of applying for a teaching job, the opportunity to move and call Bend, Oregon, home (I detail the move in my second book, *Living the Simply Luxurious Life*). And recently I retired from teaching and stepped wholly into writing.

The Road to Le Papillon

The naïve twenty-one-year-old who arrived in France for the first time thankfully did not know how difficult traveling alone might be and had no concept of the Paris Syndrome (defined as disappointment, upon arriving in Paris for the first time, when preconceived ideas about the city don't pan out). Due to blissful ignorance that I clearly acknowledge, the choice to make that trip changed the entire path of my life.

Awakening my appreciation for the lifestyle I regularly share now on TSLL blog — savoring everyday luxuries, elevating the daily routine, noticing the details of each season that last but a moment in our lives, only to return in a year's time, the culture of the French, their focus on quality over quantity, reveling in the present moment — brought great relief and gratitude as I finally felt I had found my "tribe" (I never could assimilate with my peers in the States comfortably and sincerely).

When I finally made sense of what I appreciated about my experience in France as I was nearing the age of thirty — leaving behind the angst of trying to be and live in a way that did not match my inner yearning to slow down, savor, appreciate, and be fully in the moment — the pressure was released, and the peace of being myself gradually began to return. TSLL began at this time, and France made all the difference. Shannon Before France (S.B.F.) and Shannon After France (S.A.F.).

Notice that nine years passed before I made sense of the effect and the influence France had on me regarding truths about where I would find my peace. Nine years. Simmering, or should I say resting, does indeed render delicious benefits.

In many aspects of our lives, we need patience in order to allow the new flavors to mingle and reach their full magnificence. If we neglect this step, if we turn around and walk away because it is not what we expected, because it seems too hard or fills us with fear, we miss out on something wonderful. If, as I shared in June's introduction, I had hopped back on the plane and refused to allow myself to experience France because it was intimidating, I would have lost out on an amazing, literally life-changing experience.

Remaining in Paris, with the tears wiped away, I set about to experience what would bring me comfort — touring the Jardin des Plantes, including a comforting conversation with a fellow traveler from Ireland while sitting among the summer blooms, and making a trip to the Musée d'Orsay, where I saw the originals of paintings I had only previously seen in prints hanging in my grandmother's and parents' homes.

The full potential of our life's path won't reveal itself with a Google Maps search. The key is to keep searching, letting the pieces hold space within your mind and being. Gradually, if you are patient and if you listen, and, most important, if you have the courage to trust what you discover, the next step will be selecting the best option to take, even if, in retrospect and to those around you, it would appear to be incredibly risky and without guarantees.

Gift yourself with the time and space to wander between an ill-fitting life and what you hope to achieve, how you hope to live, and who you want to become. Do not turn back; make sure to always wander forward, no matter how many meanderings left and right you may take. Have patience. Trust your intuition to head toward the life of your dreams. Give the pieces (experiences) and players (people) time to sort themselves out, and eventually everything will fall into its proper place in the most unexpectedly beautiful piece of life art.

Even though my accent, height, and big laugh leave no doubt that my citizenship is not French, each time I return to France, it feels as though I am returning home, especially when I step foot in the countryside. What do you give to a country, to a culture, that broke you open so you could live your one and only life fully? I am not sure there is an equivalent gift of gratitude, but if living each day savoring everyday moments, engaging fully in the present, and reveling in the seasonal gifts every single year as the calendar moves forward can be defined as a gift, that is what I have been doing and will continue to do. And it has made all the difference in the quality of my days.

July 1
Lessons from France

When, on April 15, 2019, I saw the flames above Notre-Dame de Paris, my mind was simultaneously taken aback and flooded with disbelief. For twenty-four hours, my thoughts and attention focused on this image and horrible event. And then I began to wonder, why? Why was I transfixed?

After all, undoubtedly many more people hold the 12th-century cathedral dear and consider it a significant place in their lives than I possibly could. I am not Catholic, and I am not French, nor do I live in Paris. So why was this event holding onto my mind and emotions and making me unconsciously long to travel to Paris *tout de suite*?

The next day, a student in my class eloquently described the *why* that answered my question — it was part of my journey, in terms of my appreciation for France, but also my re-imagining how to live a life that spoke to me and felt in alignment with my predilections and tendencies, my passions, what I valued. No, it was not precisely Notre-Dame, but rather her location, her long existence at the heart of the City of Light, and the reality that I had seen her with my own eyes during my first trip to France that held my emotions in their grip that week.

There has been controversy regarding the donations that will enable the cathedral to remain and return to its former glory. But the cathedral matters in so many people's lives, and for a reason only they can truly understand. And no, we should not become attached, but rather hold within us the values and inspiration that the past, the building, the experience brought into our lives, but what if we can save it? (We can.) What if it can continue to stand and inspire millions of others who have yet to see it in generations to come? (It absolutely can.) Then shouldn't we?

The documentary *The Rape of Europa* poses a fascinating question regarding the artwork that the Monuments Men risked their lives to recover during World War II: Is art worth dying for? The good news is, nobody died in the fire, nor was anyone severely injured, and most certainly a life should be saved before a piece of art. But perhaps the reason the cathedral's burning was visceral for so many of us is because we, in that moment, recognized the fragility of the places we have visited that played a pivotal role in our lives, and we are now more fully aware of our good fortune.

What part of your journey have you perhaps taken for granted? What shifted or awakened you to a new way of living, loving, and seeing the world? What, upon reflection, introduced you to the life you cannot imagine not living, one that you would have had no idea existed until you experienced such a moment? Today, refuse to live without awareness of the truth you have discovered, and live from this day forward with a deeper appreciation of the awesomely serendipitous "crossing of paths" that happened in your life.

Petit plaisir   Watch the Tour de France and slip away vicariously into the French countryside.

Explore further   thesimplyluxuriouslife.com/july1 (twenty-five reasons you might be a Francophile)

July 2
Contentment in the Everyday

Have you ever asked yourself why, in moments of absolute contentment, when you are able to sit down and not feel compelled to do something, you are able to be so blissful and worry free? I have a feeling that many reasons will come to mind, and depending upon the time of day and where you are in your life, you will be able to clearly explain exactly why.

One aspect of life that I have found leads to such a moment is having an outlet for your passion and being able to exercise said passion, pursuing it with curiosity and genuine zeal. When we find what truly moves us and engages our heart and our mind, after we have completed what we can during the course of a day and seeing some growth (no matter how small), it becomes possible to sit and just be.

The French culture has awakened an awareness in my life, unconsciously in 2000 and more consciously after two decades have passed — an awareness that allows me to savor the everydays, to pay attention to quality and invest in it, without strangling what I love or, in contrast, disengaging with the world.

When you too come to know the peace found in the power of giving attention to the everyday, your life elevates; you find more time to breathe, and the breath gives you the space to find your passions and your callings, as well as the energy to put toward them. What an amazing place to find.

Choose to step into your true self, sharing what longs to be expressed. Courageously let go of any false self-presentations, and the joy you feel within will expand. Whether in your own company or with others who bring you peace, revel in these moments of sincere exploration and exchange, without thought of the clock, and savor, savor, savor the everyday moments. That is true contentment indeed.

Petit plaisir While it does not necessarily have anything to do with France, Johann Sebastian Bach's French Suite no. 4 in E-flat Major is certainly worth listening to.

Explore further thesimplyluxuriouslife.com/july2 (a wise investment: understanding yourself by taking off the blindfold)

July 3
Patience

One July, my mother and I learned to make lavender wreaths on a beautiful lavender farm in the countryside outside of Walla Walla, Washington. One pristine, yet mild summer day, perfect for sitting outside under a vast umbrella, we worked away on our lavender bundles with baskets of freshly cut pieces waiting to be included.

Four hours later, after passing the time catching up, commenting on the views, and sipping lavender-infused lemonade, we each had a wreath. Four hours later. I had no idea it would take that long, but the result was

The Road to Le Papillon

impressive and well worth the time required. And the beautiful truth was I lost all track of time.

I was reminded of many lessons as I looked at my watch, hungry for what would be a late lunch but having thoroughly enjoyed the experience. The most obvious lesson was that nothing worth appreciating takes little effort. Another lesson, perhaps more important, is that adapting to something new takes time, determination, and the willingness to stick with it even when you're not exactly sure you're doing it correctly.

Many of us want to know how the things we choose to do will turn out (I include myself in this category) because we are given the illusion, due to all of the information that is available, that there is no reason for us not to know. And while I would agree that, yes, we have many more resources than previous generations have had, we must understand that we will never know anything for certain unless we try it for ourselves and stick to it, until we either finish it or reach the goal we had set.

Throwing your hands up in uncertainty stops the process of whatever you are doing dead in its tracks. But choosing to push forward, even when you're not exactly sure how it is all going to turn out, could manifest something you never thought you could achieve.

Petit plaisir Make a frittata with smoked salmon and garlic-infused spinach for a simple, yet special breakfast. Pair with freshly squeezed orange juice.

Explore further thesimplyluxuriouslife.com/july3 (remain determined and strive forward)

July 4
Freedom and Celebration

The Fourth of July piqued my curiosity more than a few years ago, at a time when I became more conscious and discerning about what I celebrated, why I celebrated, and how I celebrated.

Did you know Americans may actually be two days late in celebrating the formal day of declaration of independence? If John Adams had had his way, Americans would celebrate on July 2 rather than July 4, as it was on the second that all thirteen delegates voted for their sovereignty; however, the formal document's edits were approved on the fourth. An interesting historical footnote and an intriguing coincidence: Both Thomas Jefferson and John Adams died on July 4 in 1826.

This brief historical anecdote offers a life lesson: Much of what we celebrate, how we celebrate, and when we celebrate is subject to interpretation, but what remains constant is that there is a need to celebrate, to remember, and to appreciate the efforts and events that came before.

Very few outcomes or objectives worth acquiring or attaining happen without hard work, and most take time to blossom. So long as we appreciate the effort that precedes a patiently awaited arrival, the way we celebrate and even when we celebrate is, for the most part, irrelevant. Most important is that we appreciate how we have arrived at where we are.

The final stage of my journey to Le Papillon took four years, nearly to the day, after I had moved to Bend. And if I were to speak to my younger self in 2015, knowing I would have to wait four years would have seemed impossible, but my current self knows with confidence that my appreciation is far deeper and more cemented because of those four years of exploring, of strengthening my understanding, and honing my clarity about whether I would ever find a house in Bend to call my own.

Whether it is in honor of independence, or of a federal holiday placed on the calendar for all to observe, or simply of milestones along your own life journey, be sure to celebrate from time to time, taking into account all that is going well.

Petit plaisir Choose a day each week to feed your flowers and vegetables their regular natural food — fish, tomato, or seaweed. They will thank you by producing beautiful blooms, fruits, and vegetables long into the late summer and early autumn.

Explore further thesimplyluxuriouslife.com/july4 (tradition: to follow or not to follow)

July 5
Take a Risk, and Let Go

Life is not easy for any of us. But what of that? We must have perseverance and, above all, confidence in ourselves. We must believe that we are gifted for something and that this thing must be attained.

— Marie Curie

Have you ever asked yourself this question: "Why am I so nervous to try _____? Why am I so afraid to give it a go?" Or maybe you have even asked, "Why am I so fraught with analysis over this when others seem to be doing it with ease?"

I have discovered that the real questions we should be asking ourselves are "Why do I want to do this? Why is it consuming my thoughts?" A few years ago, I wrote a post focused on the idea that what we are fearful to try, but continue to contemplate, is exactly what we should pursue.

So often our unconscious directs us toward the life we wish to create for ourselves. Sometimes we cannot make sense of the information at the moment, but if we take the time to quiet ourselves and reflect on the "why" behind such thoughts, we begin to discover what we yearn to do, feel, and experience.

When I seriously began to consider concluding my teaching career and shifting entirely into writing and focusing on TSLL, my fear was palpable and consumed much of my thoughts during the day. However, because my exploration was sincere, my mind (the lizard mind) was doing all that it could to hold me where I had been because that is what it knows. Whether it is good or bad or anything in between, the known is often more comfortable than the unknown.

Unknowns and new paths provoke fear to raise its head, wake up, and push back, whereas doubt only arises when we have experienced the choice before and there are knowns we can concretely speak to. The feeling of fear is natural, and the good news is that it is actually quite helpful, similar to a map or a compass pointing you in the direction that your true self knows is the path you must take, if only you would exercise the courage to do so.

What is it that makes you a bit nervous to try? What is it that continues to flood your mind and beg for your attention, no matter what you do? What is it that keeps you strategizing in your head? Whatever your answer, consider that this is exactly what you should do.

What you think about, what grabs your attention without being forced, is a hint at what you are passionate about, what you are curious about, and what perks up your soul. Do it. Try it. Go there. Take that risk. No matter what happens, you will learn something about yourself, and I have a sneaking suspicion that it will be a great experience.

Petit plaisir Spend time on or near the water. Norman and I enjoy paddleboarding in the morning with the ducks, geese, and swooping birds, watching the fish jump, and greeting the day with a refreshing, grounding state of mind as we return home to work (in my case) and a nap (for Norman).

Explore further thesimplyluxuriouslife.com/july5 (build a life for ladybugs: choosing hope over fear)

July 6
Simple Things

The secret of genius is to carry the spirit of childhood into adulthood.
—Thomas Huxley

The realization that life really is about the little things is wonderful. As young children, we naturally hold our attention in the present, fascinated by seemingly ordinary details — dirt, cardboard, the birds chattering away outside at the bird feeder. So long as we are fortunate to be raised in a safe environment, the past and future are foreign concepts of time to our toddler selves. However, as life evolves, if we do not acquire and hone the skill of remaining present in our everydays, the societal expectations, pressures, and demands of the world pull us away from a skill we innately possess.

The good news is that we can reclaim this knowledge we held unconsciously as a child if we choose to search for it as an adult. The analogy to a life preserver is a fair one. The realization that the little things make the grandest difference in the quality of our lives wakes us up, helps us put things in perspective, and reveals the opportunity to make a life that brings us joy, contentment, and a deeper peace than we may have ever known.

For me, simple everyday routines bring the most joy and strengthen steady contentment — the opportunities to sip a hot cup of tea on the porch swing, watch the visitors at the bird café outside my reading nook window, savor the blooms bursting forth in the garden during spring, summer, and fall, take a morning constitutional with the dogs, and conclude the day nestled into a cozy chair by the fireplace.

Breathe, and remind yourself that life is going just fine so long as you protect your everyday rituals and routines. Savor each one as you hold yourself in the present moment.

Petit plaisir Make a chilled cucumber and avocado soup to cleanse and satiate the palate on a hot summer day (find the recipe on the blog).

Explore further thesimplyluxuriouslife.com/july6 (thirty-six ways to welcome joie de vivre into your everyday life)

July 7
Finding Your Bearings

In July, the cherry trees near my reading nook window drip with newly ripened red cherries. The birdsong is plentiful, and Norman gazes with sleepy eyes out the same window, watching the birds dance about the tree on which the bird café hangs.

The refuge of a garden — alive with birds, bumblebees, blooms, and fruits (the blackberry bushes' blossoms have speckled the green stalks with white, promising the soft sweetness that will soon arrive. I can't wait to make summer's first berry tart) — resembles in many ways a comforting hug, a feeling of reassurance, warmth, and recalibration.

Even when the world is uncertain, relationships lose their way, or our direction becomes unclear, stepping into the garden, or simply gazing out upon it, brings our focus to the present. We are reminded that life is simple. No, not easy, as the distractions that can dissuade us from this understanding are unceasing, but yes, simple. When you are distracted, parse it out: How do you feel? What has caused you to feel this way? How have you participated in enabling or inviting such an action or event to happen?

Love, respect, usefulness, curiosity. When I am perplexed, at least one of these four concepts is not present. All are feelings that, when present in our lives, create a life of contentment, but when one of the four wheels is flat or out of alignment, our lives can veer off in the wrong direction.

Take an hour or even thirty minutes today to check in with yourself. Step away from distractions that might swirl in your mind or rush through your thoughts and carefully assess each of your four "wheels" — love, respect, usefulness, curiosity. Are you feeling each one? As you make your way around to each one, take time to mentally or physically list what brings the feeling into your life. It is part gratitude exploration and part self-care check-in. If you find a "tire" that needs attention, acknowledge the need as just that, a necessity, and prioritize how to bring yourself back into your best self.

Petit plaisir Make a fruit parfait with ricotta mousse and fresh berries from the garden or the local farmers market. Don't forget the granola for a lovely mix of textures. (find the recipe on the blog)

Explore further thesimplyluxuriouslife.com/july7 (five simple changes to create immediate and significant contentment)

July 8
Visiting the Farmers Markets in France

Each day of the week, in most regions of France, there will be a year-round outdoor market for seasonal produce and goods operating somewhere within a twenty- to thirty-minute drive.

Those words — year-round — may at first seem impossible, but it is true, and it is not just in Provence, but all over the country. I gained my sea legs when it comes to market visiting while staying in Provence for two weeks during the summer of 2018. I delighted in the availability of fresh seasonal goods and the conviviality of those who were shopping, selling, and simply sightseeing.

Most markets open between eight and nine in the morning and have wrapped up by noon or one in the afternoon. If you are traveling in the Luberon region of Provence, there is a market each day of the week somewhere in the region. Simply check TheLuberon.com to see which town with a market day is closest to where you are staying.

The value the French place on fresh seasonal produce teaches a valuable lesson for everyday living. What we eat matters; regularly engaging with the local community face-to-face makes a tremendous positive difference; and stepping outside, in Mother Nature's ever-changing weather conditions, provides us with more healthy medicine than we may have thought possible for the mind.

Most of us cannot call France home year-round, but I urge you to begin to eat with the seasons and to consider growing some of your own vegetables and herbs and even fruits. You will be rewarded when you taste the depth of flavor of a tomato freshly picked off the vine in July and August.

Petit plaisir Dreaming of Provence? Read Helen Lefkowitz Horowitz's *A Taste for Provence*.

Explore further thesimplyluxuriouslife.com/july8 (sixteen tips for a successful market visit in France)

July 9
Presence: A Gift Just for You

Living in the moment ushers in a gift that we cannot buy, yet thankfully we have complete control to obtain it on our own. Simply pay attention to the world as it is in the present. That's all — just pay attention. Stop, open your eyes, and see, really look and see and savor.

At any given moment, we can witness beautiful moments or heart-wrenching ones. We can exercise the skill of being present, doing our best to step into such moments, to embrace them, to not push them aside and take them for granted, to find the beauty and be still with them as much as we can.

Witnessing a rainbow while taking a walk with my boys will always prompt me to stop in my tracks and savor. Equally, receiving upsetting news from the radio or my newsfeed will cause me to stop, listen, and try to understand. However, to linger with either a beautiful or difficult moment holds us in the past. When we are present, we are not stagnant; we are moving with life, witnessing what unfolds, taking in all of the details, and moving through it, as if capturing it, learning from it, and letting it deepen our appreciation or strengthen our awareness for better decision making.

Choosing to be present is a gift we give to ourselves. Perhaps the phrase itself is a simple reminder to celebrate each day. We become more human by letting ourselves feel what we feel — doing so in a healthy manner, walking it out, journaling it out, crying it out, dancing it out, whatever it may be, so long as we do not run from it, bury it, dismiss it, or remain embroiled in it without stepping forward. Our ability to empathize with others in the present, as well as in future moments we cannot predict, becomes more possible when we live presently.

The more you remind yourself to be human, entirely human, the richer your life becomes for a myriad of reasons. Feeling and knowing that feelings are not forever but are ever evolving and changing, just as humans ourselves grow and change, age and pass on, sets us free to live more fully and deeply in the now.

Petit plaisir For a fun French romantic comedy, watch *Tu Veux ou Tu Veux Pas* ("Do You Want It or Not?") or, the English title, *Sex, Love & Therapy* (2014), starring Sophie Marceau and Patrick Bruel.

Explore further thesimplyluxuriouslife.com/july9 (thirteen ways to attain emotional freedom and cultivate more joy of living)

July 10
Reading: A Simple and Necessary Pleasure

While I was still teaching, a student told me she had experienced the most wonderful day staying home and reading all day long. The delight on her

July

face confirmed her genuine glee of discovery of how wonderful the day was and a longing for it to happen again soon, along with a fear that it would not. I expressed my complete understanding of savoring such a day, which reminded me of how comforting, supportive, and joy-filled days such as the student described can be in our everyday lives.

Making a regular habit of cozying into our favorite chair, surrounding ourselves with books and other reading material, is arguably not a luxury, but a necessity — especially for those of us who find ourselves reenergized after escaping with a book or advancing our understanding of a topic or satisfying our curiosities.

In 2019, I read Nina Freudenberger's décor book *Bibliostyle*, and each profiled an individual's story of welcoming books into their home strengthened my motivation to create a cozy reading nook in Le Papillon. Novelist Jonathan Safran Foer recommends having "a comfortable chair, good light — these things do put you into a state of mind to better absorb ideas," and business owner Roman Alonso described his love for his reading nook, a shelf-filled room that includes a daybed, a colorful assortment of books and records, and other unique pieces of art: "I love spending time in my reading nook at home, beneath all my books, looking through them for inspiration. They are like old friends to me, and I miss them when I don't visit them." I became even more excited to snuggle up more often, carve out time more regularly, and lose all track of the passing minutes and hours. Such moments are not only invigorating but offer a grounding from which to spring forth toward a new dream or idea or to simply savor the goodness that already is, which reading makes us appreciate more fully.

Perhaps in the upcoming days you will be able to find some time to read, or perhaps you will be inspired to more often carve out time during your everyday routine to read in your favorite nook. However you welcome reading into your life, may it spark the ideas that are waiting to be revealed. And may you find comfort, calm, and absolute joy every time you snuggle in to read.

Petit plaisir If you are a gardener, continue to deadhead any roses to encourage them to bloom throughout the summer. After a rose plant's first blooming, give it its second feeding of the year.

Explore further thesimplyluxuriouslife.com/july10 (reading and curiosity: reading nook décor inspiration)

July 11
Waterfall Moments

Fly off to France and find [your] waterfall.

—Ruth Reichl

Food writer Ruth Reichl's comment, in the introduction to *At Elizabeth David's Table: Classic Recipes and Timeless Kitchen Wisdom*, was inspired by David's French food writing and how it inspired Reichl to travel to expand her understanding of food and life. It is a funny thing about France. Especially if you have a fondness for the gastronomically revered Gallic country, it brings to the surface truths about ourselves of which we may not have been fully aware.

In the quote above, Reichl is referring to a passage written by David that includes a description of music provided by a "convenient waterfall" as she and a few friends enjoy a lakeside picnic in the south of France. Unplanned, but appreciated. Beyond her control, yet observed and savored.

Elizabeth David famously and successfully used the vehicle of recipes and foods that were less formulaic and more free-form to engross the reader into the pleasures of what food can be and should be — something that elevates the everyday, and that, however fleeting, is deeply appreciated.

However, your waterfall and my waterfall will be unique to each of us. The waterfall in question is not something we can pre-plan and map out to lead us to the desired destination.

During the summer of 2019, my waterfall moment took me to France unexpectedly, following an invitation from Susan Herrmann Loomis to be a student in her cooking class in Louviers. During my trip, my connection with France deepened even more. A subtle boost of confidence for certain life decisions lying just out of my sight line gave me the courage to say yes to purchasing Le Papillon only two weeks after my return from this trip.

Our "waterfall," our bliss point of true contentment, has everything to do with saying yes and soaking up every last drop of the experience. Then, upon fully taking in all that was offered, we are more privy, more prepared, more clear and open to the next waterfall, so that we can fully appreciate it and be grateful for its intersection with our life's journey.

If someone had asked me twenty years ago to describe what my life journey would entail, what I would have the chance to do and experience, and where I would have the opportunity to live, I would not have had the vision or the foresight to consider an answer.

France and my trip to Devon have presented me with many waterfall moments during my handful of trips. In those moments, I reassured myself that I may not have explicitly dreamed about my journey decades ago, but somehow, through trusting the guidance of waterfall moments, I have created a life that I am thankful to have the opportunity to savor.

Choose to savor the waterfall moments that present themselves to you. Say yes, and be wholly present. When you do, you are in many ways saying yes to the dance that is asking you to participate. You may not know all the moves, but somehow you can figure out the rhythm, because it is a rhythm that comes from within and feels magically natural.

Petit plaisir Enjoy breakfast on your patio or porch, or near an open window. Let birdsong be your soundtrack, or tune in, as I do at this time of year, to the latest match at Wimbledon.

Explore further thesimplyluxuriouslife.com/july11 (Paris or the French countryside? A beautiful dilemma)

July 12
Trust the Timing of Your Journey

Dreams we have as a child, dreams we pack in a box for college, dreams you unpack when you move into your first apartment, who you'll meet, where you'll work, who you'll fall in love with. Think you have it all figured out? Life has better ideas. A bigger imagination takes bigger chances than someone like me a year ago moving through her forties in a cloud of old ideas. Life gives you more than you thought but maybe not in the package you expected. It's deeper than that. It's what you need underneath the want. It gives you what you can't breathe without. So go ahead and plan; just know when all your scheming, and planning, and hoping is done, life plans back.
—the character Diana from the TV series *Younger*

To this day, I do not know when visiting France — even just the simple idea of crossing the ocean to see a foreign country — crossed my mind. All I know is that when I called off my wedding at age twenty (a decision I now think of in terms of "What was I thinking if I wanted to live a full life?"), an unconscious reason (along with many others) was that, if married, I would never be able to visit Paris. (To be clear, I can only speak for myself and my own personal journey.)

It was not the fault of my well-meaning, yet naïve would-be-husband, but there came a point at which I said, I am not placing my dreams in the hands of anyone but myself.

Granted, yes, Paris was far too romanticized in my mind, as I quickly learned, but the realization that getting married at that point would negate the possibility of seeing the City of Light acted as a dog whistle: an attention grabber that woke me up and would help take me on a life journey that would surpass any dreams I could have imagined.

Six months after calling off the wedding, in the middle of my third year of college, I was checking in for my first flight to Paris to study in Angers for a summer quarter. Fast-forward twenty years to nearly the day, and if my younger self had told me I would have made five trips by the age of forty to the gastronomical capital of the world, I would have asked who you were talking about.

Life indeed seems to have better ideas, as the quote above suggests, and no, it will not arrive in the package we expect. Case in point: Each time I have traveled to France, I have flown alone, and in one instance, I traveled to spend time with an ex-boyfriend. But that's how life stepped in and revealed it had better ideas and offered (and continues to offer) what I *needed* that resides underneath the *want*.

My travels to Europe (at that point, primarily to France) have relentlessly nudged me, quite firmly at times, to blossom. I have discovered more about my truest and most sincere passions, predilections, and capabilities by traveling on my own and contrary to how and why my younger self imagined I would be traveling.

If we look to others to bring love into our lives, we are ceding an ability we have and will always have. It does not mean that we cannot feel more love while being with or around others, but we must not begin our life journey by seeking love outside of ourselves.

Thankfully (though I now know it was unconsciously exercised), I took the responsibility upon myself to call off a walk down the aisle and figure out a way to travel to France at the age of twenty. Instead of looking to someone else to bring my life goals to fruition, I looked to myself and said, Give it a go and see what happens. Perhaps, to some, this may not seem to be much of a feat. But in the days (1999) when the internet was not available or a tool for most people, and at a time when no immediate family had traveled beyond the North American continent, it was a feat for me. And in many ways, it still is.

Embracing the gift that life wishes to give is to accept not knowing what the outcome will be. I have discovered three things: *One*, **as you take the first step, you are more capable of navigating toward a desirable outcome than you may believe.** *Two*, **the life skills you lack will be given to you to learn should you want to improve your skills to enjoy fully the life you had tailored to include someone else.** *Three*, **your "love story" is your life story — or should I say your life story is your love story. In other words, you need only look to yourself to welcome more love into your life.**

July

🍵 *Petit plaisir* Add a bounce to your step as you begin the day or rejuvenate your stride when you need energy in the afternoon by listening to George Frideric Handel's Concerto Grosso, "Alexander's Feast," Andante non presto.

🦋 *Explore further* thesimplyluxuriouslife.com/july12 (a lesson from a hot-air balloon)

July 13
Everydays to Savor

As I walked through my door upon returning home one afternoon, the sun was warm and brilliant, the boys bounced and wiggled to greet me, and the birds chirped their melodies. We took a quick tour of the neighborhood, and the warmth of the sun I felt upon my face was a priceless gift from Mother Nature as the boys alternately strutted and meandered along the sidewalk.

When the outside world seems to swirl about far too quickly, I appreciate being home, settling into the pace that I have been enjoying for many years now. On that day, I quietly expressed gratitude for all that was going well, which was abundant.

Calming classical music or leisurely classic jazz often fills the house in the evenings, while Norman rests on my feet and Oscar naps until it's time for his evening snack — *de rigueur* moments that bring a smile to my face. Living well reveals itself in such moments, which are simple and full of much to appreciate.

My time in France has taught and continues to teach me the value of such living — a slow pace, holding my attention in the present, and remembering to savor fully, but letting go so as to fully experience the next moment. Each time I return, the lesson too arrives: assessing if I have learned, then applied what was shown as I made my way around Paris and the Provence countryside, or wherever the train took me when I was once again far away from "the Hexagon," the country I love.

Remember to carry with you into your everydays and wherever you call home the wisdom of slowing down, savoring, and engaging with the gifts of the daily rituals you have consciously chosen.

🍵 *Petit plaisir* Continue to stock up or add to your candle cupboard. Whenever there is a sale on a favorite brand, I scoop up one or two and tuck them away to be enjoyed throughout the year and throughout the house.

Explore further thesimplyluxuriouslife.com/july13 (how and why to transition from busy to balanced)

July 14
Take a Risk

On this day in 1789, the storming of the Bastille (a prison and a fortress at the time) took place, marking a significant turning point in the French Revolution as the people of Paris played a role, while also taking a significant risk, in changing the course of their lives and the history of their country. In total, about 100 stormers of the Bastille lost their lives on this now celebrated day, and tens of thousands would lose their lives during the French Revolution, including King Louis XVI and his wife, Marie-Antoinette, whose reign as monarchs ended in 1792; they were sent to the guillotine for treason in 1793.

What resonates with me, primarily because of the way this date correlates to my own life events, is the courage to try, the courage to take action even when the outcome is unknown and perhaps quite risky.

Le Quatorze Juillet in 2000 became the first opportunity for me to celebrate Bastille Day in France, by enjoying the fireworks display on the banks of the Loire in the town of Angers. I watched enthralled as the explosions and bursts were set to classical compositions, and I observed how similar, yet quite different, were the culture I was raised in and the culture I was currently immersed in.

Fast-forward to 2013, and again on July 14, I stood among many other tourists, and perhaps a few Parisians who had not left for their summer holiday, on a warm summer evening on one of the bridges over the Seine, taking in the production surrounding La Tour Eiffel. I had watched the military parade, earlier that day, from my apartment after sitting outside on the terrace nibbling a morning croissant. And then in 2015, it happened to be July 14 when I arrived in Bend, my new hometown, to begin a new chapter in my life.

I honestly did not purposely select a date that would hold such significance, but the serendipity delights me still. I had accepted an offer on my house in my former town, the moving sale had wrapped up, and the movers had packed up my home the day before. There was nowhere to sleep, and the road was calling on the morning of the fourteenth to move forward to Bend.

Taking a step toward an unknown way of life can be terrifying, but it can also be electrifying, even if just a few things turn out well, and even if many don't work out for quite some time.

If you have an idea, a vision, a dream, a goal, bringing it to life will take time. It can feel at times that the universe is asking us if we truly want something — not necessarily to test us, not necessarily doubting that we can handle it, but simply to ensure that we will fully appreciate the beautiful gift and opportunity it will provide.

My move to Bend has been full of amazing moments, enabling a quality of life I love, but it has also thrown some seemingly impossible challenges my way, each of which I eventually overcame after I applied new or necessary lessons. Again, I choose to see this as the universe asking if I truly want what I seek. Not once have I wavered to wonder if taking the leap to move to Bend was a worthwhile risk. In the rearview mirror, the challenges seem small. After all, now that I have made it to Bend — which at the time seemed more than just risky, and perhaps foolish — working through what life presents as I move forward, while it may be difficult at times, is something I can and have already proven I can work through.

Bastille Day involved great risk taking; it was a day full of chaos, but one that jump-started a movement of liberation, enabling a city and country beloved by millions around the world to evolve into what it is in our 21st century — by no means perfect, but oh so truly magnificent.

How about you? In what ways have you taken chances, big risks without knowing what the outcome would be? Or a better question: What risk do you want to take but haven't yet — and why?

Petit plaisir Make plans to celebrate *Le Quatorze Juillet* (Bastille Day). In 2021 I enjoyed getting together with a good friend, contributing herbed *gougères*, and savoring a long evening that drifted well into the night.

Explore further thesimplyluxuriouslife.com/july14 (twenty-four ways to celebrate *Le Quatorze Juillet*)

July 15
Everyday Routines and Rituals

One of the facts of human life is that it is short in relation to history, but it is also full, extraordinary, and constantly checking in to see if we have learned the lessons we have been given.

In other words, life is constantly asking you to appreciate the simple, everyday moments — not to rush them, because, soon enough, your life will have changed or morphed (whether you want it to or not), and if you have put into practice the art of living in the present moment, you will reflect upon your past moments with fondness and be grateful you experienced them fully.

It can be hard to enjoy the now when the future we seek appears to be so much more desirable. But let's think about it for a moment. Society and the marketing masters attempt to condition each of us to seek perfection — perfect relationships, perfect clothing, perfect families, perfect bodies. You name it and we can always improve, according to our culture, but what if today is just right? If we appreciate how wonderfully everything is going right now, would we desire more? Would we toss away that friendship, relationship, job, house, etc. for a newer and at-first-glance better model?

The attitude we bring to our everyday routines, responsibilities, and rituals is ultimately what will determine our level of happiness and contentment. Sure, we can strive to improve, but if we have not learned the valuable lesson of appreciating the now, we never will find contentment, no matter what we may gain in the future.

Do not make the mistake of putting yourself on a never-ending wheel of pursuing perfection, losing sight of all that is going well today. You are not in a relationship, so what! You have a job, friends and family who love you, and hopefully your health. Make the most of these realities that many people are not fortunate enough to have. So your kids are not bringing home the grades you want. Are they respectful? Are they kind? Are they trying?

Celebrate what is going well, and I am fairly certain you will have more to appreciate when you least expect it.

Petit plaisir Get ready to delight in the French film *Queen to Play* (*Joueuse*), based on Bertina Hendrich's novel *The Chess Player* and starring Kevin Klein and Sandrine Bonnaire.

Explore further thesimplyluxuriouslife.com/july15 (stop and celebrate)

July 16
Simple Pleasures

I will forever swear that there are magical powers in a small nibble of chocolate, freshly laundered bed linens, and a book that allows you to forget the day. And whether the day was full of exactly what you wanted or was one you want to quickly erase, the comforts of home have amazing powers.

During the summer, the linen sheets line-dry out in the garden, and slipping into a freshly made bed sharing scents of the fresh summer air is a priceless luxury. I give my house a good, thorough clean and mop every other week, and each Friday or Saturday, as the workweek concludes, sprucing up the house includes fresh, clean sheets. While I may not enjoy cleaning, what I give myself is a breath of deep restoration. Knowing that each evening, and especially at the end of the workweek, my house will be tidy, I can curl up with my dogs, slip into a comfy bed, and read a book of my choosing. I give myself a soft and gentle landing to the end of the day, no matter the events that may have unfolded.

While these are a few of my favorite simple luxuries to indulge in, you no doubt have a few you can readily name off the top of your head. No matter how full our lives become, no matter how many exciting goals we are chasing, it is when we slow down regularly to enjoy our simple pleasures that everyday life becomes more complete, more fulfilling, and all the more enjoyable. After all, if we do not allow ourselves downtime regularly, we miss the opportunity to savor the lives we have created for ourselves.

Take a moment to find your breath, sit down or snuggle in, and just revel in the life you have created up until this point. You most likely are not finished chasing your treasured dreams, but I am confident you are well on your way. And along that way, savor a chocolate truffle . . . regularly.

Petit plaisir Grow a single tomato plant in a terra-cotta pot (or many, but each plant in its own pot), add a bamboo stake to give it support as it grows, and create your own kitchen garden. In August and September, you will have tomatoes for days!

Explore further thesimplyluxuriouslife.com/july16 (simple + small = a grand and full life)

July 17
Savor Every Day

Every day is a journey. And the journey itself is home.
—Matsuo Basho

In early July each year, watching Wimbledon becomes a daily ritual for me to savor. All of its volleying and grunting play in the background on my television as I go about my day.

There is something to savor about annual events, gatherings, and dates of recognition. From birthdays to anniversaries, dates of commemoration, and especially personal anniversaries of note in your own life journey, recognizing and enjoying such events is a treat that strengthens our appreciation.

Perhaps we can take a lesson from these occasions, savoring more of what is lovely, enjoyable, and tranquil, reveling in the everyday moments that make us smile, that are going well, and that make our days all the more comfortable.

A few moments I have been reveling in since summer began are morning visits from new hummingbirds that have found the feeder outside my kitchen window. I watch them with delight as I lounge with the boys on the porch at the perfect late-morning time for soaking up the rays of the summer sun. Likewise, I take great enjoyment in just waking up in the morning and hearing the birdsong, taking the boys outside, picking up the paper, and waiting for my teakettle to sing — simple everyday things that are truly luxurious each time I experience them.

I hope you have many of these moments in your everydays as well. The simple life is a truly luxurious life if you are present, if you take the time to cultivate what works for you, establish a routine, a strong, healthy state of mind, and a community that revolves around such appreciation. May your everydays be grand, and may you even have to pinch yourself from time to time.

Petit plaisir Listen to Antonio Vivaldi's Concerto for Diverse Instruments in C Major, RV 558, to add a confident boost of joy and direction to your day.

Explore further thesimplyluxuriouslife.com/july17 (the Importance of a daily routine and how to create one you love)

July 18
Cherry Harvest

I listened to the music of John Coltrane as the summer afternoon heat was tempered by a gentle breeze. It was the middle of July, during my first summer in Le Papillon, and the cherries were nearly past their prime for harvesting. I had enjoyed a *clafoutis aux cerises* days before and wanted to enjoy more this fall and winter, so I set about harvesting the rest of the crop to pit and freeze.

July

The two trees provided a small bucketful of tart sweetness; it took only thirty minutes or so to complete the harvest.

On the day of the harvest, my seven-year old neighbor had stopped by to say hi to Norman and ended up sitting with me on my porch swing as we talked about cherries. As we swung away, she strengthened her prowess at ejecting the pit from her mouth, and she fed Norman a cherry here and there as well. It was a wonderful way to pass a weekend afternoon with no plans, and knowing I had at least done one task that was productive — the harvesting — made the leisure all the sweeter.

From simple seasonal tasks in the garden to regular weeding, creating outdoor spaces that offer both comfort and functionality (this entry was written while I was swinging) are simple luxuries that elevate the everyday tasks of my slower pace of life. British master gardener Gertrude Jekyll agreed about the value of such basic tasks: "Weeding is a delightful occupation, especially after summer rain, when the roots come up clear and clean. One gets to know how many and various are the ways of weeds — as many almost as the moods of human creatures."

As I swing, whether in the morning as the sun is rising or as the day is winding down and neighbors are heading home or setting out for an evening of fun, one of the boys (Norman) lounges at the top of the steps, and Oscar lies down for another nap on the rug near my feet. The birds feast at their café, and the cherry tree leaves sway ever so slightly.

Our days need not be full of tasks from dawn until slumber. In the evening, write three tasks you want to complete by the end of the day tomorrow on a notepad on your desk, table, or bedside table. Yep, only three. Let yourself tend to each task with full attention, and even if you only finish one by the day's end, find your "swing" and a friendly companion, and just let go of time and savor the life you are so fortunate to live.

Petit plaisir Harvest some cherries or pick up a bag at the market. Find a quality pitter and spend an hour or two pitting them. Freeze most to enjoy during the autumn or winter, then bake two reserved cups in a *clafoutis*.

Explore further thesimplyluxuriouslife.com/july18 (recipe for *clafoutis aux cerises* — cherry *clafoutis*)

July 19
Difficult Times

A week of concluding and beginning anew. A week of celebration and moments of tears. A week of ordinary that equates to extraordinary living. In order to step forward into a new chapter, goodbyes must be exchanged, no matter how wonderful the memories have been. Often it feels as though life is a seesaw, and we are merely along for the ride, but if we look closely, we have a larger influence and effect than we might imagine.

How we move forward in each of our days foretells the outcome down the road, and how we respond to events that are out of our control predicts whether the future will improve.

There will be weeks when, while I may wear a smile most of the time, bouts of frustration wiggle their way in, even if for just a moment. However, what I have recognized in myself during weeks such as this is growth. Because I have the awareness to acknowledge the good and detect the unwanted, not letting the latter remain longer than it must, and while life's challenges may be weighty, I am now better prepared than ever to handle what is presented to me. Had such moments of quandary arisen years ago, I would have had a different response, but as I apply the lessons, the outcomes improve.

Life continues to challenge us, as if to question whether we have learned the lesson. The good news is that you are capable of being prepared for the unexpected tests that come along the way. So long as you learn from the many opportunities you are given, in both frustrating and good times, you will be just fine and able to traverse through to the other side, where life is even more sweet than you might have imagined.

Petit plaisir Set aside a couple of nights and enjoy the French comedy series *Dix Pour Cent* (*Call My Agent*).

Explore further thesimplyluxuriouslife.com/july19 (why not . . . celebrate the obstacles?)

July 20
Make Room for Everyday Pleasures

One of the things I most love to do when I have free time is to read. I have a feeling this may be the same for some of you as well.

Making room for more such moments has guided me for quite some time. When I am determined to make time — to say no a bit more to things that may not be necessary or may cause me to be pulled in too many directions, ultimately reducing the quality time I spend doing the things I love — the choosing becomes easier, the design of my days richer and more fulfilling,

When I read, I never feel alone. Whether it is a book or an intriguing opinion piece, I have taught myself not to look at the clock because it will only be a reminder of how little time I have left to swim in the sea of well-crafted words, thoughts, and inspirational ideas. In fact, I have removed all blatant clock faces from my living room and bedroom in order to nurture the act of presence. Isn't that the wonderful gift of a hobby — to entertain your mind and your time in such a beneficial and enlightening way that you shut out everything else?

My garden porch often draws me, and I plop into my lounge chair, prop my feet up on the ottoman, and while away an hour or so just reading, letting the sounds of the birds swooping to and fro from the bird feeder to their roosts in the nearby pine and juniper trees play in the background. (A nap may happen during this time as well.) No clocks are present in this outdoor space, which makes it all the more special, keeping me fully in the present moment and letting my mind be held by the words on the page.

The key to enjoying anything is to make it feel like a luxury. Find a comfortable chair, enjoy a cup of your favorite tea, and play light music in the background. Be sure to do whatever you need to do to make the experience all the more pleasurable, so that you will want to carve out time each day or weekend to do so. It is worth it, and the benefits are tremendous.

Petit plaisir Tidy up an outdoor space to enjoy a meal al fresco. If you like French patio furniture, seek out Fermob for a variety of designs, be patient for your favorite color to become available, and then sit on your porch or patio or balcony, imagining yourself in the Jardin du Luxembourg or the Jardin des Tuileries.

Explore further thesimplyluxuriouslife.com/july20 (the definition of true luxury)

July 21
Make the Choice to Act

Sometimes it feels as though too many choices are a bad thing: from which vacation rental to reserve to which books to read to which thoughts to entertain. However, the fact that you have choices is an indicator that you have control over your life. And that is a very fortunate thing and one worth celebrating, no?

As I planned my 2018 summer holiday in France, I became, at first, perplexed by the multitude of options — where to stay, when to go where, what to do — but then I reminded myself that planning so far in advance was giving me the opportunity to have options, and that was something for which to be thankful.

The worry of what choice to make may cast a shadow in our minds when we are presented with a plethora of options. As I thought about this, I was reminded of something Barry Schwartz shared in his book *The Paradox of Choice*: "When asked about what they regret most in the last six months, people tend to identify actions that didn't meet expectations. But when asked about what they regret most when they look back on their lives as a whole, people tend to identify failures to act."

Robert Frost's poem "The Road Less Traveled" is open to many interpretations; one perspective is the realization that when you take one path you literally cannot take another, and quite plainly, that makes all the difference — which is neither good or bad. It just is, and it is up to each of us to make the most of the journey we have chosen. So here's to the journey: May we forever put one step in front of the other, to savor what we discover and not be discouraged to the point of stagnation.

Give whatever it is that you are entertaining a try, at least a shot. Allow yourself the chance to experience what you are curious about instead of turning away from all the options because you feel overwhelmed. If you have to, narrow them down to a handful, and then just select, letting the selecting ease your mind, as you have solidified your decision by taking action.

Petit plaisir Designate a favorite cup and saucer solely for your morning routine. In the summer, before work or the events of the day, give yourself time to sit, sip, and savor — whether outside on a porch swing or a patio chair, or indoors in a cozy armchair, gazing outside. Somehow, take in Mother Nature.

Explore further thesimplyluxuriouslife.com/july21 (action — take the first step)

July 22
Bravely Saying Goodbye

"If you're brave enough to say goodbye, life will reward you with a new hello." With these words, novelist Paulo Coehlo held my emotions in his hand, as I had been awash in feelings upon leaving Pendleton, the eastern Oregon town I had called home for nine years, and settling into my rental in Bend.

While I wholeheartedly (and then some) wanted to move to Bend, the long goodbye took its toll. It was perhaps necessary, as life made sure that I appreciated all that I had experienced during my years in Pendleton, the relationships I had built there, and the time I had been given.

For anyone who is contemplating moving, starting fresh, taking a leap, but is perhaps holding back because you think it is too late, you have invested too much where you are, let me say that, as I drove into Bend and the storm clouds and rain greeted me (have I mentioned I am a lover of rain?), I knew I was home. It may be hard to appreciate or understand, as I was not able to sleep in my actual bed for a few more nights, but in a weird way that I had not deciphered at that time, I knew I had arrived where I was meant to be.

The acts of bravery in each of our lives will be as unique as our fingerprints. For me, one brave act was fully embracing a life I love living, though I had seen no one in my family do the same. I left a secure job I could have worked in steadily until retirement, but I would not have been living true to who I was. After much reflection and contemplation, if you will be honest with yourself and listen to your inner yearnings, you will know what your bravery will entail.

And then at some unexpected, seemingly quotidian moment, you will know, without consideration or hesitation, what to do without any other vote of confidence than your intuition.

The reason the word *bravery* is synonymous with *courage* is that we often do not know what the outcome will be when we choose to act. So long as you have done your homework — taken the time to get to know yourself — you will know when you need to be brave. Get to know yourself. When you do, you set yourself on the path to living life to your fullest potential.

Petit plaisir If you enjoyed French actress Camille Cottin in *Call My Agent*, watch the film *Le Mystère Henri Pick*, in which she stars.

Explore further thesimplyluxuriouslife.com/july22 (the gift of starting over)

July 23
Daily Routines

The daily routines we put into place have the power to enhance or deflate how we feel when we wake up, when we go to bed, and everything in between. While reading an article summarizing David Buettner's successful book about how to attain happiness, *Thrive: Finding Happiness in the Blue Zones*, I began to see a lovely pattern. My journey to purposefully improve the quality of my life through conscious decisions and paying attention to the everyday routines, connections, and thoughts that run through my mind was playing a crucial part in improving the quality of my life.

Some of the changes David Buettner proposes will take time (for example, finding the town that is the best fit for you), but others can occur in a day (for example, do you have a pride spot in your home — a place where those you love and the accomplishments you are proud of are displayed so you can be reminded of what is going well?).

Your life is yours to mold into what works for you. If something is not working, do not assume you will just have to get used to it. No, you do not. It may take some deep investigating and further understanding as to how to make the necessary change, but it is possible.

Your life is yours. Live with intention. Not only will your life become more fulfilling and enjoyable to live each and every day, but you will inspire those around you to enjoy their everydays as well and make the most of the life they have been given.

Petit plaisir The next time you visit Paris, visit Parc des Buttes-Chaumont, but until then, the French candle company Kerzon makes a scent inspired by this 60-acre park. It is one of my favorites.

Explore further thesimplyluxuriouslife.com/july23 (six ways and reasons to establish a daily routine)

July 24
Routines Allow Everyday Savoring

One of my most beloved parts of the day is morning. Feeling reenergized and having a refreshed mind full of ideas waiting to be executed is a magical feeling. However, when the afternoon rolls around, I am usually quite drained; shifting to certain activities benefits this lull in my mental focus, enabling me to recharge.

Each of us has a body clock that runs in its own unique way, but regardless of whether you are bounding from bed in the morning or revved up when the evening unfolds, there most likely is a lull, at some point, when you are not feeling at your peak.

Ever since I can remember, just after lunch and for a few hours, I often need to sit down, catch my breath, and just relax. If I am able to take a nap in the afternoon when I feel this way, I take it. Now that my work schedule is my own, I take naps when my body tells me it needs it, and the latter half of the day becomes far more positive, productive, and enjoyable. While seemingly simple, just these fifteen or twenty minutes can be quite powerful. If I have a full hour, I toss in a leisurely walk or read a book or peruse a magazine.

When we become in tune with the language of our body, we are better able to care for it and respect it, and it will reward us in turn. We cannot go at Mach 80 for the entire day, every day and expect our bodies won't show wear and tear. They will, and we will then be forced to comply by slowing down, usually when we are least able.

Instead of waiting for your body to put on the brakes, take a preventive measure this weekend. Assess what you need for your body and your mind to perform at their best. If you listen carefully, you will be able to discern precisely what you need. All you have to do is take the time to listen.

Petit plaisir As a reminder to explore the countryside of France and its many wonderful towns and villages, watch Diane Lane star in Eleanor Coppola's *Paris Can Wait*.

Explore further thesimplyluxuriouslife.com/july24 (the importance of deliberate rest)

July 25
Challenges

Sometimes the challenges presented in life are opportunities that push us to grow in ways we may not have initially desired or believed we were capable of. The good news is that when we respond in a positive way, we improve the quality of our lives.

I have learned how to properly pronounce the infamous wind in Provence — the *mistral* (mi STRAL); it blows out of the northwest from southern France into the northern Mediterranean. Most common in winter and spring, it can be quite cold and strong, with sustained winds often above 40 mph. However, during the summer months (the only time of year I had been in France as of 2019), the mistral breezes (nothing beyond gentle when I've been around) have been absolutely refreshing. When the temperatures tiptoe into the nineties, the afternoons are quite sultry, but when the mistral breezes begin, my breath deepens in appreciation as they ease some of the sweat and exhaustion away. The mistral helps explain the unusually sunny climate and clear air of Provence.

While we may wish for steadiness and calm, sometimes we need a little friction, a little nudge in order to reach a true and effective balance in our lives. Most of us are in perpetual motion, and maintaining a balance is a daily act, but too much comfort or too much of a constant challenge can either dull the senses and cause us to be unappreciative or wear us down and make it difficult to rise. And while yes, the mistral winds can be devastating, so too can our lives run up against painful experiences. And in those instances, we look around, we work with others, and we rise. We strive forward to build something new, but with knowledge gained from experience.

The next time you run up against a little snag — maybe you burned the chicken you were barbecuing or maybe the balance in your checking account is running too low for you to enjoy life as you wish — take such disappointing moments as an opportunity to regain your balance, to check in, to assess and remind yourself of what is going well, what can be improved, and how good your life truly is.

You don't want to reach a point in your life when it would take a monstrous obstacle to remind you how fortunate you have been. If you will celebrate and appreciate today, find the opportunity in what is given, the universe will provide you with more goodness.

Petit plaisir Gaze at the color of the ceilings in your home. Do they work as well as they could? Ceiling color can brighten or darken, complement or distract. Simply apply a couple of coats of paint, and in a matter of a day, you can elevate a room.

Explore further thesimplyluxuriouslife.com/july25 (find your gumption)

July 26
Doing Your Best

There are many suggestions for how to best live one's life; lessons seem to be everywhere based on each person's experience. One of the best lessons for anyone — no matter what you believe, where you live, or who you spend your time with — is to do your best and then let go.

Often the reason we are unable to be present in the moment is that we are digesting, rehashing, and analyzing a past situation. When we are not present, we are robbing ourselves of the beauty that is all around us.

One of the first lessons in Jamie Cat Callan's book *Bonjour, Happiness* teaches the importance of the ability to become lost in moments — moments that will never occur exactly the same way again and that provide us with true wealth and rich lives. Unfortunately, many of us allow our attention to wander while we are with someone; we may walk down a street where fresh spring flowers have just bloomed and literally not see them, not realizing what is there to enjoy.

In order to follow the mantra of doing your best in the moment and then letting go, focus more on quality and less on multi-tasking. That will enable you to focus all of your attention, and thus your best efforts, on the task at hand. Once you know that you did your best in a particular moment, you can let it go without regret. And that is what will help you live more fully, feel more contented, and appreciate the rich life you have created for yourself.

Petit plaisir When you need a gentle boost to your step, perhaps in the latter half of the workday, listen to Johann Heinichen's Concerto no. 7 in G Major, S. 214.

Explore further thesimplyluxuriouslife.com/july26 (two secrets to living a life of quality)

July 27
Change and Growth

Those kinds of trips are memorable because they're part of you as a young person trying to discover what your place in the world is.
—Barack Obama, on the power of travel (his first trip to Europe, age twenty)

In order for any one of us to change and grow, we must be willing to step forward into arenas and circumstances that are unknown to us. Doing this can cause us to feel both excitement and fear, and even though I always plan extensively for my trips to France, there are usually moments of uncertainty, but I keep stepping forward, addressing the hiccups that arise with the determination to make it through as well as I can in order to continue to progress.

So too can you step into a new world, take a new direction, try a new strategy, even when you do not know how it will work out. One of the keys to your success is to have a drive and/or passion that is stronger than fear so that your curiosity outweighs your worry.

There is energy in curiosity, fuel in wanting to find out what you can reach, achieve, and attain when you strike out in an unknown direction. When you tap into this energy, you learn new things not only about the world you are exploring but about yourself or things you were not convinced were true until events showed you differently.

Petit plaisir Let Monty Don take you on a tour in *Monty Don's French Gardens* TV series.

Explore further thesimplyluxuriouslife.com/july27 (how to be brave: follow your "this" to live the life you have dreamed about)

July 28
Looking Forward to Monday

What would you do with your daily routine if you could make all of the rules?

This is not a hypothetical question. Give it some honest, serious contemplation, and then write down a description of a daily routine that would excite you so much you would be glad to wake up, even on Mondays. Think of a routine that would enable you to be productive, ensure you are healthy and active, but also leave you smiling at the end of the day as you drift off to sleep.

On a recent Monday, I was giddy. Why? I began, as I do each summer, my self-generated ideal daily schedule. I was exuberant, the way a child may be on the night before their birthday, as I tucked myself into bed Sunday night. Finding what it is you love doing, finding what you are passionate about, is the fuel you need in order to do what is necessary each and every day, over and over again, and to do so with sincere exhilaration.

What would you do with your daily routine if you could make all the rules? Begin with one or two small changes to shift your routine from a dream to the reality you have an opportunity to experience each and every day. Maybe it is as simple as delegating one chore to lighten your schedule, or maybe it is as grand as contemplating a move to a town that will shorten your commute and give you more time to do what you love.

July

You can cultivate a life you now may only dream of. First, have clarity of vision, and then devise the small steps that will get you to each needed stepping-stone as you take off in the right direction.

Petit plaisir Pause during your day. Step outside. Turn your face to the sky, close your eyes, and take in the luscious fresh scent and soak up the warmth of the summer day.

Explore further thesimplyluxuriouslife.com/July28 (ten ways to make Monday a day to get excited about — every week)

July 29
Rituals

The first bite into a delicate, buttery croissant, the crisp page turned in a new book, the aroma of a savory meal cooking on the stove top, and the tickle of freshly cut grass between your toes. Such simple pleasures, especially when you experience them after a long or difficult day, can bring immense happiness and delight.

We can become so wrapped up in our everyday worries and demands that we forget how easily we can welcome a moment of pleasure into our routine. Daily, weekly, or monthly rituals to look forward to are the frosting on a balanced, yet productive everyday life.

Whether it is cooking a basic meal with high-quality ingredients in the middle of the week (for example, a simple, scrumptious burger) or planning a massage to be enjoyed on the first day of the month to set a refreshed, relaxed tone, incorporating seemingly indulgent pleasures is mandatory for being your best self at work and around those you love.

Petit plaisir If you love France, art, and a cozy mystery, watch *L'Art du Crime* ("The Art of Crime") on the MHz Choice streaming service for international drama series.

Explore further thesimplyluxuriouslife.com/july29 (six cosy French mystery series to watch)

July 30
Find Contentment

In actuality, misery is a moment of suffering allowed to become everything.
—Mark Nepo

How are you doing?

It is a seemingly benign question, but when we ask it in our current times — the Covid-19 pandemic, political turmoil, the threats we face from climate change — it can be an important one and an expression of caring for those around us, in our neighborhood, community, country, and world. So again, from me to you, how are you doing? I do hope you are well and are letting yourself feel what you need to feel, but also moving through the many crises we face in a constructive way.

As I think about the isolation we have had to undergo during the pandemic, I feel that each of us will have become more appreciative of things in our daily lives that we were prevented from enjoying. I cannot just go to France or England whenever my budget or schedule allows, and that sits heavy with me and makes me more fully appreciate that once I had that ability. I also miss the hugs and sitting close to those I love or care deeply about.

But much good came out of the limitations imposed by the pandemic. I met more of my neighbors, as almost all of us were at home and frequently out walking in the neighborhood and getting to know each other better.

The stress of the pandemic has been real and unique. Even if you are like me and feel as though you have been preparing for this situation your entire life without realizing it (I thoroughly enjoy my home and yard and am an introvert), knowing you are confined and your freedom to do as you please is curtailed is unconsciously mentally taxing. However, this is when our ability to think about each other, as well as our own well-being, is tested, and we do what is best so that we can move back into the life we love with those we love. In some cases, we may realize what we can do to improve what we thought was the way we had to go about living.

So long as we do not let ourselves slip into misery, focusing on one event or tragedy that becomes the entirety of our perspective, we lift ourselves up and help ourselves progress through whatever may be unwanted, frightening, or hard to fathom. Find what is working. As Mark Nepo instructs, "Look wider than what hurts."

Finding contentment within yourself means recognizing a formidable foundation that will help to elevate you in the most trying and frustrating times. And when you do find your inner contentment, you will become more present in the moment, worry less about what

will come, and have more confidence that whatever will come, you will be able to handle it well.

Petit plaisir Find five minutes in your day to sit and be still. Listen to Ludovico Einaudi's "The Days". Then, play it one more time.

Explore further thesimplyluxuriouslife.com/july30 (unwanted moments reveal what is needed)

July 31
Lesson from an Old Copper Teakettle

Trees that are slow to grow bear the best fruit.

— Molière

I have burnt up three kettles in my history of loving tea, a mere eighteen years. There was not a fire or any big catastrophe, but I can become quite engrossed in projects, and sometimes, when I have neglected to close the spout of the kettle, which enables it to whistle, I would remember, but too late, to return to the kitchen. There are reasons electric teakettles, with automatic shutoff, are common worldwide and becoming more so in the United States: They make good sense.

But do I have an electric teakettle in my house? Nope. I always seek out the whistle and the large handle with the kettle *sans* cord. It does not make sense, but for my home, I love a traditional kettle. So after my Le Creuset teakettle became too damaged to use, I took a few months off from seeking out a new one, as I had quickly done in the past with the click of a button or two, boiled my water in a saucepan, and took a deep breath.

Six months later, I still did not have a teakettle and did not have specific plans to shop for one, until I arrived in Provence in 2018 for the first time and, on my first full day in Vaison-la-Romaine, stumbled across a *brocante* market (a French antiques market) in the town square and saw copper seemingly everywhere.

First, I came across a stunning large copper teakettle that was perfectly refurbished, dent-free, and with a price tag of upward of €700. I asked the seller again, convinced I had confused my French numbers in translation. Nope. I had heard her correctly — *sept cents*. I admired from a short distance, snapped a photo, and kept shopping.

And then I saw the in-need-of-much-care copper teakettle that would eventually make its way onto the plane as my carry-on. After a bit of bartering and handing over €35, my treasure found its new owner.

The Road to Le Papillon

In a matter of weeks, I found a retinning company, Oregon Retinners, in Hubbard, Oregon. I trusted my teakettle, which embodied the memories, the journey, and the growth from my trip in France, to strangers. I was told it would be about six weeks before it would return. I put the length of time out of my mind, pulled out my saucepan to boil water for my tea, and tried to forget about not having my new kettle in my house.

One hundred and forty dollars and approximately eight weeks later (the price included shipping), the kettle arrived home. It was akin to welcoming a child after a long absence or returning home myself after a long excursion. A small piece had been gone, out of reach, in unknown hands, but it had clearly been in good hands as the brilliance of the retinner's magic was reflected in my shiny "new" teakettle.

For approximately $200, the teakettle I had hoped for but almost accepted I would never find, one that would be able to tolerate me (copper heats up quickly, unlike my previous kettles, so forgetting I have a kettle on the stove is all but negated), found me and gained my attention. Now the teakettle in my house holds many stories, something my previous teakettles did not.

The explorer tends to find the treasures, but in order to find them, we must be open to unexpected gifts crossing our paths. We also must know ourselves well enough to judge when to appreciate from afar and when to engage. Waiting on the sidelines for anything we wish to materialize does not work, but neither does forcing something to happen. It is a tricky conundrum or an exquisite truth about life: We have to engage, yet let go, in order to find the beauty that life wishes to share with us. Both actions can cause fear, but Ralph Waldo Emerson reminds, "Unless you try to do something beyond what you have already mastered, you will never grow."

My trust in my journey deepened when the teakettle finally arrived home to stay, and I could not make my first cup of tea quickly enough.

Choose to grow beyond what you have already mastered, and who knows what treasures you will find.

Petit plaisir Melons wrapped with prosciutto. That's it. That's all. Oh! Sprinkle with some flaky sea salt, and pair with a glass of rosé.

Explore further thesimplyluxuriouslife.com/july31 (the butterfly moment in life: don't wait, just live well)

August

Be Playful as You Create and Explore

August

Cooking is the art of adjustment.
—Jacques Pepin

Dining with Julia Child quickly leaped to the top of my most memorable food explorations, even though it was only dining at the same restaurant — La Couronne — in Rouen, France, that sparked her appreciation and love for French cuisine.

Julia's first meal at the restaurant, which now pays homage to her in their dining room, occurred on Wednesday, November 3, 1948 — a dining experience that she described as "the most exciting meal of my life."

Here, from her memoir *My Life in France*, is her description of her first French meal, with her husband Paul Cushing Child, at La Couronne, after docking on the northern shores of France hours before:

> At twelve-thirty we Flashed into Rouen. [The Blue Flash was the couple's Buick station wagon.] We passed the city's ancient and beautiful clock tower, and then its famous cathedral, still pockmarked from battle but magnificent with its stained-glass windows. We rolled to a stop in the Place du Vieux Marché, the square where Joan of Arc had met her fiery fate. There the *Guide Michelin* directed us to Restaurant La Couronne ("The Crown"), which had been built in 1345 in a medieval quarter-timbered house. Paul strode ahead, full of anticipation, but I hung back, concerned that I didn't look chic enough, that I wouldn't be able to communicate, and that the waiters would look down their long Gallic noses at us Yankee tourists.

The menu Paul and Julia enjoyed has been shared many times, but it is important to consider it here:

- A half-dozen oysters on the half-shell, served with pale rye bread, with a spread of unsalted butter.
- *Sole meuniere* — Dover sole browned in butter sauce and topped with chopped parsley.
- A bottle of Pouilly-Fumé, a wonderfully crisp white wine from the Loire Valley.
- *Salade verte* laced with a lightly acidic vinaigrette. Julia also enjoyed her "first real baguette," as she describes it.
- Dessert of *fromage blanc*.
- A strong, dark *café filtre*.

Like many, I learned of Julia's experience at La Couronne from Nora Ephron's film *Julie & Julia*; the first scene depicted was inspired by this excerpt from Julia's memoir. The curiosity, fascination, and clear love for what she was eating is palpable in the pages, and Ephron and Meryl Streep bring it to the screen in such a way that your appetite is immediately whetted, even if you have just eaten.

It may seem silly or "touristy" to want to visit the destination of the first meal of someone you hold in high regard, but first impressions leave a mark on an individual's memory. For Julia, the meal was extraordinary, while for any French patron, it most likely was quotidian, but knowing the French and their love for food, it was most certainly appreciated and slowly savored.

The more I read about Julia Child — her memoir, the many biographies, as well as her cookbooks — the more her sincere passion for food and curiosity about the culinary world and its flavors are apparent. That she was thirty-six years old and just arrived in a country that, unbeknownst to her, would offer a life-changing opportunity, is a lesson to us all to keep following our curiosities. Refuse to throw in the towel, and continue to pursue what tickles your proclivities.

Beginning at 1:00 p.m. on Friday, July 13, 2018, I dined for more than two hours. I chatted with the head waiter, Gosé (he had worked at the restaurant for thirty years); an assistant waiter, Romain (he was a delight and happy to pose for a picture, which you will see in the video; follow this link: https://thesimplyluxuriouslife.com/august), who had worked there for three; and the hostess, Darbin, who was friendly and welcoming, sharing Julia's menu with me and answering my questions. I primarily sat, sipped a glass of champagne and then one of Chablis, and absorbed all that I could in a seemingly ordinary moment that was for me extraordinary. In that same space, seventy years ago, Julia's meal was life-changing.

Perhaps we embark on such sojourns to understand that it is not necessarily the destination that is exceptional, but the chemistry of the individual we admire, the time in their life's history in which they had to be open enough to take in what was offered, as well as the seeming ordinariness. What I continue to realize is that so long as we remain brave, so long as we do not hold on too tightly to what we think "must" happen and instead, along the way, engage with the experience and enjoy the journey, our lives will often turn out to be more grand than we might have imagined.

For me, and whether it was silly or profound, watching Ephron's film ignited a curiosity not only for blogging (the film premiered during the summer of 2009, and I founded TSLL in late 2009), but a curiosity to know the woman called Julia Child and what she loved about French cuisine.

I am thankful I had the opportunity to go, to see, to be, and, if nothing else, to understand that, as Thoreau shared in *Walden*, we can "meet with a success unexpected in common hours." In this case, it was just a Friday, and for Julia, it had been just a Wednesday; for both of us, it had merely been lunch, but oh, what a grand lunch it was. Every single bite.

Certainty evades us when we follow our curiosity, and that is a gift. Often our perspective of possibility is far too narrow to see the potential that awaits if only we would let go, step forward, and try something new that has captured our attention. Food, France, and Julia Child captured my attention as my fourth decade of life began, and my life has changed for the better ever since.

August 1
Create Your Own Recipe for Life

Recipes are a helpful tool when we are learning how to cook a new dish we have never attempted. But, like training wheels, following a recipe can hold us back from experimenting and discovering new flavor combinations once we have mastered the basics that please our palate — and even more when we muster up the courage to cook or bake by memory and engage in creative experimentation.

Recipes — ones we use in the kitchen or recipes for life, as we listen to those we love, absorb the advice of books, and look to the world around us — are important to give us options and ideas. But we should not forever adhere to someone else's recipe. Why? Because that particular recipe was made for someone else.

There is no other person like you. No other human being has genetic coding precisely like yours, nor was anyone else born, raised, and shaped by the events, people, and conversations that have formed you as you have walked your journey thus far through life.

Consider all of the elements mentioned above as the ingredients and yourself as the cook. The *pièce de résistance* will be the outcome when you take on the challenge of making sense of the magic that resides within you.

Petit plaisir A new month, a deep breath to take in all the possibility. Upon listening to Georg Philip Telemann's Flute Quartet in G, TWV 43 G10, there seems to be even more possibility to seize. Be sure to listen to the third movement, Vivace.

Explore further thesimplyluxuriouslife.com/august1 (how to set yourself free)

August 2
Favorite Foods

My first taste of sweet, luscious lemon-meringue pie began my lifelong love affair with pies and tarts. As a child, my first concoction in the kitchen was a crust I made myself, and I can remember having a picture taken, posing with my very own handmade lemon meringue masterpiece (well, at least to me it was).

Similar to tasting something that you immediately fall head over heels in love with is the feeling when you experience a taste of the life you desire to live. It may be visiting a new city that just speaks to you, causing you to realize, then and there, that you will someday call it home. It could be interning in a particular field of study and becoming mesmerized by its energy and captivated by your ambition, ultimately studying for a degree that will allow you to pursue a similar job.

Or maybe it is the first time you house-sit in a home that requires you to take responsibility, but at the same time revel in the comforts of a beautiful, welcoming sanctuary, prompting you to vow that someday you too will own your own home and customize it to the life you love living.

Whatever it is you taste and realize without a doubt you want to incorporate into your life, listen to the calling. Your intuition is speaking. Listen and then examine what it is saying to something inside you. Your life is speaking to you, trying to lead you to where and what you should be doing. Trust it. Investigate it. And then act upon it in some way.

Petit plaisir Explore the books published by Persephone in Bath, England. I recommend *A House in the Country* (1942), by Jocelyn Playfair, to begin the exploration of their reading material.

Explore further thesimplyluxuriouslife.com/august2 (intuition and the truth about daring to take the winding trail)

August 3
Knock on the Door of Genius

Genius is the ability to renew one's emotions in daily experience.
—Paul Cézanne

August

As I stepped into my vacation rental just two miles outside of Gordes, nestled in the Provençal countryside and surrounded by vineyards, my breathing deepened, and I released a long sigh. I had no set plans for the foreseeable duration of my stay at this particular destination, so I nestled in and played as though this "home" was my own. Except, this time, my home was in Provence, specifically the Luberon region.

During my travels, it is impossible for my mind not to seek and eventually find deeper insights into what I am seeing and experiencing. Instead, I ask repeatedly, How would this experience — the feelings I am feeling, the sensations my body is comforted by — be possible to recreate when I return home. Some may say, Well, that is impossible; after all, there is only one Provence, and I would agree, and that is what makes it special.

But Provence shares its goodness with us, and for us to return to our year-round homes without taking the gifts it offers, the lessons it wishes to share, would be to negate some of the experience. In fact, we can bring aspects of the Provence way of life into our everyday routines.

Keep meals simple, yet seasonally flavorful. Pick up a small serving of dessert from a beloved *patisserie*. Take a bath on a summer afternoon when a soft breeze comes through an open window. Read in a relaxing chair with a great view. Enjoy *petit déjeuners* (breakfasts) outside on the *terrasse*, and elevate an everyday lunch with a small glass of wine and flavorful food selections. Take time to reflect on the morning and rejuvenate for the afternoon. Keep watches and clocks out of view, and let your body clock be your guide as you get lost in projects and follow your curiosity.

I agree with Paul Cézanne, a post-impressionist painter who spent much of his life in Provence: When you master savoring everyday moments and elevating your experiences, you are knocking on the door of genius.

Petit plaisir Welcome a simple bouquet of sunflowers into your home. Keep recutting the stems and refreshing the water, and they will last for weeks (especially if there are buds on the stems as well).

Explore further thesimplyluxuriouslife.com/august3 (escape to Provence and explore the above-listed items further)

August 4
Your Journey

The big, significant steps or decisions in life may not appear as such in the moment. Rather, only in hindsight do we sometimes realize how influential a seemingly small decision — taking advantage of an opportunity, listening to our intuition, or doing what made the most sense — affected the trajectory of our life.

I have been thinking about Julia Child lately, and as I reread her memoir *My Life in France*, I was reminded that she had no idea deepening her knowledge of French cuisine would lead her to write the tome revered by generations of cooks throughout America who wish to sharpen their French culinary skills. But she did listen. She listened to her intuition, to an understood need in society, and to a recognition of what she had to offer, without hesitation or someone else to lead the way.

Julia Child was a pioneer in many ways: as a cook on a successful television series; as a cookbook writer who tirelessly tested her recipes and applied careful attention to the language in her instructions so that they would assist, not confuse, the home cook; and as a woman who would chase her dreams without apology.

Julia's life story reminds us of the vital importance of investing in ourselves and our dreams. After the successful launch of *Mastering the Art of French Cooking*, coauthored with Simone Beck and Louisette Bertholle, even after they received their first royalty check, the authors were still saddled with a debt of over $600 to cover the remaining expenses of writing the book. To absorb this fact is crucial. After spending more than seven years writing, testing, rewriting again, being rejected and doubted, the authors continued to invest in what they wholeheartedly believed was beneficial to home cooks. Based on their efforts, research, and thorough attention, the remaining balance was quickly paid off. But they had to invest first.

Choosing to invest in an unknown venture at first feels risky, even foolhardy, as knowing the outcome is impossible. But, in truth, everything beyond today is unknown. Outcomes are never guaranteed, even when they are similar to past choices. What makes any foray worth the venture is how it brings you to life.

What awakens you when you merely think about the possibility? Whether it is a change to your life or the larger world and community, what excites you and points to somewhere inside you where there resides a belief that you can make a difference? To take Julia as an example, what if a French cookbook were to be written in English? Wouldn't life be all the more delicious? Choose to invest, despite the temporary roadblocks that may seem cemented into your path. They

are not, and you can navigate around them if you believe in your purpose wholeheartedly.

Petit plaisir Read Noel Riley Fitch's *Appetite for Life: The Biography of Julia Child* or *The French Chef in America: Julia Child's Second Act*, written by her nephew Alex Prud'homme.

Explore further thesimplyluxuriouslife.com/august4 (the world needs you — all of you: how not to become a commodity)

August 5
Keep Working, Despite the Unknowns

It was amazing how you could get so far from where you'd planned, and yet find it was exactly where you needed to be.

—Sarah Dessen

As a reformed planner now heeding Oliver Burkeman's advice in *Four Thousand Weeks: Time Management for Mortals*, I am letting go a bit more and letting life unfold as it will, finding the balance between being prepared and being open to life's magic; after all, as Burkeman notes, all a plan can be is "a present-moment statement of intent . . . The future, of course, is under no obligation to comply." However, I know it can be frustrating when things don't go as hoped, especially when you have invested many hours, computations, and analyses into the outcome.

Your hard work, your passion, did not go unrewarded. While it may not have worked out exactly as you had planned, something is still churning beneath the waters of what you may see as a failure. In fact, I would wager that your expectations were not unrealistic, but perhaps not big enough.

While you will not know why things did not work out immediately, most of the time, as months and years pass, if you continue to strive forward, hold your head up, and have faith, you will look back fondly on the experience. Had you not tried to accomplish it, you would not have set yourself on the path that merged with the one you were meant to be on to help you reach your dream.

Life is funny that way. It basically asks each of us to have faith in what will be, what is possible. It asks us to always put our best foot forward, to quickly assess what we can improve upon, and then move forward with something similar to blind trust. This can be frightening. It can cause nights filled with tears and questions, but if you trust yourself, if you tend to what you are doing and focus on the positive, beautiful things will materialize.

A few days ago, I read a journal entry from when I was traveling and going to school in France. It allowed me to step back into who I was at the time and realize that so much of what I now have experienced in my life were things I did not expect to happen, things I could not have even fathomed. But I kept moving forward, kept wiping away the tears, moving through the frustrations, and kept believing in myself. These moments in my youthful past, seen twenty years later, buoy my confidence that, while there will be confusions along the way, the future is not something we can predict, and that means beauty and awe await so long as we hold ourselves in the present, step out of the past, and refrain from looking too long into the future.

Sometimes it can be hard to believe that something better awaits you, but the truth is, right now is pretty awesome if only you will take responsibility for your present state and how you hold yourself in it.

Petit plaisir Make a simple roasted sweet potato salad with French lentils and spinach. Dress with a couple of tablespoons of red wine vinegar or lemon. That's all. Enjoy.

Explore further thesimplyluxuriouslife.com/august5 (recipe for sweet potato with French lentils and spinach salad)

August 6
Cooking and France

Lately, I have found considerable comfort in some noteworthy food and cooking programs, as well as cookbooks — from Samin Nosrat's docuseries *Salt, Fat, Acid, Heat* to Tuesday evening's *Chopped* series on the Food Network and Richard Olney's *Simple French Food*. More specifically, the food, the creating, the gathering, the enjoying, and the learning have grabbed my attention.

Perhaps it is just a natural extension of my life's journey and my discovery and now sharing of more food-focused posts and episodes, but I don't think I am alone.

Homemade, thoughtful meals are a means to not only nourish ourselves, but to bring loved ones together with camaraderie, goodwill, and pleasure. This is not a return to the past of traditional roles for women or men, but rather an awareness of the importance of eating well, and also being well together and not just with our families, but with the people who are in our communities, the people we work with, and the people who

August

make our lives a bit brighter. Food is powerful and a powerful means of communicating conviviality and platonic affection. A bond of recognition. A recognition of humanness.

Among the memorable parts of my trip to France during the summer of 2018 were meals I shared with those who call France home — dinners that stretched from evening into the night, a leisurely approach to time, thoughtful, playful conversations of affection for the world, food, and life. No rushing, no expectation except to enjoy the seasonal food, good wine, and the chance to enjoy being together.

Explore ideas for enjoying food with people whose company you enjoy. Be prepared with simple food when an unexpected guest drops by (I keep herb *gougères* in my freezer and place them in the oven for twenty-seven minutes when a guest arrives; by the time we have enjoyed the first glass of wine, the warm savory bites are ready to be devoured, and the conversation continues). Or organize a small dinner party just because, make time to gather. Keep it simple, express your appreciation for those you have invited with the food and drink you have prepared, and let go of time.

Petit plaisir Listen to jazz vocalist Melody Gardot's album *Sunset in the Blue*. Especially listen to "From Paris with Love." Each year, during the second full week of August, TSLL's Annual French Week takes place, and this song sets the tone well.

Explore further thesimplyluxuriouslife.com/august6 (how to plan a meal with multiple courses)

August 7
Aha Moments

In the blink of an eye, your world changes. Where once there was a blur and a lack of understanding, clarity suddenly dawns.

Oh, that is what a croissant is supposed to taste like, I think, as I take the first bite of a croissant in Paris from La Maison d'Isabelle and savor each subsequent bite and gaze at the Cathédrale Notre-Dame de Paris while sitting on a bench in the Square René Viviani.

From knowing what a good croissant is, to knowing the work that puts you in a state of flow, to distinguishing the difference between secure and insecure individuals so as to ascertain who to engage with for any relationship — when you have clarity, the trust in the direction you choose to follow becomes far less friction filled.

A valid question is *why?*, and often the answer is simple: You have reached clarity about what you wanted, gained necessary knowledge and skills you previously lacked, and now trust in yourself and those around you to have the patience to finally bring forth the desired change.

No, you did not know how it would look. No, you did not know for certain it would occur, but you kept striving forward anyway.

The moment of clarity will come not when you expect it. But even so, when you experience it, you — the doer, the believer, the one who kept striving forward — will know, without question, the reason it has appeared.

Pocket these moments, write them in your journal, imprint them in your memory because, as you continue to move forward on your journey, these moments of clarity and discovery will be a reminder and a source of calm as you go about your life, grounding you to trust that you know how to navigate your life and navigate it well.

Petit plaisir As summer winds down, the opportunity arises to take stock of your garden — what is doing well, what would complement what you have, etc. Knowing the needs and hopes for your garden, place orders now for perennials you want to plant in the fall so they can firmly establish themselves and share their beauty in the spring. The butter-yellow hue of the Julia Child shrub rose has pride of place at Le Papillon and was the first plant I put in the ground in 2019. In 2021, I chose to welcome two more; they create a soft, cheerful edge to my east-facing cottage garden.

Explore further thesimplyluxuriouslife.com/august7 (how to continue to strive forward)

August 8
Experience Pleasure, but Keep Striving Forward

The moments when you have achieved victory, have deposited the paycheck, felt the kiss of someone for the first time, or simply enjoyed your favorite dessert are evanescent; they do not last forever. Such moments drown out anything else that may be going on and allow us to lose ourselves in the present, savoring all the goodness that such a reassuring, pleasure-filled moment creates.

Such moments are so pleasurable that we may try to recreate them by taking a few more bites, then a few more, and then one too many until we are miserable. Why do we do this to ourselves, and how can we become disciplined so as to enjoy just enough, but not too much?

M. Scott Peck's *The Road Less Traveled: A New Psychology of Love, Traditional Values, and Spiritual Growth*, first published in 1978 and still worth reading, recently provided me with a moment of *aha* about love and personal growth that, until then, I had known intuitively but could not articulate. I took that moment as proof that, if we refuse to be halted in our search to find the answers, we will eventually find them. In finding them, our lives will have permanently been moved forward, leading us closer to understanding, clarity, and contentment about the life we have the potential to live and appreciate.

Back to those pleasure-filled moments. Pleasure is evanescent, unlike true personal growth, and to choose to stay in moments of pleasure is to become stagnant and actually prevent future growth. We must move beyond a delicious first kiss and actually get to know the person — their awe-inspiring self as well as their flaws; we must invest our money wisely and not squander it away frivolously, longingly waiting for next month's paycheck to arrive. We must enjoy the dessert but not live on dessert alone.

While pleasures are an important part in life — ultimately, humans live for food, sleep, and sex — if we chose to subsist on these three elements alone, nothing would get accomplished, and our clothes would never fit (at least the clothes we love).

Remind yourself that life will never stop throwing questions at you, but have faith that if you keep searching, the answers will come, and they will permanently change your life for the better. Do not be afraid to enjoy the occasional pleasures along the way, but make sure not to indulge too much.

Petit plaisir In the Northern Hemisphere, we are in the last full month of summer. Remind yourself to let go and just be a little while longer as you listen to Giacomo Puccini's Nessun Dorma from *Turandot* — Act 3 (Luciano Pavarotti's performance is phenomenal).

Explore further thesimplyluxuriouslife.com/august8 (thirty-eight invaluable lessons about attaining happiness)

August 9
Be Your True Self

Clear priorities simplify decision making. It has been my experience that, when I unwaveringly know the order of my priorities, I can recognize my errors or missteps clearly upon reflection — from understanding why I was ambiguous about where and with whom to spend my time to wrong decisions about my desired direction.

Hindsight offers us brilliant *aha* moments, insights into how to improve our journey going forward, and when we define a priority list, along with a purpose for each item on the list, we shed the unnecessary, radically reducing our stress. And as we do so, the strides of our journey moving forward become longer and stronger.

Once I realized the sincere joy and pleasure cooking brought into my life, I kept stepping forward, either by investing or by saying "yes" to opportunities to expand my experience, deepen my knowledge, and share what I have discovered. The hesitation was all but nonexistent. I began purchasing fewer shoes and more copper pans and cookbooks.

But I want to ease your mind as well. When it comes to aligning with our truest self, knowing what our priorities should be and what we think they are is the difference between a perfectly fitting sneaker and the pair of heels we cannot wait to take off.

Knowing our true priority list is not a piece of information that materializes in our minds on demand, much like a "to do" list. Rather, a true priority list materializes with time and life experience. The attempt to reach simple (and luxurious) living will be successful when we first understand and cultivate true contentment in our lives. That is when the true priority list becomes clear.

As you continue along your journey, the knowledge you gain gives you the ability to hone your list of priorities down even more concretely, making decision making simpler with each passing life experience. May each day of your journey lead you closer to clarity, and may you enjoy what you discover.

Petit plaisir Read, enjoy, and be inspired to cook recipes from *In A French Kitchen*, inspired by Susan Herrmann Loomis's friends and neighbors in Louviers, France.

Explore further thesimplyluxuriouslife.com/august9 (remember to embrace your unique journey)

August 10
Find Your Happy Place

I gazed out the window of my home, which offered a view of my two cherry trees, where my bird feeder hangs, and saw not one, not four, not even just six, but eight and sometimes ten birds dancing about the feeder, waiting to enjoy a nibble. To say I was giddy would be to understate my exuberance. My smile stretched from ear to ear, and eventually, Norman gazed at the birds outside our window and appeared to be delighted as well, or at least mildly curious.

In the past four or five years, I have come to realize with great clarity that I find much joy in pottering about my home, whether working on projects, tending to the yard, planning a décor project, or simply sitting and relaxing while the world happens just outside my window. Even when I travel, I enjoy settling into a vacation rental, exploring the immediate neighborhood, and then cozying back into my temporary sanctuary.

Perhaps it is the gift of the internet, but I never feel disconnected (if I do not want to be) even when I stay at home because we now have ample means to communicate with others, whether work colleagues, friends, or family. Now of course, I do travel and leave town regularly, and I explore my town of Bend on a regular basis, but I also find great joy in just being at home; the tranquility I find when I am at Le Papillon grounds me in the gifts the everyday holds, and my appreciation and ability to savor each day strengthens.

Each of us will find a unique happy place. I recognize that not everyone enjoys spending so much time at home. I have no doubt that part of my comfort comes from my childhood, as my brother and I could easily entertain ourselves on my parents' 20-acre property out in the country. Knowing how to pluck ideas from my imagination and to also set my curiosity free were skills I learned largely from my parents in their creative pursuits in the garden, in the woodshop, or in the house.

The way we engage with the world and enjoy time at home will be different for each of us; each individual will strike their own balance. Once you find your bliss point, make no apology and savor, savor, savor.

Petit plaisir Search for a one-of-a-kind vintage or consignment piece of furniture. Disregard the fabric. Then find your favorite upholstery. In time, you will have a signature piece for your sanctuary.

Explore further thesimplyluxuriouslife.com/august10 (why not . . . create a happy place?)

August 11
Understand the Root of Wants

Once or twice a year, I spend the entire morning or afternoon cleaning out my *épicerie* (aka pantry or home grocery) and organizing it. While it takes some time, afterward, the *épicerie* becomes my favorite room in the house. Well, not really, but it is a place I then love going to because it is tidy and free from clutter, and only contains what I use. What an immensely helpful feeling.

For me, there has always been a certain comfort to be gained from simplicity — fewer items to care for or find a place for. When I exercise the patience to wait for exactly what I want or need, I have often realized, while I wait, that I really don't need the item and thus save myself more than a few pennies.

The grand lesson that I am finding to be true, time and again, is that we do not need as much as we think we need. Often the feeling that we need something is simply a want, one that will eventually result in clutter we will have to clean out and pass along to someone else who may or may not want it. At its core, advertising aims to create anxiety within the consumer, a feeling of lack, and while yes, there are essentials, items we need that can only last for so long — many clothing items, for example, if they are worn frequently — acknowledging the role of the advertiser and distinguishing our needs from their claims are essential to simplifying well. When we realize that each of us is enough just as we are and embrace our self-worth, we become more discerning, more patient, less flappable, and more clear-eyed about the difference between a need and a want as we strive to live a life of true contentment.

We need to prioritize our time so we are able to spend it on the things that matter in order for our relationships to grow more deeply, and we should also follow the same approach when it comes to bringing items into our homes and our lives. While they are just things, they take up space, they clutter, they distract, both literally and mentally; they take time away from the priorities we know hold great value, complicating our lives unnecessarily.

Define *wants* versus *needs*, honoring your true self by doing so. Then take a moment to contemplate anything you are considering purchasing. What was the genesis of the desire? Do you consider the purchase a want or a need? Why? With future purchases, give yourself at least twenty-four hours before clicking "Buy now." When your choices honor your truth, comfort rather than clutter will follow.

Petit plaisir Make a flourless chocolate cake (it requires only a handful of ingredients), and let yourself melt into its rich, decadent flavors.

Explore further thesimplyluxuriouslife.com/august11 (recipe for TSLL's flourless chocolate cake)

August 12
Follow Your Curiosity

I devour nonfiction books that offer insight and information about how to improve the quality of our lives. TSLL blog is, by design, a destination where readers will find tips, ideas, and inspiration for living a life of contentment. And while seeking knowledge will, I wager, be something I will always do, often when we seek information, we find that much of what we need already exists within us.

The books, the blogs, the lectures, the sessions are merely the keys opening the door to understanding how to see what has always been there, waiting to be discovered.

For as long as I can remember I have been in awe of chefs who can whip up a savory wine sauce for their entrées — or a sauce of any kind, for that matter. With no recipe in sight, they let taste and experience be their guides, and the resulting dishes satiate and satisfy. Similar to an artist in their atelier, cooks and chefs in the kitchen seem to stand in a space of revelry and magic.

In 2011, I set the goal of publishing my first book, and if I met my objective, I would reward myself by purchasing a place in one of Patricia Wells's cooking classes in Provence. Fast-forward to 2015. My first book had been published in 2014, and I attempted to gain a spot on a class list that fills up within minutes when she opens registration. No luck. I was placed on the waiting list for a class to be held in 2017. The classes opened up again during the summer of 2016 for courses two years in advance, and this time, I signed up immediately, just in time to secure one of the eight to ten spots offered. Classes would begin in 2018, but the waiting was actually pleasurable, as learning how to cook with the seasons from a woman who had lived in France for decades and cooked alongside some of the top chefs in the world filled my thoughts in the day and my dreams at night.

My weeklong course with Patricia Wells in June 2018 exceeded expectations. And to this day, I understand that the impetus to take her class was the curiosity to become a cook who dances in the kitchen and does not need to rely on a recipe, one who relies on seasonal offerings and relishes the opportunity to share food with those she loves.

If a curiosity about how to improve your life keeps tickling you, investigate. If after much reading and searching, you cannot dismiss from your mind what you are confident would be a significant improvement, take action. Stretch yourself. Eventually, you will find what you are looking for. And in that moment, you will begin to trust your curiosity, and yourself, and you will move forward more resolutely.

Petit plaisir Let summer continue to sweep you away and listen to Louise Farrenc's Etudes, Book 1: no. 12, Moderato.

Explore further thesimplyluxuriouslife.com/august12 (cooking in Provence with Patricia Wells)

August 13
Patience and Intention

If you know French patisserie, you most likely know what a *palmier* is. Savory or sweet, these lovely, delicate puff-pastry cookies contain layers of either the simplest of ingredients — sugar or, for those with a taste for the savory, meats, mustards, and cheeses. As I shared in a recipe post some years ago, this French treat is simple and mouthwatering, but it takes time.

If you make your own puff pastry, which I prefer to do, the layering of the butter takes three different rolling-and-waiting sessions as the pastry chills in the refrigerator. However, this part of the process is where the magic happens.

The puff-pastry process parallels nicely with life. Patience and intention. Application of effort, and then patience with a purpose. Why do we wait? Because we are confident we know what is likely to transpire if we do.

Sometimes we get busy with our daily life, and the waiting period stretches longer than expected, but the pastry is still there and may be even better than it could have been because we gave it more time.

I celebrated my fortieth birthday, in February 2019, on the fourth snow day of the week in Bend, where we received 3 feet of snow (that's no typo, 36 inches is correct — gorgeous and "yikes!"). Consequently, I had much time to enjoy my home and my neighborhood, write in my office, work on the blog, and reflect. And it seems to me that clarity is the key to becoming comfortable with patience.

If we have a recipe, or some kind of knowledge, about what we are trying to build, even if we do not know exactly how it will turn out, we at least have our purpose. And we can live with purpose, letting the days unfold as they will, with many variables we cannot control. When we discover our purpose, the clarity provides a peace of mind, a contentment, and that is a wonderful gift to give ourselves and those in our lives.

While I encourage you to make some *palmiers* (I enjoy offering savory ones as a treat for out-of-town guests upon their arrival), I also encourage you, once you know your purpose, to relax, enjoy, and savor the moment you find yourself in right now — and again tomorrow and the next day and the next, because this calm you bring to your life is magical.

Petit plaisir Grab your trug and small pruners, and spend the evening or morning dead-heading roses. Listen to the sounds of Mother Nature, and if you have a pet, invite them to luxuriate with you outside as you potter about.

Explore further thesimplyluxuriouslife.com/august13 (*palmiers*, a simple French treat)

August 14
Remember to Play

When I was teaching, as the summer days slowly and leisurely passed by, without a need to constantly glance at the clock, I had to remind myself to appreciate and savor such a schedule. Before I knew it, I would be back into the throes of fewer vacations and more work on my desk.

So when I heard a recent NPR broadcast, "Play Doesn't End with Childhood: Adults Need Recess Too," I stayed in my car to finish listening to what the researcher had discovered, and I was not surprised. After all, when we are just playing, we are doing what comes naturally; we are not pushed or required to act in a certain way. When we embrace the joy of play, we lose track of time and can stumble upon new discoveries, talents, and curiosities.

When my niece and nephew were younger, I took them to swim lessons during a week when their parents had other obligations, and watching them have so much fun in the pool made me want to jump in as well. Both were attentive and eager to try what the instructors were showing them, but in the few minutes before and after class, each explored a bit more on their own — just playing. They began to discover new things they could do in the water when they moved their arms this way or that way, and you could see their eyes light up when they made a new discovery.

We should not let go of such excitement and playfulness when we become adults. While there are certain expectations of behavior for adults, allowing ourselves regular "play" time relaxes us, helps us regain our equilibrium, and brings us back to who we truly are.

This weekend, allow yourself some play time. Forget the rules and responsibilities and just dance on the beach, do a cartwheel on the lawn, run with your pups, or explore on your canvas. Reinvigorating your everyday with play not only will enhance your peace of mind; it will also enrich your connections with other people.

Petit plaisir Pick up the first book of the cosy mystery series set in Aix-en-Provence by M. L. Longworth (did you know her novels were turned into a BritBox cosy murder series?). Check out *Murder in Provence*.

Explore further thesimplyluxuriouslife.com/august14 (listen to my conversation with author M. L. Longworth; she talks about her Provençal mystery series coming to the small screen)

August 15
A Lesson from Julia Child on Her Birthday

The rains came, soothing heat-stressed residents of the Pacific Northwest and providing a bit of a respite from unrelenting heat. The air's freshness reminded me that even when we think nothing will change, eventually it does, and we are usually more appreciative when it occurs, so long as we are prepared at the most basic level — our safety, finances, sense of self, self-confidence, etc.

With change comes a wealth of opportunities, and while it is easy to understand why some people are uncomfortable with change, more often than not, change can bring many wonderful gifts into our lives. Perhaps a change in your life will demonstrate the lessons you have learned, take your abilities to the next level, or allow you to experience something you never before felt to be possible or to live in such a way that until now was out of your peripheral vision.

Along the way, as change occurs, it is helpful to have a few people supporting you and cheering you on with sincerity and excitement, but so long as you trust in yourself, based on what you have accomplished this far, you will indeed find the goodness that life is eager to bestow upon you. Now it is up to you to accept the offering.

Stepping into a new culture, beginning to build a life in a new country, requires a steeled determination to be open while maintaining a sense of self. Today is Julia Child's birthday. She had worked in China during World War II, during which she met her husband Paul Child. Following their marriage after the end of the war, Paul was assigned to France, French being a language he knew well, unlike Julia. Not speaking the language and not knowing what to do with her time while in Paris, she followed her passion and did not apologize for being exactly who she was — extraordinarily tall and extraordinarily curious about French cuisine.

Whether it is the abrupt arrival of a summer rain, a relationship change, a career shift, or a relocation to a new town or country, look for the sweetness, look for the opportunity. Trust me, opportunities abound.

Petit plaisir In celebration of Julia Child's birthday, read, savor, and be tickled by her memoir *My Life in France*.

Explore further thesimplyluxuriouslife.com/august15 (six ways to handle unwanted change well)

August 16
The Comfort of the Kitchen

Stepping into the kitchen swaddles me in the comfort of a good friend meeting me at the arrivals gate at the airport after a long journey home. It is familiar, it is happy, it is warm, and it provides sustenance to restore me.

Whether I have had a restless night's sleep or a deep restorative slumber, I step into the kitchen each morning to make what, yes, is the same breakfast nearly every day of the year, and I am filled with joy. The crack of the eggs, the whisk tinging against the bowl, the steel oats simmering, the sizzle, and then the ritual of sitting down and savoring the after-much-practice properly seasoned eggs, salted butter smeared across toasted artisan bread, and sips of freshly squeezed orange juice — fantastic! Having made it myself makes it better.

You don't need to sweat and strain and stress about how to make good food. The sequence of tasks becomes the dance that, when you understand their function and what they can bring or create to the table, is a pleasure to practice and hone.

Petit plaisir Whenever possible, have fresh fruit on hand. Make two of whatever you are preparing — two fruit tarts, for example — and freeze one to be enjoyed later in the year when time is short and fresh fruit is no longer available.

Explore further thesimplyluxuriouslife.com/August16 (my daily morning breakfast and more morning meal ideas — cooking video)

August 17
The Kitchen as a Space for Presence

Fridays have been one of my favorite days of the week (the others being Monday, Tuesday, Wednesday, Thursday, Saturday, and Sunday — because how lucky are we to be alive to enjoy them!); for years, they marked the end of my workweek, and a bit more loosely, they still do. Friday offers a space to celebrate, and during the summer especially, it was always a day when I would cook something special. One memorable meal was pan-seared scallops sizzling in French unsalted butter for only two or three minutes on the first side (be sure to season and pat dry before putting them in the pan) and one or two minutes on the second.

The fishmonger at Bend's Newport Avenue Market raved adoringly about the scallops, which were quite fresh. I was more than willing to bring them home for myself, and the sauce reminded me of how simple it is to create delicious flavors. A quality sherry, one shallot, and cream, reduced to perfection, and voilà. Let me stay home every Friday night because it does not get more delicious than scallops and a simple starch topped with a sherry cream sauce. Oh my goodness.

The kitchen provides a space of presence for me. Whether on my own, which is normally the case, or cooking with company, the rest of the world, the rest of the day, the latest news crises all vanish. I am all in and reveling in the goodness that hopefully all will enjoy when the tinkering and tossing and searing and boiling come to an end.

I usually have a film or recorded show waiting to be enjoyed with my meal and a glass of wine. Tonight it was a 2019 French film starring Juliette Binoche and Catherine Deneuve, *La Vérité* (*The Truth*). If I am honing my French while I am watching and dining in front of the television, it cannot be a bad habit, non?

Typically, the meals are simple to prepare, and the requirement for the deliciousness is quality ingredients. However, when I step out of the kitchen, no matter how hungry I am and curious to try the dish, part of me still wants to be dancing about with the food and the pans and the flavors as they come together.

Even if the kitchen is not the place to hold your presence, find the room, the nook, the outdoor space, anywhere where you can most easily stand in the present moment fully. Choose to spend time in this space often, and let it teach you how to hold yourself in the present wherever your days take you.

Petit plaisir Bring into the home or the office a small bundle of lavender sprigs freshly clipped from the garden. Only a small handful is necessary to add a calming scent to the room.

Explore further thesimplyluxuriouslife.com/august17 (recipe for seared scallops with sherry cream sauce)

August 18
Mise en Place

Mise en place translates as "set in place" or "everything in its place." Perhaps part of the reason cooking and baking can feel rewarding as well as relaxing is that there is a science to it, and the unofficial scientific approach to preparing a dish, something even the most novice cook in the kitchen can quickly learn, involves *mise en place* (the preparation and organization of ingredients). But what exactly is it, and what is the art of a truly effective *mise en place*?

When I attended both Patricia Wells and Susan Herrmann Loomis's cooking classes in France, *mise en place* was *de rigueur*. Each day upon arrival at our respective kitchens and assigned cooking stations, the ingredients were already either prepared and arranged in the necessary bowls or, at the very least, waiting to be prepared and placed in the bowls. As well, the recipe was clearly typed and propped up and ready to go to ensure ease of preparation.

I was in awe and absolutely inspired by the organization in both kitchens. From Patricia Wells having multiple ceramic canisters complete with labels for multiple spatulas, peelers, and any other tool her students would use, to Susan Herrmann Loomis's knives neatly and safely stored in the middle of her custom wooden kitchen island, every kitchen tool had a home, and all of the items we would need or that were regularly used were easy to find and thoughtfully placed where they would be the handiest to grab while cooking.

While *mise en place* often brings our attention to the recipe or meal we are cooking at the moment and the ingredients that are needed, in a larger context, it *is* your kitchen: how you arrange it, how you work within it well, and the tools you welcome into your artistic space — your *batterie de cuisine*.

    The primary purpose for *mise en place* is to make your time in the kitchen successful. The dishes and multi-course meals the people in each class would enjoy when we sat down to dine at first glance would have seemed impossible, but when the process is broken down into clear steps, with ingredients and amounts prepped and ready, it all seems quite possible indeed.

    As you approach your favorite meals and recipes, what small dishes, organizational containers, and particular placement of tools would make you feel as if you were dancing in the kitchen? Create a *mise en place* that works for you, and discover how it can elevate the enjoyment you experience each time you step into your kitchen.

Petit plaisir Enjoy breakfast outside on the *terrasse*, garden porch, patio, or however you can in order to feel morning sunshine and take in the fresh air and birdsong. Dress a simple table with a cloth, add a small vase with one or a few rosebuds paired with salvia sprigs (or any flower from your garden), and savor.

Explore further thesimplyluxuriouslife.com/august18 (thirteen ideas for creating your own effective *mise en place*)

August 19
Motivation

Motivation is a powerful tool prompting us to do things we either do not want to do or, for whatever reason, feel we are unable to do, whether that is true or not. Case in point: I didn't want to sell my house in eastern Oregon, but the motivation of a better life in Bend (central Oregon) was my motivator, and it had to be strong because I adored my house, especially after renovating and customizing it to fit my lifestyle. On a smaller scale, it can be finding motivation to complete a daily to-do list or to live healthily when it comes to eating and fitness.

    Small, everyday motivations can enhance our lives, as no matter where you live or what stage in life you occupy, feeling productive at the end of the day is priceless. In fact, when we feel productive and achieve a sense of completion, gradually our confidence builds, and we begin to realize we can create an amazing life even if it is not within arm's reach at the moment.

Even when your life is running smoothly, with no significant strife, completing small goals or tasks feels good. They may involve building a respectable reputation for your small business or establishing a strong bond in a relationship. The tasks may be things nobody else will notice but us — for example, the food we choose to eat, the thoughts we allow to whirl around in our minds, the choice to tackle a few items of a long-term project before it needs to be done — but they are tasks that eventually yield significant results that play a large role in the quality of our lives.

What works for me is to dangle a carrot. The carrot might come in the form of time to read without interruption or taking a favorite hiking path with my dogs and not worrying about how much time it will take; it may be as simple as watching a favorite show that I have recorded. Whatever it is, having the self-discipline to not indulge until I have done what I need to do provides double the satisfaction when the task is complete. Not only is my job done, but I also get to revel in the prize.

Recently, one of my prizes has been paying for and attending either a yoga or Pilates class at a studio here in Bend. I set myself the tasks that I need to complete, outline my days and jobs that need to be done, and if I am able to check off these to-dos, I hop on my MindBody Connect App and sign up for a class. Right now, that is truly like eating chocolate. My enthusiasm for this particular carrot may wane in the coming months, and if it does, I will find a new motivator, but the intent is to reward myself, and in the end, it's a twofer.

Whatever type of carrot you choose to use, make sure it is one that is beneficial as well as enjoyable. It need not cost a dime, but it can be something worth investing in to improve the quality of your everydays.

Petit plaisir Gift yourself a favorite teacup and saucer or coffee mug from Gien Faïencerie, a French company established in 1821, the largest faïence-making factory of its kind in Europe. Gien symbolizes elegance, luxury, and the unique *art de vivre*, the legendary French way of life. Be sure to look for their tiles the next time you travel to the City of Light; their work is abundant in the Parisian Metro stations.

Explore further thesimplyluxuriouslife.com/august19 (six essentials to create a life of fulfillment)

The Road to Le Papillon

August 20
Savoring a Beloved Memory

I fell in love with France on my first trip there in 2000, even with all of the frustrations born of being a first-timer and moments of longing to return home. Many more trips have followed, and I have enjoyed several journeys to the Gallic country that has captured my appetite and my affection.

During the summer of 2020, the first in decades when Americans were not able to travel to France for a holiday getaway, Le Papillon was a way for me to escape to France. I prepared a simple feast for one: a baguette, a French brie, a bottle of rosé from Provence, sole for the making and savoring of sole meunière, along with herbed couscous, a recipe I learned while cooking with Patricia Wells in Provence. The memories flooded back while I cooked in my kitchen.

Better still was another memory I savored that day — my arrival in Bend five years ago. I left my previous home, with my belongings all packed up in one large truck, and arrived in Bend, Oregon, to begin the next chapter of my life.

The power of food as a memory-savoring opportunity elevates your everydays all the more as you celebrate your life's journey and the moments that have brought you to where you are, the ways you live well, and what makes your life so truly special. Along with all of the other holidays, your personal holidays of recognizing and remembering are dates to place on your calendar each year and savor, savor, savor in your own special way.

Petit plaisir As you move through your day, turn on Johann Sebastian Bach's Oboe Concerto in F, BWV 1053R. It will keep your spirits up and steady your energy.

Explore further thesimplyluxuriouslife.com/august20 (fourteen ways to eat like the French — savor good food, don't fear it)

August 21
Doubt the Default

A nail is driven out by another nail; habit is overcome by habit.

—Erasmus

August

While traveling in France during the summer of 2018, I found that I was finally able to default in conversation to a handful of expressions to demonstrate, on the most basic level, that I comprehended what was being said — *bien sûr, absolutement, parfait, oui, je comprends, merci, de rien, à demain*. When those words or phrases were warranted, there was no longer a pause. I no longer had to think; I just spoke.

In this instance, I was tickled. Finally, an aspect of the French language, after many years of sporadic studying, was becoming a default in my brain. A muscle had been strengthened to the point of habit. But, again, my responses were basic, simple, superficial.

"Doubt the default." When I heard Adam Grant utter this simple, concise, alliterative statement in his TED Talk about original thinkers, my attention was captured.

Nearly seven years ago, upon arriving in Bend and moving into my rental home, I ran into a new neighbor. We did not know each other, and in conversation with this perfect stranger, I uttered, "Trust me, I understand what you mean." At the time, I did not really consider the weight of such words; I just said, "Trust me" out of habit, out of default. And I would not have even reflected upon this fact had the woman engaging me in conversation not said, "I don't know you well enough to trust you." The topic of our conversation was about our dogs, but the truth was, she did not know me, and she was fully present in the conversation. While I thought I was, the words I chose said otherwise.

Ever since this conversation, I have thought carefully about what I say in conversations out of habit — filler, silence enders, placeholders. I have done my best to eliminate words such as "like" from my informal speech after I recognized how many times I would say it when, had you asked me, I would have guessed I never used the word. Aside from the words I chose, I began to dive into my living habits and my thinking patterns, and with my trip to France, I recognized many cultural defaults as well that I had not even considered addressing.

Another word for "default" is "habit." By definition, a habit is something that frees up our mind to focus on other tasks. So as long as the habit is helpful and contributes to the quality of the life we desire, a habit is a very good thing. Selecting water as your drink of choice, looking for the positive, smiling instead of frowning, wearing the same uniform to work to eliminate wasting time in the morning — all are very helpful habits. But habits, defaults, can also be hindering our ability to live a better life, a more thoughtful life, a more engaging life, especially when we don't even realize we have these unhelpful defaults.

Following is a list of potential defaults that may already be in your life, inspired by what I have seen, experienced, and caught myself doing without thinking: engaging in speedy and surface conversations; not taking a grocery tote into the market; expressing negative energy during a first impression; driving faster than necessary; not greeting the shopkeeper, artisan, taxi driver, etc.; assuming a market will always be open; eating the same food year-round; believing that drama is necessary and thus inevitable; assuming you are incapable of something.

Adam Grant was right. We should doubt our defaults; when we don't, we are either living unconsciously or not living as full a life as we could if only we had more information to make different choices and take different actions.

When you doubt the default, you are choosing to be selective about the behaviors you allow to be habits in your life. It is when you do not know you have these habits that you step on your own toes, so to speak, and trip yourself up without realizing you are the one slowing down your progress. And that is great news: You have the skills and the opportunity to stop tripping and start striding into the life you love living.

Petit plaisir Pick up fresh blueberries at the local farmers market or harvest them from your garden. I often will walk by mine and give myself a morning snack.

Explore further thesimplyluxuriouslife.com/august21 (live deliberately rather than by default)

August 22
The Perplexity of Becoming an Expert

In order to be an expert in anything, we must become a student, and forever maintain this approach even if people eventually call us an expert in our field. As children, we are hardly stymied by the status of being a novice. *Of course we don't know! So let's have fun trying!* That seems to be the mantra that children abide by. But when, as adults, we try to learn something new — perhaps something other people around us know how to do or that people who are experts know how to do very proficiently and we do not — it can take more courage to admit, "I am a student. Please teach me."

I was reminded of this novice feeling during a week when a part of my podcasting setup sputtered, screamed static murder, and promptly died without telling me exactly which piece of the puzzle was no longer playing its necessary role. I was flummoxed. I no more knew what had broken than how to speak in Tagalog (the language used by a quarter of the people of the Philippines).

Feeling perplexed and stumped, and realizing I needed to become better versed in podcast setup lingo and know-how, I went about gaining more knowledge (and trying to fix my system as quickly as possible). After more than a few days of troubleshooting, talking with what felt like every help desk of each company that made a component of my setup, I narrowed it down. I found the broken link, and I was able to rectify it.

Along the way, I learned far more about my system than I had known in the past, and perhaps that was the unexpected by-product of this hiccup. I now know by heart how to set up my system (mixer, ¼-inch mono cord, XLR cord, stereo out outlets, USB external adapter, etc.) without even blinking an eye. If ever I have to transport it (podcasting in France? *Oui! Oui!*), I will not hesitate to unplug it, as I know how to set it up again in a heartbeat.

While I would not call myself an expert, I now step into my office to record episodes, trusting my ability to troubleshoot the fundamental hiccups that may arise from time to time.

But here's the thing: We all have to be students before we can become experts, before we can make that video that others trust to learn from. We all have to be okay with saying, "I don't know, but I want to learn." That is what will ensure that we can become the expert in whatever new field or skill we are trying to master.

Consider the knowledge you want to gain, the skill you want to acquire. Are you taking classes to learn? Are you practicing? Are you trying? If not, why not? So long as you try with an open mind, a positive attitude, and a dose of patience, you will surprise yourself with all you can learn.

Petit plaisir Looking ahead to September and stepping into the autumn schedule from perhaps a leisurely summer, read Oliver Burkeman's *Four Thousand Weeks: Time Management for Mortals*.

Explore further thesimplyluxuriouslife.com/august22 (the gifts of knowledge)

August 23
The Cook's Garden

An American would call my garden a yard, because it is primarily a small lawn with rock terracing. I do not have raised beds or plots of soil that are dedicated solely to growing vegetables. My garden is indeed small, but as I wandered around the outdoor space multiple times prior to the closing of the purchase of my home, I began to appreciate more fully the thoughtful landscaping that had created what the French would call a *potager* serving the original purpose of an English cottage garden.

The fruits and vegetables planted among the trees and shrubs utilize every inch of soil: the edging of one border entirely consists of strawberries, while the blueberries make up another short border, and the rhubarb sits right among the roses and tall, swaying Karl Foerster grasses. Even the peach tree, carefully placed on the east-facing side, protected from the wind, and the cherry trees provide privacy as well as beauty. The garden at Le Papillon exemplifies function married to aesthetic beauty.

More so than ever, this home felt as though it was meant to be mine. Before I even signed the documents to make it so, I had purchased a journal that would be reserved entirely for my notes about my garden — what was planted when, harvested when, blossomed when, what succeeded, what would need tweaking. I also knew I would put my herb garden close to the kitchen.

I had read Rosalind Creasy's *The Edible French Garden* and *The Edible Herb Garden*, as well as Judith Hann's *Herbs*, and the previous year I was inspired by French chef Robert Arbor's *Joie de Vivre: Simple French Style for Everyday Living*, in which he describes his own *potager* in the French countryside. I excitedly planned the herbs I would plant and where; I would need to grow others from seed, as they are hard, if not impossible to find as starter plants in local nurseries.

As I open my screen door onto what I call my garden porch, outside my kitchen, to my left are sorrel, lemon verbena, Genovese basil, and French thyme, to my right an overflowing pot of chervil that needs to be planted into the ground (the chervil, not the pot), more basil — both Genovese and opal — dill, chives, and lemon thyme. I have planted sage and more thyme in my sunshine garden, to edge the lawn and provide a contrast of color with my Julia Child rose; the herbs are adjacent to the border where my four tomato plants are planted and appear to be quite happy.

No matter the size of your outdoor space, windowsills, or balcony, what can you plant that you enjoy eating and enjoy seeing? Marry your appetite and aesthetic preferences to create a cook's garden of your very own.

Petit plaisir Add a well-made lumbar pillow to your favorite chair, whether at home in a favorite settee or reading chair or in the office. The support provided will bring much comfort, and it will add an extra layer of design detail.

Explore further thesimplyluxuriouslife.com/august23 (ten plants — herbs, vegetables, berries, and flowers — that I grow in my *potager*, and you can too!)

August 24
Dreams Become Reality

On July 20, 2020, the renovations on Le Papillon's kitchen began. By August 24, just over five weeks later, the kitchen was complete. It is my playroom, my atelier, my artist's studio, whatever similar term that means a space where I can play, create, explore, make mistakes, try again, and be fully present, all the while shutting the door on the day's events and thoughts of the future. I finally had my space.

I can remember that first week as work began: It felt surreal, but at the same time, as I gazed from my living room to my kitchen (I have an open floorplan for the main living spaces) — at first, without a stove or a microwave, with only the silver liner of a new hood placed at 6'3" so that I would not bump my head when I wore heels — I knew that the process was real, and that soon I would be able to cook on a French La Cornue gas-top stove.

It took twenty years for this particular dream to become reality. The dream wavered and was momentarily forgotten, but it never fully left my mind. The pleasure and joy I find while cooking — whether for myself, for others, by myself or with others — is the most natural and delicious activity in my everyday life.

Watching Julia Child in many episodes of *The French Chef* furthered my fascination with cooking, as did many episodes on the Food Network over the past couple of decades. With each dinner party I have thrown, no matter how many dishes I have to clean at the end of the evening, I revel in the opportunity to bring people together, gather them around with food and wine, and express my appreciation for their friendship and love through food.

Not every dish is spectacular or even good, but the memories always seem to be, and I am grateful for each of my guests over the years — from my neighbors in Pendleton, Bend, and Portland, and colleagues over the past twenty years of teaching, to my family and friends — for accepting my invitations. Their presence is a gift, and I can only hope I am lucky enough to host more such occasions to celebrate the everyday lives we have the opportunity to live.

Dreams rooted in love that enable sincere self-expression honor your true self. Find the courage to bring them to fruition, while exercising patience. Even if those around you may not understand, if a dream has been present in your being for years, there is a truth it is trying to share. Honor it by bringing it to life.

Petit plaisir When she realized that women music instructors were paid less than the men, French composer Louise Farrenc, a professor of piano at the Paris Conservatory, advocated for pay equal to that of her male counterparts. Listen to her Nonette in E flat Major, op. 38; at its premiere, Farrenc credited this composition with solidifying her pursuit for equal pay, which was granted following the premiere of the Nonette.

Explore further thesimplyluxuriouslife.com/august24 (take a tour of the kitchen at Le Papillon)

August 25
The Pleasures of the Fading Summer Season

The temperatures are subtly dropping, and the sun is peeking over the horizon ever so slightly later each morning. Kids become restless, and most are silently excited for school to begin, while families hustle to enjoy every last ounce of the easy summer days.

During the twenty years I taught in the classroom, there was something very sweet about this time of year, as I looked ahead to a season I loved, being with a new group of students, and lingering in a season that brings so much freedom to create, travel, rest, and explore. What better quandary to be in?

The simple pleasures of life, the walks in the morning that don't require you to rush, the taste, before going to bed, of an artisanal chocolate truffle that melts in your mouth, and the leisure to flip through the multitude of magazine issues that pile up in your mailbox day after day — we savor all of these at this time of year.

For each of us, there are specific simple pleasures that need not be rushed or very expensive, yet that bring absolute delight. As soon as the next season arrives, there will be other pleasures, but each season is uniquely its own, as reflected in the weather and the schedule you keep.

At this time of year, while I am now retired from teaching, I savor the shift of what the French call *la rentrée* (the return from vacation to a regular working schedule). Cutting sunflowers from the garden to brighten the house and hanging on to the summer for just a few more days; gentling pulling on a ripe tomato to harvest it from the garden, then enjoying it with fresh basil, a slice of mozzarella, sprinkled with a pinch of flaky sea salt and finally drizzled with balsamic vinegar; refreshing my wardrobe for the autumn and winter months, beginning with a closet clean-out and edit, followed by investing in a few quality pieces; harvesting peaches from the two trees in my garden. Each of these activities bring moments of pleasure that can only be savored at this time of year.

Before rushing off into autumn, savor one more time (or a few more times) those simple pleasures that will be unavailable to you until next June.

Petit plaisir Welcome the sea into your dinner plans by making a comfort food favorite of mine — spaghetti *vongole* (with clams).

Explore further thesimplyluxuriouslife.com/august25 (thirty-two ways to savor the sunset of summer)

August 26
Your Voice Is Enough and It Is Powerful

On August 18, 1920, the 19th Amendment of the U.S. Constitution was ratified, declaring that women in America have the right to vote — not without controversy, and not to mention follow-through to ensure that indeed all women would be able to vote without harassment, fear, or suppression. The progress toward equality deserves commemoration, and in 1973, the U.S. Congress designated August 26 as Women's Equality Day, so designated to remember and hold with awareness the certification of the 19th Amendment.

I have never had the opportunity to vote in-person in a voting booth (but I remember vividly going with my mother to the courthouse and watching her pull the curtain and cast her ballot) as Oregon became the first state to vote by mail prior to my turning eighteen. I have voted without interruption every four years, and for every mid-term and every local election. The more I learn about the journey to gain such a seemingly simple, yet irrefutably vital exercise of one's voice to wield change in a government that only remains a democracy if people participate, the more I realize how important the right to vote is. If people learn the skill of critical thinking, refuse to jump to conclusions based on assumptions or cling to slippery fallacious arguments, and instead engage civilly, they will understand that while the majority may win the vote, the minority is protected as well and not forgotten or dismissed. In fact, it is the minority at any given point of history that ensures that a democracy remains.

Being in the minority is a misnomer. While its definition literally equates to "less than the majority," that does not mean that its connotative value is any less important than that of the majority. More of something does not make it better or "more" right. It literally means that more people have a certain opinion. Whether or not that opinion is founded in fact and is well-researched, and considers all of the complexities of the people or options in question, is not considered in the equation.

All of this is to say that your voice matters when it comes to your life journey. Michael A. Singer writes in *The Untethered Soul*, "You have to realize that you really only have one choice in this life, and it's not about your career, whom you want to marry, or whether you want to seek God. People tend to burden themselves with so many choices. But, in the end, you can throw it all away and just make one basic, underlying decision: Do you want to be happy, or do you not want to be happy? Once you make that choice, your path through life becomes totally clear." In other words, stop seeking approval from others to gain a "consensus."

Some may argue this is selfish thinking, but the truth is that happy people — or to use TSLL's term, *contented* people — are not miserable people. Quite the contrary, they are at peace, and what guides them to that peace is not following what others advise if it does not align with what they innately know to be true about themselves. In other words, know yourself, listen, and then courageously journey toward what piques your curiosity.

When you let go of trying to gain approval from those others, you not only free yourself; you free others as well, and you will experience more peace.

Petit plaisir Carve out ten minutes and listen to the ebbs and rises of Fanny Mendelssohn's Overture in C-major, her only known orchestral work.

Explore further thesimplyluxuriouslife.com/august26 (how to let go of comparison? heal thyself)

August 27
Finding Peace by Honoring Your Needs

On a Friday morning in August 2020, I woke early but fully rested. The day before, I had made a decision and communicated it to TSLL readers, and doing so infused me with more peace than I have ever felt since starting to share my life on the online platform that is blogging. It was potentially a risky business decision, and typically I do a lot of contemplation prior to embarking on any decision that involves financial aspects, even if I do decide to proceed. However, this time was different.

Audibly exhaling deeply in the presence of only my boys that night, following posting the decision, I revealed to myself that the peace I experienced in my everydays was not exchangeable.

Unable to go back to sleep, I was bursting with energy. My copper teakettle began to softly sing on the stove top, the morning's classical music hummed throughout the house, and I nestled up next to my picture window to watch the birds arrive for breakfast and say their hellos.

Norman kindly joined me, taking an extra snooze on the ottoman, nudging himself against my feet. Hearing the garbage collectors going about their weekly rounds was music to my ears. After all, they are literally enabling a clean, fresh new start to the next seven days. The melody of everyday life.

The business decision I implemented officially in October 2020 was to place a soft paywall in front of the blog's content. Primarily the choice was for privacy, as I wanted to share my home and life journey with readers but not the entire world; it was also to value the content I had created over the previous decade. What buoyed my assuredness in my decision was the understanding expressed by long-term readers and even most readers who had only recently been introduced to the blog. I may have lost more than a handful of readers during this business-model shift, but what I gained was priceless daily peace and a significant elevation to my quality of everyday life.

While some people will honor and respect you without being asked, others may need you to show that you honor and respect your own value in order for them to recognize it. Some will resist having to exchange something — a raise in salary, more time off, better working conditions — for what you can provide, but more often than not, with clear, measured communication, those who are seeking what you offer will make the exchange.

~A *special surprise gift to you: Enjoy two free months of TOP Tier Membership reading of TSLL blog when you use promo code* MERCI3rdBook *upon signing up for a monthly membership.*

~Sign-up here https://thesimplyluxuriouslife.com/subscribe

Petit plaisir With September nearing, France's annual transition back into the regular work schedule (*la rentrée*) comes to the forefront of my mind. Mark Nepo's *The Book of Awakening*, a daily meditations book, fosters rejuvenation, brings more calm, and strengthens mindfulness.

Explore further thesimplyluxuriouslife.com/august27 (say *au revoir* to these seven unhelpful defaults)

August 28
Follow Your Passion Regardless of Whether the Crowd "Gets It"

One of the most exciting and memorable dishes I have ever made was a summer salad that called for blanched peas. Why was this dish so memorable? The peas were blanched on the La Cornue gas stove top that Julia Child purchased for her Provence home La Pitchoune in the late 1940s for $425 (to see this photo, check out episodes beginning in season 4 of *The Simply Luxurious Kitchen*; it hangs just left of the stove top). This stove was the same one she used when perfecting her *pain Français* (French bread) recipe; as she shared in her memoir, she went through hundreds of pounds of flour until she finally achieved the composition and flavor she knew to be truly French.

Little did I know that I was going to be one of the lucky few to cook on this stove during our weeklong class, as tasks were assigned at random to the students in Patricia Wells's cooking class in Provence. By the end of the week, only three or four of the eight students had been given such an opportunity (although we all made sure to take our picture with the stove).

Immediately upon seeing the stove, my eyes widened, and my jaw dropped in disbelief. A fellow student took my picture, and I took hers. Her photo of me (find it on my Start Here: Introductions page on the blog; scroll to the bottom) was anything but staged. I hugged it. I gave it an air kiss. And on the last day of class, I gave it another hug and said a few words that will only be known to Julia and myself.

A few months later, when the fall teaching schedule began in 2018, our administrator, during the "welcome back" days for staff, asked if any of us wanted to share a memorable moment from their summer holiday. I had never shared before, but in this instance, I was compelled. Julia Child's stove! I cooked on Julia Child's stove! Well, I did not take my own teaching advice, as I had not considered who my audience was, and when I shared that I had not only cooked on but had also hugged and even kissed the stove (I did not mention it was an air kiss), my administrator looked at me with concern, said, "Okaaaay," and quickly moved on. I was crushed for a moment or so, and my respect for my administrator waned.

Upon reflection, I realized that no one can know or fully understand why we are passionate and incessantly curious about a particular thing, and that is okay. When it comes to our passion, our job is to not be deterred or halted by those who do not understand or try to impede our pursuit. Whatever fuels your curiosity is what you should feed, and did I ever feed myself well during that week in Provence with Patricia and Walter Wells and my classmates.

Whatever is speaking to you, whatever keeps presenting itself to you, if you are drawn to it, step toward it. You may not know where it will lead or what it will reveal, but if my life journey is any indication, it will delight and surprise you in the most wonderful (and delicious) of ways.

Petit plaisir Make a classic French amuse-bouche — shredded celery root dressed with white wine, Dijon, and a touch of mayonnaise. Top with pieces of fresh crab.

Explore further thesimplyluxuriouslife.com/august28 (the power of finding your passion)

August 29
How to Make Progress

From time to time, Bend experiences summer days when the temperature reaches triple digits, but not often. And with the dry heat we do have, few Oregonians have air-conditioning. So for someone who does not especially enjoy the heat anyway (bring on the rain and temperate spring and fall days anytime), this was uncomfortable. But it was probably far more uncomfortable for my dogs.

I share these few days of high temperatures experienced while still living in my rental because Norman kept waking me up overnight, begging to go to the back screen door — not to be let out, but just to sit and take in the cool night air, which was far more abundant at this spot than in my primary bedroom. So I stayed with him. In fact, I took my pillow and comforter to the dining room, and then Oscar followed me, and we all fell asleep there. I never would have expected this, but I had one of my best night's sleeps in a long while.

Whether this was because of the temperatures being far cooler or because my jet lag from a recent trip had finally worn off or a combination of the two, I will never be sure, but certainly moving to a different location and trying something new and different made all the difference.

While it is impossible to prove the negative when we do not move or try something new, if you have ever chosen to make a change in any capacity and experienced improvement that you did not expect, you know that sometimes, even when you do not know what will result, if your conscience (or your pup) is pulling you to try something, why not give it a shot? Why not at least explore it? If the door you are pounding on won't open, look for an open window somewhere or a neighbor to let you in.

On the flip side, sometimes we try to fix things that are not broken but are just going at a slower pace than we would like. But if something is broken and will not work, try something different. Each of our individual scenarios will be unique, but perhaps take a moment to step back and examine which category it falls into: slow, but progressing, or stalled and potentially quite stuck.

If you are stuck, trying something new is a step in a different direction because at least there is movement, and the only way to make progress is to move — even if it is pulling back to take a great running leap.

Petit plaisir Add pep and motivation to try something new by listening to Franz Benda's Flute Concerto in E Minor.

Explore further thesimplyluxuriouslife.com/august29 (five simple new ways to invigorate your everyday)

August 30
Savoring Joy

The further I step into my journey, practicing more daily presence and savoring the everyday moments, the more moments, days, and weeks I want to figuratively frame upon reflection. In August 2018, a week unfolded in which I would not have changed a thing. As I sat in my office during an afternoon when the blue sky was fighting through the haze (successfully so), Norman's gentle snoring provided the background music, while Oscar silently slept in peace. Syncopated jazz music subtly filled the room, and I sipped hot tea from Paris. The afternoon was mine to fill as I pleased, and I knew that this was bliss. Yes, more days such as these, please.

On the outside, it would have appeared as nothing special to most people, but to me, it felt significantly unique and not at all ordinary. To me, this is reason to celebrate because when we find something to be lovely all on our own, without someone telling us that it is lovely, we are experiencing true joy. As discussed on the blog, joy is different than pleasure.

Joy (and I like to couple contentment with joy) is found within each of us. It is not guaranteed; we need to learn how to cultivate it. But we will find it only within ourselves. It is authentic. It is truly of our own creation. And a feeling of joy, in part, is a realization that no matter what is going on around us, we are settled within ourselves; we are at ease with ourselves and how we will navigate whatever might come our way or whatever we might be introduced to. Feeling joy is the mind telling us (so therefore, we are telling ourselves), "You've got this. You have figured out the skills to be more than just okay." At least that is what my joy is telling me. For each of us, our joy will have its own narrative voice and style, but the message is essentially the same. I might describe it as an inner calm and a celebration, like a happy dance, that no one else will see (so it is quite fabulous and original, *bien sûr*).

Now to my week, mentioned above, when I experienced this feeling of joy. It was not anything extraordinarily grand that created the joy, but rather realizations of great growth that were grand to me. While we travel in this world along with others, we travel every day and every moment with ourselves. This fact demonstrates the importance of continually being on a quest for understanding, for learning, for self-growth — because if you think your life is grand now, it can truly only improve, but only if you choose to be open to all that is available to further understand. And that choice to stay open is frightening at times, which is why many stop and remain where they are.

The rainbow that appears after a frightening storm is there every time (in fact, there is always a double rainbow; it just isn't perceivable to the naked eye). So in actuality, there is a double dose of awesome to experience so long as you refuse to remain still and agree to walk through the unknown, even if the world around you does not know why you are doing what you are doing.

Petit plaisir Examine your fall capsule wardrobe and invest in a key piece (or two or three) to elevate your outfits.

Explore further thesimplyluxuriouslife.com/august30 (twenty-seven *petit plaisirs* for you to enjoy)

The Road to Le Papillon

August 31
Cooking as a Way of Life

Cooking used to be, with the exception of emperors, kings, and royalty, a frugal everyday affair . . . [a] scrappy approach that was both local and personal. Julia [Child] single-handedly got Americans cooking again but with an imported cuisine, one that was deeply personal to her. The lessons of the past, I think, are clear: cooking thrives when it speaks to our soul, to our heritage, and to our landscape. Cooking is not a hobby. It is a way of life.

—Christopher Kimball

A confluence of many inspiring food influences have cultivated within me a love for cooking, making it a way of life that elevates one's entire existence. Christopher Kimball, cookbook author and founder of Milkstreet Radio, describes this approach in the quote above.

It was not until I moved out of my family home and was well into adulthood that I began to more fully appreciate what my mom and dad had offered my brother and me — the daily sit-down dinners and special holiday meals with friends and family gathered around a family table full of my mother's home-cooked fare — from the first crown roast, complete with white paper chef hats for the legs of lamb; the oyster stew based on a recipe from my grandfather, who was inspired by Emeril Lagasse; the "super nacho" recipe we only enjoyed on the day we would bring the Christmas tree home.

My parents continually supported my curiosity in cooking, whether it was letting me cook the meal for a small dinner party, being my sous-chefs for a catering event for the members of the local nine-hole golf course, or my dad asking when I would visit and cook something he saw me post on Instagram that looked delicious. But they also inspire my cooking. My mom will try making elderberry vinaigrette with her equally curious friends and give me a jar. Her homemade huckleberry jam — made from berries found only once or twice a year, if they are lucky — is a treasure to bring home, and when she sends me off with an extra cucumber plant from her greenhouse, I feel as though I have struck gold.

I have so many memories of watching my mother — canning local produce every year, making my dad's favorite salsa from tomatoes from her garden, or harvesting the strawberries with the family dogs and cats (the dogs nibbling on a few that don't make it to the basket). The more I reflect on my childhood and young adult life, the more I realize how much I was unconsciously inspired by the local, personal approach to cooking.

Cooking may not play as integral a role in each of our lives as it did for Julia Child or does for Christopher Kimball, or entice you as much as it does me, but we all need to be nourished, and it is wonderful

to recall or create memories to elevate the necessary daily occurrence of dining. It need not be complicated; it only asks you to be present.

Petit plaisir A simple idea for adding luxury to your home: add something in pairs — lamps, chairs, vases, etc. Otherwise, avoid the matchy-matchy, and instead adhere to the same tonal hue throughout the space.

Explore further thesimplyluxuriouslife.com/august31 (how to create a sanctuary for your senses)

September

Be Strong and Soft, and Think Critically

September

All I had were terrible ideas. I hated them all. I was just about to drop the class when she said something to me that changed everything. She said, "Terrible ideas are like playground scapegoats. Given the right encouragement, they grow up to be geniuses." She told me to take one of my terrible ideas and work on it.
—Under the Tuscan Sun

"Terrible ideas. Don't you just love those?" Lindsey Duncan's character, Katherine, suggestively utters these words in the film *Under The Tuscan Sun* to Diane Lane's disheartened and disbelieving character, Frances, whose life journey, unbeknownst to her, is on the brink of blossoming.

For years, I dismissed a deeply held but rarely outwardly shared dream of being a writer, but kept working solitarily to one day be able to bring to life that may have seemed to many to be a terrible idea — the best and only true calling that lifted my days, energized my spirit, and soothed my being, especially during the most confusing times of my life journey.

Over many of our annual sessions, my accountant, who had become accustomed to my regular teaching salary and secure job, and who while an expert in tax law, had dealt only limitedly with those working in the blogging world, stated without hesitation that my idea to leave teaching permanently was a non-starter. In February 2021, I delivered the news of my "terrible idea" to my accountant. As I predicted, he objected, but without hesitation, I stood by my decision.

Leaving the public school classroom after twenty years of teaching high school rhetoric and humanities concluded my professional career as a teacher, but as I wrote in my resignation letter, "I see my new dedication to my website, blog, and books, all focused on how we live our lives, as strongly related to the role of an educator."

Terrible ideas reveal more about the environment in which they exist than the reality of their substance.

Inviting curiosity to be our companion through life affords us the gift of forever being a student, and if we choose to forever be a student, the way we live our lives demonstrates that we can also be a teacher. How? When we befriend our inner growth, sit comfortably with the truth, and grow consciously into our better selves, every day forward is full of more contentment and a deeper quality of living.

Consciousness reveals to us, the student, when the lesson ends; then we have to find the courage to sign up for the next class. We have to find the courage to express gratitude and move forward, to dedicate ourselves to continual learning. My formal teaching career may have ended after twenty years, but I forever take with me the education I had the privilege of receiving. Yes, the education, I received while I did my best to be an educator in subjects I had the privilege to teach.

September 1
Celebrate the Return: *La Rentrée*

As September begins, schedules change, growing fuller, and many see a bit less of the sun (but for my Southern Hemisphere readers, more sun is coming!). I must admit, I find some comfort in my September schedule, as it kicks off autumn.

The attitude we approach anything with undeniably plays a role in how successful the endeavor we are embarking on will play out. Here in the States, businesses do not shut down entirely for the month of July or August, as they do in France. But when Labor Day travel winds down, there is a shift in everyday routines and expectations at work and at school, and a mental shift occurs.

The French expression *à la rentrée* (literally, "at the return") loosely translates as "See you in the fall." It is understood that September is the point at which all will return — from extended vacations, from the respite from school, to the everyday expectations and regular activity that occurs the other ten or eleven months of the year.

Studies have shown that taking time to literally get away from work — putting down the technology and truly being on vacation — can be highly beneficial for the brain. When we allow our brains to rest and think freely, problems magically seem to have solutions, creative ideas spring up like daffodils in early spring, and we are renewed and reenergized.

No wonder the French celebrate the return from their vacations. Beginning in September, we have an opportunity to put our best self forward. And while nothing will ever be perfect, improving and fine-tuning will always bring different results than if we did the same thing over and over again.

As you step into September, consider ways to welcome the new season — perhaps creating a bedtime ritual; revamping your schedule to find more energy by letting go, tweaking, or adding activities; purchasing a few new capsule wardrobe items; creating a food shopping plan; perusing new releases of books, films, plays, exhibits, and shows to enjoy (visit TSLL every Friday for the *This & That* post for just such news); stocking up on your favorite teas and coffees; sprucing up and stocking up your everyday tote or work bag items; and finally, but most helpfully, setting an intention for the season.

How do you wish to engage with the life you have before you? What do you wish to receive and/or achieve? Any new season brings with it wonderful opportunities, but, indeed, there does seem to be something special about the autumn season — specifically the beginning of September. When we are mindfully aware of our preparedness, our attitude, and where we wish to go, we have a much

greater chance of it materializing before our very eyes. May *la rentrée* treat you well.

Petit plaisir Make a simple fruit tart from fresh seasonal strawberries and blackberries picked up at the market or from your garden. At Le Papillon, peaches from my trees are ripe, so I also throw them into a simple pastry shell, then add a bit of lavender and nutmeg. When the baking is done, I pair this rustic tart with a hot cuppa.

Explore further thesimplyluxuriouslife.com/september1 (how to prep for *la rentrée*)

September 2
The Brilliance of Chosen Change

With "fresh start" opportunities — perhaps new faces in our lives, new or adjusted schedules, and a shift into a new season — this time of year gives us the potential to make our lives brilliant. Not brilliant as in perfect, but brilliant due to the possibilities to explore and thus brighten our days with curiosity, growth, and serendipitous moments of awe.

When my schedule changes, some years I make a simple alteration in my everyday life by rearranging my living room furniture, always making sure the new configuration works well and that I am not making unnecessary tweaks. Often when I do so, I ask myself why I have not considered this arrangement sooner as it feels quite well suited for the way I enjoy spending my evenings relaxing and unwinding: settling into a cozy armchair, feet up on an ottoman, the boys napping on their favorite pieces of furniture. I sip a cup of tea while either reading or watching a taped episode of the *Great British Bake Off* or a US Open tennis match.

You often cannot know what you will see from a new vantage point until you actually arrive there. Continue to gather up your courage and step into new experiences, attempt new challenges, and discover what you are truly capable of. Who knows what you will discover and how your life and its quality will change.

Petit plaisir Listen to a popular piece of classical music, Mozart's Eine kleine Nachtmusik ("A Little Serenade"), in G Major, K. 525 – first movement (Allegro), one of the composer's best-known works.

Explore further thesimplyluxuriouslife.com/september2 (five ideas for strengthening your courage)

September 3
Signature Style

People think costumes are fun; it's fantasy, and it's sort of frivolous, but it is an integral part of good storytelling.
—Sarah Jessica Parker

Dressing each morning or evening, or simply stepping outdoors with my dogs to take a walk always prompts me to consider what I am wearing. It may be simply because I love clothing and the beauty of a well-put-together outfit, but also I recognize that what I wear is a means of communicating with the world without saying a word. For example, if I step outside in the morning to collect my paper in my robe, someone who sees me may assume I have just woken up. If I leave my home in a tailored ensemble, dressed to the nines, onlookers may surmise that my destination is important to me.

What we wear communicates a great deal about what we feel our role in society is. And while our actions make a significant difference, we forget that while we may not come into contact with everyone who sees us, we are, unconsciously and consciously, influencing others around us in a variety of ways.

Malcolm Bernard, the author of the seminal book *Fashion as Communication*, puts it this way: "We communicate a society's beliefs, values, and experiences through practices, artifacts, and institutions. Where, in this case, the practices, artifacts and institutions are fashion and clothing."

The power of presentation enabled by our sartorial choices offers an amazing tool we can all use. What do I mean by presentation? In this particular case, how we dress and carry ourselves throughout our day. By no means should our clothing be the sole and primary mode of communication, but understanding how our ensemble choices introduce us strengthens our self-awareness and thus gives us one more tool for the life we wish to live.

The combination of how we appear in terms of style and how we carry and present ourselves in our behavior ushers in positive results when we realize we have control over these two aspects in our lives.

A first impression is a real thing, and as long as you follow it up with expertise, a sound mind, and thoughtfulness, you are helping yourself move head in a positive and promising direction.

Petit plaisir Add one new habit or replace an old habit that was unhelpful in living well. For me, making a weekly capsule menu on

Sunday/Monday afternoons (check out my template here: https://thesimplyluxuriouslife.com/product-category/capsulemenus/), followed by visiting the market, assists me in eating well all week and feeling great in my skin.

Explore further thesimplyluxuriouslife.com/september3 (ten tips for evolving your signature style)

September 4
Tasting Success

There is nothing quite as gratifying as seeing your tireless efforts toward a particular goal pay off. However, while you are striving toward a deadline, it is easy to forget how wonderful it will feel to see everything come together. Often doubt rears its ugly head and tugs at our efforts, asking for the pace to let up or stop altogether. But upon finally reaching the day that has been marked on the calendar and knowing that you have given your best effort to ensure success, you will feel a quiet sense of confidence, and amazing things will happen that are often beyond your expectations.

The confidence to forge ahead toward new goals becomes easier with each success, but it is important to taste success, and sometimes a flawed approach can keep this from happening.

If you set ginormous goals, without a clear plan broken down into small steps, it will be quite difficult to succeed. I look back on my efforts to try new things and set lofty goals, and the knowledge of my success in achieving prior goals has helped me believe I can accomplish anything I set out to do. However, the key is to taste success.

How can we find success, little by little, in our lives as a way of fueling the belief that we can achieve even bigger goals in the future? First, be your own cheerleader. When you finish something you have told yourself you will do, celebrate — make your favorite dinner, have a glass of wine, purchase that dress, handbag, or pair of shoes you have your eye on. Allow yourself to feel good. Second, make sure you have small goals as well as grand ones; they truly do help keep you on track, and we should celebrate these small victories as well as larger accomplishments.

While this may sound too simple, the euphoria of realizing a goal is an adrenaline rush (as many of you undoubtedly know) and has an amazing influence on your mind, helping you to believe ever more in your abilities. Taste success, and you feed your confidence for persevering toward future, grander goals.

Petit plaisir Pour a glass of wine or a hot cuppa, settle in after a task has been completed, and just savor the magnificence of Vivaldi's Violin Concerto in D Major (op. 3, no. 9).

Explore further thesimplyluxuriouslife.com/september4 (twelve ways to make your mornings magical, mindful, and the foundation of a great day)

September 5
The Mindset of Abundance

Life can genuinely be astounding. Life lessons are regularly tossed into our path, and the same ones will keep appearing until it is clear we have absorbed the objective. For example, staying in the mindset of abundance, rather than scarcity, is a lesson to be applied in every aspect of our lives.

When we embark on any new venture or are introduced to new people, disciplining ourselves to stand confidently in the knowledge that we are enough puts us in a position of attracting wealth. This wealth may come in the form of money, but more often it will be experienced as healthy relationships, respect, and a promising outlook.

Choosing to view our lives as already abundant, regardless of what others may think, means pausing, taking a step back, and allowing the people we are introduced to and the situations we see for the first time to reveal themselves to us instead of feeling that we must prove that we should be there.

When we allow a bit of mystery about ourselves at the outset, the interest of the other party will likely be piqued. We have chosen not to behave in a desperate manner, but instead to act as we would like to be treated — with the respect and genuine interest we deserve. The mindset of abundance means that, just as we are in that moment, we are enough.

When you stand back and take the time to let the other party reveal themselves, you are able to make a better decision on how to move forward in a way that lets you remain comfortable yet continues to hold their curiosity and/or respect. It also allows you to decide whether to remain engaged with this individual or situation. Yes, this approach takes patience, but view it as an investment in beautiful things to come down the road.

Petit plaisir Add a single hydrangea bloom to a vase — tall or short. Place it anywhere to brighten your day.

Explore further thesimplyluxuriouslife.com/september5 (twenty-six ways to ensure happy singledom at any stage of one's life journey)

September 6
The Power of Presence

During an unexpected situation in which I had a choice to inflame, to stand aside, or to engage to provide calm, I discovered the necessity of living in the present moment in order to live a life of contentment.

The situation was a department meeting while I was still teaching high school English. Choosing to inflame would have been quite easy. I would not have needed to keep my emotions in check. Instead, I would have only been rash and reactive, and I would not have thought about likely consequences. If I had chosen to stand aside, my attention could have wandered to the future, making plans and getting excited, and even wandered to the past, as I removed myself mentally from the situation, attempting to avoid excess stress or strife.

Instead, I chose to engage in a manner that provided calm to as many people in the situation as possible. This meant taking a risk that I might have become a target of others' anger or frustration, but it offered the greater potential of allowing all involved to avoid inflicting more pain and of preserving, as much as possible, the respect of everyone in the room.

When we choose to engage, we must be fully present in the moment. We must listen attentively, actively, and compassionately. We must listen not only with our ears but with our eyes — observing mannerisms, facial expressions, and nervous tics. In tandem, we must apply knowledge we have from previous occasions that might be helpful in understanding the stress, strain, or sensitivities that have been triggered. So long as we act in good faith to help more than just the "side" that we may favor, we can actually help everyone.

How is this possible? When we are present in such a way, we know what to say, we know how and to whom to say it without further fueling the contention in the room.

When we stay present so that we may engage in a manner that provides calm, we reduce the stress in the room; we demonstrate that there is more than meets the eye to the casual onlooker; and we acknowledge that humans have bad days as well as triggers we may not fully understand. And we can be more aware and not feed the flames that will lead somewhere far worse than would make sense to the unknowing newbie who blindly stepped into a situation, unaware of a hornets' nest —

a perfect storm of triggers, sensitivities, and long-held pain that had not been dealt with.

Choosing to be present in your everyday life not only helps you elevate the life you have thoughtfully curated and enjoy living each day. It also helps you better navigate the difficult moments that arise among others as well.

Petit plaisir Welcome in your home a handful of sunflowers. Place them in a vase at an entry point — foyer or mudroom or the dining-room table — and smiling will ensue.

Explore further thesimplyluxuriouslife.com/september6 (how to have a difficult conversation)

September 7
A Sound Structure for Flexibility to Soar

A strong yet pliable foundation provides structure yet the flexibility to move with the dynamic nature of life. The U.S. Constitution, in the final paragraph of Article I, Section 8, grants to Congress the power "to make all laws which shall be necessary and proper for carrying into execution the foregoing powers," in language that is often referred as the Elastic Clause. Our founding fathers crafted a document over two hundred years ago that, while tested severely over the centuries, has moved in one way or another with the significant changes generations have brought before it, and it still stands today.

No document of foundation is perfect, just as the best parents in the world are not perfect. Neither can our daily lives be perfect, and to take on perfection as a goal is foolish. When we pursue perfection, we end up with something that will be perfect only for that moment and may not suit our future needs. The combination of flexibility, clarity, and an open mind enables us to strive forward with our lives and discover the gifts it will introduce to us.

With each passing year, I am more grateful to my parents for providing me with a childhood that allowed me to feel safe, yet to explore, dream, make mistakes, and continue to grow. Like all parents, they were not perfect, but I know, now more than ever, that they gave and continue to give everything and more.

As adults, we can cultivate our own strong, yet pliable foundation from which we can dream, leap, experiment, and bounce back as we learn from our mistakes. Such a foundation can materialize in a variety of ways:

financial, in the form of a large cushion of savings; *structural*, in the form of a physical home for which we can pay the rent/mortgage without worry; *communal*, in the relationships we build and maintain with friends, colleagues, and family; and *educational*, as we build our confidence, savvy, and skill in fields that enable us to travel, explore, and try new things.

Not everything in our lives needs to be a work in progress in order for us to always be a work in progress. Even if we know life will change eventually due to age, death, retirement, etc., having some constancy helps us cope with the foreseeable and inevitable. So long as we have one solid and pliable foundation in our lives, we can learn the new skills, achieve the new tasks, and accept new lessons in order to be ready when our structure changes. Sometimes we will provide that structure for those we love, and if we are given this responsibility, we must be both pliable and strong.

Be courageous enough to reach your full potential, but gentle and open-minded enough to understand that you may not always know how the journey will unfold. Keep striving forward, and you will continue to create and strengthen the necessary foundation.

Petit plaisir Find a book or two to read in Will Schwalbe's *Books for Living*.

Explore further thesimplyluxuriouslife.com/september7 (why not . . . leap from a solid foundation?)

September 8
Dreams: Fashion Week

It is a funny thing about chasing after a dream. In the beginning it seems impossible, but what the heck, we say to ourselves, why not try? As you continue to work toward it, while doubts may arise from time to time, you also witness how much of your effort, resources, and time are expended toward something you are not sure will happen. Observing your investment strengthens your ability to toss aside doubts that pop up every once in a while and to continue forward because you have momentum toward a dream you set in motion.

As you near the date or the outcome you have worked toward for so long, moments of disbelief may materialize; however, such materialization further demonstrates the truth of your capability. In such moments, we finally see ourselves differently, and if we are being honest with ourselves, we will acknowledge that sometimes we do not fully know what we can do until we give it a good, determined try.

Early in my blogging venture, one dream I floated in my mind was to travel to New York City and take part in the Fashion Week festivities. In 2011, I secured my hotel, and in September 2012, I stepped onto a plane headed to the Big Apple during our school's weeklong holiday break, which coincided with Fashion Week, a bit of serendipity I was not going to ignore.

Simply walking through Central Park put the grandest smile on my face because I was actually there — to feel the energy, the creativity, the competitiveness, the collaboration. After ten long years, I was finally able to return to a city that has always piqued my interest and stirred my passions. That is the beauty of working hard to make something happen. You appreciate it all the more. You are less likely to toss it aside and take it for granted.

No matter where you are in the journey, you can do it. I know you can. Anything that tugs at your heartstrings and never lets go will always call you until you do something about it. Don't stop. Before you know it, you will be facing a dream that is now your reality.

Petit plaisir Heading to the Oregon coast is a seasonal ritual for me, and whenever I visit, one of the recipes I make, after picking up fresh seafood, is anything that lets me savor mussels (*moules*). *Moules Provençal* is a simple, flavor-filled appetizer, perfect for settling into restful time spent along the Pacific.

Explore further thesimplyluxuriouslife.com/september8 (recipe for *moules Provençal*)

September 9
Time to Put Together the Pieces

You know the feeling: You are at a gathering with a laundry list of people, and you see someone you recognize, but you are not sure from where. You may even know their name, but for some reason, your mind is drawing a blank on why you know them. It is frustrating when you know something but cannot piece it together at the moment. Then, at a random time, when you are no longer at the event, the name and all pertinent information flash like a bright sign in your mind.

While we may have all the necessary information to figure out a particular life question or problem, often we need time to put the pieces together. I often wonder, why do we need this time, this delay, this pregnant pause of wonder connecting the information we seek? Why can't we just discover the lessons immediately?

The answer to each question is that, for whatever reason, we are not ready to accept the answer or appreciate all it has to offer. In other words, we are being given a grace period to take the time and understand why this particular lesson is a wonderful piece of information, once we acquire it, so that we don't have to be taught the lesson again.

The tough part for me is always that limbo time between gaining all the information and the *aha* moment when I finally learn what I was supposed to see or understand. It is frustrating, yes. It feels excruciating, and during such times, often I do not get much sleep because I am trying to work through everything and make sense of the new information. Most people refuse to go through this limbo period because it is not easy; it often creates more questions, and it is often difficult to take an honest look at ourselves — our needs, our passions, our priorities.

But if you continue to trudge through this valley of ambiguity, when the lesson is realized, it will feel as though a burden of uncertainty has been lifted from your shoulders. It may be only a single layer of that burden, but the removal of that one layer is proof that you are choosing to grow into your best self, a wiser self.

Whenever you find yourself trying to learn a lesson but are still unable to determine what it is, do not give up. Like the revelation that hits you the next day while you are sitting down for breakfast, the lessons that will help you make the best decisions for your life will arrive when you least expect them. But they will arrive when you are ready to receive the full *aha* lesson, so do not give up trying to unearth the wisdom.

Petit plaisir Slip away to the English countryside in 1932 and solve a murder with *Gosford Park*, a classic Julian Fellowes' film.

Explore further thesimplyluxuriouslife.com/september9 (how accepting your mortality sets you free to live more deeply)

September 10
Finding Peace with the Unknown

Jumping to conclusions is the result of needing to know, even if "knowing" is not possible just yet. It may sound impossible initially, but peace of mind already resides within us; during times of uncertainty, we don't need to seek it outside of ourselves from other people or events.

Often society, those we converse with, and even we ourselves want to know the answers before they are available: *Why did this happen? What is this particular news story truly all about? How can I ensure this will or will not happen again? Who is responsible? Who deserves the credit?* But rushing to judgment when we are frustrated by something stems from mental laziness. Life truly is more spectacular than mere black-and-white options. We can all explore a full spectrum of the colors of life, and this exploration will take time.

Whether you seek an answer about your future, about your past, or about the world, trust that any knowledge worth seeking, even if it makes perfect sense eventually, takes time to be revealed.

I regularly told my students, when they were examining a story line in the news, a new article, speech, or any medium of rhetoric, to "look behind the curtain." In other words, look for what is not being immediately offered. Finding the motivation for any occurrence takes time when it involves more than yourself, and understanding the full context is often more complex than it would at first appear.

Being quick to judge, quick to leap, quick to find an answer may feel like the solution, but too often it only reveals our own bias, while we remain ignorant of it. Such a revelation is not always necessarily bad — it can reveal our true passions, true hopes, etc. — but such a practice of rashly jumping to conclusions can make you look like a fool who has not done their homework, which is how our credibility can be tarnished.

The next time a current event that sparks a conversation on social media or a seemingly too-good-to-be-true opportunity presents itself or life throws you a curveball, take a breath, let go of reacting, and practice responding when you are ready in a way that allows you to not only go to sleep with a clear mind, but to awake without doubts.

Petit plaisir One weekly ritual I savor is reading the papers on Sunday morning after a long walk with Norman. If you too enjoy an exploratory and informative reading of the morning papers, you will appreciate Johann Strauss II's "Morgenblätter" ("Morning Papers Waltz").

Explore further thesimplyluxuriouslife.com/september10 (the benefit of resisting the urge to judge)

September 11
The Importance of Knowing Your Audience

My first year as a teacher in the classroom was 2001. I was in graduate school observing and then teaching, with supervision, middle and high schoolers. My mentor teacher, Ms. Robert, demonstrated the skill of knowing your audience on the day that marks the beginning of my teaching career.

Before us that Tuesday morning on September 11 were thirty eighth-graders. They knew something had happened, so she did not dismiss it, but she knew what they emotionally could handle or should have to handle on a day when they woke up intending to see their friends, learn something about English and social studies, and socialize some more before heading to sports or music practice. The principal, who was closely monitoring all classrooms on this heartbreaking, fear-inducing, and confusing day, walked through the room and stopped next to me. She nodded at my mentor teacher, who was in her final year prior to retirement, and told me, "Watch her. Watch how she handles the emotions and the instructions today."

With stoic support, the principal stayed for a few minutes and watched Ms. Robert's confidence, her awareness of each and every student and their body language, not ignoring their questions, but also not dwelling, as a lesson needed to be taught and attention given fully to what we knew, which was little at that time. Focusing on what the students could do, and what would bring calm and steadiness exhibited her professionalism, compassion, and leadership during an unprecedented moment. The principal then moved calmly along to the next classroom.

Taking the time and energy to know whom you are speaking to, whether at work or in your personal world, shows you are invested in creating a positive engagement. When you speak without showing awareness of whom you are speaking to, you can seem self-centered, which may or may not be true. Sometimes you are nervous, and so you talk about what you know — yourself; but at other times, you talk about yourself because . . . well, that is something only you will know, and why self-awareness is equally important as being aware of your audience.

Exhibiting emotional intelligence benefits your relationships with others as well as the one you have with yourself. It is a skill and must be strengthened with conscience effort, but it is a worthwhile investment of your time and energy.

Petit plaisir *Courgettes* (zucchinis) are in abundance in most gardens and markets. What to do with them? Make this recipe: *courgette*, basil, and ricotta tart.

The Road to Le Papillon

Explore further thesimplyluxuriouslife.com/september11 (recipe for *courgette*, basil, and ricotta tart)

September 12
The Value of Routines and Stepping Away from Technology

I am a fan of podcasts. As many readers know, I produce my own, *The Simple Sophisticate*, and listeners often ask for recommendations of podcasts similar to mine, but my recommendations usually veer into topics slightly different than the category my own podcast falls under as my content is an accumulation of what I have learned on specific, yet varied niche topics — food, travel, gardening, politics, history, French culture, etc.

I frequently look to podcasts for ideas, inspiration, and instruction on a skill that interests me. Whether I am at home, on a walk, or in the car, I seek out ways to feed my brain.

One podcast I listened to recently recommended the book *Daily Rituals: How Artists Work* by Mason Curry. One method many of the artists suggested was adhering to regular routines that take the decision making out of the "have-to's" in our day-to-day lives, as those routines free their minds for the creative process. Another suggested waking up early to savor the silent sweetness of the day, freedom from interruption, freedom from obligation, freedom to let your mind bring forth creative ideas without fighting for your attention.

I could not agree more with both of these suggestions. While I continually fine-tune my regular routine, waking up early has consistently been part of my schedule. I find early morning to be the most tranquil, yet productive part of the day. Even while traveling, I enjoy the morning most; lines are shorter or nonexistent, and the natural beauty of the locale — the gentle sunrise, the birdsong, the few fellow early risers proceeding uninterrupted by the hustle and bustle that often develops later in the day.

Just as vital as working diligently to meet our goals is taking a needed respite from time to time. Visits to the Oregon coast in September are a favorite annual ritual of mine. An early-morning walk on the beach — listening to the soft roar of the ocean as the dogs romp, free of the leash, on the soft wet sand — slows my racing mind's pace and holds me in the present. September at the coast is a special time, as summer warmth still lingers, but children and families are back in the school routine, so crowds are smaller. A September beach visit subconsciously signals an end to summer and a gearing up for the fall season.

Often, my students would teach me something I appreciated immensely and would apply in my own life. One year I visited with a handful of my former students, and they inspired me with something they shared regarding technology. When out for a meal together or sitting around having their lunch, they held a common agreement to place their phones in the middle of the table, so that they actually are looking at each other instead of at their phones and each other's social media pages. What a savvy and simple idea. And when there is buy-in and an understanding of the benefits from the majority of the group, it is that much easier to do. So I want to send a thank-you to my students for teaching me something yet again. They never cease to amaze me.

While, like so many of us, you have no doubt become accustomed to the benefits and extra information at your fingertips that your devices provide, stepping away from them regularly or establishing tech-free zones cultivates deeper conversation, more beneficial rest, and complex thought and understanding on anything you may be wrestling with.

Petit plaisir A new season of *The Simply Luxurious Kitchen* cooking show kicks off on TSLL blog each year on the second Saturday of September. Discover how to incorporate seasonal fare to enjoy stepping into your kitchen.

Explore further thesimplyluxuriouslife.com/september12 (become the master of your smartphone)

September 13
Worth the Struggle

Welcome the struggle.
What??!!
During the final couple of years of my teaching tenure, as a medium to teach the variety of rhetorical devices involving repetition, I would have my students analyze the song "My Shot" from the Tony-award winning Broadway musical *Hamilton*. One of the song's resonating themes is the understanding that a struggle will need to occur; the colonies will, in order to break free from the British monarchy, choose to wander into a state of anarchy if they hope to reach the other side and become a sovereign state. As Hamilton ponders,

And? If we win our independence?
'Zat a guarantee of freedom for our descendants?
Or will the blood we shed begin an endless cycle of vengeance and death with no defendants?

The Road to Le Papillon

A sagacious and discerning observation. No, we do not know what the outcome of our efforts will be when we begin. When we look the struggle in the eye and decide to step into it, at that moment, we cannot be certain of the outcome; however, we can be certain of our determination.

Your current way of life may not suit you; it may not make you feel at peace or fulfilled, or it may keep you in a constant state of discontent (perhaps about the state of your health, the attitudes you bring to the day out of habit, or the state of your relationships, to name just a few examples). In order to change your way of life, a struggle must occur.

Take, for instance, the struggle to lose weight, reduce body fat, and build muscle mass and strength. In order to build muscle, we must exhaust and tear it (using either light or heavy resistance). When muscles become torn, they swell with water, and lactic acid builds up . . . temporarily. Often, we are sore, especially two or three days after we have worked out; however, then the muscle will begin to rebuild itself and become stronger. If you pair your physical workout with a healthy eating regimen, the results become noticeable in four to eight weeks. But first the muscles must endure the struggle.

When we decide to walk away from whatever it is that is no longer serving us well, there is an initial moment when we can breathe more deeply, as if a burden has been lifted. But then, if we are truly choosing to strive toward a better way of living, we will face a struggle — perhaps an unknown feeling or an unknown experience repeated often, both of which we do not have the tools to navigate effectively . . . yet (the key word in the sentence).

Yes, we will have to acquire new tools, learn new skills, and become aware of defaults that need to be consciously shifted in order for us to successfully move through the struggle.

Continuing the muscle metaphor, we may have to hire a trainer to show us how to properly tone our bodies. We will have to prioritize our days differently, but so long as we keep in mind why we choose to experience the struggle and understand it is temporary, we can push through it and come out successfully on the other side.

What is worth the struggle for you? Even when you choose to embrace a struggle, giving yourself time to breathe, moments to relax, and opportunities to savor are essential in order to maintain the energy to continue to strive forward.

Petit plaisir Oboes are one of my two favorite instruments to listen to, and Giovanni Benedetto Platti's Oboe Concerto in G Minor reveals why.

Explore further thesimplyluxuriouslife.com/september13 (through struggle comes success)

September 14
Change

The things we often think we need are sometimes the things that keep us trapped in an unfulfilled life.
—Bronnie Ware, author of *The Top Five Regrets of the Dying*

There is a reason a car cannot go in reverse at high speed: It was not designed to be driven backward. It is the same for us humans. While we need to assess our progress and reflect from time to time, if we gaze too long on the past for positive or negative reasons, we cannot make forward progress. Life is designed to move forward, unless you are a character in *Back to the Future*.

Part of the reason we focus energy on what we would like to change is because it is a known entity. It exists, or did exist, and so it is clear to us. It is known to us. The future, what we would like to see become a part of our life, is not yet crystalized, does not exist for us to experience and trust. And so, we cling, consciously or unconsciously, to what we know out of a desire for comfort.

In other words, we are fearful that what we hope to alter will not change. It is important to remind ourselves of the difference between fear and doubt. Feeling fear due to unknowns is a very good thing and a sign that you indeed know what you want; you just do not know how it will materialize because you have never had it in your life before.

The gift we give ourselves when we focus our energy on what we want is that, with each day, we lose sight of what we do not want, and it therefore can then become permanently a part of our past.

Reflect upon your life five, ten, or twenty years ago, on a behavior that was not helpful and that is no longer part of your character and/or behavior. It may take some time to home in on such behaviors because you have not thought about them for years, even decades, and that is of benefit to you. What we focus on materializes. What we feed, grows.

As I tried to go through such an exercise, I reflected on my life in Pendleton versus my life in Bend; more than six years have passed since I first called Bend my home since 2015. A simple positive change has been how frequently and how often the boys and I walk or are outdoors. Immediately upon moving to Bend, each day we walked outside, explored, walked further, tried a new trail here and there, and were able to take excursions where the pups could be off leash.

Instead of focusing on the way of life we used to live — walking solely in our neighborhood, so about a mile and a half each time, and always with the boys on leash — I focused on the opportunity provided and seized it. Norman immediately became more fit and trim (Oscar, with his high metabolism, typically always has been), sleep became deeper and restorative for all of us, and my stress levels lessened overall as well. In no time, it seemed, a positive change had become a permanent part of our lives.

Understanding why you are seeking change is paramount to altering the way you used to do something or how you relate to something or someone you want to let go of. Since the change you seek is new, it will initially take more energy and more focus, so any distraction or energy you expend looking backward will reduce the speed of your progress and the cementing of the change you seek. Be patient but clear-eyed with your persistence, and before you realize it, your life will change — and for the better, because of your conscious choices.

Petit plaisir Watch the French film *Le Prénom* (*What's in a Name?*), a lighthearted comedy set in a cozy Paris apartment full of food and lively conversation.

Explore further thesimplyluxuriouslife.com/september14 (unbecoming who you are not in order to remember who you are)

September 15
Find and Embrace Your Dharma

Passion + Expertise + Usefulness = Dharma

Jay Shetty, author of *Think Like A Monk*, defines *dharma* as written above. The good news is that your dharma already exists within you; your task is to discover it through courage, stepping into fear when it presents itself, and being patient until you find out what it is. Shetty explains, "If we keep our minds open and curious, our dharmas announce themselves." But do not stop there. "Pursue it."

A founding premise of TSLL is recognizing society's expectations and then becoming clear-eyed about what will truly fulfill us. The difficulty comes when we observe that some of these expectations are not

September

aligned with what we want to accomplish in our lives. Our task then becomes to do the work and find the strength to honor our truest selves in order to find what we innately possess that fires up our curiosity while positively contributing to society. Not an easy task.

Difficulty abounds when we try to identify beliefs and norms we have blindly accepted. One of the easiest ways I have found to see whether we unconsciously adhere to societal constructs is to travel to a different country or any place we are not accustomed to and just observe: the pace of the day, how people spend each day of the week, the traditions they follow, behavioral norms, etc.

Reading Vishen Lakhiani's *The Code of the Extraordinary Mind* reminds me of the power we let slip away — whether it is the defaults we keep lockstep with, the treatment we put up with or dismiss as okay, or the habits we follow when it comes to structuring our day, building our relationships, or completing our work.

At one point, the author writes, "We don't have beliefs so much as beliefs 'have' us." As he later shares, "Each of us lives by thousands of rules. When we aren't sure what to do, we follow the example of those who came before us." In order to not live blindly and to flip this "belief" truth, we must question our inherent beliefs. Nothing is excluded: from why you work Monday through Friday and not Wednesday through Sunday, to why you think a particular age is when something has to happen or will happen, even to your religious, spiritual, and political beliefs. This most likely will not be an easy or a short task, but you will discover what you truly believe is best for you and what you may have blindly accepted.

I have examined and am still examining the beliefs that seem to assist in my decision making about life, career, relationships, the world, etc. This process keeps you on your toes, and it certainly is humbling. But it also makes it easier to identify when others have not thought through why they do or speak or live the way they do. Being thoughtful is an active, ongoing process that requires us to be present and pay attention not only to the world around us, but to our engagement with it each day, from the thoughts that pass, previously unchecked, through our minds, to the words and tone we use when we speak or respond to others.

Consider something that is giving you a headache, causing frustration or angst, and challenge yourself to check your beliefs about the situation and how you think you should handle it. Perhaps adopting a different perspective will shed new light on ideas you have not yet discovered, or maybe it will eliminate the need to see the issue as a frustration.

Petit plaisir More *courgettes*? Make Nigel Slater's orzo with zucchini and parmesan. Pair with a glass of oaked chardonnay (the same one used in the recipe — yum!).

Explore further thesimplyluxuriouslife.com/september15 (recipe for zucchini and pancetta orzo with parmesan)

September 16
Growth

Progress, no matter how much or how little, so long as it is going in the right direction, generally results in a positive outcome.

When it comes to life advice, one popular maxim is that lessons repeat themselves until they are learned. While I have heard this before, I often felt there was a negative tone to the reappearance of a life lesson that we had experienced before — as if to say, You failed, so let's try it again. When we look at any life situation through such a negative lens, it can be difficult to have confidence.

My yoga instructor framed this life-truth in a different way. She began class with the statement that our lives are full of spirals, events, situations, and lessons that reoccur for us to apply the knowledge we did not have the first time around. I appreciated her reframing of this concept. After all, we can only do our best at the time the lesson presents itself. To ask for more would be impossible. But when we have experienced the lesson previously, we possess information that will enable us to do better the next time a similar situation arises.

Part of the reason my instructor began class with such an idea was to let us know that we would be revisiting poses throughout the class, and we should notice that, with each attempt, our bodies will be more comfortable, more at ease, and better able to hold the pose or go deeper into the pose. She was right.

The skills you have learned — beginning with smaller challenges that at the time seemed insurmountable but that you indeed met — have helped prepare you to be better suited to know how to handle even bigger challenges down the road. In this case, and in the parallel I have chosen to take on in my own life, the key word is *choice*. You may have the option to sit back and not look another challenge in the face, but why waste the knowledge you have gained? Why not continue to pursue a goal if it is something that is speaking to you and will not relent?

Life wants to prepare you for what you are capable of realizing, but it is up to you to hang in there, to keep learning the lessons, and to

keep striving forward. So far, in my experience, it has been more than worth it.

Petit plaisir Take a moment to settle somewhere peaceful — indoors or out, at home or out and about — then let your mind relax so that it can soar with possibilities.

Explore further thesimplyluxuriouslife.com/september16 (nine life lessons to learn, and apply, before it's too late)

September 17
Don't Worry, Be Productive

All of a sudden, a fall chill has arrived. The house needs to be warmed up when I walk through the door. I crave something warm to sip as the day winds down, and the duvet, pulled from the closet where it resides during its summer respite, returns to the bed.

As the weather becomes cooler, we find ourselves searching for different ways to strike a balance of productivity and rejuvenating rest. I find it a treat to curl up in my favorite chair with a hot cup of tea and a pile of newspapers, magazines, or a favorite book. Each of us will have our own preference. Find time to dive into your hobbies, your loves, your goals, and your passions. Become so immersed in what you want to create and cultivate for your life that idle gossip, the weight of the news of the world that is beyond your control, and unnecessary worries have little to no effect on you.

While I firmly believe we all need to find time to relax and unwind, often when we do not have something that engages our minds as well as our hands, our minds can wander to topics and ideas that are worrying, wasteful, and draining. Whether it is by reading a book that takes you away from your own head or focusing on completing a goal that contains many small steps, continuing to exercise your mind will allow you to feel productive, and perhaps you will have learned something new along the way. The rest that follows such productivity arrives more swiftly and deeply, and balance is restored.

When I head to bed at the end of a productive and mentally and/or physically exhaustive day, I sleep better, as my mind craves time to be rebooted. Conversely, when I have not challenged my mind or done something productive, my mind can wander and worry endlessly and unnecessarily, keeping me awake to toss and turn.

Strike a balance of working toward goals that interest and engage you, so that you spend your energy in a beneficial and life-enhancing way.

Petit plaisir Dahlias continue to bloom at this time of year. Whether you have them in your garden or find them at the market, two bouquets — one for your home and one to share — are sure to delight.

Explore further thesimplyluxuriouslife.com/september17 (twenty ways to banish worry)

September 18
Living Firsthand

It is a common aphorism that when the learner is ready, the lessons become available. Based on my experience, I realize that life lessons have presented themselves often, but it has taken time for me to understand what I was experiencing.

Even though it would be wonderful to not have to learn everything firsthand, often the most powerful lessons are those we experience with our own eyes and hearts. Because when we only live vicariously, we cannot truly know what it feels like to be in the room when the event occurs. We can guess what it might have felt like, but often in order to change our world, to adjust our mindset and approach, we must be present.

A description of how delicious and satiating a French croissant is cannot convey the experience of enjoying one, that has to wait until we take our first bite of the flaky, buttery quintessential crescent pastry while visiting France. Being kissed for the first time by our love surpasses all daydreams we might have held in our mind's eye. To experience is to live, and in order to learn, we must take an active role in our lives.

You have to put yourself out there, take the necessary risks. You have to be willing to see things with your own eyes if you are to live a contented and fulfilling life. When you spend your life sitting on the sidelines, you wonder and regret based on what the media projects and what other people tell you. However, when you take the initiative and put yourself in the game, you learn lessons you might not have expected. And when you apply these lessons, you are able to live a most contented life.

Petit plaisir Listen to Felix Mendelssohn's Symphony no. 5, *Reformation*, in D, op. 107, second movement, and savor the balance of strong and gentle rhythms.

Explore further thesimplyluxuriouslife.com/september18 (shedding the layers of your old self: necessary, temporarily uncomfortable, but absolutely worth it)

September 19
Be Present

One of my students studied in Argentina, and I had the fortunate opportunity to be working with them in an independent-study blogging class in which they wrote posts, shared them online, and built their own presence virtually. In one of their posts, they shared an interesting quip about Americans planning as if they can ensure the future — if they just do everything right, they will be able to relax.

As I read the line (I paraphrased, but the gist is that we spend so much of our life planning for the future that we forget to let life flow and enjoy the "now"), I smiled, then read it again, then chuckled out loud. While the source was a teenager with far fewer worries and responsibilities than an adult would have (as it should be), the thought they shared held my attention.

How much of our time do we spend in the present and how much do we spend planning, imagining, and maybe worrying about the future and thereby ruining the present? While planning is not a bad thing, the tendency in America leans heavily toward productivity for a profit rather than connection for emotional well-being. I would argue that planning is why America inspires individuals to dream, because amazing dreams do indeed come true, albeit sometimes in forms other than what we might have imagined. But do we take it too far?

Each year, after sitting down with my accountant, I take time to reflect on the trajectory, goals, and realities of how I spend my time. One realization that jumped out at me a handful of years ago had to do with how working harder can work against you if you do not do it with forethought and clarity of vision. In response to that idea, I was reminded of my clarity regarding two of my visions, but perhaps I needed to adjust the others. Perhaps I needed to just relax a bit, let the reins hang a bit looser, and allow the life journey I am on unfold as I savor each present moment.

Deciding to do that last bit sounds serene, doesn't it? But it can be scary. It can be hard to trust. It is somewhat similar to trusting people after you have been hurt repeatedly; it can be hard to trust that life will unfold in a way that it has not before, and as it does, that you will know how to navigate successfully. But a trusting attitude toward life is not equivalent to trusting a person who has betrayed you. When you change your approach to living, you are engaging differently with life, and welcoming an entire new world of opportunity and energy.

The key to easing your mind — and I was reminded of this by someone close to me who repeated my worries to me, allowing me to see that indeed I was being a bit absurd — is this: So long as you trust yourself, you will be just fine. In fact, you will be more than fine.

You have made it this far. You have traversed, swerved, and soared to arrive at the moment you are at right now, and while you may wish to continue to strive forward, let your past success and wisdom be the peace of mind to keep you grounded as you let the reins hang looser. It can be that easy. You just have to trust yourself and then trust the life journey that unfolds.

Petit plaisir Read two books by David Richo: *Daring to Trust: Opening Ourselves to Real Love and Intimacy* and *How to Be an Adult in Relationships: The Five Keys to Mindful Loving.*

Explore further thesimplyluxuriouslife.com/september19 (relax, you're doing just fine in this thing called life)

September 20
Understanding Ourselves

There are many ways we come to understand ourselves. Sometimes it is through following our curiosities and paying attention to the discoveries that delight us. Sometimes we hear people who may see us more clearly than we see ourselves talk about us or comment on our actions and behavior. The opportunities to better understand our innate abilities, our strengths and weaknesses, are vast, but in order to deepen our understanding of ourselves, we must be present with each of these opportunities. We must be in the moment, paying attention and being open to what we may discover.

A couple of years ago, I was standing in the hall during my prep period and noticed a former student who needed a respite from their day. Their anxiety was palpable, and so I offered breathing room away from the hustle and bustle in a quiet classroom. It was clear the student wanted to decompress, but not being a counselor, I quickly reached out to those in our building who were. In the meantime, while we waited, the student began to share, and gradually, their tension began to subside. I did my best to listen, as I recognized in that moment so many similar moments I have had in my past, distant and recent; there was no real possibility a listener could understand what I was trying to say, as the words I was using were vague, pained, and perhaps confusing, even to the speaker. However, what I was seeking at that moment was to be seen and to be heard by someone who knew me prior to that moment.

Like this student, in such moments, we can all of a sudden find ourselves in a ball of angst or a quandary of uncertainty, forgetting that the only source of true, lasting reassurance comes from within ourselves. However, the moment of perplexity clouds our knowledge of this fact. Until we learn the fundamental truth, we seek out individuals who already understand such wisdom and are thus lifesavers.

I did not meet my lifesaver until I was in my early forties. My counselor taught me to sit with myself, and at such perplexing times, when I doubted myself, to remove myself as much as I possibly could from the moment of subjective worry and speak to myself as an outsider observing all that was swirling about in my mind.

What do you know to be true about yourself? What do you need to hear in such a moment to be reminded of your true strength and capability? When you give yourself reassurance, you ground yourself in your truth; you shut out the ignorant pushers of worry and doubt and you find your peace.

When we can teach ourselves the skill of providing our own reassurance, we become more capable of empathizing with others who are in a similar state, one we might have been in prior to learning that helpful practice. In such moments, if we are truly present, our empathy deepens. We not only become a better person for others to engage with but a better friend to ourselves as we begin to understand our own language far better than we might have comprehended.

In a matter of fifteen minutes or so, the student's anxiety had visibly lessened, though not everything was resolved; however, it appeared that they regained a bit more self-confidence as they felt heard, seen, and supported. They thanked me and went about their way and their day. When the counselor arrived, I provided an update.

Life has a funny way of teaching us something about ourselves, as well as reminding us how to better engage with the world, how to be a better human to other humans, and how to best speak up and support ourselves. When we can fully understand ourselves, we can more helpfully and healthily engage with others. We may not solve the other person's problem, if there is one — only the individual who is going through their frustration can do that — but we can perhaps be fully what only we can be and, along the way, offer a healthy helping hand.

Lessons to learn more about yourself are always present if you will just open yourself to their gifts. Enjoy the journey of discovery, and see the moments of growth as you step into your fullest realization of all that you are.

Petit plaisir Enjoy a fresh and simple dinner of grilled, spice-rubbed salmon dressed with tomato and avocado relish and placed atop a bed of black rice. (Find the recipe on the blog.)

Explore further thesimplyluxuriouslife.com/september20 (an essential skill for the most peace-filled and resilient life)

September 21
Honoring Your Emotions

When the end of the school year would wind down in May and my classes had completed all or most of the required reading and coursework, I would assign a few of my classes to read *Tuesdays with Morrie*, a memoir by Mitch Albom about visits he made to his sociology professor Morrie Schwartz. The juniors who received this assignment were typically first a bit quizzical about the prospect of reading it — *a book about an old guy who is dying?* — but then were pleasantly surprised to see that the book contains gems of wisdom they can apply to their lives.

One of the many pieces of wisdom from Morrie Schwartz that are sprinkled throughout the book is the idea of allowing yourself to experience the emotions you are feeling, letting them wash over you (allowing yourself to experience them fully), and then detaching. When we hear the word *detach*, it can have a negative connotation, but in this instance, Schwartz is suggesting that we step into the emotion we don't want to feel. In so doing, we respect and acknowledge what we are feeling by choosing not to let it control us longer than is necessary, and instead feel it fully and then move through it and past it.

Regardless of the outward emotions we express — jovial celebration upon reaching a goal, utter anguish and pain due to loss, and anything in between — allow yourself to be human, because no matter how amazing you are on your best days, you are human. Showing your emotions in a healthy, constructive way does not mean you are weak; it means you are human. You have a heart, you have dreams, you have feelings. Listen to it, follow them, feel them.

One of the benefits of learning to detach is that you also know that each emotion you feel — good or bad or a long list of any one emotion in between — will subside as emotions are impermanent by nature. If you are in a state of euphoria, revel it in and soak up every last drop, as it will not last forever. And if suffering engulfs you, be comforted by the fact that it will subside in time.

Knowing how to effectively handle your emotions affords you an invaluable key to true contentment. Having emotions and being human are a package deal, and once you learn how to understand what your emotions mean and how to express and manage them, you will be able to feel much more content and at peace at your core.

Petit plaisir As a new season arrives, perhaps hang a new wreath on the door to welcome autumn. Or add a few pumpkins to your stoop.

Explore further thesimplyluxuriouslife.com/september21 (give yourself the gift of true contentment every day, all day)

September 22
Pay Attention to What You Want to Grow

If the nails are weak, your house will collapse. If your verbs are weak and your syntax is rickety, your sentences will fall apart.
—William Knowlton Zinsser, author of *On Writing Well*

Words build our reality. While actions have their rightful place, so do the words we send out into our daily lives to the people we work with, the people we love, and the people who help us all make it through the day.

When we acknowledge a behavior — with our comments, our reactions, anything uttered — we increase the chances that it will be repeated, whether our commentary is positive, negative, or observational. For example, if instead of expecting proper behavior from my students and saying nothing when they behaved as I had hoped, I sincerely and specifically praised the behavior I expected with compliments and appreciation, it was more likely that I would see that behavior again.

Another example gives me the opportunity to talk about the beloved four-legged gentlemen in my life, and it is one I have seen work without fail when followed consistently. I have raised three spaniels from the age of eight weeks. When I acknowledge and pair my attention with love for doing something constructive (coming when I called, going to the bathroom outside), the puppy began to realize that the behavior would be rewarded with a treat and endless love and attention, and they wanted to repeat it.

The Road to Le Papillon

Many of the people we interact with during our daily routine respond in very much the same way. When we focus on something of importance to them, if we extend appreciation conveyed with sincere compliments or statements, we increase the likelihood of continued positive responses. The key word is to communicate *sincerely*. An observant person can quickly discern a brown-noser, and nobody wants to be labeled as such. If we take the time to be observant, focused, and fully engaged with people in any transaction, conversation, or situation, we will make an authentic connection.

Another way this approach plays out is in the media we watch, the activities we enjoy, and the things we buy. Whenever we place our focus on something, we are promoting, validating, and justifying it. In other words, if we want to live in a world of civility, kindness, and compassion, we must support shows, products, and businesses that do just that.

Living a life with integrity, compassion, and purpose takes forethought, and when I am trying to find inspiration, I often think of Harper Lee's character Atticus Finch in *To Kill a Mockingbird*. He held himself to his own high moral compass and was strong enough to rise above extreme adversity, even when the society he lived in would have looked the other way if he had chosen to lower the bar.

Practice conscious engagement in your daily life. When you engage with the moment, the people, and the opportunities that surround you, you are holding yourself in the present. Assisted by a clear and grounded sense of self and your values, you begin to engage constructively with an open mind, listening but not following, thinking so as to respond with consideration rather than reacting. When you become the voice of inquiry — Why are we doing this? Is this who we are? What values are projected when we take this action? Are we making this choice out of expediency and less friction or because it is the best decision for all involved, not just the few? — you open a window for others to pause as well and to respond instead of react. You begin to nurture the culture of civility.

Petit plaisir Listen to Carl Philipp Emanuel Bach's Flute Concerto in A Major, Wq 168, a piece included in a list of music that encourages one to fall in love with symphonic music.

Explore further thesimplyluxuriouslife.com/september22 (responding versus reacting: the difference)

September 23
Perseverance

As much as children, teenagers, and even adults do not want to hear it, in order to become proficient in any task or ability, we must battle through an initial phase of frustration as we learn the new skill and keep working at the task in which we wish to become an expert.

In refusing to give up and walk away, we recognize that we must continually look for knowledge to improve our abilities, approach, and techniques. Most important, we must be willing to practice endlessly.

The fourth time I attended a conference on teaching advanced-placement courses, I finally realized some growth, truly feeling as though I had a firm grasp on how to approach the content I was teaching. You might think I would have felt this way upon my second or third visit, but instead, it took some time.

Did I then feel that I had nothing else to learn? Hardly! As the maxim states, "The more you learn, the more you realize how little you know." But what I am describing was my ability to finally see growth from where I had started four years earlier. In anything we do, it is who we were yesterday and what we knew yesterday that we must compete with, not others, as we can never know how far they have come, what they have overcome, or what they already knew innately. When we realize that the only person worth competing with is the self we were yesterday, our ability to forge relationships, whether at work or in our personal lives, becomes much easier, and we free ourselves from unnecessary stress.

If in the midst of trying to become proficient in something you love to do, you find yourself yet to produce the results you know you are capable of, hang in there. As Malcolm Gladwell shares in his book *Outliers: The Story of Success*, it takes 10,000 hours of doing something before we can become experts. Even though subsequent studies have challenged Gladwell's finding as oversimplified, the underlying truth remains: While you may not become an expert, you will become better than you were yesterday. And along the way, new avenues of information and discovery are revealed, potentially revealing the path that better aligns with your true gifts.

And simply because you are passionate about something does not ensure it will come easily. In fact, it is better if it does not, so you will know if you truly love whatever it may be as much as you say you do. The good news is that finding your passion and turning it into what you do for a living follows a simple equation, as shared in the September 15 entry, so long as it provides usefulness to the world: Marry your passion with expertise and usefulness, and you will have found your dharma.

Petit plaisir Snuggle in for an Italian film to savor, *Viaggio Sola* (*I Travel Alone* or *A Five-Star Life*).

Explore further thesimplyluxuriouslife.com/september23 (six key components to becoming the director of your life)

September 24
Kindness

In 2019, upon the death of my beloved great aunt, I received comfort from someone who gave without expectation and from a place of sincerity. It buoyed the start of my week and strengthened collegial relationships.

The paradox of comfort presents a life-truth — that often we can gain it by giving it to others who need it as well. Perhaps we know that someone may be exhausted, scared, hurt, or worried, and we know because we are riding the same wave of emotions. In these moments of giving what I myself need, I have found something quite surprising: When we are observant of others' feelings and offer comfort in a way that is within their boundaries and our abilities, we experience the side benefit of receiving comfort and a deep breath of peace ourselves.

We may never know exactly how much or how little our offering helped, or even if it helped at all, but when your giving is done sincerely and gently, and without expectation, and is welcomed by the recipient, you may just be surprised by the strength you have gained.

You may never know how far your kindness will extend, as it may inspire other acts of kindness. The maxim "Pay it forward" comes to mind. What an awesome energy to put out into the world.

Petit plaisir If you are looking for inspiration to take a risk — you may be questioning whether it is worth the stretch as the outcome is unknown — read *The War of Art*, by Steven Pressfield and Shawn Coyne.

Explore further thesimplyluxuriouslife.com/september24 (extending kindness: the path to deepen contentment)

September 25
Change and the Unknown

"Live by design, not by default." This axiom could spur many long and thoughtful conversations, but here is my simple interpretation: The best lives are those lived consciously, not simply in imitation of what has been done in the past.

Stepping outside of our comfort zone and doing something new can be daunting. We may be met with naysayers who are comfortable with the status quo or tradition, but we should never be held back by these contrarians. If we discover, after an extended period of time, that the change we desire cannot be accomplished where we exist — whether within a relationship, at a particular job, or in the town where we reside — we must find the courage to redesign our lives.

When we make this decision to change, there often is not a roadmap of certainty. We may be able to do homework ahead of time to help yield the best results, but we cannot know for sure what those results will be. We must welcome such an unknown as a gift, because it is amazing how the universe provides what we need; it often exceeds our expectations, if we are willing to let go and show we truly desire what we seek.

You cannot proceed half-heartedly. You must have faith — in yourself, in your intuition, and in the world — that something better can exist that will answer your yearnings. Because it does.

Petit plaisir Harvest fresh strawberries and turn them into a decadent French dessert that is simple to make: a strawberry tart with crème fraîche whipped ganache. Dominique Ansel's cookbook *Everyone Can Bake: Simple Recipes to Master and Mix* is my trusted go-to for upping the baking game in my kitchen.

Explore further thesimplyluxuriouslife.com/september25 (how to create a new normal)

September 26
Embracing Your Truth

It took me thirty-eight years (thirty-eight and a half years, to be precise), but I finally saw and more fully came to understand something about myself that I had not fully grasped earlier.

What is the necessary component of connection that makes it beneficial? I had appreciated being woken up by Susan Cain's *Quiet*, which provided an awareness and peace that I had not found until I read her best-selling book. But Michaela Chung's *The Irresistible Introvert* is the manual I needed as it speaks to readers clearly and conversationally about the language of introversion.

The aspect that I regularly pushed back upon was that "everyone" needs social connection, meaning a connection to other people. And while I have always agreed we don't want to *not* be around people entirely, I do enjoy others' company; it was hard to explain the connection I felt in my own company, which is to me priceless and absolutely necessary to thrive. Chung made me realize (and it was with a huge relief that I clearly understood and agreed wholeheartedly) that, as an introvert, my time alone *is* a source of connecting, and when it is limited or taken away consistently, the best I can be is negated.

I share this, assuming that not all who are reading this are introverts, because all of us understand truths about ourselves that we do not always know how to explain. And sometimes it takes a sage outsider, someone we may never meet face-to-face, to speak or write in a way that connects with us to shed light on something we need to understand in order to find tranquility.

Each of our journeys will be unique if we are being true to what we have to offer the world. The obstacle we must overcome is passively sliding into the journey that was laid before us. Because while our story as we progress through life may have similarities to those who came before, it will never be exactly the same so long as we are listening to our own marching band.

For me, in some ways, it was acknowledgment that I was not misunderstanding myself. Instead, I simply did not have the translation for what I was experiencing, but all along I knew what journey I should be traveling, and how I needed the journey to be.

What is your language? Take the time to observe when you feel most at peace, and honor what you discover as fundamental to a key component for living well.

Petit plaisir Food for thought: Read *Happy Ever After: Escaping the Myth of the Perfect Life*, by Paul Dolan (and listen to episode 262 of *The Simple Sophisticate* podcast, where the book is the focus of the discussion).

Explore further thesimplyluxuriouslife.com/september26 (nine ways to let go of the myth of a perfect life)

September 27
Patience

You can't rush something you want to last forever.

Whether it is friendship, a romantic partnership, a hard-to-attain goal, financial security, anything pertaining to your ideal life, it will take time.

A maxim I often questioned was that if something arrives without effort, it must be questioned. Not that I will toss it away, but in order to be assured of its legitimacy, I must question it. As I reflect back on my life — the houses I have purchased, the ideal rental that I feel fortunate to have found in Bend prior to buying Le Papillon, the dear friends and relationships in my life, and now the blog's loyal readership and sincere interest from you, the reader — it is something that did not occur without effort, time, and a testing to see if indeed I truly knew and would appreciate what I was seeking.

As a result, I have discovered that life offers us choices. Depending upon where we are in our journey and what we have learned so far, life will offer temporal pleasures that immediately grab our attention, and if we are ignorant about what they truly offer, we often bite until we are bitten. Life will offer us a treasure to appreciate only once we have either learned the lesson or exhibited patience to wait for and gradually discover what is worth discovering. But even if we know what is worth the wait, it will take time to acquire and enjoy.

Such a simple life-truth often has to be learned firsthand. When we are ignorant, it is because we are insecure in who we are, what we want, and where we want to take our lives. As we travel along, making discoveries and memories along the way, temporal pleasures are a comfort. And this is not all bad. After all, often we do not know what we want, and in experiencing these short-lived moments of pleasure, which will become nostalgic memories to reflect upon when we are wiser, we often learn a very valuable lesson: perhaps something about ourselves or the direction we know we must or must not travel.

To have clarity, make waiting no longer a bother — because you know it is worth it. There is comfort in knowing you have found your way, no matter how long it took. My hope and wish for you is that you will find this happy place of being comfortable with patience, because that will speak volumes about your peace of mind concerning the direction of your life.

Petit plaisir Find inspiration to make your dreams part of your everyday while listening to Mozart's Symphony no. 20 in D Major, K. 133, which he composed at the age of sixteen.

Explore further thesimplyluxuriouslife.com/september27 (the benefits of patience)

September 28
Feeling Comfortable with Feeling Uncomfortable

The tagline for Nancy Meyers's movie *The Intern* is "Experience never gets old," and as we move into autumn here in the Northern Hemisphere, I urge you to contemplate this simple truth.

No matter when we acquire wisdom, we have been gifted a treasure. It is important to note that simply growing older in years does not make us wiser. We must choose to grow, choose to learn, and accept challenges and new ventures when we could, at times, easily settle for what is comfortable. But here's the catch: We cannot acquire wisdom if we choose to stay put. And the frosting on the cake is that when we welcome wisdom, when we choose to accept the initial uncomfortable feeling that comes with doing something new and letting go of what we know, we become more alive.

Remaining curious fuels us to gain wisdom, and so long as we remain in such a state, we can never truly be old. As we gain new wisdom, we shed our old selves and start anew. While at times we can feel vulnerable, it is also what makes us feel alive and helps to hold us in the present moment.

My challenge to you — and to myself — is to become more comfortable with feeling uncomfortable as you acquire new knowledge, experience new ways of going about your daily routines, and — the big one — accept not knowing how tomorrow will unfold. Often the anxiety you feel about plans for the future and whether they will work out is your recognition that more skills need to be added to your toolbox. In my second book, two chapters focus on building a toolbox of skills and strengths beneficial for living a life of true contentment. Understanding the key to stocking our toolbox is a choice and an investment each of us chooses to make.

I hope you find some comfort in the unknown, perhaps more so than you have before. That comfort begins with feeling secure within yourself and comfortable with the choices you make, confident that you have the skills to navigate whatever tomorrow brings and letting go of outside approval.

Petit plaisir Understanding how to be a secure adult in order to build secure and healthy relationships is a priceless skill to give yourself. Read *Attached: The New Science of Adult Attachment and How It Can Help You Find — and Keep — Love* by Amir Levine and Rachel Heller, but first, listen to episode #318 of *The Simple Sophisticate* podcast. as an introduction to the book.

Explore further thesimplyluxuriouslife.com/september28 (how to build a grounding peace of mind and six ways to bring it into your life)

September 29
A Work in Progress

The world is what you believe it to be, and it changes as you change.
—Byron Katie

My new washer malfunctioned. Sopping wet clothes. No spin cycle to perform the function that, nearly every other day, I take for granted. It's Friday. I'm frustrated. Clean clothes are all I want. It's one month to the day after installation, and my washer is defunct. Or is it trying to teach me something?

Byron Katie suggests four questions to ask anytime a thought we allow to hold center stage in our mind creates a world of despair. (1) Is it true? (2) If it is true, can you absolutely know that it is true? (3) How do you react, and what happens when you believe that thought? (4) Who would you be without that thought?

My first response, which stemmed from mental fatigue at the end of a productive, yet taxing week, was, "This *always* happens to me. This is going to cost a fortune to repair. I already paid a decent price for the new washer. The repair consultant will take forever to schedule, and they'll make me pay more than I can afford. Argh!"

Right out of the gate, my first response to Katie's first question in her series of inquiry was a simple "no." I had not thought twice about my washer for eight years until my old one broke down a month earlier and was declared beyond repair.

I then jumped to question 3: How do you react, and what happens when you believe that thought? My response: I become unnecessarily stressed, laser-focused on the negative, and not someone I enjoy being around. In other words, in such moments, I can be far from my best self, and now that I know what I believed initially is not true, I was frustrated with myself for going down that path.

Moving on to question 4: Once I saw that my initial thought was void of truth, I could jump straight to problem solving, avoiding the unnecessary acute raising of my blood pressure and coming closer to the solution by seeking out an expert who knows more. Hmmm . . .

At any given point in our lives, no matter how young or old we are, we are each a work in progress, because if we are fortunate to be alive, we have the opportunity to grow. Acknowledging this life-truth, we exhibit awareness of self and a desire to grow, and we demonstrate that we know we have the ability to grow. Because we do.

Katie's questions have the ability to change your approach to the everyday in a profoundly positive way. She reminds us, "Asking the questions — that's what changes lives. Every cell in your body is awake with inquiry. And you cannot believe the old thoughts again."

How is this possible? When we stop reacting, living by a default that does not serve us well, we begin to shift the defaults into intentional thought patterns to create a constructive approach of engaging with the world and, most important, engaging with ourselves and our minds.

The washer will be fixed. As it is under warranty, it will not cost me anything, but I will be confirming the length of the warranty and options for when it expires in order to save money should an issue arise down the road. Our unhelpful defaults also reveal what we fear most and what gets in the way of our positive progress. Katie's four-question inquiry turns the unwanted moment into a nugget of gold to propel us toward a constructive outcome.

When you add Byron Katie's four-question inquiry to your skill sets, you add a valuable tool to your critical-thinking toolbox. This tool enables you to question your own thinking, so you don't get in your own way. Write the four questions down on a piece of paper, if you would like; laminate it, if that would be helpful; and place it where you can easily see or find the questions quickly until they are ingrained in your memory. Once you are habituated to the questions, your mindfulness practice strengthens, and the quality of your days improves because you begin to trust yourself and understand how to navigate well in your everydays.

Petit plaisir Watch *Home Again*, directed by Nancy Meyers's daughter Hallie Meyers-Shyer and starring Reese Witherspoon. It looks at a woman returning home to create her own life and does not end with a traditional romantic ending, but perhaps an even better one.

Explore further thesimplyluxuriouslife.com/september29 (twelve life-truths to remember about making progress)

September 30
Opportunity

Being observant of how you live your life — what works and what does not — is a worthwhile practice for a variety of reasons. Reflecting on how something worked well provides an opportunity to apply the methodology to future tasks. The opposite is also true: If something did not work out as you had hoped, you can learn from your mistakes.

However, sometimes we do not recognize when we have become too analytical, especially if doing so is a habit we practice regularly. It often takes unexpected occurrences to remind us to stop analyzing and just strive forward, trusting in ourselves. Letting go of knowing keeps us in the present to fully experience our lives and opportunities, while trying to perfect or predict the future stunts the possibility for future contentment and, most important, present peace.

I was reminded to let go of worry when a horrific wildfire erupted on September 2, 2017, in the stunning, majestic Columbia Gorge. Along with what became named as the Eagle Creek fire, twenty-five other fires simultaneously burned in Oregon, until rain finally came, pounding the ground with long-overdue moisture to aid in extinguishing the flames.

For a handful of hours, the sky was clear of smoke, the air was fresh, and the drastic contrast deepened our appreciation for Mother Nature, and the need to care for her if we wish to savor what we love (and need).

Many events, including those orchestrated by Mother Nature, are out of our control, but many are subject to human intervention. With education, curiosity, and courage, we can put the odds in our favor and help the world, specifically the natural world, as we do. When we accept that we are, at least in part, the masters of our fate, we can achieve the tranquility we seek.

If you are deep in thought, perhaps even worry, take a moment to reflect on what you are doing to put the outcomes of life in your favor. Then relax, enjoy, and remember this: You never know when Mother Nature will give us the unexpected goodness we long for. When it does arrive, be able to recognize it — stop and soak it up.

Petit plaisir On this date in 1868, Louisa May Alcott published *Little Women*. Read it, or read it again, closely. Savor the way Alcott crafted each character uniquely, yet authentically.

Explore further thesimplyluxuriouslife.com/september30 (the truths and myths of the independent, single woman)

October

Lead with Your Humanity as You Pursue Knowledge, Understanding, Bravery, and Kindness

October

Humanism is the philosophy that you should be a good guest at the dinner table of life.

—A. C. Grayling

Randy Pausch, in his book *The Last Lecture*, written for his children prior to his passing from pancreatic cancer at a far too early age, pointed out how self-esteem is not something we give to someone else — our children, our students, our loved ones — but something "they have to build." Building self-esteem is a learned skill taught by teachers — formal teachers in the classroom or fellow human beings living around the globe: parents, friends, mentors, aspirational individuals who have preceded us in the journey to acquire a strong and healthy self-esteem.

When I was a teacher of rhetoric, the introduction to the art of persuasion was the foundational coursework for advanced-placement Language and Composition. I included lessons on exigence (the motivation of the speaker/writer) along with Aristotle's rhetorical triangle — the necessary components to analyze writing, speeches, art, video, film, décor, dance, clothing, any mode of communication to determine the intended message, both blatant and indirect — as an introduction to identifying the basic appeals (emotion, logic/reason, credibility) that advertisements bring to the forefront, especially for teen audiences, but other age groups as well. The assumption in ads is that a person is lacking in something, and the proposal is that the presented product will fill the void and solve the problem. The common refrain of insufficiency and deficiency rings loudly. As if to say, you are not enough, but you will be when you purchase this product or sign up for this course (or trip, appointment, procedure, etc.).

Once the students understood the strategies being employed to persuade them to purchase or accept the advertiser's claim, their objectivity arose, and their temptation to accept the falsehoods dissipated. And, similar to toning a muscle, repeated practice ensured they would hold themselves in conscious awareness of the devices used. It is when we are vulnerable, when we hold doubt in our heart about our abilities and self-worth, that the persuasion brings us to doubt ourselves.

Such doubt and feelings of being lacking, when not combatted with the help of loving and wise teachers who tell us how to build our self-esteem, strengthens what weakens not only us, but our relationships, our community, and our world. An insecure world gives rise to a vast array of ill deeds, angry words, deflecting behaviors, and choices; it is a world in need of more love, more acceptance, and more awareness that each of us is enough just as we are.

An insecure society is much more comfortable laughing or poking fun at something other people are laughing and poking fun at as well. An insecure society is easily motivated to follow what another person — one who is perceived as having more status, power, or acclaim — says is cool. In an insecure society, it is easier to act as others expect than to think before acting. But simply because something is easy does not mean it is for the best if we are seeking a civil society. Simply because it will be accepted does not mean it will sit well with you when you are in your own company.

In coming to terms with these observations, I have concluded that living a life that is one to be proud of, creating a legacy that leaves the world even just a smidgen better than when you were born, takes bravery.

However, learning to build self-esteem on our own is difficult, if not nearly impossible, which is why we need each other. We need to acknowledge the humanness in others. We need to be brave in letting go of those who hurt us because, in fact, they are hurt, they are in pain and need to find the courage to heal themselves. But we must also be brave in embracing what can help us. When we are strengthened, we can teach with a loving, open hand the skills that will give the freedom of self-esteem to others.

We do this by stepping away from one side or the other. Yet another common refrain in my advanced-placement Language and Composition classroom was that we must not dismiss the shades of gray that may exist regarding any one issue. The gray area is where the understanding deepens, and even if we do not wholly agree on any one point, often we find a sliver of similarity, and that reminds us of our humanness. That connects us. But when we push people who are the "other" aside, we become too removed to see any similarity.

Actor and producer Tyler Perry, upon accepting the Jean Hersholt Humanitarian Award at the 2021 Academy Awards, implored the audience: "Stand in the middle because that is where healing happens. That's where conversation happens. It happens in the middle. So anyone who wants to meet me in the middle, to refuse hate, to refuse blanket judgment . . . this one is for you."

Remaining with one "side" or the other feels safe; however, what most people desire by holding fast to one side stems from insecurity planted within us from a host of sources. Even though many share beneficial and desired support — from society-at-large, institutions (religious, family, economic, education, government, local community, ethnic or cultural groups), friends, media in all of its forms — they are not part of who we innately are.

Psychotherapist David Richo teaches what all humans desire when it comes to being human and connecting in a healthy way with others: attention, acceptance, appreciation, affection, and being allowed to seek our deepest needs and desires. This much more individuated approach for a global community in need of massive healing on multiple humanitarian, economic, and environmental fronts can at first seem incongruent, but look closely. Our world consists of humans, and when we begin to acknowledge this undeniable truth, we discover how to receive what is being communicated and then understand how to connect for mutual benefit.

This is not an easy task, but with more people founded in such awareness, with a desire to honor what none of us can escape: that when we exercise the bravery to proceed with self-esteem, grounded in the truth that we are enough just as we are, we empower ourselves and others to live in a kinder, more loving world. As Amanda Gorman, National Youth Poet Laureate, states in her poem "The Hill We Climb": "If only we're brave enough to see it. / If only we're brave enough to be it."

October 1
The Power of Perseverance

My abiding hope, my abiding prayer, is that we emerge from this ordeal with a new wisdom, to cherish simple moments, to imagine new possibilities, and to open our hearts just a little bit more to one another.
—Kamala Harris, at the Covid-19 Victim Memorial, January 19, 2021

In 2016, the Chicago Cubs, after 108 excruciatingly long years of waiting to earn the title of World Champions, finally captured the elusive Commissioner's Trophy.

I tuned in with the many on that long-awaited Wednesday night of victory for what turned out to be one of the best, if not *the* best baseball games I have ever seen. (The Boston Red Sox also had a few when they too rewarded those loyal fans who refused to believe in "the curse.") One of the many parts that struck me as worthy of celebration was the response of the defeated Cleveland fans. The Indians put up a whale of a fight. Chicago had to unquestionably earn this long-sought dream (and now Cleveland is the team with the longest drought, with seventy-four years since their last title), but the residents of Cleveland, being the true sports fans they are, tipped their hat to their rivals. After all, leaving the battle on the field is the mark of true sportsmanship.

I could not help but contemplate that span of 108 years. Mark Twain, one of my most beloved American authors, was still alive, and sadly, women were not even allowed to vote yet in the United States in 1908 (the 19th amendment, in 1920, gave us the right). So much has changed, so much has been discovered, learned, and created since. Perhaps there are many lessons we can derive from the Cubbies' victory, but one sticks in my mind: the lesson of perseverance.

Sometimes we are not ready. Sometimes the world is not ready for what we have to offer, but since we can never predict when a fortuitous confluence will arise, we must refuse to give up. We must, once we know what we seek, ardently pursue what we know is possible for ourselves, our lives, our world. We must not give up. We must not lose hope. Even at the bottom of the eighth, when Cleveland evened the score at 6-6, true believers and, most important, the players, did not give up.

Doubt only has power if we feed it. Stop fueling what you do not want in your life, and start feeding what you do. Good advice from a team that never gave up hope.

Petit plaisir Plant English bluebells for a mid-spring bloom next year. I plant mine among my daffodils, as the bluebells provide a wonderful pop of color after the daffodils have flowered.

Explore further thesimplyluxuriouslife.com/october1 (the difference between being scared and having doubts)

October 2
Feeling Unsettled: A Precursor to Change

On one of my daily walks, I came across a lot in which the developer had just begun to break ground to build a new home. After the first day of prepping the land for construction, the ground was torn up, and innumerable building items, as small as tools to as large as bulldozers, lay haphazardly about. In the neighborhood of this building site, beautiful homes sat tended to and respectfully cared for. And I began to contemplate the idea of change.

Whenever we choose to undergo a change in our lives, we initially imagine the final outcome, the time when everything is as we want it to be — perfectly transformed, flawlessly finished, and precisely as we expect. During this time of excited planning, we may forget that, in order to attain the outcome we seek, we must first go through times of turmoil, unrest, and upheaval. As with the construction of a new house, ground must be moved, and necessary tools and scaffolding must be brought in to ensure that everything is in place and properly put together so that when the final structure is complete, it is sound and sturdy.

A sense of unsettledness will undoubtedly set in at the beginning, in the middle, and just before the end of any meaningful change we seek. So long as we know this truth at the outset and keep such wisdom in mind as we move forward, we will be able to resist the desire to stop and retreat to what once was. After all, when we initiate change, we acknowledge through our action that the current state of our life is not working and express resolve to improve. In time, the new home will appear, as complete as the houses neighboring it.

Patience, perseverance, and understanding will be the keys to your certain success, and your life will be transformed into the remodeled version you know it can be.

Petit plaisir Find reserves of energy to move through your day with more buoyancy when you listen to Concerto Armonico no. 6 in E-flat Major, composed by Wilhelm van Wassenaer.

Explore further thesimplyluxuriouslife.com/october2 (eight ways to tame the overthinking mind to maintain creativity and find mental tranquility)

October 3
Avoid Being Passive

Fight for the things that you care about, but do it in a way that will lead others to join you.
—Ruth Bader Ginsburg

Similar to a dogged advocate who sticks up for rights they ardently believe in or a leader who keeps their focus on what is best for their constituents, letting criticisms from the opposition sting less and less, we need to stick up for ourselves and not succumb to personal attacks.

Maintaining a steady, ever-present self-esteem requires a stubborn resolve. There will be times when it is easier (when things are going well, and people support and accept us for who we are), and there will be times when our inner strength will be tested (others expressing disapproval regarding how we live or what we believe).

Understanding that the road will be both tranquil and rocky is fair warning because once we ground ourselves in self-respect, we will certainly be tested. Whether it is a colleague who refuses to entertain our ideas or a friend who disregards our needs or preferences, when such opportunities arise, we must refuse to allow ourselves to be cowed.

I am not suggesting that we act aggressively, but I am recommending that we summon a good amount of gumption and refuse to continue to passively agree in order to avoid upsetting someone. But, to again quote Ruth Bader Ginsburg, "Reacting in anger or annoyance will not advance one's ability to persuade."

As long as you approach a situation with tact, respect, and civility, go ahead and ruffle some feathers every once in a while. If others still ignore or disregard you, then you might want to consider different options to deal with them more effectively, or you might want to remove these people from your life altogether.

Petit plaisir For late-summer and early-autumn flowers, explore preordering dahlia tubers to plant in the spring.

Explore further thesimplyluxuriouslife.com/october3 (twenty-six ways to create the life you want)

October 4
Living Consciously

My life journey of trusting myself and fully and sincerely expressing myself parallels in many ways my journey with meditation. Beginning in my twenties, I attempted meditation, but the ignorant student I was at the time found it to be impossible. Yet I persisted, because something rang true. Different teachers inspire different students, and often it takes time for two paths to cross at the right time, which is why we must keep trying. By my mid-thirties, I began a regular daily meditation practice of five to ten minutes.

As my practice has strengthened, I have found that my awareness of my mind and my ability to bring it back from wandering from the present moment impart a steady being to my days. I find myself stepping into a deeper level of appreciation for everyday moments, an improved level of calm, and the capability to hold myself in the present moment more often than in the past or jumping to the future. Even when I catch myself thinking something unproductive, such thoughts last but a moment as my mind catches itself and refocuses.

Living mindfully versus mindlessly sounds quite minor on the surface, but a sizable chasm exists between the two in terms of the quality of one's life. I have by no means mastered the skill of living mindfully, which the tool of meditation strengthens — being conscious, remaining present, and avoiding blindly living by default.

To live mindfully is not easy at first. It is a skill we must learn, but it becomes easier as we awake to what our lives can become when we put in the effort, when we understand how to move past what we once thought was unsurpassable: our worries, our fears, the false limitations we have placed upon ourselves and the world.

Once we begin to live more mindfully, we observe our lives with a clarity previously unseen. We make different choices, engaging more productively, and may even begin to let go of a variety of choices, tasks, people, and routines we previously felt were part of how we had to live.

Stepping back and not going with the flow when it does not suit you initially will be difficult, but having made such decisions to honor your truth, the peace and grounding calm you find will be the reward. That well-made decision will make future shifts and changes far easier.

Stepping away and being honest about why is difficult at first, but when you recognize why and realize you are stepping toward a more fulfilling life, you begin to find more answers to the questions that previously may not have made sense about how to travel your unique journey.

Petit plaisir Enjoy a weekly (or twice weekly) at-home facial. Clean, exfoliate, steam, and apply a masque (or two). End by nourishing your visage and décolletage with moisturizer.

Explore further thesimplyluxuriouslife.com/october4 (twenty-two French beauty secrets worth the investment in time and money)

October 5
Marrying Comfort and Curiosity

When is it time to take a leap? When is it time to change? Is it okay to become comfortable? When is a change too much? When is a risk too great?

The gift of comfort provides ease and allows us to relax. Our shoulders drop away from our ears. Our breath becomes deeper, steadier, slower. When we relax, we think more clearly, practice more patience, and make better decisions as we give ourselves time to contemplate the potential benefits and/or drawbacks of the choices presented in our daily lives.

A certain level of comfort is necessary to take risks, to say yes to change. That comfort comes when we have had time to contemplate with a clear mind what we want, what we can handle, and whether the change we seek is a reaction to fear (not confronting a challenge, running away from it, and not learning the lesson) or a response based in trust in our hopes (moving toward something we desire and know to be more true to who we are).

To feel comfort is a privilege not afforded to everyone. But once we have attained comfort and have time to think more clearly and step closer to self-actualization, we are given the privilege to help those without comfort through no fault of their own.

As well, when we become too comfortable, the temptation to settle arises. "Too comfortable" will be different for everyone, but it is a place of ease that does not inspire growth or encourage curiosity, a place that keeps your feet in concrete. Being too comfortable can disengage us from the world and isolate us, ultimately, removing the ingredients necessary to live a life of contentment — engagement, change, and curiosity in pursuit of the unknown.

Choose to feed your curiosities. Examine where you can contribute to a better world, and devise solutions for avoiding stepping into concrete and, worse yet, letting it harden. Our curiosities will continue to remind us how extraordinary and potential-filled life is, no matter how small or large the question is that we are asking.

Whether the leap you wish to take appears to others as large or small, to you it will seem significant because you have never done it before. Follow your curiosities, and if taking big leaps is not something you are wild about, just follow the seemingly small tickles most of us sometimes feel: What is this? How does this work? Why does this happen when I do this? Those little curiosities will take you quite far.

While each of us has our own journey to follow, so long as you remain curious, you will be amazed at where you will end up. And, at that moment, you will be able to realize that you did take a leap, you did choose to change; it just happened in small, steady increments. In the end, it does not matter whether you arrived at your destination in one large leap or many small tiptoes; in both scenarios, you arrived.

Petit plaisir Read and give yourself time to absorb all that is shared in Viktor E. Frankl's book *Man's Search for Meaning*.

Explore further thesimplyluxuriouslife.com/october5 (lessons from Viktor E. Frankl's *Man's Search for Meaning*)

October 6
Be Yourself

The ability to be unabashedly oneself is more difficult than it sounds. While it is easy to dance around the house when no one else is there, it is quite another to speak up for ourselves when others make incorrect assumptions about our beliefs, preferences, education, or interests or when they make ad hominem attacks unrelated to the subject at hand, but meant to shake our confidence. It also takes great courage to voice our ideas and dearly held passions and risk criticism.

I recently had a conversation with a reader of the blog; she is a talent in her profession, and I greatly admire her. We had been acquainted for a handful of years, and when she spoke honestly and kindly offered a lovely compliment, I unexpectedly found myself choking back tears. I was completely thrown by my response and had to ask myself later why I became so emotional. Let me explain my response.

Often, our lizard mind, if we are not conscious of its survival approach, grabs fervently onto the few negative items of feedback, dismissing many more positive ones. Throughout the duration of TSLL, the predominant feedback from readers has been positive and gratitude-filled, but far fewer negative e-mails and comments are sent my way as well. The choice to open the door to my life, ideas, and discoveries welcomes opportunity to connect, grow, and explore far more than if I cowardly refused to embrace being vulnerable; however, because of the personal nature of what I do, one sting of disapproval carries a heavy dose of "ouch."

When we put our true selves out in public, saying, in essence, "Here I am, love me or not, I can't be anybody else," we open the door to meeting people who genuinely respect our efforts. Why? Because when we read about or see someone who's life rhymes with our own, a connection takes place, an appreciation that further nudges us to take the chance we have only previously just considered, but perhaps not seriously. We see another in the middle of taking the risk of being themselves and chasing their dreams, or someone who has already done so, and we are encouraged to embrace the risk as well. Such was the case with the e-mail I received from the reader of the blog; it reminded me that, even though there will forever be unconstructive critics, my purpose is to inspire just one person to find more contentment in their lives by sincerely living my own.

On the flip side, when we choose to hide our true self, even to disguise it, choosing to be someone we are not in order to please those we think we need to impress, we only end up building a life on shifting sand. But insecurity built on a façade cannot materialize into something great because sand is not a firm foundation. Growing into greatness and building trust take time, and when we are not ourselves, a single storm can demolish the false self we have presented, and we build something different to avoid the same outcome. However, only when we choose to take a deep breath and step out as we are — when we take the risk to become the tech genius, the golf prodigy, the pastry chef, the lover of fabulous interiors, the travel guru — will life open its treasure trunk, as we will be building on solid, stable ground. It is a courageous person who has the courage to offer their true talents and selves, and I know you have it within you.

The Road to Le Papillon

The risk of revealing ourselves can be great, as people can be rude, inexplicably baffling, and hurtful; however, bear in mind that hurt people hurt people, and their actions reflect their own current place in their life journey and most likely nothing about yours. The sweet rewards for embracing your truth — rather than following society's dictates and marching along safely, yet insincerely — yield all the more inspiration to celebrate what you discover about yourself.

Petit plaisir Make a batch of Morning Glory Muffins. Freeze whatever batter you don't need for enjoyment later in the fall.

Explore further thesimplyluxuriouslife.com/october6 (recipe for Morning Glory Muffins)

October 7
Be What You Want to See in the World

A simple life. No grand, thirty-room mansion or five-car garage. Not a housekeeper or butler to be found. Reading *Tuesdays with Morrie* always reminds me that a life of simple and intentional living nurtures true wealth and contented living.

As mentioned in earlier entries, when I was teaching, each May, as a way of wrapping up the school year, I assigned my upper-division classes to read Mitch Albom's collaboration with his professor Morrie Schwartz. The pace of the memoir is unusual, the approach unique; yet Morrie grabbed the attention of many of my students, and they often finished the book in only a weekend when they were given a couple of weeks to complete it.

While I cannot speak for my students, I can speak for how this book makes me feel. It offers reassurance for choosing a life that will nurture a quiet, yet engaged and curious individual, one who is sensitive to the pain of the world, yet is determined to offer ideas for comfort and peace.

We each need to create a nurturing culture and cast aside the feeling of lack that advertisers, naysayers, and cynics encourage.

We will have to make tough choices, and it is a matter of letting love win, so we must be conscious in our decision making. We must take time to be at peace with ourselves, yet courageous in our life journey because if we do, when we leave the world, or at least the community we live in, we will most likely leave it a little bit brighter and a touch more hopeful.

As its subtitle states, *Tuesdays with Morrie: An Old Man, a Young Man, and Life's Greatest Lesson,* is a book of lessons on living, and the life lessons just keep coming. It is a book that reminds us all that the richness of human existence is in how we live our day-to-day lives, in the little decisions that can seem insignificant. It is about being strong, listening to yourself, and being the example of the kind of person you want to see in the world.

Petit plaisir Make your own lavender spray, using true lavender essential oil. Use this calming scent on pillowcases and linens, and in powder rooms. It is a simple home-care item to make and have on hand.

Explore further thesimplyluxuriouslife.com/october7 (eight unique small décor ideas that make a signature difference in your sanctuary)

October 8
The Curiosity to Invoke Change

When we seek change in our lives, it can be daunting to make a move. After all, what if the change we seek is not guaranteed to be better, will involve considerable work, or be confusing because it is unknown or takes time to learn?

While uncertainty comes attached to change, it has been my experience that if a particular desire for change keeps occurring in your mind and is not merely a one-time thought, then it is something to explore. Ask yourself: Why do you desire this change? What about your current situation is not working for you? How do you hope to improve your life?

Often our subconscious knows what we need before we accept the reality in our conscious state, and when such a desire for change keeps popping up, we must explore further. There will be times when the change we seek turns out to be unnecessary or ill-advised, but it is in the exploration that we will find the answer and often learn far more than had we never embarked along the journey.

Rather than simply desiring change, take the time to dive deeper and explore further the matter dancing around in your head. Gather the necessary information, and then make the best decision for your life and the direction you wish to travel.

Petit plaisir Listen to Vivaldi's Cello Concerto in C Major, RV 398. It is gentle and swift. It is soothing, yet it will propel you through your day.

Explore further thesimplyluxuriouslife.com/october8 (how to make change happen and how to make it stick)

October 9
Slow Down and Breathe Deeply

Take a deep breath. Now, one more time. Too often, I forget to practice such a simple, yet rewarding mindful activity — meditative breathing. The practice of mindful breathing can happen anywhere — while you are snuggled up in bed, at work behind your desk, on the bus or subway (stay alert, however) — but you get the idea.

While meditation may sound intimidating or unnecessary, it is actually a simple way to bring calm and peacefulness to everyday life. Whenever I find myself feeling harried or busy, prompted by a change in my regular schedule, for example, or anything that rachets up my breathing, I remind myself to sit down and just breathe. I count my breaths, and just breathe again — deeply.

The beauty of the breath gives us time to truly consider our actions before we put them into play. It allows us to think seriously about what to say before we inadvertently put a foot in our mouth.

I continue to work on going one step and one breath slower. It never does harm, and it may make all the difference. After all, taking the time to respond thoughtfully, gently, and respectfully can turn someone else's day around, not to mention your own, and making a wise decision, rather than having a rushed, snap reaction can eliminate regret or remorse down the road.

Even if you do not practice meditation, remember to be conscious of your breath as you go about the day; it is a simple way to slow yourself down. Slow down enough to act consciously and not out of a knee-jerk reaction, and act in accordance with who you know you are capable of being.

Petit plaisir Create a cozy side table next to your favorite reading or relaxing chair. Provide space enough for a cuppa, some reading material, a small treat, and a candle or a vase of flowers.

Explore further thesimplyluxuriouslife.com/october9 (letting go of the busy mentality)

October 10
A Solvable Puzzle

In October 2011, news of the death of Steve Jobs, one of the great innovators and creative minds of our time, was announced to the world, a world in which so many go about our lives using a device he engineered. Jobs's life trajectory, while extraordinary in both its successes and struggles, reminds us that sometimes all we can do is seek out the answers, plan for the future, while reminding ourselves to live in the present, doing the best we can by exploring what truly captures our minds and our hearts.

More than anything, what I was inspired by as I worked with young students during my teaching tenure, was how malleable the world is. We truly can make it what we want it to be. If nothing else, Steve Jobs demonstrated what following your passion can accomplish. We too can create our own amazing legacies.

After all, the ability to listen to our callings, be curious about where they might lead, and choose to strive forward will make for an amazing story as we reflect in the coming years. I often reminded my students that, in order to complain, you must have first made an effort to improve or change the situation that is irking you.

What I indirectly try to suggest is that if you are busy trying to fix the problem or create a life full of purpose and meaning, you do not have time to complain. Besides, in complaining, we are wasting time that we could better spend accomplishing the tasks in front of us.

Even though Steve Jobs lived only fifty-six years and his mode of interacting with people and family left much to be desired, his contribution to society was abundant. He did not waste his time on earth. Whatever path you choose, find what sparks your curiosity while also positively contributing to the lives of others.

I find life to be a puzzle that continually reveals itself in subtle ways as I try to navigate my way successfully along a path best suited to my talents, goals, and personal fulfillment, and, more important, to figuring out how I can contribute to this grand world in a helpful way.

Ultimately, it comes down to your perspective. The power of the mind is an amazing thing, so why not encourage yours to think "I can" and imagine yourself doing what you wish to accomplish? In hindsight, you will be able to say you gave it your best, rather than having sat back as a spectator.

Petit plaisir Snuggle in to watch new or old episodes of *The Great British Bake Off*.

Explore further thesimplyluxuriouslife.com/october10 (six unwanted life scenarios and how to dance with each one by positively moving through and past them)

October 11
Tending to Emotional Ups and Downs

There are times when I discover that I am more wrapped up and invested in something than I realized, only to discover, when it is all over, the emotional toll it has taken on my mind and energy.

As a rhetoric and civics teacher, I regularly kept abreast of current events, local and global, as well as columns written by top journalists across the ideological spectrum, trying to stay at least one step ahead of my students and prepared for any questions they might ask.

From election fatigue to pandemic updates, cultural awareness, and issues long in need of investment and progress, as well as our own personal emotional journeys navigating relationships, career, and family — knowing how we can exhaust ourselves emotionally plays a vital role in managing our life well so that we do not become overwhelmed.

In a variety of situations during the past six years, I lacked an emotional awareness of my own fatigue. In some cases, my emotional strength had to break before I realized that I had not been managing it well. In such moments, I looked for the lesson in my exhaustion and quandary, and this is what I came up with: Discovering what grabs your attention, makes you care beyond expectation, and reveals something you may not have known about yourself, your community, and the world in which you live is a priceless gift not to be squandered.

When you become engrossed and passionate about something, sometimes you do not realize the energy and emotions you are expending in its pursuit, almost as if time is not a factor because you are doing what you enjoy, what holds great purpose. That is a wonderful thing. However, we must monitor our investment (our emotional engagement) if we are to be able to forge forward effectively, and with a sound mind and measured responses, to bring the desired progress to fruition.

Emotional ups and downs come with living, being human. However, you *are* human, and that means you must deepen your emotional intelligence so that you do not exhaust yourself to the point of being ineffective in the calling you pursue.

Petit plaisir Read a new issue of Sharon Santoni's *My French Country Home* magazine to calm the day and sweep you away to the French countryside.

Explore further thesimplyluxuriouslife.com/october11 (how to create a healthy approach to staying abreast of the news)

October 12
Taking a Leap

"What if . . . ?" We often pose this question to ourselves before we leap, and sadly, it can be a question we ask when we look back in regret at not taking a chance on something that captured our full attention and tickled our curiosity.

When we ask, "What if . . . ?" before we launch into an activity with an unknown outcome, the question is fueled by excitement, as well as a touch of apprehension, because the outcome is opaque. Conversely, when we have let an opportunity pass us by, a "What if . . . ?" can sit in our stomach like a badly digested meal and remind us that playing it safe might have been the wrong choice.

Life speaks to us, gives us opportunities, and reveals paths we may not have known were open or available as other possibilities. Often when we awake to potential we previously ignored because of society's expectations, mores, or judgments, the universe encourages us to broaden our perspective and look beyond the box we have chosen to keep ourselves safe, or so we thought.

But if something speaks to us — a dream that will not leave our imagination, a hobby we eagerly want to try, or an undertaking that would be riskier not to try than to attempt — we must consider leaping. We must consider trying.

While we may end up disappointed, with onlookers saying, "I told you so," the thrill, the excitement, the adrenaline rush, and, most important, the experience is worth it. Why? Because we stretched, we grew. Even when we do not reach the objective we sought, we still had to step beyond our previous limits, and similar to a ball of pizza dough being stretched and thrown to widen its diameter, before you know it, if you keep trying, stretching, and moving beyond your limits, you will discover you have grown beyond what you may have thought possible.

Life can be terribly short, even if we are fortunate enough to live an average human lifespan. If we go about our business assuming that we have years and decades to live, we may miss a beautiful chance to have an extraordinary life. In my own life, stretching has included choosing to study abroad even though nobody in my family had ever traveled to Europe, let alone knew a foreign language. At the time of that first effort, I assumed I had failed in that particular leap, but it turns out that my takeoff had just begun into an extraordinary exploration and appreciation for a culture that changed my life for the better in innumerable ways.

Today, consider what excites you, what tugs at you to try. Then ask yourself, What if it should all work out? On the chance that it will, the mandatory response is to leap.

Petit plaisir Plant the foxgloves you grew from seed this summer (June 4). As biennials, they have spent the summer establishing themselves and should flower next year.

Explore further thesimplyluxuriouslife.com/october12 (seven tips for a successful leap)

October 13
Take a Risk on Yourself

As our modern world invites us to design our best lives, the idea that perfection is attainable can feel possible. Yes, we have access to more information than ever. Yes, we have more options when it comes to clothing, food, relationships, and travel destinations. And yes, we have more awareness of the myriad of ways life can be lived, but as Barry Schwartz points out in his best-selling book *The Paradox of Choice*, that may be precisely what is abetting our lack of satisfaction and contentment.

By no means should we choose to remain ignorant and shut ourselves off from the world. Part of why I write each week on TSLL blog is to inform, teach, and inspire readers in discovering and successfully traveling their unique path to cultivate their simply luxurious life. However, when we do finally make a decision and encounter a first bump of discomfort or frustration, rather than looking to other options, we would be better off examining the hiccup, understanding what happened, navigating through or around it, and then continuing to strive forward. So long as we have done our investigating, research, and homework beforehand, we can trust that we are on the right path.

Could that path end when we aren't ready? Sure. But any decision — whether it involves a relationship, a skill, or finishing a project — more often than not can be strengthened when we address the temporary faults and move past them.

Obstacles often present themselves to strengthen, not stop. You can cultivate deeper connections, achieve awe-inspiring goals, and find greater confidence if only you will shift your understanding of the purpose for obstacles. If you instead leave or give up when things become difficult, you will never see the beauty that could have blossomed had you chosen to weather the temporary discomfort. Why not let your life blossom?

Petit plaisir Time for pizza and a luscious glass of red wine, but not just any pizza. Make a French twist on a classic margherita pizza by adding béchamel sauce.

Explore further thesimplyluxuriouslife.com/october13 (recipe for margherita pizza with béchamel sauce)

October 14
Charging Up Your Courage

Self-provoked change presents the opportunity to welcome a richer and deeply fulfilling everyday experience. Whether we want to improve our health, strengthen our relationships, hone our craft, or simply know more than we did yesterday, change presents the foothold for an elevated life and lasting contentment.

And — good news — drowning or exhausting ourselves in order for the change to occur is not required; however, we do have to be consistent and purposeful in our efforts. In other words, we must push past the limits we thought existed: Hold that downward dog in yoga class just a little bit longer, pause or bite our tongue before we say something without thinking it through, or eliminate a favorite food from our diet that does us no favors.

One additional element enables the change you desire to occur with more ease: having a cheerleader, someone who encourages you and is as confident as you are in your ability to change. Let's take yoga. The cheerleader — in this case indirectly — is the yoga instructor. When I finally happened upon an instructor who gave me the knowledge to work with my tall frame when it came to properly holding poses, I felt seen; I felt accepted and thus inspired to dig in a bit more and hold the poses that stretched my previous abilities.

A recent study revealed that, in order for people to change, to try something they do not feel comfortable doing or are not sure they can do, they must feel safe. In other words, when we have someone who will not laugh at our attempts, will disregard our awkward first go-rounds, and will offer encouraging support, we are more likely to continue to move toward the change we seek. It may be gradual, but with consistent effort and someone to hold our coat of courage and offer it when we cannot seem to find it, we are bound to be successful.

If you want to change in one way or another, or if you know or love someone who would like to change, keep in mind the power of an encouraging partner, and never underestimate its strength.

Petit plaisir Paris in the spring. Paris in the fall. Paris anytime. Listen to the Hot Sardines' "Wake Up in Paris." Be sure to also tune in to their track "French Fries and Champagne."

Explore further thesimplyluxuriouslife.com/october14 (eight ways to be more courageous)

October 15
Stop Living as You Think You Should

Patience holds a permanent place as a requisite for a life of contentment. Whether while putting in the necessary effort to achieve our goals or biding our time, waiting for life's events to unfold, having patience will eventually prove to have been a valuable investment. It could be that exercising patience gives us time to learn the necessary lessons, or perhaps it allows us time to realize we are on the wrong path. Either way, more often than not, patience is a gift we can appreciate only in hindsight.

While I practice patience, and gradually have become more adept at not acting rashly, I am also reminded that part of feeling more content is accepting "not knowing" as a part of life.

While we practice patience, we also most likely accept that life will unfold in its own time, so long as we have assembled the necessary ingredients to produce the desired result. Akin to baking a soufflé, we must mix the proper ingredients and, once it is in the oven, not peek until the timer goes off. However, even when we have patience, sometimes the outcomes we seek are fulfilled in a way we had not expected. Sometimes we turn the oven temperature to the wrong setting, or we read "tablespoon" instead of "teaspoon." In such cases, the outcome is not what we expected, though sometimes a beautiful accident occurs or a learning opportunity presents itself.

Our life journey unfolds without our knowing if what we have put into our days thus far will work out in a way we have imagined; however, our imagination is limited to our life experiences thus far. The first time I made my own French croissants, I had no idea how they would turn out; however, I put the odds in my favor and purchased the best butter I could find — a French favorite — and high-quality flour. And guess what? While they may not have looked Paris-boulangerie-presentable, they tasted mouth-wateringly out of this world. The best ingredient you can put into your life journey, while patiently waiting to see how it will unfold, is to be your full and complete self — *oopses*, strengths, awesomeness, and all.

I have discovered that one of the best ways to be at peace with uncertainty is to stop editing myself to meet with society's approval, to stop living in a way that I feel I *should* act or behave. In other words, if an event or moment moves me to act, and the action is respectful and aligns with my path and priorities, why not? So what if it does not align with what I had previously planned or what others expect or will approve?

Your life speaks to you. That may sound absurd at first, but think about it. If you can understand who you are when you silence your busy life and remain happy with your own company from time to time, the only way you can know which way your life should go is to listen to the moments that bring you *to* life. Have patience and become comfortable with not knowing how all of the pieces will come together, but know that you are putting the odds in your favor. They will come together magnificently so long as you are being yourself.

Petit plaisir Turn on Miles Davis's "So What." Settle into a café or sit outside under a *terrasse*'s awning as the rain falls, sip a hot cuppa, and just tap your toe.

Explore further thesimplyluxuriouslife.com/october15 (recipe for *soufflé au fromage avec herbes* — cheese soufflé with herbs)

October 16
A Pursuit Misunderstood

It's the very pursuit of happiness that thwarts happiness.
—Viktor E. Frankl

I vividly remember, as a teenager in high school, mindlessly scribbling on my binders and notebooks the statement "Be Happy." From my naïve perspective, who wouldn't want to pursue happiness? After all, it is stated in America's Declaration of Independence. But after reading Auschwitz survivor and prominent psychiatrist and neurologist Viktor E. Frankl's book *Man's Search for Meaning*, I became more convinced than ever that instead of pursuing happiness, it must be a by-product of the life we lead.

Happiness, by definition, is an occurrence of luck ("hap" is an Old English root for "luck" or "chance"), and with all of the time we devote to making our lives supposedly happier, what we are really pursuing is fulfillment and contentment.

"Happiness as a by-product of living your life is a great thing, but happiness as a goal is a recipe for disaster," says Barry Schwartz, professor of social theory at Swarthmore College.

Why? Because the very occurrence of happiness is dependent upon outside forces, events, and people, all of which are beyond our control. On the other hand, contentment is found within each of us. Happy moments absolutely should be savored and reveled in when they occur, but they cannot happen every moment of our lives. Contentment, on the other hand, regardless of the circumstances on any given day, can be with us at all times. Why? Because it is a mode of travel, whereas happiness is a sight we see as we drive along the road of our life.

Moments of happiness lie around us at any given moment if we choose to look for them — watching our children sleep soundly after a long day full of play and excitement, picking up a book that we cannot put down, having gas in the tank to go where we want to go, and having a healthy body to live life the way we desire. The difference between happiness and contentment resides in a dichotomy of external versus internal — what is in our control and what is not. There will be more moments of happiness to celebrate and savor when we strengthen the skill of cultivating contentment in our lives. True contentment cannot be understood until, when we tumble, we find a resilience within ourselves to navigate well through unwanted situations. While we may not want to experience such moments, if we do not let them discourage us, they will strengthen our contentment and open up more moments when happiness might occur.

As you travel through your days, seek not moments of happiness, but rather moments to savor. In so doing, refrain from clinging and, rather, just appreciate. When you remain open, you exhibit contentment with how you travel, rather than what the outcome must be, and what you will draw to you will be elevated as well.

Petit plaisir Enjoy learning the skill of savoring. Listen to episode #323 of the podcast and discover 6 everyday moments to savor.

Explore further thesimplyluxuriouslife.com/october16 (from seeking happiness to cultivating contentment: a shift in pursuit)

October 17
Intention versus Expectation

Author Tracy McMillian shared a helpful tool to aid in setting intentions rather than holding on to expectations. Whether approaching small or large decisions, she includes in her spiritual practice the simple statement "Show me." It allows her to let go of all that is out of her control and to be open to possibilities or the truth of others and the world around her. It may seem daunting at first, but her suggestion, shared on Oprah's *Super Soul Sunday*, may be something to try.

Living a life with intentions facilitates our ability to be full of gratitude, even for the simplest of details: good weather, friendly customer service, a cheerful fellow walker, no traffic, etc. When we set the intention, for example, to remain congenial and optimistic, we recognize that we do not know what the day will present to us, but we intend to greet it with something we can control — our attitude of optimism and congeniality. What comes out of the interactions that follow is unbeknownst to us, but at least we can sit well with how we have engaged with the world.

You may be wondering, should I set goals? Absolutely. The key of incorporating goals into this mindset is to be firm on the general destination, but not on how you get there.

For example, your goal may be to attain financial stability. Initially, you thought a particular career path would do that, but perhaps that has changed. Or maybe you were certain buying a home would guarantee your end goal, but you realize that building a business that you will eventually sell is a worthwhile idea as well. In other words, be flexible but focused.

Consider shifting to setting intentions for your days and your short- and long-term goals rather than grasping for expectations that, if not met precisely, may dim your ability to appreciate the outcome, as well as lessen the quality of traveling along the journey to the goal.

Petit plaisir Seek out hassocks or ottomans to prop up your feet as you sit in your favorite chairs; they also serve as helpful step stools for pups to climb into their favorite chairs.

Explore further thesimplyluxuriouslife.com/october17 (choose a life you love living each day — yes, it is possible)

October 18
Seizing a Second Chance

The events a single week can encompass quite often astound me. Sometimes their breadth can change your perspective, your direction, and your attitude, and either squash or boost your confidence.

Often life leaves it up to us to determine whether events will be judged as positive or negative. As we consider the possibilities, we become the captains of our lives, the conductors of our very own symphony, sailors navigating toward or away from catastrophe. Such moments reveal how we choose to travel through life, and if we choose to work with rather than fight what already is, we may not need to learn the lesson again. Or if a challenge does re-present itself, we can proceed confidently, without worry, as we know how to manage forward successfully.

Second chances happen, but they are not guaranteed. A significant, life-changing second chance arrived when a year after I had an unfruitful interview for a teaching job in Bend, I was given a second chance, and I prepared far more thoroughly than I had previously. Thankfully, they hired me for a teaching position of my dreams. To have another chance to get something right or a chance to have a clean slate requires each of us to do something differently, and you are the best person to know what that might be. You will not know for sure if the change will make the difference, but if you listen to your intuition, you will have a fighting chance. And again, none of this is to say such a chance is guaranteed, but when good fortune arrives, dawdling would be unwise.

Perhaps life has dealt you a dilemma you have faced before or taken you to a familiar fork in the road. Whatever you choose, refrain from doing the same thing and expecting a different result. While unknowns are frightening, they are your chances to get it right. Even if the outcome is not perfect (it never will be), it will most certainly make things better and more enlightening than before. Here's to the journey and for doing it better the second time around.

Petit plaisir Plant snowdrop bulbs, hellebores, and daffodils in your garden now for late-winter and early-spring flowers.

Explore further thesimplyluxuriouslife.com/october18 (twelve ways to learn the lesson)

October 19
Setting Your Boundaries

In order to define its territory, a country must have boundaries indicating the land that is its sovereign right to rule. Once boundaries have been established, as in South Sudan (the most recent country to be recognized by the international community as a sovereign state), they will be tested, and fiercely. After all, seceding from a founding fatherland is most often not an amicable separation. It can result in a loss of control and of economic wealth, and may require unforeseen readjustments.

However, in time, if new boundaries are defended effectively and with clarity as to why they were established in the first place, they become respected, and the outside world learns to not question them, at least not as often or as intensely.

The same can be true in our lives. Boundaries are imperative in our social circles, in attaining the respect we seek, in building lives that honor what we value. We have discussed the importance of boundaries many times on TSLL blog, but as with a new country that is establishing itself, it takes time to firm up the boundaries and for them to be recognized. Along with clarity of purpose, patience, and determination, these ingredients will in time ensure that the new boundaries will be respected by others and will rarely be questioned.

As I have built TSLL, it has taken a certain effort for others, and even myself, to respect the boundaries I have placed around my time — the time needed to create, find inspiration, and rejuvenate so that each week the content will be something I am proud of and, most important, something you as a reader can find inspiring and applicable to the life you are living and building.

As you go about setting and adhering to the boundaries that will help you cultivate the life you strive for, have patience with yourself, refuse to become discouraged, and trust that you know what is right for the life you live each and every day — more than anyone else ever could.

Petit plaisir Pick up Elizabeth Gilbert's *Big Magic* to validate the big dream, idea, or wish you ache to explore. Then trust the magic.

Explore further thesimplyluxuriouslife.com/october19 (how to welcome the magic into your life)

October 20
The Gift of Obstacles

People often hope that life will present them with an untroubled path, a path free of obstacles, tribulations, and growing pains. I absolutely understand this sentiment and have wished for the same thing more times than I can count. However, the reality remains that we will run into moments of frustration, occurrences we would rather not deal with at some point throughout our lives if we are daring to chase our dreams.

While we can certainly prevent many unfortunate events from happening with planning, knowledge, and foresight, there will always be hiccups we cannot predict or avoid.

A sign of progress and of growth is running into these roadblocks, kinks, and initial problems, for it is only when we choose to change and improve our lives that we run up against things we have never experienced before. And it is in these moments that we learn, grow, and surpass these teachable obstacles that nudge us ever closer to our desired dream.

Life never offers us an obstacle we cannot handle. It is as if life knows our strength before we do and often presents obstacles as a way of placing a mirror in front of us and awakening us to a strength we did not know we had.

So today, tomorrow, or anytime in the future, when you run up against something that at first you do not have the answer to, have faith that there is a solution, and be thankful that you have been given this opportunity to grow. After all, life is simply an opportunity to step more fully into who we have the potential to become.

Petit plaisir Turn on Nina Simone singing "Feeling Good" and reignite your inner confidence.

Explore further thesimplyluxuriouslife.com/october20 (five ways to harness the power of your mind to improve your life)

October 21
Conquer Fear with Perspective and Connection

One of the easiest ways I have found to dilute fear's power is to broaden my perspective and seek connections with those who are rational, have more experience than myself, and have proven themselves to have integrity regarding the issue at hand.

October

When I do these few things, in what feels like the blink of an eye, my fear dissipates, and I breathe far more deeply and can escape the swirl of anxiety that had been threatening.

Fear and those who encourage it do not want us to step outside the box they are trying to place around us. So long as the environment is under their control, they can limit the information that is shared. As soon as we step outside the box — pick up a book, gain information from a credible expert — the fear loses its grip, and we can combat the threats that are being used to hold us in place and keep us in line.

Often we hold on to fear because we lack the energy to look beyond what we are accustomed to or an ability to understand that there is more to know or how to acquire such information. And while it may seem initially too difficult to seek beyond the box in which we find ourselves (it can seem to be a secure space), especially if we have been there for a long time, we can become unburdened and liberated from fear.

Wherever you run up against fear — at work, in a relationship, after reading the news, in social situations — remember that you hold more power than you realize to step out of the circle of perpetuated fear. By seeking to broaden your perspective and by speaking and engaging with others you trust and who perhaps have successfully navigated the same situation, you deflate the power of the fearmongers.

Knowledge is power. Knowledge enables us to find true peace. And knowledge conquers fear. When a temporary moment of fear presents itself, seek out more knowledge before you act in the way the fearmongers want.

As I share in my first book, *Choosing the Simply Luxurious Life*, fear never evaporates entirely. Rather, we become better at mastering it. Instead of letting it drive your life, put it in the back seat and take it for a drive. While you are at it, let it fuel you, as often the dreams we are afraid to seek are exactly what we deeply desire.

Petit plaisir Visit a local antiques or consignment or thrift shop. Explore the paintings. Who knows what treasured original piece of artwork you might find. Pair with a custom frame to fit your home's aesthetic, and add a signature touch at an affordable price.

Explore further thesimplyluxuriouslife.com/october21 (eight ways and reasons to display art in your home)

October 22
Everything Is Invented

When I entered my second year of living in Bend, Oregon, and realized how powerful the first year had been for meeting new people, my reflections on first impressions gave me great pause. The gift of a first impression is that you can be almost anybody. The catch is continuing to be that person, as eventually the true you is revealed in one way or another.

It is easier to just be yourself from the beginning. When you have the opportunity to rebuild a life from what can feel at times like the ground up, you can be who you truly are without your former selves holding you back.

Each of us must examine where we have come from, heed the lessons that come to us along the way, and recognize why we act and think the way we do, yet too often we disable ourselves by holding on to these former personas. And they are — now, in the present — former personas. We all can grow, and we should take all opportunities to grow and therefore surpass who we were yesterday to become more fully ourselves today.

When I began my life anew in an entirely new town, it was very much a fresh start. The new location in many ways made it easier, but a fresh start does not need to require uprooting from where you call home.

Why not attend a new activity or event and reach out to new people? Why not introduce your new and current self to them? Why not let go of the selves that are no longer serving you? Because you do hold the power to change the quality of your life. In many ways, it begins with how you perceive yourself and requires discipline to not revert back to old, unhelpful habits that did not serve you well.

In *The Art of Possibility*, Benjamin Zander writes, "Everything in life is an invention. If you choose to look at your life in a new way, then suddenly your problems fade away. One of the best ways to do this is to focus on the possibilities surrounding you in any situation rather than slipping into the default mode of measuring and comparing your life to others."

Consider for a moment who you are today and who you were a year ago. I have no doubt you have grown and progressed in some fashion. However, are you still hanging on to old habits that are part of the old you and that no longer serve you? Why not let those habits go? Why not begin to live your life in a manner that is more truly in alignment with who you are now? The quality of your life will benefit, and that is absolutely the reason to let go.

Petit plaisir Make a lentil, olive, and raisin salad, and discover how decadent a healthy salad can taste.

Explore further thesimplyluxuriouslife.com/october22 (recipe for lentil salad with olives and raisins)

October 23
What Are You Being Given: Comfort or Growth?

There can be a tug of war between comfort and growth.

I was to attend my regular weekly yoga class at the end of the day. I had carefully planned my work schedule to ensure I would be done in time to partake in class, return home afterward, and relax without any unfinished writing to tend to. However, when yesterday afternoon arrived, I was eager to stay at home, unwind, cook a good meal, and relax with a hot bath.

In the back of my mind, I knew how restorative, necessary, and worthwhile attending yoga class would be, but oh my goodness, did I not want to go.

But I did, and as soon as I sat down on my mat and went through my own personal regimen of stretches before class began, I knew I had made the right decision. The class exhausted me, challenged me beyond what I was capable of doing, but I was present the entire time. I gave myself the ability to be present in that room with a handful of other people also working through their yoga practice, stepping away from their lives for an hour and fifteen minutes. I had accepted the gift of going to class: the opportunity for growth.

My yoga instructor began class, incorporated throughout class, and completed class with a central question. At each segment of our vinyasa practice — when we were holding poses that our breathing enabled us to do, when we were folding our bodies in half, and when we were completing the session in savasana — she asked us to ask ourselves, "What am I being given in this moment?"

What a necessary question to guide us through our days, and especially through moments we may, in the past, have deemed stressful, unmanageable, and irritating. Thanksgiving is nearing here in the States, so the mantra of inquiry seems pertinent, but why not pose this question throughout each of our days all year long?

When we ask, "What am I being given in this moment?" we are removing future worries and past pains and reflecting on what is going well, what is enabling us to live our lives in the present moment. Maybe you can be thankful only for drivable roads to get to the market to pick up food (such as during Bend's snowpocalypses of 2017 and 2019), or maybe the gift of sight will be the best you can muster, but there is, as my instructor reminded us, always something to be grateful for.

As I attempted to hold some of the more difficult poses, the question danced in my mind. And in that most unwelcome moment of focus — my muscles were screaming, and I wished that class was over — I was reminded to be thankful that my back no longer hurts, and that I have a body that enables me to try these poses, no matter how discombobulated I may look.

Keep the question "What am I being given in this moment?" alive as a regular bit of self-inquiry. Perhaps you will begin to notice yourself lighten, the angst in your step lessen, and the joy of your days expand.

Petit plaisir Explore planting Rozanne geraniums — hardy perennials that provide lovely groundcover in rose beds — for a flood of purple blooms from June to September.

Explore further thesimplyluxuriouslife.com/october23 (the necessary ingredient in luxury — comfort)

October 24
Taking Action

Merely by doing absolutely nothing, we can easily create problems and obstacles in our minds that do not exist. In other words, when we face a daunting or intimidating new task, the longer we do not take action to tend to it, move past it, or examine exactly what it is, the more we build it up in our minds as something horrendous or life-shattering.

In everything — from dreading seeing the score we earned on an exam to uncertainty about the future — the unknown can take many forms, and we can gravitate toward the negative if we have never experienced the success a reward or boon can bring into our lives. After all, we know what our lives are like right now, at this moment. But we do not know what our lives will be like when the homeowners say yes to our offer to buy the house, the boss says yes to our request for a raise, or the coach/trainer pushes us beyond our preconceived limits and enables us to experience what we can achieve.

We thrive and step closer toward our best possible selves only by trying something new, taking action, and making ourselves vulnerable.

But we also need to be in the right frame of mind to receive the information we need, to move forward successfully.

As I watched the documentary *RBG*, which profiles the late associate Supreme Court Justice Ruth Bader Ginsburg, I was reminded that often our best self is revealed when we adhere to what we uniquely can do best. Instead of physically joining the protests in the streets for women's equality during the 1960s and '70s, Ginsburg took part by becoming a teacher (she was one of only twenty female law professors in the country when she began teaching at Rutgers in 1963) and by practicing law to challenge legislation that suppressed women's rights. We take action in different ways, large and small, but taking action is the path toward reducing stress, making progress, and reducing our fears and worries.

It can be tempting to do nothing when the unknown appears to be horrendous, but the life we desire lies on the other side of struggle — waiting for us to take action and persevere through strains that will only be temporary.

Perhaps you are on the other side of the struggle and nodding in agreement that, indeed, in hindsight, the struggle was absolutely worth it. I can attest that sometimes it does not feel that way when you are in the middle of it, but the discomfort will not last long as you strive forward through the challenge and then overcome it.

Petit plaisir On this date in 1960, John Coltrane recorded "Body and Soul," a lovely jazz track. Close your eyes, and just let your body sway to its syncopated, yet steady rhythm.

Explore further thesimplyluxuriouslife.com/october24 (the choice, the struggle, and the reward)

October 25
The How of Change

Motivation + Ability + Prompt = Lasting Change. BJ Fogg teaches this equation for change in his book *Tiny Habits: The Small Changes That Change Everything*. Most important, he says, we must begin with a clear idea of the change we wish to make.

Fogg uses the analogy of designing a garden we wish to grow into a beautiful and abundant space. Once we know what we want to grow, we can begin cultivating the behaviors that will enable what we plant to successfully reach its fullest potential.

The Road to Le Papillon

Where to begin? Start small. Again BJ Fogg instructs us: "Start where you want to on your path to change. Allow yourself to feel successful. Then trust the process." Start so small that it may seem almost too unfathomable to believe you are creating new habits to bring about the change you seek. Success on the first attempt creates momentum, thereby removing the "demotivators." "Once the 'demotivators' are removed, the natural motivator (often hope) can blossom, which in turn can sustain the new behavior over time." Once your motivation begins to rise, you begin to see your confidence in your own ability to make the necessary change rise, and you begin to understand that you can usher into your life the change you seek.

With motivation and ability figured out, now all you need is a prompt. "The skill of redesigning your environment makes your habits easier to do." Cultivating an environment that encourages the change you seek is the final ingredient for lasting change to occur. For example, if you are working on taking time to slow down every day, create a beckoning place in your house or in your garden to sit and relax.

A friend of the podcast, the founder of The Confidence Project, Tracy Hooper shared that, to achieve this goal, she plants zinnias in the summer outdoors near a sitting area she sees from her kitchen window. The space is tidy, colorful, and offers a comfortable place to sit and just be still. Throughout the year, the plants change with the season, but the goal remains the same: a simple daily prompt — natural beauty — reminding her to rest daily. Each day she is in her kitchen. Each day she looks out her window. Each day she knows the peace she will find when she sits down in her curated tranquil space. Boom! A new and positive change, a lasting change, occurs.

Take time to consider the demotivators versus natural motivators surrounding you to live the life you imagine. Thoughtfully edit and create the positive prompts that encourage you to begin experiencing "easy" successes that will bolster your motivation, thus encouraging you to continue until the change you seek is your reality.

Petit plaisir Enjoy an apple *tarte tatin*.

Explore further thesimplyluxuriouslife.com/october25 (recipe for apple *tarte tatin*)

October 26
Mental Scripts

What scripts do you hold in your mind that you have accepted as truth without questioning? Initially, this can be a hard question to answer because when we do not know that we have accepted something, how can we be aware of it?

I have been thinking about scripts that I have let myself accept, and with the help of others I trust, I have been able to identify certain beliefs about what I can and cannot do, what is and is not possible, what is and is not true about the world we live in. Identifying these aspects of my life has brought me even more peace and comfort for my everydays.

Perhaps you too have scripts you have accepted that are not beneficial to living your best life. Maybe you have accepted a script because others are following it or preaching it, and not following it would initially be stressful, exhausting, and perhaps ostracizing. One key to detecting when we are following an unhelpful or self-destructive script is when we do not understand our own strengths and uniqueness. In my second book, *Living the Simply Luxurious Life*, I devote a chapter to helping readers unearth the strengths that already exist within them. Our discoveries will be unique to each of us, but being conscious of what they are and discovering how to strengthen them can be life-changing — for the better.

Erasing the scripts that we have accepted without question and that confine us to a life lived beneath our potential liberates us to finally see and experience what previously had seemed impossible or unknown. Find some time to sit with yourself and list the truths by which you live your life. Then examine the ones that set you free and the ones that cause you pain, angst, and worry. As entrepreneur Marie Forleo shares, fear is good when it is tempered by the hope that it will lead to expansiveness, but it is something to relinquish when it comes from a place of retraction.

The same can be said for the scripts we allow to be part of our lives: If a script is limiting, we need to question its validity fiercely. And if a script enables us to stretch ourselves, perhaps we should at least get to the truth of where it came from, so that we can find a more stable foundation from which to spring.

Petit plaisir To inspire you to sit down for dinner with neighbors and friends more often, read Isabel Vincent's memoir *Dinner with Edward*.

Explore further thesimplyluxuriouslife.com/october26 (ten ways to cultivate a mental diet that elevates the quality of your life)

October 27
Keep Going

It never feels it will be done until it is.

When we take on a demanding project, task, or goal, the outcome can feel elusive. However, so long as we continue to step forward (occasionally stopping to catch our breath, refueling as needed, resting regularly), we eventually feel something that is hard to understand until we find ourselves near the end of the route: the lifting of a weight or expectation (some may call it a burden) slowly rising from our shoulders.

When the end is in sight, when the finish line is within reach, an adrenaline surge helps us to push through tasks we never imagined we would be capable of tending to well or at all, after experiencing so much exhaustion and sometimes pain. When we are in the middle of selling a house, searching for a job, building a relationship, or completing a long, arduous project, it can feel as though it is never going to end. But it will.

The renewed energy you will feel upon not only seeing the finish line but crossing it will boost you to heights of creativity, hope, and playful giddiness you might have never known you could feel. From finishing a wallpapering project even though my shoulders felt like jelly (I dreamed of sleeping in a bedroom filled with more light and beauty) to crossing the finish line of a marathon in which we weathered deluge after deluge of rain, the adrenaline fueled by sincere desire seems impossible to imagine until you experience the moment.

No matter where you are in your journey, I hope this offers some encouragement, a deep breath of reassurance in yourself, and a pat on the back for choosing to see what you are capable of, and persisting. I know you are going to be successful.

Petit plaisir Victoria and Albert — their paired names can be found in a variety of venues — from museums to soaking tubs — and their love affair still intrigues. Watch the series *Victoria*, starring Jenna Coleman and Tom Hughes.

Explore further thesimplyluxuriouslife.com/october27 (be the hero of your own story — why and how)

October 28
Extending Kindness

Extending kindness — not because someone deserves it, but rather because we wish to extend it — requires that we be self-actualized, self-aware, and cognizant of more than just that one moment.

Often when we are on the receiving end of rude behavior, we respond with a cutting remark thrown back in return or an equally rude response. After all, it was warranted, no? In actuality, when it comes to sincere kindness, it is important to understand that the reason the other person chose hostility rather than kindness has nothing to do with you. You simply gave them an outlet, and as a way of release, they chose to take it.

Choosing kindness is easy when the people we engage with are equally kind or more so, and when kindness is not expected, that is often when it is most needed. It is in such moments of need that kindness has the most power — maybe not in the moment, for the person on the receiving end, but perhaps for people looking on. Watching someone extend kindness when it was not expected can be a profound, life-shifting experience.

Kindness is powerful. And whether you believe in karma or anything else that dictates your moral code, you can never choose badly when you choose the path of genuine humanity — thoughtful compassion and kindness. Whether it be a smile extended to a stranger or perhaps refraining from a teasing chuckle and instead offering a pat on the back and reassurance that someone's efforts were appreciated, kindness is priceless.

Depending upon your sensitivities, you will pick up — immediately or eventually — on sincere kindness extended your way. Repay the favor. And that does not mean you have to extend it directly to the giver. Pay it forward. Move it along and spread the kindness. Kindness really does beget more kindness, in one way or another.

Petit plaisir Settle in and be still while listening to Duke Ellington (piano) and John Coltrane (tenor saxophone) as they pair up for "Sentimental Mood."

Explore further thesimplyluxuriouslife.com/october28 (the difference between kindness and pity)

October 29
The Realities of Being Human

Our minds are powerful motivators or manipulators, depending upon how well we understand them. When things are going well, it can seem that everyone must be feeling the way we are or has felt what we are feeling, but when things are upside down and we cannot seem to make anything work, we can convince ourselves that we are the only ones who have ever felt so horribly.

The truth is that we all are experiencing the realities of being human, and we all feel, at some point, excitement, anxiety, relief, doubt, validation, and rejection. Each of these feelings — positive and negative — are felt by just about anyone who has lived a long life. You are not alone.

It can be hard to remind ourselves of this truth when the cards do not seem to be falling in our favor; it is much easier to believe it when they are. But the reality is that we are never alone in feeling what we feel. While yes, each of us is unique and has particular strengths and talents, human emotions are not unique. The moments and reasons we feel them will vary, but not what we feel.

Knowing this fact brings relief to my mind every time I remind myself of it, and then I rebuild my courage, give myself a good pep talk, and face what I am about to encounter.

A similar truth regarding worry and doubt is that we can create what we tell ourselves and can help manifest the outcome we hope for or avoid the outcome we dread. How? We put on filters and look for either positive or negative signs, embracing or ignoring the script we have allowed to run through our minds. When you know this, it is all the more important to choose hope rather than dread, faith rather than fear.

Look at the worries that consume your thoughts. Then remind yourself of the two life-truths discussed above. Now, seek the life and the thoughts that will bring you more peace and contentment. I know which I will be choosing, and I have a feeling you do too.

Petit plaisir Make a mushroom risotto paired with a favorite glass of chardonnay. Sip as you stir and unwind at the end of the day.

Explore further thesimplyluxuriouslife.com/october29 (recipe for wild mushroom risotto)

October 30
Invest without Guarantees

Releasing a hot air balloon into the sky, enduring months of training prior to an athletic event, feeling secure in a healthy, loving relationship. The main requirement for each of these worthwhile ventures is investing up front.

In order to attain the success we seek, we must be willing to expend energy initially without being certain about how things will work out. However, if we do our homework beforehand, the results will eventually be positive if we have patience.

Whatever you wish to materialize in your life, be willing to invest in it. Whether spending money to set up a business venture, dedicating your extra time to training for a marathon, or setting your relationship as a priority to allow it to become the bond you seek, you must be willing to put forth the necessary energy.

As tempting as it is to look into the future to see if expending your hard work and resources will be worth it, it is impossible to gain such advance knowledge. It is the power of your thoughts, the belief in yourself, and the dedication you put forth that will ultimately determine your success.

Petit plaisir Frame a quote, an illustration, a picture, something that reminds you that you are living the life you thoroughly enjoy. Place it where you will see it during your moments of pondering.

Explore further thesimplyluxuriouslife.com/october30 (inspiration for investing in yourself)

October 31
Embracing Risk

There is something exciting, childlike, and intriguing about Halloween. Maybe it is the opportunity to dress up as an entirely different persona, no matter your age, or maybe it is knowing that something (that won't hurt you) will catch you off guard.

While many aspects of this holiday intrigue and offer enjoyment to many, it also reminds us what it means to take risks, what it feels like to be uncertain and maybe a bit scared, even if we know that, no matter what happens, we will be okay.

The Road to Le Papillon

Accepting a certain level of risk is necessary in order to live fully and up to our maximum potential. Calculated risk — most definitely. Spine-tingling risk based on curiosity — absolutely. After all, it is only when we jump that we cover amazing distances. Yes, sometimes we will miss the mark, but with each leap, we gain experience and confidence, and understand how to fine-tune the next leap we most certainly should take.

While it is easy to go about life following the same routine, walking in the same path day after day, we waste the opportunities our one and only life can bring if we do not stretch our boundaries, act a bit more boldly, and do something even when the outcome is not certain.

Consider a risk you have been contemplating more seriously than you have before. Whether it is something small (say, allowing someone new to get to know you) or grand (presenting an idea to your boss or submitting an application for graduate school), give yourself the chance to excel.

Petit plaisir There is disagreement regarding where Mozart composed his Piano Sonata no. 12 in F, K. 332 — was it Salzburg in 1784 or Paris in 1778? Either way, it is a treat for the ears.

Explore further thesimplyluxuriouslife.com/october31 (five reasons to take the risk)

November

Explore and Discover Yourself and the World

October

Some vital life lessons take an extraordinarily long time to learn. My course — I call it Shannon's Peace and Trust in Herself — required twenty years for me to become proficient and graduate.

The lessons offered as part of my particular course (and required to pass it) came in many mediums, but the arts played a particularly large role — from exhibits in the handful of towns and cities I have called home, to nonfiction books, biographies, three Broadway plays (I still pinch myself when I recall seeing them), films, documentaries, classical music and jazz, and yes, even gardening was a teacher as well.

Travel certainly provided a significant portion of the curriculum, as did language teachers and cookbook writers who welcomed foreigners, complete strangers into their homes in France and taught us not only how to cook, but how to live well. Yes, the arts — from culinary to film to paintings to music to writing — were my teachers, and I am grateful to have had the opportunity to learn.

What did I learn? This book and my previous two contain the lessons I discovered. One of the most valuable — required before I could don the "cap and gown" and step forward toward a life I had dreamed about but did not feel would be possible — was how to hold my joy.

As a child, I unconsciously discovered how to find joy in my everydays. As a teenager and young adult, I lost track of that knowledge because I did not fully realize how valuable it was. In my late twenties, I stepped back into the course of learning how to live to experience true contentment. The blog was born, and the lessons built upon themselves, and I have shared 99 percent of them with the TSLL community.

Once I began to experience a life of contentment in my everydays, I wanted to share what I had discovered with not only my readers but the people in my life, but sometimes, when I did, my joy was diminished because of the insecurities held by some of those people. I wanted to share my joy with others — wouldn't doing so only multiply it? — but I finally realized, guided by my counselor, that what I was really doing was seeking approval for my joy. Ahhh.

After I gained this insight, it still took me nine months to consistently not seek approval to feel my joy fully. When I finally did, I strengthened my trust in myself — most important, my trust in my voice and my intuition — and came to know a truth I had held, but did not trust: that public school teaching was no longer my path. I could not change the past. Being a teacher was the journey I needed to take to pass the required course for a life of quality and true contentment. What I had not done for twenty years was, first, to fully and completely listen to my voice and, second and most important, to trust my voice.

My feeling joy — something not derived from what is outside of me, but wholly from within and unique to me — was enough. Joy arrived, and it remains when I trust myself even, and especially, regarding how I will navigate many tomorrows.

Having put into practice the vital life lesson I finally learned, I listened. I listened to myself without outside influence (the pandemic helped here, as it freed me to think without limits). I listened, and I knew it was time to leave teaching. I listened, and I feel joy in my everydays more regularly than I have ever felt joy.

And when I feel the urge (out of habit and conditioning) to unconsciously seek approval for feeling such joy, the arts are my outlet. I write it out. I put it on paper or in the computer or into an idea for the blog. I spend time pottering in the dirt in my garden — feeding the roses, planting seedlings after the first frost, and planning my garden for next year. I turn to works created by others and soak in what they share.

The arts reveal insights and unexpected truths that are often obscured by master marketing techniques and cultural expectations, ranging from the latest fashions to the life-trajectory path we must follow. Whether it is our career path, our love path, or our life path, if it is not our own, and we unconsciously allow ourselves to be nudged and pulled and coaxed in directions and accept beliefs that shroud our true selves, we can turn to the arts. They deftly wave a magic wand of sorts, providing insight and motivation to gather up our courage to explore the feelings they provoke.

The arts also, and most important, inspired me to further explore a variety of things on my own after the play concluded, after I finished the book's last chapter, or viewed the final painting in the exhibit. Many times, I was my own company, and this too was a grand gift that demonstrated to me the power of letting myself be wholly myself, of following my curiosity without approval from another or trying to impress someone. Yet another important life lesson.

The road to Le Papillon wound through many mediums of art, and without them, I would not have arrived where I am. I would still be lost, insecure, and mistrustful of myself and my voice, but the arts *were* there. I stepped forward toward the opportunities they offered, and my entire life expanded, strengthened, deepened, and became a joyous everyday experience.

November 1
The Courage to Create Your Life

Creativity takes courage.

—Henry Matisse

November

In the last house I decorated, the last home I owned, I played it safe in the living room and the kitchen. I kept to beige in the living room and white in the kitchen — walls, furniture, dishes, you get the idea. After all, I told myself I needed to think of the resale value.

In my current home, as I go about making decisions about wallcoverings and furniture and appliance colors, beige and white are set aside. However, even the choices I am making, while they may seem bold to some and tame to others, to me now, after having traveled far more than I had thirteen years ago, the decisions I am making seem natural and intuitive because I have seen them before in beautiful spaces.

Often our courage comes from observing others exercise their courage (or what appears to be courage, as we would have been too timid to try) in arenas we are exploring ourselves. Perhaps it is décor or painting or screenwriting or graphic design. To explore art history, architectural design periods, and clothing trends we see it takes courage exercised frequently and without exception.

Mihaela Ivan Holtz, PsyD, LMFT, has written, "Courage is an energy that you can connect with when you find comfort in your fears, insecurities, or anxieties. When you tap into your fears and allow them to fuel you rather than paralyze you, you are finding and using your courage."

The muscle of courage is toned and kept in shape by continuing to explore, to learn, to witness, to travel, to read, to inquire, to keep an open mind. Everything we will experience or witness will not speak to us, but we will begin to understand what works well together and why, and if we want it to work that way should we bring it into our home or projects.

Observe the performers at the next concert, play, or lecture you attend, soak up the aesthetics in the vacation rentals, museums, and hotels you visit. As you flip through magazines, décor books, and cookbooks, what sparks your interest? What holds your attention? What spontaneously earns your appreciation? Without warning and almost naturally, you will begin to observe courageous choices being made, but no more will they seem courageous to you because they simply make perfect sense as you live your life and cultivate your sanctuary sincerely, thoughtfully, and intentionally.

Petit plaisir Let Handel's Concerto Grosso in B-flat Major, op. 3, lift you as you begin to explore without hesitation, and let your curiosity take you where it will.

Explore further thesimplyluxuriouslife.com/november1 (thirty-four inspiring daily rituals to ignite your creativity)

November 2
The Purpose of Tension

Novels generally include a plot, an expected trajectory, and a buildup of tension. In fact, a central aspect of most pieces of enduring art is a need to relieve tension, but first the tension must build. A need unfulfilled creates tension. A desire unrequited creates tension. An injustice creates tension. Whether the author, playwright, screenwriter, or artist in any medium aims for the world to better understand, wants to deepen the audience's compassion, seeks to celebrate a truth, or explain the "why" of events that seem to consist of nebulous complexities, the brilliance of art resides in its ability to serve as a tool to awaken society, but before artists relieve tension, they must present a quandary.

Each of our lives can be a work of art. We each are a masterpiece, should we choose to work with the tools we have been given.

Tension can appear and remain in our lives indefinitely if we do not live a life of awareness and presence. However, when tension arises, we generally want to relieve it, and the ways we relieve tension will determine the quality of our lives.

As with stress, small amounts of tension can assist us in completing tasks well or surviving unexpected emergencies. However, persistent stress — caused, say, by job exhaustion and a failure to balance work expectations with what we need for well-being — can reduce the quality of our lives. My writing, the blog, and its related projects became my tension relievers. I would go to school to earn my paycheck and give 110 percent to my students, come home drained, and fuel back up by sitting down and writing. Tension relieved.

However, while the relief part of the equation felt incredible, the endeavor to find balance began to wear me down. I needed too much relief, more than I could find, more than there was time for. So I began to be brave and explore the role tension should have in my life.

In hatha yoga, the goal is to build tension through the poses, challenging your muscles, pushing them beyond what you once thought were their limits. The balance of creating this tension is knowing you will let it go. The release will be exhilaratingly soothing and calming.

We each need to learn how much tension is healthy for us. Healthy tension can bring to life brilliant works of art, thought-provoking and emotionally riveting plots, and character journeys toward truth and insight. But refusing to acknowledge that we are continually running up against the same tension is not healthy.

Tension that is healthy stretches us, expands us, strengthens our minds and our understanding of the world, our skills, what we are capable of, and the possibilities waiting to be discovered. Your art, your form of expression can actually be your tension relief, explored while you stretch yourself.

Stretching myself involved stepping out of my comfort zone, concluding my public school teaching career after twenty years, and accepting that I would feel tension temporarily as I began a new chapter. I knew the tension would be minimal so long as I chose to be a student of the journey.

Choose to acknowledge that, while tension may be a temporary part of your journey, it should not be the same tension each time if it is the right type of tension. The right tension expands you and enables you to grow into your full potential. Being in the grip of a negative tension depletes you and leaves you exhausted with life, unable to pursue what you wish to explore.

Petit plaisir Make the classic French seafood dish *moules marinière à la crème*, paired with artisan crusty bread and a glass of white wine.

Explore further thesimplyluxuriouslife.com/november2 (recipe for *moules marinière à la crème*)

November 3
A Day to Yourself

The piece of art that you are requires thoughtful care and attention. Depending upon my schedule, I reserve full or half days to rejuvenate my mind and body, and do so regularly. Whether it is the afternoon for my seasonal facial, popping into a favorite bookshop, taking a leisurely stroll at a park full of autumnal colors, then returning home, skin nourished, and making a simple, yet flavor-rich meal that I enjoy while watching a cosy mystery or a documentary, or spending a full day at the coast walking with bare feet (summer) or wellies (for wading in the incoming tide), returning to my cottage only to write, sleep, and cook a good meal — such necessary moments restart a source of creative energy that allows me to put my best ideas and best self forward.

On a consistent basis, as you observe your schedule and responsibilities, insist on taking a day or half a day to focus solely on yourself, a day when your responsibilities have either been delegated or put on hold and you can just let the day unfold. Over the years, I have witnessed great benefit to my interactions with others as well as the quality of my work when I prioritize my well-being.

Often, our lives take on a momentum of their own, and it is not until we consciously pause and take a breath that we realize a breath is very much needed — maybe two breaths. For some, the ability to put on the brakes and schedule time for ourselves may be easier than we expect, while for others, it is more difficult for any number of reasons.

Wherever you lie on the continuum of being able to regularly carve out a day for yourself, be assured that it is not selfish to take a day just for you. It is actually necessary for you to gain back energy, your *joie de vivre*, and a sound and alert mind. By an alert mind, I mean being aware of where you are heading and that it is in the direction you want.

Days to yourself — periodic pauses to refresh your vision and avoid the need for backward steps further down the road — affirm the necessity and the value of your role in your life. It may seem obvious to point out our role in our own lives as valuable, but when we hold space, we model ways for those around us to also value themselves and to honor what they need, creating a positive snowball effect of healthy relationships that include self-respect as well as respect for others.

Schedule a day to be yours completely. Whether you stay home or go out or mix and match, let yourself be fully present to follow where you need to go for your well-being, and observe what presents itself.

Petit plaisir No matter how large or small your garden, add soil conditioner or organic compost wherever you have plants, shrubs, trees, borders, boulevards, or garden beds. Your plants will thank you with their nourished beauty in the spring.

Explore further thesimplyluxuriouslife.com/november3 (five reasons to revel in solitude)

November 4
Give Yourself Space to Create

Have you ever wondered why you are more creative at certain times of the day or during certain period of your life? In a 2003 article in *Time* magazine, Jeffrey Kluger describes findings that when we free our minds of unnecessary worries, clutter, and busyness, we free ourselves to think creatively and connect the dots, producing more than we may have thought possible.

This study was designed to explore whether those who are retired are more likely than their younger counterparts to create amazing works of art and, in doing so, lengthen the years of their lives. From my own experience, each time a school holiday or summer break arrived, my time was wide open, and my mind opened as well, sparking seemingly endless ideas I could not complete entirely before the break would end and the classroom would call.

Kluger explains that the reason for more creativity in later years is that, by then, many responsibilities have been completed (raising children, paying the mortgage, etc.). And while this study was directed at the Baby Boomer generation and beyond, there is a lesson in it for all of us. The more we fine-tune and simplify our lives, the more of an opportunity we offer ourselves to live creatively and more fulfilled because we are doing what we love. In doing so, we lengthen the duration of our years as well as improve their quality.

Take a close and honest look at your schedule: Where can you open a few windows, even just a smidge? In other words, what can you remove that holds less value than the value of improving the quality of your everydays?

Petit plaisir Is there a picture that captures your joy — unedited, unposed, and unabashedly true? Frame it well, and hang it where it suits your daily life to extend the joy into your everyday routine.

Explore further thesimplyluxuriouslife.com/november4 (ten life choices to simplify and welcome calm and contentment into your everyday life)

November 5
Self-Care Means Listening to Yourself

Our bodies and minds speak to us, telling us what they need. We simply need to listen.

During the months leading up to the release of my second book — *Living The Simply Luxurious Life: Making Your Everydays Extraordinary and Discovering Your Best Self* — I gave my attention and energy predominantly to launching the book. With the help of a publicist, I introduced TSLL concept to new readers, media personalities, and writers. My family came to Bend to visit and help me send out the books that blog readers had preordered. I was humbled by their support and by my readers' enthusiasm and interest in the book. All of this positive energy buoyed my energies higher than I expected.

With new readers exploring what living simply luxuriously is all about without having first spent time on the blog or listened to the podcast, I felt a little more vulnerable, and over time, I realized I had become emotionally raw. Sharing intimate, honest glimpses of ourselves is not easy. But as I watched the critically acclaimed film *Can You Ever Forgive Me?* starring Melissa McCarthy, I was reminded that being vulnerable is hard. In fact, it is the courageous thing to do. And because it is hard, we may become more exhausted than we expect, even though it is "only" emotional energy we are expending in extra doses. The truth is, emotional energy is still energy, and we need to replenish our reserves in order to keep sharing ourselves with others.

What is your body telling you? Are you listening? Is it bursting with energy and eager to share in the holiday spirit that is approaching? Or perhaps you need a bit of rest, maybe just an afternoon, an evening, or a blissful morning to be still or at least slow down. The holidays are tremendously exhilarating and exciting, but we need to take care of ourselves so that we can enjoy them.

Frequently, my first step of self-care is a bubble bath. The hot water encompasses my body, soothing music removes the day's events from my mind, and the darkened room, alight with flickering candles, helps any headache I may have subside. And I regain perspective.

Especially when you choose to be vulnerable and share yourself with others, remember to care for yourself as well. You have expended much, and it is a wise investment to make. In doing so, you increase the potential to improve the quality of your life as you connect with others. But you will always have yourself; therefore, tend to yourself well, regularly, and often.

Petit plaisir Let the rainfall of the season nourish you. Pull on a pair of galoshes or wellies (favorite French brands: Aigle, Le Chameau; British: Hunter, Barbour), don a hooded raincoat, or open a sturdy umbrella (one from James Smith and Sons is an investment but will last a lifetime), and wander, letting the drops wash away worries that need not be yours and reveal the beauty of the life that surrounds you.

Explore further thesimplyluxuriouslife.com/november5 (sixteen ideas for simple everyday self-care)

November 6
Be Present

Soft rains falling on trees that have turned exquisitely golden and ruby-red perform a melody for the senses akin to an opera singer expertly sharing her talent surrounded by brilliant costumes and sets. Taking my dogs on a walk with my feet in my favorite yellow wellies, taking a drive as the windshield wipers sing their tune, or simply sitting in my large armchair next to a picture window overlooking the garden while I sip something warm and listen to the raindrops tap on the windows — these are the simple luxuries of coziness and tranquility during this beautiful time of year that make me smile and elevate my everydays.

It is easy to miss such moments because one minute the weather is warm and beckoning, then the next it is frigid and the trees have been blown bare. By slowing down and taking the time to absorb my surroundings, I am able to enjoy these fleeting moments nature has to offer, no matter what may be going on.

Whether you learn the lesson of living in the moment and appreciating what it offers via experience or observation, heed what it is trying to teach you. Lift your eyes from your smartphone, take your fingers off your tablet, and look up, look around, before such beauty transitions into winter.

Petit plaisir To relax, listen to Arabesque no. 1 in E Major, by Claude Debussy.

Explore further thesimplyluxuriouslife.com/november6 (the hygge phenomenon and living simply luxuriously)

November 7
An Exhaustion to Be Treasured

During my trip to France in the summer of 2019, I greatly anticipated returning to the Musée d'Orsay for the first time since 2000. Since that earlier visit, the museum had come to hold the largest collection of impressionist art in the world. A new fifth-story pavilion was added during a 2011 renovation, hidden from the main public area, but once you find it, the iconic see-through, floor-to-ceiling clock in the impressionist's wing's foyer grabs your attention, and you too will likely want a picture of it or with it as it looks over the Seine and toward the Tuileries on the other side of the river.

Upon arriving, I discovered a special exhibit, the first of its kind since the mid-20th century, dedicated entirely to a lesser-known impressionist painter, Berthe Morisot. She knew she was as talented as the better-known, predominantly male impressionists (who immediately recognized her as one of the group's most innovative artists) and did not let a lack of approval thwart her from pursuing her passion. I toured the exhibit with awed fascination, reminded how art from decades and

The Road to Le Papillon

centuries ago can open our eyes to realizations, insights, comfort, and new ideas we may have never explored.

I have found, after heeding suggestions by readers of TSLL blog who live in or near Paris, that a museum is often more satisfyingly enjoyed in small doses, and I walked through other rooms throughout the museum to say hello, for example, to Jean-François Millet's *The Gleaners*, which holds a special place in my heart as the first print of a painting I remember seeing as a young child in my grandparents' home. For some reason it captured my attention, and seeing the actual painting in 2000 and then again in 2019 brought thoughts of my grandparents.

After visiting a museum, we are filled, we are moved, but we are exhausted from taking in a vast amount of input and the exercise of our eyes and mind, even if we have visited the same galleries before. I am always grateful for such exhaustion; it means I have surrendered myself to the museum's visual and intellectual treasures.

Consider exploring a local art exhibit or check your city's arts calendar to plan ahead as you look forward to exploring works that will stimulate your mind in ways you may never have imagined.

Petit plaisir Take time to walk among the fallen leaves. Choose paths where the deciduous trees share a symphony of color to hold you in the present and deepen your appreciation for the seasonal beauty and being alive to savor it.

Explore further thesimplyluxuriouslife.com/november7 (the impressionist artist Berthe Morisot's exhibit at the Musée d'Orsay)

November 8
Books as Necessary Sustenance

It matters because it's an open door to a real life . . . it's an open door to discovery and wonder and fascination and figuring out who you are, why you're here, and what you came to do. It's an invitation to life, and it feeds you forever.
—Oprah Winfrey, speaking about reading and education

The catalyst of an idea springing into my mind often eludes me upon reflection. However, my ideas are usually generated in one of two ways: My curiosity has been piqued, or I have encountered a question I cannot answer.

It was 2016, and I had finally secured a spot in one of Patricia Wells's cooking classes in Provence, after setting it as a reward in 2011 for a goal I wanted to achieve. All things Julia Child had become my fascination, and

November

I read not only the autobiography she wrote with her nephew but a handful of biographies. For two years, I waited with great anticipation and appetite for my return to France for the first time in six years, and my first visit to Provence. Cooking on Julia's stove and listening to Patricia and Walter's stories of their times with her were like being held enthralled by an able storyteller.

Julia Child first tickled my curiosity when I read a book in 2013 titled *Julia Child Rules: Lessons on Savoring Life*, by Karen Karbo. For some time, I had been searching for a town and place to call home, as I never felt truly at ease or content where I was. Bend, Oregon, was always on my list of communities where I might seek out a teaching job. And when I read in Karbo's book that Julia and Paul Child had driven through Bend, Oregon, just prior to being wed in 1946 after a cross-country road trip, someone I wanted to know more about felt in a small way like a kindred spirit.

It was Julia Child's life story, her journey, springboarded by her love of and learning about French cuisine, that fueled my continued curiosity. From her height, to her physical awkwardness, to her determination and zeal, as well as her politics and handling of struggles, I wanted to know more. Thus began my interest in reading books about her life.

The luxury of reading is a priceless gift that can often require money. When I was younger, I had a limited ability to acquire the books I wanted to read. Even with visits to the local library in every town I called home, finding the book I was seeking was often frustrating, time-consuming, and fruitless. For much of my twenties, while I lived in Portland and near Reno, Nevada, I always spent my weekends at the local bookstore to gather titles that captured my attention, find a corner in the shop, and settle in with the only thing I could afford — a hot cup of coffee and a sweet treat to nibble on as I lost all conception of time. Rejuvenating, comforting, insightful, and inspiring, these bookshop weekends fueled me for the coming workweek, even if I did not return with material to read at home.

One of the biggest luxuries I am most grateful for as I advance in my career is the ability to purchase my own books and gradually build up my library. While a consistent handful will be consigned back to Powell's Books, in Portland, for credit so that I can buy more volumes, having a book always at the ready has been the most comforting gift I have welcomed into my life.

To look over a person's library is to perhaps see a glimpse of who they were, who they wanted to be, who they have become and are. Arguably, books are not a luxury, but a necessity for you to breathe and live and wander, seeking answers, throughout your life journey.

Petit plaisir Enjoy a simple, yet delicious appetizer by sautéing sliced oyster mushrooms (three cups) in unsalted butter. Once the mushrooms are nearly cooked down, add one or two handfuls of white rice flour for a nutty flavor, sprinkle with flaky sea salt, and cook until lightly brown. Add more butter, if necessary, and more rice flour, if you want a nuttier flavor. Dish up and sprinkle with freshly chopped parsley.

Explore further thesimplyluxuriouslife.com/november8 (recipe for sautéed oyster mushrooms)

November 9
Our Unacknowledged Gifts

There was no one near to confuse me, so I was forced to become original.
—Joseph Haydn

My students became my teachers when it came to classical music. At the start of each year, we would analyze a musical selection and a handful of adaptations to introduce the concept of tone as it contributes to rhetoric. The students who were enrolled in the school's band and symphony courses taught not only me but the rest of the class new and precise vocabulary to strengthen the analysis of each piece — staccato, decrescendo, forte, vibrato — a handful of the terms written on the board, discussed and brought to life with a brief performance exemplifying each term, followed by discussion of the composer's purpose in using it.

I attended performances of the local volunteer regional symphony, made up of adult musicians from around the community, and occasionally a student would be part of the ensemble. Watching and listening, seeing the young talent take part in bringing musical beauty to so many people reminded me of the life-truth that each of us has a unique talent that we may be unaware of because we have been exercising it for such a long time. Our abilities can seem commonplace, ordinary to us, but to onlookers, our unique abilities shine brilliantly.

Each of us innately possesses, from the day we were born, unique strengths and capabilities. In my second book, *Living The Simply Luxurious Life*, I discuss the idea of a toolbox and stocking it well with our strengths and skills — what we are given by nature (strengths) and what we nurture within ourselves (skills) — to reach our full potential and create a life of true contentment.

Haydn's quote is a reminder of the gift of being in one's own company. From time to time, I tried to explain to extroverted colleagues who had a hard time understanding my choice to live on my own the gift of fruitful solitude and creativity that I enjoy when I choose to be in my own company. To me, it makes sense, and my life thus far is evidence that it works. Time with ourselves, letting our curiosities lead us, frees us from following and gives us permission to try, to explore, to dance with ideas that present themselves without worry of what others are doing or might think.

Many of the students who taught me to appreciate the music they played exhibited a quiet confidence, a trust in themselves to think for themselves, to share their ideas even though they may stray from the common refrain heard from most students, and to exhibit a strong work ethic due to a variety of factors, including the abilities to focus, organize, and ask questions if a topic needs clarifying. Studies have shown that musicians have an increased ability for emotional and impulse regulation, improved memory and spatial learning, improved verbal memory, literacy, and verbal intelligence, improved focus, and an ability to listen as well as to connect disparate ideas. What is even more exciting is that such benefits are not reserved for the young. Picking up an instrument as we age has proven to be beneficial as well.

However, each of the positive benefits shared are skills each of us can learn. The dance of strengths and skills produces our gifts, ones we may not have known or even thought existed.

Spend more time in your own company, revel in solitude, and observe where your curiosity wants to lead you. Follow it, dance with it, explore what is introduced. As you build your confidence to give yourself permission to pursue ideas those around you may not support, give yourself more time than you think you deserve. The truth is, you do deserve it. You have something awesome to share. Give yourself the time to find it.

Petit plaisir Ask yourself the question "How do you keep your heart alive?" Prioritize time to answer honestly, and honor what you share by including it in your everyday life.

Explore further thesimplyluxuriouslife.com/november9 (eight ways for introverts to thrive in the workplace)

November 10
Striking a Self-Nurturing Balance During the Holidays

During the Thanksgiving and winter holidays, I enjoy the opportunity to focus on kindness, gratitude, and compassion. With the arrival of the holidays in the final two months of each year, a direct reminder presents itself that we can either acknowledge or dismiss. We are each given this precious thing called life, and I often ask myself, Am I making the most of it? Am I contributing in a manner that is fulfilling not only for myself, but for others as well?

With each year, I hope I have made progress as I strive to come ever closer to living the life that sits most comfortably and authentically with my true self. After all, trying to be someone we are not is exhausting, and it can rob us of many amazing opportunities.

When I read Twyla Tharp's *The Creative Habit: Learn It and Use It for Life*, what spoke to me immediately was Tharp's embracing of who she is and what she loves to do, her refusal to apologize for it and for making it her life's work. Tharp speaks to the daily rituals and habits so ingrained into her routine that they are a comfort, and they prep her to be the creative talent she is.

When we tap into our creative self, we realize that work can be fun, and as a result, life can be amazingly fulfilling. But more often than not, accessing our creative side will take a tremendous amount of discipline and focus, and will often mean choosing to ignore those who do not understand. It is not our job to explain ourselves to each person who stands in our path or snickers from the sidelines. It is, however, our job to keep striving forward relentlessly.

What does this have to do with the holidays? Celebrating the holidays can cause me to lose my balance, so that I often play expected (but not authentic) roles and do not stay true to who I am, which can prompt a grumpy mood or a feeling of suffocation under all the "have to's." What I have discovered, and with each year am fine-tuning, is that finding a way to keep my balance — enjoy the holidays, but keep my creative rhythm, what I love most about my life — is vital to making the most of this time of year.

I still have moments in the midst of the holidays when I have to step away and catch my breath. Often, I can tell I am off kilter when I notice that my dogs are on edge as well. (It's funny how we first notice an emotional state in others before we notice it in ourselves.) In that moment, I ask myself, How did I let it happen again? Thankfully, with each subsequent year, and with strengthened self-awareness and honoring my needs, such unwanted moments of fatigue and emotional exhaustion occur less frequently.

The key to finding the ideal balance is continuing to get to know ourselves, continuing to ask important questions. Why do I feel comfortable or at peace doing [insert activity], but not what is expected of me? When do I feel free to be myself and just be? When do I feel uncomfortable and out of my element? Why?

November

When we are honest with ourselves and ask these questions, we can begin to experience a holiday season and a life that correlates with our values, our authentic self, and begin to create the life that brings genuine contentment.

I wish you well on this journey, and if you have achieved it, I tip my hat to you. Enjoy and encourage those around you to find their contentment as well.

Petit plaisir Make a savory mushroom, thyme, and leek galette. Perfect for vegetarians, absolutely delicious for all.

Explore further thesimplyluxuriouslife.com/november10 (recipe for mushroom, thyme, and leek galette)

November 11
Yes, and . . .

Life is a lot like jazz . . . it's best when you improvise.
—George Gershwin

When I moved into my house in Pendleton in my late twenties, I received a beloved housewarming gift: a stack of CDs containing the music of the big band and jazz albums my Great Uncle Rufus had on vinyl in his collection (he and my Great Aunt Betty also lived in my new hometown). He kept his vinyl, understandably, but he knew I enjoyed his music, and I appreciated the time it must have taken him to create these CDs.

One New Year's Eve before I moved to Bend, the boys (Oscar and Norman) and I spent the evening with Betty and Rufus. Aunt Betty poured the two of us each a glass of wine, Uncle Rufus made himself his preferred mixed drink, and we all headed into their daylight basement, where shelves and shelves of records were organized. We turned the record player on, I pulled out the vinyl albums that caught my eye, and we sat, listened, sipped, and laughed. The boys too enjoyed snooping about, and they prompted many a chuckle out of Aunt Betty, who adored animals. To this day, Norman still knows her name when I say it out loud — his ears perk up and his eyes look around (she always treated them well, and not a Christmas went by without stocking stuffers for my boys).

Today is her birthday. Our family said goodbye to her in 2019, just before she turned 96, and her passing hurt deeply. During my adult years, she became my grandmother and fervent supporter. After I moved to Bend, I could no longer visit her and Rufus a handful of times each month, which I had done when I lived in Pendleton. I later heard from my mother that, while Aunt Betty missed me and the boys, she believed in me without hesitation, stating, "That girl can do anything."

Aunt Betty's life and mine may appear to have had different paths. Born during the 1920s, she enjoyed working as a single woman, but when she was married, she was not allowed to keep her job due to laws and cultural mores of that time. However, Uncle Rufus was a businessman, and she worked for him at their place of business. She and Rufus had stayed in the same town where they were raised, and though they had a long marriage and wanted to have children, the latter was unable to transpire. Instead, she gave her love to her pets, her husband, her church, and her many grand- and great-grand-nieces and -nephews.

So much of our life unfolds beyond our control. Just as Aunt Betty, part of the Great Generation, grew up and built a life surrounded by certain mores, values, and gender roles, she also improvised in such a way that her love of life and what she valued shone forth. Love and kindness directed her days, and she danced jovially through her full and long life.

Dreaming and planning and hoping play a role in living well, but then we must let go and learn to improvise with what life presents to us.

Following the advice of Tina Fey, Amy Poehler, and so many Second City–trained actors and comedians for onstage success, choose to acknowledge what is, and then add yourself. Simply say, "Yes, and . . ." Step forward into life; become a part of it rather than sitting on the sidelines because a particular moment, event, etc. did not go your way. It may just be the best thing to happen to you, and you will never find out unless you accept the invitation to take part.

Petit plaisir Sit back, put your feet up, and enjoy Stéphane Grappelli's "Sweet Lorraine" performed by the Formosa Quartet with Ru-Pei Yeh on cello.

Explore further thesimplyluxuriouslife.com/november11 (a quiet holiday playlist for jazz and classical music lovers)

November 12
Habits versus Change

Any habit that has become ingrained into our "muscle memory" can be difficult to rewire, even when we know the habit is a reason we are unable to materialize the change we seek. Immediately apologizing, even if we are not to blame, fidgeting when we are nervous, doubting ourselves when we are pursuing something we passionately desire — these behaviors, habits that we repeat unconsciously, can be defensive or survival behaviors.

The difference between surviving and thriving is vast. Which is why we must become aware of the habits that are causing us to stumble and rewire our brain to be rid of them.

In an article posted in 2013, I shared specifics on how to rewire our minds and behaviors in order to starve out bad habits and become acclimated to new, beneficial ones:

- Realize you can change almost anything about your behaviors and habits.
- Give new habits lots of energy by practicing them or imagining doing them.
- If they require self-control, work on only one or two at a time.

The change we seek is possible. However, we must accept that it will initially take a lot of energy to establish new habits. In the end, it will be worth it; the immense energy invested will yield beneficial and long-lasting positive results.

The first step is recognizing which habits do not represent who you are or who you know you can become. You are a confident individual, but when you are placed in challenging situations, do you lose your ability to speak up with resolute certainty? Do you immediately assume the worst, no matter what the situation, and cloud your ability to see the truth?

You can retrain yourself out of detrimental habitual thinking, and I am confident you will tap into the courage to make that change a reality. Your life will be far richer and more fulfilling as you align your thoughts with behavior conducive to the life you wish to create.

Petit plaisir Listen to Carl Friedrich Abel's Symphony in F Major, op. 1, no. 4, as you let newly formed ideas and habits take hold.

Explore further thesimplyluxuriouslife.com/november12 (eleven tips to cultivate good habits)

November 13
Say Yes

Some years ago, I had the opportunity to listen to comedian and writer David Sedaris at Cordiner Hall at Whitman College in Walla Walla, Washington. Nothing short of hilarious, insightful, and oh-so-crassly

The Road to Le Papillon

humorous about life's everyday hiccups, Sedaris spoke with his one-and-only Billie Holiday-esque voice for two hours and probably could have gone on for more.

He had the sold-out audience in stitches as he read his essays, which had appeared or would appear in *The New Yorker* and on his English radio show *Meet David Sedaris*. But a particular statement he made about why so many adventures happen in his life, giving him endless fodder for his writing, caught my attention toward the end of the evening.

"If you say no, you don't have a story to tell. That's why I say yes. The less control you have, the more adventure you have."

It is the last part that is frightening, no? Giving up control is something I have worked hard for when it comes to the security of my job and home. But when it comes to relationships and working with other people, we cannot control anyone but ourselves. So maybe he has a point. Instead of pre-designating in our mind how things should unfold with the people around us, maybe we should say yes (unless, of course, we know better based on previous experience).

Again, when we make assumptions about how something will turn out or should turn out, we get in our own way. I will admit, I have done that many times, and upon reflection, what I was doing unconsciously was trying to protect myself and gain a peace of mind that is impossible to acquire, as I was looking outside of myself rather than within. Accept what is impossible, and say yes anyway, so long as any part of you is the least bit curious about what might unfold should you do so.

Maybe the life lesson or takeaway is to not only say yes initially, but to keep saying yes as more of the adventure unfolds. As I type this, I am trembling a bit because doing this requires a lack of control. But I will try. I am saying yes. Will you?

Petit plaisir Reach for Richard Olney's cookbook *Simple French Food*, which has pride of place in my kitchen library. Peruse until you find a recipe that speaks to you. Be brave, read all of the directions, and then give it a go. His flavors rarely disappoint.

Explore further thesimplyluxuriouslife.com/november13 (why not . . . say yes?)

November 14
Trusting the Unknown

Enjoying the everyday. Being able to savor each moment, not dwelling on the past or worrying about the future. In reality, such simple tasks can be quite difficult, so much so that when we are able to appreciate the present — savor it, revel in it — we need to congratulate ourselves. Have you been able to do this lately?

Allowing myself to let go of expectations is something I have worked on for years, though I still catch myself holding on to them from time to time. For whatever reason, I am able to move forward from the past without much difficulty, but ever since I was a young girl, I have always planned, dreamed, and prepared. In fact, I consider planning to be a hobby, not a chore. But there comes a point when we need to relinquish planning and looking to the future.

Once we know our future is secure, or as secure as we can make it in the present moment (saving for retirement, tending to our health, doing our best professional work, investing and engaging in healthy relationships, etc.), we then need to give ourselves permission to take a deep breath and trust ourselves. In order to truly trust ourselves and where we currently are, we need to be present.

For some, this is an easier proposition than it is for others. I place myself in the "others" category, but it is becoming easier for me to let go — to not worry, "What will my future look like?" and instead trust that it will be just fine due to my efforts, the savings I have invested, and the education I have garnered.

Part of why I bring up the idea of living in the present is that often, if not most of the time, we do not know what life has in store for us. Yes, we have control over much more than we realize, but realistically speaking, we just cannot predict the future.

Give yourself the biggest gift of all this holiday season and establish a future plan; put in place a blueprint for savings and an outline for your life's direction. Then let go, and be present as often as possible. Your life will allow you to experience amazing moments of rhapsody and cultivate unforgettable bonds and memories. Root yourself in trust in yourself, and then let go.

Petit plaisir At a dinner party, make toasts expressing hope for those you have gathered and the journeys they are traveling, as well as gratitude for the present moment, then celebrate with the food and drink that brings you together.

Explore further thesimplyluxuriouslife.com/november14 (ten tips for hosting a wonderful dinner party)

November 15
Responding Rather Than Reacting

Excitement and sadness, exhilaration and frustration, confidence and fear. When opposing emotions enter our lives simultaneously, it can be hard to know how to react. The Charlie Hebdo attacks in Paris in January 2015 firmly held my attention when I first learned of them, and my heart was heavy for longer than I could have imagined. As well, it took even more time to understand what I felt and why I felt it so deeply.

Conflicting emotions can make it hard to maneuver through the everyday, but the better course of action is to recognize and acknowledge our emotions, take time to understand them, but refuse to be their servant. After all, with a clear mind, we know what particular scenarios require of us. We know that when suffering occurs, we must provide comfort and support in a way the griever needs, but we also must honor what we can wholly and lovingly give. We must be professional at work and not take our roles and responsibilities lightly. And we also know that we need to find outlets to unwind, celebrate, and relax. Balance is crucial.

Awareness and common sense are two qualities that require us to be present and to respond as necessary. We cannot simply allow life to toss us about or lead us around by the nose. When, instead, we carefully determine how we will respond, we achieve better results, feel more at peace, and achieve a sense of true contentment.

Find the courage both to strengthen your emotional intelligence (awareness of your own feelings) and to understand how to deepen your awareness of the world around you. These two skills alone will radically improve the quality of your life and the ways you engage with both unwanted events and those you yearn to experience.

Petit plaisir Put a tap in your step as you listen to John Coltrane's "My Shining Hour."

Explore further thesimplyluxuriouslife.com/november15 (the benefits of self-awareness)

November 16
How to Start the Day

I often wake up before the sun rises. This habit began when I had to rise early and commute to teach school. But since my retirement from teaching, my two pups' sleep clocks have become mine. When their appetites tell them it is time for breakfast, they stand in bed (politely, yet insistently), reminding me that mealtime is upon us. I oblige, and quite honestly, I adore my mornings.

I turn on my classical music station (KUSC or WRTI), and my day begins with a gentle bounce as I listen, say, to Tomaso Albinoni's Concerto for Two Oboes in F, op. 9 (allegro). With music in the background, one cannot help but be hopeful for a grand day.

Should I wake up and find that my mind is not in its strongest state (that would be Brain 3.0: The Inner Sage, as defined by Due Quach, founder of Calm Clarity and author of the book of the same name), after feeding my boys, I pour myself a hot cup of lemon water, snuggle back into bed with the window open and the curtains pulled back, so that when the sun rises, I will be able to savor it. Then often I read a book that buoys my resilience.

As TSLL readers will confirm, over the past twelve years, I have shared and recommended nonfiction books far more often than fiction. On my bedside in 2021 were Norma Kamali's *I Am Invincible*, Jay Shetty's *Think Like a Monk*, and Monty Don's *A French Garden Journey*. Each, in its own way, is joyful, uplifting, and insightful.

If we live consciously, we understand that our mind will ebb and flow and not always be in its highest state, but with intentional practice can reside in an inner sage state most of our waking hours. When we choose to dance with life rather than react to it, we bring quality into our everydays.

Determine when your mind may not be strongest, and then devise practices, rituals, and routines to help bring it back to a firm position. Something as seemingly simple as classical music and a good book have worked for me.

Petit plaisir Watch the multi-award winning British drama *The Crown*, created by Peter Morgan.

Explore further thesimplyluxuriouslife.com/november16 (twelve ideas for jump-starting the day well)

November 17
Trusting the Tug of Your Curiosity

We seek what we wish to find, the oft-cited saying reminds, but sometimes poignant serendipity dances into our lives, and we cannot help but acknowledge what is extended to enrich our journey moving forward.

Leading up to my long-anticipated trip to Provence during the summer of 2018, a locally owned boutique theater screened a series of documentaries profiling renowned artists: *Manet: Portraying Life* (2013), *Cézanne — Portraits of a Life* (2018), and *Rembrandt, Exhibitions on Screen* (2016). I am not an artist, but my attention was captured; I became engrossed with these life journeys, fascinated by what inspired the three painters to create and how they navigated the world that surrounded them. The thirty-minute drive to the theater — in the middle of the week after a day of work — provided moments and memories that I savored and that built up my anticipation for my upcoming trip all the more.

Rembrandt chose to leave school at the age of thirteen to pursue painting. Paul Cézanne spent most of his painting days in Provence; he often depicted Mont Sainte-Victoire, which overlooks Aix-en-Province. Édouard Manet was influenced by Cézanne. Each artist adhered to their internal compass, no matter how their life decisions strayed from the expectations of the times or family, yet during their lifetimes each of their choices proved successful. Such inner clarity is what captured my curiosity. Where did they find the tenacity, the courage, the gumption to pursue what many may not have understood or necessarily supported?

At the time, as I traveled along my own journey, the idea of writing tickled the edges of my possibility radar but remained a dream. But with each exploration — watching these documentaries and many more, along with reading about the lives of individuals who trusted their chosen way, even though it did not align entirely or at all with those favored by society — I began to trust my intuition. I began to not ignore what refused to be dismissed.

We cannot know how choosing to follow our curiosity will feel until we finally courageously take the step, but the beautiful truth for myself has provided a wash of contentment, a steady calm that sits at my center, no matter what is swirling about with any project I am working diligently to finish. Such a steadiness, such a grounding in contentment is a peace I did not know at any time during my early adulthood and now will never throw away. Because while tomorrow is unknown, what I know is that I will see it through. I will find a way.

Your tug of curiosity may not be pulling you onto a dramatically different life path, and even if to an onlooker what you are considering in terms of changing course may not seem drastically different, making

the choice is not always easy. One reason is that when you choose to take your own path, you are expressing through your action a trust in yourself, a trust in what you cannot be certain will work out, but you are also expressing what you value — honoring your truth, honoring something inside you that desires to be shared.

Petit plaisir Invest in a luxurious cashmere stole or scarf. Choose a favorite print or versatile neutral to wear on walks, and tuck it into your wool coat when you head to work.

Explore further thesimplyluxuriouslife.com/november17 (how to let your truth emerge)

November 18
Second Chances

Life does not often offer second chances, but I am beginning to think that when they do come around, it as if life is saying, "This is important. Try again and do your best. I know you can do better." We do not always know why we need to learn that particular lesson at the time, but usually, we do find out down the road or during a second opportunity as we witness a different result.

I recently had an unexpected second chance, and the serendipity was that I had recognized after the first opportunity that I had not done my best. I did my best at the time based on my ability, energy, clarity, etc., but in hindsight I knew why it had not gone well.

Since then, I have been dialoguing, examining, and writing it out, trying to make sense of why I did what I did and how to refrain from repeating the mistake. One recent significant *aha* for me coincided with the concept of the art of attraction: We attract what we think about. After all, so much of what we see is what we are looking for. Many things are happening all around us, but we sometimes do not see them because we either do not know what we are witnessing or we are looking for something else and miss what is right in front of us.

Why not attract what you want rather than what you don't want? Why not imagine your success? Why not choose good outcomes instead of bad? Why not relinquish cynicism regarding the motivations of others' behavior and instead simply stick to your tasks and let others tend to theirs? Why not expend your finite amount of energy on figuring out scenarios in which it all works out rather than sabotaging yourself before anything has even occurred?

As I continue to grow, my internal voice — the one that tells me to refrain from past unhelpful habits of self-protection — has come to have quite a strong volume. Rather than waste energy on my worries, I let go of expectations about the outcome and expend energy toward my hopes. Even in moments of weakness, I can, at the very least, acknowledge my regression and stop myself from giving fuel to old habits that were not constructive.

After all, continuing to imagine the life we want does not mean everything will work out each time. It will not, but eventually, when you have a hopeful, determined attitude, when your energies intertwine with those of another with similar ideas, the moment will seem almost magical. Again: It cannot happen if you are not looking for it. That is the law of attraction.

Think about what you want to attract rather than what you want to avoid or never experience. Let go of what is weighing you down and blinding you from so much that wants to go well. Then, when the good, the hoped-for materializes, you will be present fully and entirely to witness it, savor it and appreciate it.

Petit plaisir Upon reaching personal decisions after much contemplation, celebrate them in a way that only you may understand.

Explore further thesimplyluxuriouslife.com/november18 (seven ways to become the person you were truly meant to be)

November 19
Self-Care During the Holidays

Self-care is tending to what we need in order to be more engaged with the world and therefore experience it fully and constructively. Whether meeting with good friends, taking a breath and stepping away from the computer, or diving back more fully into a hobby that engages your passion and attention, when you practice regular self-care, you right the rails, correct any leaning off into a wrong or unhelpful direction, and reboot your determination, enlivening yourself for the holiday season.

The month of October through the middle of November is a beneficial time to examine and implement self-care practices, perhaps a bit more intentionally and emphatically than throughout the rest of the year. After all, the winter holidays offer an abundance of festivity, gaiety, exchange of love, and good cheer, but each requires an investment of human currency — time, presence, and attention. Keeping that in mind, preemptive fueling up is a worthwhile investment not only in ourselves, but in a memorable time with our loved ones.

How are you doing with your self-care regimen? Sometimes, as the year winds down, we are exhausted, but with so much to celebrate and so many loved ones to celebrate with, our energy ironically needs to be as full as possible in order to arrive on New Year's Day refreshed, exhilarated, and grateful for a brand-new year.

Before you hop on the train or plane or into the car to travel for the holiday season, or before tending to your abode, if you are the host of the gatherings, make a self-care checklist, and ensure it is a priority. What can you do for yourself that will ensure a joyous and happy holiday season?

Petit plaisir Make a bourbon pumpkin tart with gingersnap crust. Don't forget to add spice-infused whipped cream on top.

Explore further thesimplyluxuriouslife.com/november19 (recipe for a bourbon pumpkin tart)

November 20
Let the Universe Know What You Long For

Finding peace, and even making it, yes, and also metamorphosis can be time-consuming undertakings.
—Margaret Roach, *And I Shall Have Some Peace There*

Throughout the early days of my exploration of blogging and even when it became a second career and a second source of income, I had compartmentalized my teaching and blogging, so much so that I did not talk about my blog at school. If a student asked about my blog, I let them know I would be happy to talk about it, but not during class time. I gave my attention fully to school when I was at school, and I would savor and fully immerse myself in my writing the moment I stepped off school grounds.

I chose to compartmentalize, in part, because most people do not fully understand blogging and how it works (I myself was learning each day as I went along), but I deeply wanted to express my enthusiasm for the new world I was exploring and experiencing. After a few attempts at sharing my giddiness for a new pastime I thoroughly enjoyed and seeing vacuous expressions as people wondered why I was so excited about blogging, I stopped and kept the two separate. My blog was by no means a secret, but I kept my delight and curiosity to myself and solely in the space of the blogging community and TSLL reader exchanges.

Eleven and a half years into blogging, I wrote my resignation letter and, with the encouragement of my editor, included specifically why I was leaving: "to pursue an even greater love: my website, blog, and books, all focused on how we live our lives." Without realizing I was doing so, I lifted a burden and gave myself permission to be fully Shannon, not worrying about whether some folks understood blogging or my website's focus. Finally, I communicated what I have always loved — being a detective of life, seeking out how to live with true contentment, and using the medium of writing to communicate what I learn.

Since sharing my news of stepping fully into a new chapter, I feel as though I am introducing myself for the first time to people I have long known. And for new acquaintances, no longer do I lead with "I am a teacher," which while true, never felt entirely accurate.

In order for others to trust us, we have to show that we trust ourselves. We have to take the first step, introduce ourselves, share with the world a dream, a desire, a wish we may think the world will not "get." Because somewhere inside we know it will be part of our journey, we must step forward and let the world know we believe in ourselves.

From my editor's support during an emotionally intense time to my family's excitement to students I had taught during three of their four high school years saying "Good for her" when they heard my news, my connections with others were more sincere and full of more depth with those who "got" it.

Let the world know who you are, and do not seek its approval. Your sincerity will inspire actions and choices you may never see or learn about, but the reactions you receive from those who see the truth of you will open windows and doors of connection you never experienced while you hid your true yearnings.

Petit plaisir Listen to Johann Sebastian Bach's Concerto in C Major for Violin and Oboe, one of my favorite Bach oboe concertos, and lighten up the day as you take a few deep and restorative breaths.

Explore further thesimplyluxuriouslife.com/november20 (discover yourself and set yourself free)

November 21
Heal Yourself

Have you ever had a sore back that inhibits you from doing what you had been unconsciously doing without realizing how and what your body needs to move well?

Hopefully you have never had to feel a subtle, yet excruciating back pain that seems to slow down everything in your life and, especially, interrupts a full night's sleep, but if you have, you know that, until your back heals, you cannot fully experience or enjoy so many other aspects of living the life you love.

When an ache in my lower back gave me pause a while ago, I was reminded of a life-truth regarding symbolic "backaches." When we have not dealt with something, when we keep avoiding something or denying a conversation or choosing not to correct something that requires our attention before we can move past it, the quality of everything else in our lives is put on hold. Sometimes we recognize this fact — we cannot fully engage because our minds are wrestling with something that is nagging at us — but sometimes we don't know how our lives are being hindered until we take the time to be honest with ourselves.

The good news is that when we do confront what is limiting us, bothering us, impeding our ability to progress, our world becomes brighter, our responsibilities become doable, and the hope that returns is empowering.

If you have been feeling that something is holding you back or holding you down or preventing you from truly engaging in your everyday life and savoring it, ask yourself what you need to heal. Whether it is literally your back or addressing a skeleton in your closet, start anew this month, and walk toward it and explore it. Often, what is required and what you have most feared will not be as horrifying as you had imagined. Regardless of whether you encounter a molehill or a mountain, choosing to traverse it is a practice of self-healing, so that you can walk through it to the life you wish to be living.

Petit plaisir Cut some magnolia branches, full of their magnificent leaves, and arrange them in a large vase.

Explore further thesimplyluxuriouslife.com/november21 (the wonderful truth about health, happiness, and getting older)

November 22
The Wisdom of Desire

The more time and dedication one gives to the sport of chess (yep, a sport, as it is an exercise of the mind), the more skilled and successful a player becomes, the further ahead they plan their moves. A match can be thought of as the game of a solitary player mastering many possible plays. Another game of the mind, bridge, is likewise complex. A game of trick making, it requires players to be in pairs, and success depends on a sound playing partner. Applying the rules of chess to bridge (or vice versa) would be futile and pointless. Yet, as we strive forward to cultivate a life that aligns with our strengths, enables our passions to be pursued, and reveals our unique gifts to the world, if our lifestyle does not adhere to the life rules others believe we should follow, our way of life can be defined as inferior, or not enough, or lacking. In truth, what is lacking is an open mind.

No two people have the same awesome gifts and talents to share with the world, just as no two days in a calendar year are precisely the same. We too can limit ourselves when we measure our life against "societal rules" that dismiss our strengths.

Neither chess nor bridge is better than or superior to the other. You can learn, master, and enjoy both. What distinguishes them for you is the desire you have to play one game over the other, based on which leaves you feeling most fulfilled, most alive, most truly you.

Honor your truth, dismiss those who compare and rank, and you will become an expert in your own life journey, savoring every step along the way.

Petit plaisir Begin watching the Emmy-Award-winning mini-series *The Queen's Gambit*, starring Anya Taylor-Joy. Based on Walter Tevis's 1983 novel of the same name, it is the story of an orphaned chess prodigy struggling with addiction in a quest to become the best chess player in the world. The final episode is my favorite.

Explore further thesimplyluxuriouslife.com/november22 (set the world on fire: be who you desire to be)

November 23
The Mind as Architect

Your thoughts are the architects of your destiny.
—David McKay

November

On my last day of teaching in 2021, prior to students taking their semester final, a student asked if it was true that I was moving to France after I concluded my career as a teacher; she had heard that this was the case. I smiled from ear to ear. Living in France, if only for a portion of the year, has been a dream of mine for some time. However, I said no, at this time, I am grateful to be staying in Bend and look forward to traveling to France again in the near future, and hopefully quite frequently, as I indeed adore the culture.

Upon hearing our conversation, a nearby student said with a smile, "Well, maybe you'll manifest it into being, Ms. Ables, as it is something you want." This student was speaking my dreams out loud, and over the years, she was not the first student to predict that I would live in France after teaching. Hearing others — in this case, students who know me quite well, including my love for France and my curiosity about the world — say this made such a dream more of a possibility, one that I would pursue in the future. It will be only a matter of how badly I wish to make it my reality.

When we look at the paths we have traveled to arrive where we are today, we can look back and examine what we believed to be possible. This is not to say that we wanted pain, hardship, inequality, or injustice; rather, we can appreciate how we navigated despite the opposition — whether based on society's ill treatment and prejudice or self-created. As Madisyn Taylor writes in her book *DailyOM*: "Focusing our energy on fear can actually create what scares us."

We lack direct control over much in our world, but we can control our minds. Being present in our everydays is crucial to living well, and our everydays are a result of what we have imagined they can be. Motivational speaker Earl Nightingale put it this way: "Whatever we plant in our subconscious mind and nourish with repetition and emotion will one day become a reality."

A year after purchasing Le Papillon, I looked at the list of desirable qualities I hoped my future house would contain. When I made that list in 2018, I did not know where in Bend my house would be located, but I knew what I wanted, what would attract me to look more closely and seriously consider making an offer.

Small space for a garden. Check. Small in square footage, but made large due to oodles of windows and natural light. Check. A front porch with potential for a swing. Check. An attached garage for safe entry of the pups to the house. Check. Many more details, seemingly like magic, kept my attention and eventually prompted me to make an offer on the house.

I acknowledge that a house is a thing, and holding tightly to material objects is a practice that will leave our lives stagnant and prevent growth. However, if we understand that "possessions are only representations of energy at work in our lives," as Madisyn Taylor teaches in her book *Daily*

The Road to Le Papillon

OM: Inspirational Thoughts for a Happy, Healthy, and Fulfilling Day, "we are able to shift our attention to the right and proper place." I became clear about what would bring me stability and strengthen an awareness of the world around me as well as about how I was traveling along my journey. For me, having a home to call my own, from which I could spring more freely and sincerely into the world, would mean more than four walls; it would be a space to manifest ideas to share with the world and ground myself in everyday contentment.

We cannot predict. We cannot force. However, if we will conceptualize with patience, keen self-awareness, courage, and visualization, the life we imagine can take shape. We cannot manifest people or events; such specifics are too concrete, but also not enough. Our ideas, our imagination are much bigger, much more magnificent. What we can manifest, what we want to manifest by supposing it is people or events, is actually most likely love, kindness, sincerity, compassion, joy, peace, and abundance.

Le Papillon was a hope, and at times a hope I let doubt push out of the forefront of my mind, but I never fully relinquished my deep-held wish. Thankfully, I did not because on that day when I did not have house-hunting on the mind, I asked the question I hoped would be met with a yes, and everything unfolded in dream-come-true fashion. Maya Angelou was right: "Ask for what you want and be prepared to get it."

Become aware of your thoughts, and if your thoughts focus on a life you want to live, on events and outcomes you hope will occur, hold fast yet with an open hand to those ideas. If you are inundated with fear, worry, and cynicism, let go, for you will only create what you least wish to become your reality. As Ralph Waldo Emerson said, "A person is what he or she thinks about all day long." Think about and expend energy on figuring out how to bring to fruition the everydays you long to experience.

Petit plaisir Purchase or cut a basketful of fresh sorrel (a perennial herb) from the garden, and make sorrel chicken. Nest it on top of angel hair pasta, and pair it with a favorite glass of white wine.

Explore further thesimplyluxuriouslife.com/november23 (recipe for sorrel chicken)

November 24
Letting Go to See Anew

When learning how to ride a bike without training wheels, you probably felt the supportive hand of one of your parents on your back to help ease your mind, even though, technically, the hand on the back is not there to help you stay vertical but to nudge you forward, give you momentum so that you can acquire your balance on your own.

When deciding to conclude my career in the classroom, the helpful, supportive nudge came from a few trusted people. They did not tell me what to do, but understanding the path I wanted to take and how I wanted to use my creative energies, they stood with me as I cemented my decisions — writing my resignation letter, submitting the letter, and remaining present to savor my last week in the classroom.

Mark Nepo, an author on spirituality, writes in *The Book of Awakening*, "There are no wrong turns, only unexpected paths" that require choices; he suggests that every choice available to us is neither a good or bad choice but "when we believe that only what we want holds the gold, then we find ourselves easily depressed by what we lack." When we shift our approach from making choices in our lives to one of opening up our lives, as opposed to limiting what we will label as success, we expand the possibilities for reasons to celebrate.

When you let go of required outcomes, when you gather up the courage to take a new path, you choose as well to let go of mandatory requirements. In other words, you trust your decisions. Having taken the time to do your due diligence, you know whether this is the best decision for you, just as you know a bike can be balanced on two wheels so long as it is moving forward.

Vow to yourself to continue to move forward and enjoy the ride you have chosen. When we couple our courage with acceptance of uncertainty, we make way for a future full of possibility, unexpected reasons to celebrate, and opportunities to step into our truest selves.

Instead of reflecting on and lamenting your past choices, step back into the present and see all that you have gained because of those choices — lessons, deeper awareness, strengths, etc. Then permit yourself to become excited about the unknown potential lying before you, ready to be savored so long as you expand your lens to see all that can be.

Petit plaisir Read Marshall Rosenberg's *Nonviolent Communication: A Language of Life* and discover how to choose responses and approaches that make life wonderful for others and yourself.

The Road to Le Papillon

Explore further thesimplyluxuriouslife.com/november24 (how to let go of self-imposed limitations)

November 25
The Spontaneous Gifts of Presence

The first thing I tend to do when I arrive in Paris, unless it is the middle of the night, following dropping off my luggage at my accommodations, is to wander about the neighborhood that is my home base. Such was the case in July 2019 when I began to do my best flâneuring in the 5th and 6th arrondissements as the afternoon turned into evening.

Having enjoyed *moules mariniere et frites* on the *terrasse* at Huguette with a glass of white wine, satiating my starving, confused appetite after a day of travel, I began to wander, and discovered that a young cellist would be playing five of Bach's concertos in a local *petit venue* near the Sorbonne. It would begin in under an hour and required a nominal entry cost, so I bided my time with pleasure. After all, I was in Paris. At 19:00, the concert began, and though there were fewer than fifteen listeners seated in the audience, the musician played with rapt attention. The acoustics of the cello's voice bouncing about the centuries-old interior engulfed me in what felt like a warm welcome, and I found myself closing my eyes to absorb the moment more fully (checking with myself that it wasn't jet-lag-induced shut-eye).

I could never have planned, predicted, or hoped for such a pleasurable, multi-sensory arrival, but I seized the opportunity, walked through the door, sat still, and remained present.

In the pursuit of tomorrow's gifts, we may forgo today's. As you move through your everydays and your days while traveling, choose to leave space to engage with what the day offers. It may be an ordinary, steady day without friction, which is reason enough to celebrate. It may also be an unexpected concert shared with fellow aficionados in a historic space and town that will elevate the day in ways you could have never imagined.

Petit plaisir Find a moment to snuggle up with a hot cuppa, a favorite shortbread biscuit (Walkers are a go-to staple in my house) and be still.

Explore further thesimplyluxuriouslife.com/november25 (discover nine places in Paris I recommend for dining, sleeping, exploring, and finding the perfect croissant)

November 26
Handling Unfamiliar Situations

Thanksgiving is one of my favorite holidays, in large part because it focuses on time together rather than tangible gift giving. Okay, maybe the food counts as a type of gift, but there are very few occasions I enjoy that do not involve wonderful, satiating fare, various wines paired with each course, and, of course, lively conversation.

 Whether while teaching and having the week off to celebrate or savoring a handful of days free of outside expectations, I enjoy a slight change in schedule, if only for a short period of time, and an opportunity to spend time with my family. However, many of us have family members we normally would not choose to socialize with; for one reason or another, there will be people in our lives whom we must spend time with who do not add something positive to our daily experience, whether at work or in social situations. While it is advisable to keep such people out of our lives, the holidays may make that impossible.

 If you will encounter such people, note what you can control: your attitude, your reactions, and your behavior. The way others respond to your behavior is their responsibility and will reveal more about their true character.

 While it can be tempting to offer a knee-jerk reaction or to speak up in defense of yourself or others, try to hold yourself to a standard that you will be proud of. You cannot control anyone else's behavior, only your own. But when we engage lovingly and provide a welcoming space for others to relax and be themselves, we may share the best gift of all.

Petit plaisir Watch the Danish political drama series *Borgen*, which takes viewers behind the scenes of coalition politics in Denmark. Grounded in personal and gender realities, it follows the life of the unexpectedly victorious Birgitte Nyborg, who becomes prime minister.

Explore further thesimplyluxuriouslife.com/november26 (how to engage in respectful communication in your relationships)

November 27
Make Your Own Traditions

Here in the States, the turkey has been carved, enjoyed, and prepared for leftovers; the wine has been poured and savored; and the pie dishes hold just the crumbs of buttery, flaky crusts. If you have taken part in a traditional Thanksgiving celebration, you may also be enjoying the deep sigh of relief that many exhale after the guests have returned home and the house is now a place of refuge — though now with endless snacking available.

Each year, as I grow older, I try to create a more memorable, authentic, and less "crafted" affair. While the holidays offer an opportunity for nostalgic moments, often the expectations, pressures, and hype can strangle the beauty that such times can offer. The holidays are unique to each family and each individual based on their values, personalities and temperaments, and life experiences. To become a cookie cutter, and trying to match what "should" be, is to weaken the gift the holidays offer.

Perhaps you regularly wake up at dawn on Black Friday to take advantage of the huge sales and finish the afternoon by stopping in for a pre-arranged pedicure with your best friend or your mother or other family members. Or perhaps Black Friday is nowhere near your radar, but instead is reserved as a day to hike to the highest peak to burn calories, let the dogs run, and spend time with those who have traveled to see you and yours.

The essence of the holidays is to take the traditions that may come with expectations of a certain design, and instead edit, tweak, or toss, so that you and those you spend the holiday with can find joy during a time of year full of potential for memorable connection and exchange of good tidings.

Petit plaisir Designing your own traditions for the holiday season — whether with family and friends or alone — can be deeply enriching and uplifting when the mind shifts beyond the limited definitions of what "must" be. Thank yourself for courageously living a life that is wonderful for you and those you love.

Explore further thesimplyluxuriouslife.com/november27 (five French-inspired ideas for creating new holiday traditions)

November 28
Choosing to Be Self-Full

It is true that water will flow indifferently to east and west, but will it flow equally well up and down? Human nature is disposed toward goodness, just as water tends to flow downwards. There is no water but flows downwards, and no man but shows his tendency to be good. Now, by striking water hard, you may splash it higher than your forehead, and by damming it, you may make it go uphill. But is that the nature of water? It is external force that causes it to do so. Likewise, if a man is made to do what is not good, his nature is being similarly forced.
—Mencius (4th-century Chinese philosopher, disciple of Confucius)

TSLL's mission statement, which I wrote in 2010, says: "The simply luxuriously life is something that I believe every one of us can attain if indeed we are seeking . . . a truly fulfilling life instead of being led around by the nose; thereby, creating a life of true contentment." Recently, a reader expressed dislike for the phrase "being led around by the nose." However, I had paid careful attention when I chose that wording, and it remains. It can be a hard truth to acknowledge that we have lived unconsciously, but when we do, we set ourselves free.

Pulling back when we have initially gone along with what society nudges, dictates, or requires may cause immediate pain. If something is attached to your nose, the instinctive response is to walk forward and follow, if for no other reason than to avoid pain and feel immediate comfort. To endure the unease, at the very least, of "being led around by the nose" is a choice to endure temporary pain, to experience unknown but certain struggle, yet it is the only way to discover a fulfilling life.

However, let us not forget the unnecessary pain inflicted upon ourselves and, yes, others when we pull away without knowing *why* we are pulling away. If we pull away, rebel, protest, resist, simply because it is what others we wish to be aligned with are doing, then we are still following. How do we ensure we are conscious and knowing in our stepping away from being led around by the nose? Be like water.

Mencius says that each person embracing their full and true nature is the single best gift we can give the world; it is an act of kindness and a necessity for a more peaceful world. In his statement "if a man is made to do what is not good, his nature is being similarly forced," the phrase "not good" is anything that goes against one's innate being.

As we begin to explore ourselves, our talents, our strengths, and our curiosities, it can be incredibly difficult and sometimes seemingly impossible to know what goes against our nature. But so long as we choose to do the homework of getting to know ourselves, we begin to understand conflicting approaches or ways of living.

In my own life, each time I took a step that was more aligned with my true temperament, curiosities, and strengths, the "water" flowed more freely and seemingly effortlessly; thus the tranquility of my days improved, as did my ability to strengthen my skills and, most important, improve how I treated both myself and others.

"Not being led around by the nose" reminds us to get to know ourselves, to speak truthfully and kindly to ourselves, and to find the courage within ourselves to live in alignment with what we discover. Certain aspects of society will contend that your choice to honor your truth and care for yourself is selfish, but the opposite is true. You are self-full, not full of yourself, but acknowledging and honoring who you are, sharing it with the world, and thus positively contributing in both your personal and professional life.

Choose to be curious about you. Explore, wonder, ask questions, try, attempt, trip, and keep going. Your discovery will take you to an inner peace and grounded clarity, establishing a life compass that will elevate every arena of your life.

Petit plaisir For cosy mystery enjoyment, read Richard Osman's *The Thursday Murder Club* and subsequent books in the series.

Explore further thesimplyluxuriouslife.com/november28 (the necessity of personal privacy: a delicate and important dance)

November 29
A Thoughtful Approach to the Holiday Season

The holiday season has officially begun. Can you feel it? Do you like it? Or do you at times feel out of sorts? For me, it depends. Each year is different, but with each year an opportunity is presented: to reassess, to reflect, and to appreciate.

Holiday celebrations may go as planned or run completely off the rails. But, if during the rest of the year, you have found a balance, a routine that is productive and rejuvenating, you can more easily enjoy the holidays and create memories to savor years down the road.

As well, the gift of understanding your own language and your needs, and distinguishing them from wants, can provide inspiration for tailoring a holiday season that works well for you and those you love. When we remember that our loved ones desire us to be happy, we can give them the thoughtful gift of our full attention, time, and engagement.

When you do not place too much expectation on the holidays to produce magical results, solve your ills, and leave you miraculously better off than you were before they began, you will be better able to sit back and just enjoy.

Set an intention for what you hope the holiday season will be for you and those you love. Do not forget yourself, but be sure to include activities you know those in your life will enjoy as well. When everyone feels seen and is allowed to contribute to the festivities, love is felt. Isn't that what the holidays are meant to strengthen?

Petit plaisir Make a pear and blackberry tart with hazelnut crumble topping drizzled with blackberry sauce.

Explore further thesimplyluxuriouslife.com/november29 (recipe for a pear and blackberry tart)

November 30
Be Yourself

Each of us has a unique journey. If we want it to lead to our true potential, and if we want to experience a contentment we doubt may be possible, we must have courage. That means thinking for ourselves, stepping outside the "this is what is done" box in order to discover what truly aligns with who we are and what we can uniquely bring to the world.

During my seven years in Bend, I have spent four Thanksgivings on my own — intentionally and with great appreciation for the opportunities, insight, and enjoyment I found.

Some readers new to TSLL blog may initially say, *That's just sad* or *Why would you want to be alone?* or *How could that be enjoyable?* The truth is, for me, many Thanksgivings were not the joyful celebrations typically depicted by the media. They were not bad or miserable; they just felt forced, days of feeling uncomfortable, conversations in which I tried to defend my life choices to people who meant no judgment, yet conveyed it unconsciously in their questions.

There were a few Thanksgivings that I most definitely did enjoy, and those were at my parents' home in Wallowa County (Mom, we should have more there in the future), but because Wallowa County is literally at the end of the state highway, and the roads require a steady and alert driver, it is difficult for many people to travel there in November. But I will always travel to Thanksgiving in Wallowa County.

The Road to Le Papillon

I spent one of my most treasured Thanksgivings in Britain, a country that does not celebrate this American tradition. I am not married, nor do I have children, so I can design my holidays as I like, but truthfully we all can do this, no matter what our relationship status, by designing holiday celebrations in our own way. In the past, I only had a few days off from teaching, and the additional two days off meant more stress than respite, so upon arriving in Bend, I said nope.

In 2017, I had a full week off for Thanksgiving, and I took the opportunity to spend four days in north Devon overlooking the Bristol Channel. Whiling away my days and nights walking while it rained on the sloping green fields and rocky beaches and then returning to my cottage to soak in a hot bath while the rain pelted the windows, I reveled in a new way to enjoy the holiday.

Along my journey, I have found more peace, more reason to celebrate, more calm within myself when I make choices that may not make sense to the outside world. For me and the life I love living and sharing with others, my choices make complete sense, and they have strengthened my relationships with those who respect my journey, even if it does not resemble their own.

Remember that you are learning as you go, and the biggest lesson is how to reach your full potential, all the while being kind to one another but not forgetting to be kind to yourself too.

Petit plaisir To prepare for the holiday season, read Beth Kempton's *Calm Christmas and a Happy New Year: A Little Book of Festive Joy.*

Explore further thesimplyluxuriouslife.com/november30 (tour my Devon holiday cottage)

December

Find Peace, Calm, and Sanctuary: Become a Butterfly

December

Fall into a life you love by continuing to step toward it. One's home is meant to be a sanctuary, a place where you find immediate comfort and peace, a place that allows you to shed any façades and outer shells, and just be yourself. When we create a sanctuary for ourselves and those we love, we give ourselves the ability to recharge, relax, and unwind.

Even as we intentionally and consciously begin to build a life of quality over quantity — letting go of over-scheduled days and replacing them with days filled with tasks and responsibilities aligned to what we value and what ensures a healthy well-being — each time we step outside our home, our sanctuary, we have a finite amount of energy to expend. And even if what we engage in outside of our sanctuary refuels us, knowing our home is a dependable, consistent source of respite sets us free to fully engage with the outside world, which is why we need to create an environment within our home that allows us to sigh with relief, to savor beautiful memories, and to know we are safe.

The power of a home's aesthetic can be amazing, and I had been favored by the original design of Le Papillon. The Craftsman house and its surrounding landscaping gave me two things to work with in indulging two aspects of my temperament and passions: the Francophile (a *potager* garden) and the Anglophile (the Arts and Crafts interior design principles).

Within the first two months of moving in, my corkboard was in place, and samples for everything from wallpaper to fabric swatches, pictures of a dream stove, furniture, and other room ideas were pinned in their designated room categories. My mind danced with the potential end results during the day and even through the night in my dreams.

My life leading up to the moment I laid eyes on Le Papillon in July 2019 gave me the ability to see that indeed this was to be my lifetime house, my "settling-in" place. Many aspects of my life — from my travels, to the people I have met, loved, and lost, to my beloved pets and other animals, to fully understanding which activities fuel me and free me, much like a puzzle actually designed for me — allowed me to know that I had found my home.

The large aspects of the design (the house is small but grand, with tall, sloping ceilings), the details (oodles of natural light), the basics (enough bedrooms to support myself, occasional guests, and a work office) — I was able to appreciate all of these because of my life leading up to this one moment at the age of forty.

Having a space and then understanding the gift of peace and freedom it offers, no matter what the outside world claims to be "acceptable," is priceless. Yes, our sanctuaries may require paying rent or taking out a mortgage or leasing our home as a vacation rental, but understanding that we have found our place makes it priceless.

Our lives change when we understand how powerful and life-lifting a sanctuary can be in the design of a truly fulfilling life, a life of contentment experienced and appreciated every single day, no matter how high or low events take us. We begin to honor the space in a way we might not have understood previously. We exercise the practice of presence, design a life we love living, and refrain from rushing through our days and our lives. Knowing our sanctuary's benefits to our well-being, we more freely and sincerely engage with the world beyond our four walls, which requires emotional energy along with physical exertion. We knowingly expend energy in worthwhile connections because we trust our sanctuary. When we return home, we reenergize and are restored for another day.

As I stepped into my adult life, I came, unconsciously and gradually more consciously, to know the power of a sanctuary. In every rental, I painted walls, decorated rooms with garage-sale and hand-me-down finds, and made a space that set me free each time I returned home or woke up in the morning.

I say *set me free* because throughout nearly the first full twenty years of my adult life, I was regularly poked fun at, laughed at, seen as not enough, silly, someone in need of help or guidance, when I expressed how I adored simple pleasures, such as being at home, doting on my dogs, truly living the life you see on TSLL.

You name it, I heard it and felt it, so I dove into my writing of TSLL, trying to strengthen my understanding of myself and stand strongly on my two feet — whether I was out in the world away from my sanctuary, welcoming others into my home, or just being there myself.

Today, the determination that existed inside me has never left — that I am enough in being someone who enjoys solitary pursuits, revels in simple pleasures, vividly sees the world in all its beautiful detail, loves to be loved, and gives love exuberantly when in a relationship, but not at the expense of losing myself to fit the world's traditional, often limiting definitions of a woman.

I am fully Shannon, whether at home, out in the world, or sharing ideas and posts or podcast episodes with readers and listeners of TSLL. I am home not only in my physical space, Le Papillon, but in myself, wherever I am in the world at any given moment. At times the journey seemed it might never arrive at the desired destination of contentment, but in hindsight, it was the journey that provided the curriculum I needed to understand, and I am grateful I stepped forward into the course believing I was worth the investment.

Whether you are on your way toward true personal freedom or have arrived, nurture the space where you find yourself today — where you rest your head, where you make your meals, where you return home at the end of the workday. With each intentional tweak, adjustment, or change, not only will your space physically change, your trust and your strength in yourself and your journey will change as well.

December 1
Detours Along the Journey

In 2015, I sold my house of nine years in Pendleton, Oregon. It was a 1930s, Norman-style home, complete with a great room showcasing extraordinarily high ceilings, a picture window that welcomed loads of northern light, hardwoods throughout, and a fireplace with artisan tile dating from the early 20th century. When I arrived in Bend, I was determined to buy a house, but rented for what I thought would be a couple of months, maybe a year.

Within a month of arriving in Bend, the owners of a house that was ideally located, fair in price, and complete with a butler's pantry, open kitchen, and cozy reading room had my accepted offer. But it was not meant to be as an all-cash offer from another potential buyer was too good to pass up after I requested more time to close. My first mistake was thinking I could go it alone, without a realtor; another was not taking more time to understand my must-haves in a home (for one, space for a garden with a southern exposure).

As much as we may want to plan, we cannot predict all the details that will best lead us to our fullest potential. We cannot predict what our journey will reveal to us about ourselves, much like a treasure hunt, with delights unearthed along the way.

I am incredibly grateful the house I thought would be perfect did not work out in my search in 2015, because eventually I stumbled upon the ideal house for the person I realized I was — someone who cannot imagine not gardening, someone who needs a little bit more space from my neighbors but not too much, someone who is uplifted each day by seeing the sky and moon and sun and all of the weather patterns through the east-, south-, and west-facing windows that frame my main living spaces, someone who has a net-zero home, meaning that my home's use of energy is equal to the amount of renewable energy created by my house's solar panels.

Remind and reassure yourself of your journey. Loosen the intense grip you may have on your future, releasing control of what must be. Often what your life reveals when you do not reach a hoped-for outcome is an opportunity for a richer awareness, increasing the quality of what you will experience in the future, but only if you remain open and trust your journey.

Petit plaisir Splurge on white truffle butter and make the pasta dish tagliarelle with truffle butter. Add a favorite protein, if you like, and a side of roasted vegetables. And don't forget a glass of crisp chardonnay.

Explore further thesimplyluxuriouslife.com/december1 (recipe for tagliarelle with truffle butter)

December 2
Finding Your Home

Gently falling snow lays a blanket of calm upon my neighborhood, which quietly goes about its business in all sorts of weather. I went to bed when gardens and front porches were bare, and woke up to a generous covering of snow — one of the best ways to start a December day.

I turn on the stove top to boil the water for my standing breakfast of toasted steel-cut oats, a dash of chia seeds, and a smidge of salt for flavoring, along with a teaspoon of honey, toasted unsalted almond slices, and raisins, paired with a two-egg omelet and a small glass of freshly squeezed orange juice. I settle into my Cabbage & Curtainrail cow-face-patterned armchair by the fire, with the boys snuggled into their spots — one in the partner chair and the other squeezed in by my side. All the curtains and blinds are pulled open, even though the sun has yet to appear, and I delight in the snow softly, steadily falling, covering the fence posts with white stocking caps and creating an unplanned, yet welcome cozy moment.

As it is a special occasion on an everyday — it snowed! — I add bacon to my regular breakfast menu, and its sizzling provides music throughout the house as we sit. (Okay, Oscar is roaming around, determined to find the bacon, a rare scent in our house. Rest assured, a slice is reserved for each pup.) Norman snuggles in, patiently knowing his breakfast treat will come, and I savor every single detail of this moment that comes along only a handful of times each winter.

When we are at home, we can relax, be ourselves, and just breathe without explanation. The comfort of hot tea in the morning, snuggling with the dogs, or listening to casual conversation about the day's events on the radio — this is what home feels like to me. For the first time in fifteen or so years, I feel as though I have my own home for the holidays. Having found a hometown of my own, after much searching, is a priceless feeling.

If you have not found your "spot" when it comes to settling into a town, a house, or a group of people, trust me, you can find it — if you keep searching. Just do not give up.

Petit plaisir Explore classic skiing and take a leisurely touring session out through snowy trees and fields (or simply through your neighborhood streets on a snow day). Bring your pup along if they love the snow as much as Norman does.

Explore further thesimplyluxuriouslife.com/december2 (take a photo and video tour of the excursion to find a tree for the house while touring in the Bend mountain snow)

December 3
Curiosity as Medicine

I have found the cure for nearly all of life's woes. Okay, maybe I am exaggerating, but I have found a cure, free to all, for much of what often frustrates us or causes us angst.

If you have been following TSLL, you know that in 2015 I basically hit the ground running in my new town, Bend, Oregon. Whether it was paddleboarding on a high lake, taking in an opera via the Met's Live in HD theater presentations, or visiting a nearby farmers market, I wasted little time making my rental house a home, exploring the town, and walking all ten of our legs off (my two dogs' and mine — get it?).

As I was on Cloud 1200 (way beyond Cloud 9), I needed to be taken down a notch, and I was. While just about every experience I have had in Bend has been stellar, one caught me by surprise. While I won't go into the details, in retrospect, I am glad it happened. No place is perfect. There will always be quirks and frustrations, but what we can do is find and help to create a community and a space that is perfect for each of us to thrive. But how?

Finally, I am getting to the cure-all, which is curiosity. I recently came across a quote by Diana Vreeland that gave me pause: "There's only one thing in life, and that is continual renewal of inspiration." You may be wondering what this quote has to do with curiosity, but let's think about it.

The only way to continue to be inspired, to have hope, to discover new ideas, is to seek new experiences, meet new people, and evolve so that we can see through different eyes. That is when inspiration strikes, and that is how we cultivate a space and community that fits us. We approach these new experiences with an open mind, our sincere selves, and — this last one is important — gratitude for simple actions and kindness, even when it may not seem warranted.

If we can approach each tomorrow and every person we encounter with such an attitude, our world will brighten and open in ways we may not have foreseen.

The Road to Le Papillon

If you feel that your season, year, or life is in a rut, start your engine of curiosity, and seek out what tickles your mind. You may never know where your search will lead, but if you keep the basic approach in mind (an open mind, sincerity, gratitude, kindness), your life is sure to improve.

Petit plaisir Step into the holiday season and listen to Handel's Water Music, Suite no. 2 in D Major.

Explore further thesimplyluxuriouslife.com/December3 (an ideal day in Bend: TSLL's itinerary)

December 4
The Feeling of Coming Home

Encountering a butterfly is the sign of the transition from an old life to a new life, from a state of ignorance to awareness, from a hard life to a better life . . . The butterfly . . . remind[s] us that each of us transforms through multiple stages in our life. It is only through exertion that we emerge into who we will be next.
—designer Danielle Fichera

What is home? There are concepts of home that others insert into our vocabulary, and thus our subconscious, because of what they know to be true for them or what they know will appeal to a particular audience, and sometimes we will trust their definition. After all, ours cannot be that much different than theirs . . . right?

Oh, but we would be mistaken. After all, home is a place that offers sanctuary — allows us to be untethered, to be our most sincere selves, to be certain of security, to be at ease and fully capable of being present without pretense or building walls.

Yes, sometimes home is where we grew up, and sometimes it is a far-off destination, but always, home should be our very own skin in which we live every single day. While we can amplify our home in an environment we inhabit, knowing we can be at home wherever we may be is a most powerful and soothing gift to ourselves.

I once felt that another person offered the feeling of coming home. Sadly, I was mistaken, but I learned an amazing lesson from that error. The gift was realizing I was more at home in my own company and needed to acknowledge this fact more consciously.

The ability to find such calm, clarity, and peace in our own company is a means to knowing with less doubt where else we may find ourselves to be at home. However, if we begin the search without realizing we need to find home within ourselves first, we will never truly find home elsewhere because our compass will never accurately be calibrated.

When I first "met" Le Papillon in July 2019, my ability to trust I would be able to step into my new chapter had followed years of exertion and, finally, awareness about the progress and changes I needed to make to experience daily contentment. Knowing I would be able to purchase a house in Bend, Oregon, applying the lessons I learned along the journey (working with a trusted realtor, lesson learned!), while they took time, strengthened my courage to step into another significant change for the better in my life journey.

My home is not actually the four walls that surround me each night; my home is my internal peace and contentment, and I carry that with me wherever I go. Symbolically, purchasing the structure exhibited that I consciously understood and acknowledged a shift, a trust in myself.

May you find your "home" and continue to reside within it and take it with you wherever you may travel or reside.

Petit plaisir Make Christmas stollen for the holiday season to be enjoyed in three weeks' time, as the bread becomes better after resting a while.

Explore further thesimplyluxuriouslife.com/december4 (recipes for Christmas stollen and more holiday desserts)

December 5
Time to Yourself

Simplicity, simplicity, simplicity.
—Henry David Thoreau, *Walden*

Whenever my life becomes a little too harried, too over-booked, and my body cannot seem to catch up, I look to Thoreau's quote. Then I also remind myself of the even simpler adage "Keep it simple, stupid." I'm not stupid, and neither are you, but sometimes the obvious way to live evades us as we try to please everyone and make each occasion we are involved in perfect. As a result, we become drained physically and emotionally. Especially during the holidays, we must keep our balance; as much as we want to be super heroes, even they need their rest.

Be sure to find time to just be by yourself. Treat yourself to a cup of *chocolat chaud* and pull out your favorite book or a magazine full of dreamy images to get lost in. Perhaps splurge on a pedicure or a massage, or take an hour for an afternoon nap to rejuvenate — and refuse to feel guilty for slowing down.

It is vital to maintain a stable state of mind and, most important, to be aware of how you are feeling. Take note when you feel you are not performing up to your full potential, and catch your breath. Those who love you will understand and appreciate your maturity in recognizing that sometimes we say yes too often, but that it comes from a place of good intentions.

This holiday season and year-round, consciously be aware, on a regular basis, of your energy tank and seek to keep it stable through balancing work, play, rest, and exertion.

Petit plaisir Add a jovial jolt of energy to your step when you listen to Tomaso Albinoni's Trumpet Concerto in B-flat Major.

Explore further thesimplyluxuriouslife.com/december5 (new and trusted holiday traditions)

December 6
Live the Life You Need

Workweeks or weekends full of unwanted or unexpected emotional strain drain our resources to be self-aware of what we need in order to refuel. More than anything, such times call for the warmth and support of those we love, and for reminders of all we can be thankful for, what is going well, and how we can bring more love, kindness, and compassion into a world that often seems out of control.

The holidays create an opportunity for reflection. For some, the past year may have been a whirlwind of amazement, dreams coming to fruition, and countless blessings, while others may still be in the middle of their journey or may have experienced unwanted or disheartening events. Regardless of where this time of year finds you, seek out those who love and understand you, find time to be and do what you love, and always remember the opportunity of a fresh new day and your choice for constructive engagement to benefit not only others, but yourself. Most important, today be the person you wish to be, to create the life you want and live in a way you can be proud.

Life will present challenges, moments that provoke anger and frustration, as well as times of sobbing, but look for the lesson, look for the love that is available and wants to be welcomed into your life. So long as it is authentic, undemanding, and true, let it in. And know that

it is always a good time to bring more kindness and love into the world. We can never have too much.

Petit plaisir Purchase a bottle of Châteauneuf-du-Pape for your next dinner party or special dinner for one or two at home.

Explore further thesimplyluxuriouslife.com/december6 (sixteen ideas for enjoying a simply luxurious winter holiday season)

December 7
Exploring

Observing or participating. Following or leading. Consuming or creating. Opposing forces typically are needed for the cycles of life, business, progress, and entertainment. This idea tickled my thoughts during the spring of 2014, the year before I knew I would be relocating to Bend, Oregon. The primary question I asked myself was which part of the cycle should one dedicate their life to in order to be fulfilled?

Think about all that we consume in our everyday lives — food, entertainment, news, etc. It is much easier for us to consume rather than create. Creating requires us to set a wheel in motion. And in order to create something that we want, we must be very focused and clear in our purpose. Having a clear focus and not letting distractions detour us requires that we understand why we are pursuing something.

When I first toured Bend with an eye to living there, I observed a city in which people live purposefully. They participate in the development of a community they are proud of rather than just observe the world as it turns; they lead by example rather than follow blindly and simply exist, and they create businesses, homes, and opportunities for fellow and future Bendites, even after the economic crash of the Great Recession.

Such a dedication to creating is electric, and that energy draws people from around the state and the country. But just as this community did not just happen, neither can our lives become our dream unless we are clear about how we wish them to evolve. We may not know precisely how it will all work when it comes together, but we must start somewhere.

Not everybody wants to live in a town like this, but what Bend revealed to me in my first real exploratory visit was that in order to know what you want, you first have to have a conversation with yourself, and then you have to be willing to step forward, even if you are not accustomed to heading in that direction.

The Road to Le Papillon

Do the necessary homework, investigate, ask questions, and then go back to your practice field and prep until you can take the first step toward your dream. It will happen. It will not be easy, but it will happen.

Petit plaisir Watch a favorite holiday or winter film. Here are a few that grab my attention at this time of year: *The Holiday*, *Grumpy Old Men*, *The Shop Around the Corner*, *The Apartment*, *Love Actually*, and *The Family Stone*.

Explore further thesimplyluxuriouslife.com/december7 (what to do when you don't know how the future will unfold)

December 8
Reaching a Dream

I learned this, at least, by my experiment: that if one advances confidently in the direction of [their] dreams, and endeavors to live the life which [they have] imagined, [they] will meet with a success unexpected in common hours.
—Henry David Thoreau, *Walden*

Fast-forward from 2014 to 2019.

Dreams can come true. I have held the above quote, which I shared in the introduction to my second book, close to my heart and journey for years, and it continues to ring true. Extraordinary things indeed do happen in the most ordinary of moments.

On the day I signed the papers to purchase Le Papillon, for me, an extraordinary moment occurred, but no one else knew how extraordinary it was. As I step forward into a new chapter in my life, I have discovered that when we maintain clarity, patience, and confidence in ourselves, as well as an openness for learning and evolving, dreams do come true, and often more easily than we had imagined, with the support of special individuals along the way.

The grand and most momentous and life-changing chapters in your life need not be acknowledged by the outside world. However, choose to acknowledge, celebrate, and commemorate these events, for they are your dreams coming to life.

Petit plaisir Read Anita Brookner's *Hotel du Lac*, a classic that inspires us to trust our journey and seek independence when our intuition tells us to do so.

Explore further thesimplyluxuriouslife.com/december8 (seven truths about experiencing happiness)

December 9
Take a Risk

During my senior year of college, I decided to try a few different pursuits. After all, I had just called off an engagement, changed my major to English from elementary education, and was determined to be accepted into graduate school — three things that, a year earlier, were not at the forefront of my mind.

One of the new pursuits I decided to tackle was a dance class. Mind you, the first dance class I had ever taken in college (as a young girl, I had had much experience, but that was more than a while ago), and then I found the wherewithal to try out for the school's annual musical production. What was I thinking? And then I made it, mainly because I could jump — high (having been a forward for my high school state basketball team caught their attention); still, I made it. I have always loved to dance, but being tall does not lend itself well to what many choreographers have in mind, even if I can find the beat innately.

For as long as I can remember, I have loved to dance, move, let go if only for a moment, and step away from the world. It can be a mini vacation of sorts or a way to celebrate without saying a word. And what I have discovered as I navigate this adventure called life is that it is a dance as well.

In order to perform a dance someone else has choreographed, we must figure out how to move with the music and our partners, and follow preordained steps. We cannot know for sure what these will do or require from us. We cannot know until we try, until we attempt to move to the beat.

We may be inexplicably drawn to someone or to music, and heeding this magnetism is part of the dance and the adventure. And while the dance movements or our partner's understanding of the choreography may at first be hard to grasp, so long as both parties are willing to try, the results can be magnificent. The key is being willing to try.

Our life journey has the potential to be a magnificent, breathtaking choreographed piece of art; we just have to figure out how to dance to the music it is playing. And that can be hard, especially when the notes are not given to us beforehand. But keep trying, refuse to give up, refuse to let a chip form on your shoulder, and always come to practice sessions with a smile and determination to figure it out.

We need to bloody our toes at times and stretch and strengthen our muscles. In doing so, we will come to realize that life does not want us to fail; it just often has higher expectations of what we can do than we might once have believed.

Won't you join me? Won't you keep trying to learn the dance of life? Each of our choreographed routines will be different, but life wants you to dance. You must, because that is the only way to have moments that will sweep you away.

Petit plaisir Consider sending your version of a holiday card to loved ones. Set aside an entire morning or afternoon to savor this ritual — pair with festive surroundings, music, and ambience. I often conclude my morning of holiday tree hunting out in the snow with an afternoon of decorating the house and an evening of writing my holiday cards — and immediately I am in a festive mood.

Explore further thesimplyluxuriouslife.com/december9 (four reasons why it's okay not to know)

December 10
Serendipity and New Life Chapters

During the early fall of 2018, I shared a photo I had captured inside my home that I would have never imagined in my mind's eye. I found a new bed for my primary bedroom. A mahogany bed, complete with carved butterflies. Perhaps it was serendipitous that it arrived in the days leading up to the launching of my second book, or perhaps that was just coincidence, but I am choosing the former.

The arrival of the new bed was a changing of the guard and promised more comfort, but I also reveled in the fact that the mahogany frame reminded me of France but was made in my childhood hometown by an artisan I highly regard.

It's funny how certain details in our lives shift in parallel to significant life moments. Things come into or leave our lives when we least expect them; at the same time, they prompt us to reflect how such a shift or change in our lives may hold some sort of powerful significance.

When we commemorate something in our mind, we pay attention to our lives. We are present. We notice stages of growth, opportunities to expand or become more aware of the life we want or perhaps realize we are already living. Somehow it is a shedding of some part of the past we may have been unconsciously holding on to, and such a shift somehow gives us permission to let it go and move forward.

December

  Take a moment to consider objects, habits, or routines that do not fit the new life you have chosen to live, and find new ones that align more fully with your true and sincere self. Consider letting go of what no longer supports your journey forward to give yourself space to fully grow into the life you have begun to build.

  Petit plaisir Listen to trumpeter Wynton Marsalis's "Winter Wonderland" and discover yourself fully stepping into the holiday season at a crisp pace and with cheerful energy.

  Explore further thesimplyluxuriouslife.com/december10 (becoming your best self and embracing the transformation process)

December 11
Live the Life You Want

Take into account that great love and great achievements involve great risk.
— Dalai Lama

  What *shoulds* are you following? In other words, how are you letting yourself be led away from your authentic direction, voice, and inklings? How are you being subconsciously swayed by outside dictates and voices? Sometimes all it takes is slowing down, being still, and answering these questions honestly.

  As a teenager, I happened upon the quote shown above, and I still consider its wisdom whenever I am considering (or am already immersed in) a decision when fear is present. There have been a handful of years in my life when I forgot the wisdom in this quote, but thankfully, I have returned to it, having recognized why it rings true for what I desire my life to become.

  Any time I ask myself which *shoulds* I am following, the Dalai Lama's statement begins dancing around in my mind. Doing anything that is uncertain is definitely frightening, but having chosen the safe route for a couple of years, I can attest that, as a general rule, doing so means that nothing worth achieving or experiencing will materialize to strengthen our contentment. I will temper that by saying while that this is what fits my temperament, tastes, and preferences, one person's definition of risk may look completely different.

  Risk taking stretches you, takes you out of your comfort zone, because when you choose to grow or attempt to change your life, you can become a tad trepidatious. However, it is at such moments that life

can become exhilarating and pinch-me moments can occur. Such an approach has been a fundamental part of the life I love living. What we fear is often a sign of what we hope will be our reality if only we could figure out how to gather up the courage to explore the unknown that is tickling our curiosity.

Petit plaisir Make a lusciously decadent tomato soup and pair with a croque madame sandwich.

Explore further thesimplyluxuriouslife.com/december11 (recipe for lusciously rich tomato soup)

December 12
Unexpected Surprises

Have you ever had one of those months, weeks, or years when it seems nothing is going your way, from little things, such as facing a red light at every intersection, to large, life-altering events, such as a relationship or a job ending or a pandemic? When difficulties persist, our sense of hope and motivation to continue pushing forward can be shaken.

Thankfully, prior to 2013, I had not experienced any catastrophic events, but during the winter of that year, my patience was tried as the boiler in my beloved eighty-some-year-old home gradually gave up the ghost. For about three months, my mind was not entirely at ease because I was not sure how it was going to hold up during our cold spells.

A house needs a heat source, so even if I wanted to throw up my hands and forget about it, I couldn't. To make a long story short, with the help of someone I trust in the business and with a refusal to be taken advantage of when it came to seemingly exorbitant estimates, I ordered a boiler that was within my budget.

Did I plan on paying for a new boiler? Absolutely not. I had planned travel to France the following summer, and I had to postpone that trip. But the good that came out of this unexpected event was that the value of my home increased, which ensured a swifter sale two years later, and I slept peacefully during the next cold season.

More important, I learned to trust myself. I learned to be intuitively watchful of those who might be taking advantage of the situation, yet equally more open to trusting others who have given me no reason to do otherwise. I also learned that I could rely on myself to figure out something I initially knew absolutely nothing about.

Life will test you. Life will question if you really want or need something, and it will reveal the answer based on how you respond: Do you give up or do you continue to look for answers? While you may not be able to plan for everything life has in store for you, you can still navigate through the obstacles and arrive at the destination you had in mind.

Petit plaisir Adorn your front door with a fresh wreath of pine or cedar boughs or magnolia leaves.

Explore further thesimplyluxuriouslife.com/december12 (nine ways to trust your inner compass)

December 13
Finding Home

She had not known the weight until she felt the freedom.
—Nathaniel Hawthorne, *The Scarlet Letter*

Sometimes we do not know what we are missing until we feel or experience it firsthand for the first time.

This is not to say I did not love my life in Pendleton and, prior to that, Portland, Oregon, but it was not until 2015, when I was returning home to Bend, with my dogs, from the Oregon coast, a place I adore, where I always am able to relax and unwind, that I ached to cross the threshold into my home.

While rejuvenating, I not only longed for my new rental house, where I was living at the time, but I was eager to walk around town, pop into my favorite shops and bakeries, all now for the first time in one town. That same feeling is now amplified, knowing I am returning to Le Papillon, a house that is actually mine.

Sometimes we do not know what we want, but rather we know what does not fit quite right. We cannot always explain it, but intuitively something is ill-fitting, irritating, even if we cannot quite put our finger on why. I am tickled that I re-stumbled across Bend after unconsciously being drawn to it during my childhood. It was the jolt of an *aha* moment that showed me what I was missing.

If such a feeling persists for you after a long period of time, consider exploring. Often you do not know what you need until you stumble across it. The key is to listen to yourself, trust yourself, and then step forward in exploration. Be brave.

Petit plaisir Read *The Tao of Pooh* by Benjamin Hoff and discover contemplative and inspiring insights for living well.

Explore further thesimplyluxuriouslife.com/december13 (seven life lessons from *The Tao of Pooh*)

December 14
The Journey

The rejection, the acceptance, the progress, the struggle.

Life can sometimes feel as though we are on a roller coaster ride, completely at the mercy of the conductor. Sometimes the journey is uphill and slow, testing our patience; at other times, it is exhilarating, surreal, and moving so fast we wish we could slow it down to savor it all the more.

I remind myself of the roller-coaster analogy when it feels as though the efforts I have put forth are not bearing the fruit I had hoped. In reality, it is simply that things are moving, progress is being made, but at increments that are hard to observe with the naked eye or behind the scenes where we do not have access until they reveal themselves.

On the flip side, the good will arrive, and while the pace will be seemingly fast and furious when it does, I am reminded to savor, stay present, and not dismiss all that is going well or take it for granted. More important, I am reminded — now that I know myself, my introversion, and HSP (highly sensitive person) tendencies, more thoroughly — that choosing a less "thrilling" or speedy ride is quite alright. You may need to proceed through life at a different pace in order to not be scared to step onto the ride in the first place.

Everyone's roller-coaster ride will involve different twists and turns, rises and falls, but so long as we come prepared for the ride, put the odds in our favor, do our homework beforehand (in other words, buckle up and hold on tight), we will be able to navigate successfully the moments when we need to work, stay focused, and not lose heart.

Life is not for the faint of heart; it is for those who are full of courage. If you will embrace life, remain hopeful, and let go of stories that do not serve or support the life you wish to live, an amazing life awaits, and you will find yourself better able to enjoy every moment and, at the end of the ride, arrive safe and sound with a super-sized, uncontainable smile on your face.

Petit plaisir Read *The One Thing: The Surprisingly Simple Truth Behind Extraordinary Results*, by Gary Keller, as you begin to look ahead to a new year.

Explore further thesimplyluxuriouslife.com/december14 (why not . . . celebrate the struggle?)

December 15
Gifts to Yourself

The funny thing about traditions and social norms is that, while it may feel intimidating to do something that challenges expectations, usually it is far more difficult to make the decision to act or live differently than it is to actually embrace and live the change we seek.

For example, the conventional wisdom about the winter holidays is that you will spend time with family and/or friends, exchange gifts, spend far too much money, and stay awake until midnight on New Year's Eve. Each year since living in Bend, I have consciously tried to tailor my winter holidays in a way that honors my ability to enjoy them. Each time I do this, I am far more at ease, content, and thankful for having the courage to listen to what I had been trying to hear for a long time.

Perhaps there are smaller traditions or ways of living that just do not work for you. Maybe you don't know exactly why they always feel like they are a size too small or a touch off key, but you are curious to try something new, something different, something that has piqued your interest for quite some time. However, every time you consider taking action, you think about the consternation it may cause for those around you. You worry that making the leap will cause alienation or leave you regretting your decision in some other way.

While you will never know unless you try, if you sincerely know something is not working for you, anything you try will probably be better if your mind is set on making it so. From my experience, part of the reason we hang on for so long to what is not working is that we have told ourselves we have to, and when we let go, we allow our minds to be riddled with guilt. That guilt is fueled by a culture that does not have your peace of mind and contentment in mind and that plays the role of a bully to corral you into following its dictates, even if they make you miserable.

The courage to trust yourself, even and especially when it goes against cultural norms, strengthens with time, and each time, when you honor what brings you joy, those who love you will feel that joy expressed toward them. If, as part of how to celebrate any holiday, each of us considers those we love and how they feel joy, the holidays and their traditions may be filled with even more joviality for all.

Change your mind, become its master, and choose to honor and then explore a new idea for celebrating or spending time during the holiday season. Most likely, if you have been contemplating making a change to your holiday celebrations for some time, you do desire a change. Leap. Be brave. Respect your one and only life, and live in a way that allows you to come alive and be yourself. It is a most, if not *the* most, wonderful gift you can give yourself.

Petit plaisir Make a quadruple chocolate cookie, and melt in pure satiation with each bite.

Explore further thesimplyluxuriouslife.com/december15 (ten ideas for holiday rituals to savor)

December 16
A Snowstorm's Life Lessons

The lessons of life exist at every turn, on every day we live; they are merely waiting for us to pay attention. In January 2017, Mother Nature brought around-the-clock snow to the small town of Bend, Oregon, and after twenty-four hours of consistent snow showers, I measured 19 inches on my back porch. I was astonished.

I was able to stay home when the winter weather arrived. I shoveled my driveway, sidewalks, and walking paths a few times throughout the day before going to bed and waking up to 6 more inches. However, those last 6 inches were much easier to shovel Thursday since I had shoveled as much as I had the day before.

As I drove around town, running a few errands and seeing how Bend had fared, I observed a variety of things. There was less traffic and slower, more attentive driving. And while I was fortunate to have the day off, many people had to go in to work and postpone snow removal until they arrived home that evening. Nonetheless, the large amounts still remaining in many driveways gave me pause.

The first life lesson I observed that day: The small, incremental steps we make toward the results we seek eventually add up. The snowfall was steady, unrelenting, and beautiful as it created a majestic, mesmerizing wintery wonderland. And when it was all said and done, the amazing accumulation left me in awe.

The second lesson: Doing the necessary work, training, or practice repeatedly — even when the results may seem to be minimal even after hours, months, or years of attention — makes it all the more certain that you are closer to seizing the opportunity when it presents itself than if you had not taken the time to practice.

Not only was the snowstorm magnificent, but it offered many life lessons, certainly more than two. One of the most amazing gifts life gives us is the chance to experience it, truly be present, and observe its magic. **Especially during this season, but throughout the entire year, keep looking around you, and you too will see the lessons, the *aha* moments that can deepen the quality of your everyday life.**

Petit plaisir For a cozy evening in, make a flavor-rich French onion soup. And don't forget to pick up a freshly made, crusty baguette.

Explore further thesimplyluxuriouslife.com/december16 (recipe for a simple and luxurious French onion soup)

December 17
Be Love

The simply luxurious life, when attained and truly understood, prompts you to savor every moment. Not all will be positive and joyous, but every one will offer something to appreciate, enjoy, and perhaps learn from. Part of living simply luxuriously is understanding how to savor life. So often we get caught up in the whirlwind, the have-to's, the must-do's, and we forget to be still, listen, and then act through love toward ourselves and others.

It can be easier to live in fear than to live with our heart extended, knowing it may be hurt or broken. But to not live and act through love shuts the door to a life full of great joy and contentment. Love's gift, one of the many, is that it changes us forever and for the better.

There are only a handful of humans I have loved deeply, and very few, thankfully, have passed away. Conversely, there have been many animals and pets, whose lives are destined to be far shorter than our own, but perhaps we can learn how to be more fully present for them, savor our time together, and not take for granted what we have been given. I am not sure how to learn the lessons love teaches without experiencing real love personally, but I do know that the only way to feel love is to be love.

Being love can be misunderstood if it is too narrowly defined. One necessity for embodying the "being" is to express your sincere and true self. Take off the façade, remove the figurative masks and false selves, and courageously, without guarantee, share yourself with the world around you.

As I continue to grow, learn, and become more courageous in sharing my true self in my daily life, I find the relationships, the connections, the exchanges, I encounter have more depth, more beauty, and thus more love (of any kind: love for community, love for the beauty of the day, platonic or romantic love). If such a connection or relationship emerges but then ends — someone moves away or dies, someone leaves the place of work that brought you together — the loss we feel pains us more deeply.

When a relationship in which we have given of ourselves changes in unwanted ways, it can feel as though a piece of us has left us. But when that happens, our heart, ourselves, our being — whatever breaks because of the change — has grown far more than it would have ever done without the shared connection.

If you have lived long enough, you know that you will not always find people who have the best intentions when it comes to your love. You know that your love can be squashed, taken advantage of, and even laughed at — by someone with a callous heart or by an insecure individual who is too afraid to love, so they do not trust the love you wish to give.

We all have to work through what we are insecure about when it comes to expressing love. All of us, albeit for different reasons, have insecurities, doubts, and fears, but we must not give up entirely the hope that we will find other individuals who are sincere, genuine, loving, and secure within themselves.

I encourage you to choose to love and to be love in your daily life. Be open to the potentiality of whatever may cross your path, without assumption or expectation. Simply be love — in your words, your thoughts, your actions, your hopes, and your handling of your emotions — as you navigate pain as well as exuberance. I do not know what will unfold when you choose to be love in your daily life, but I know it will bring a life full of many moments of joy to savor in the moment and after their passing.

Petit plaisir Turn on Count Basie's Orchestra's rendition of "Let It Snow" and let it spark you to dance about the house, perhaps with a hot cuppa or an aperitif in hand.

Explore further thesimplyluxuriouslife.com/december17 (twenty-six ways to love fully)

December 18
A Fresh New Day

Each day, we wake up and have the chance to do better than yesterday, do better than last year, do better than our much younger selves of years ago.

Before I wake up each morning, I give myself about thirty minutes to just be. I switch on the bedside lamp, turn on a classical music radio station, and just lie in bed. Each day is a little bit different, but one aspect that is the same is that I am preparing. It is nothing dramatic or rehearsed, but I am giving myself time to step into the day, rather than push myself out, ignoring the importance of being kind to myself.

For me, easing into the day, no matter how early I have to wake up, helps immensely, as I can make sure I am aware of my schedule and mentally prepared for what I need and hope to accomplish, enabling me to step out the door feeling able and ready to do my best. I am inspired by the four components of the morning-routine acronym TIME coined by Jay Shetty (author of *Think Like a Monk*): Thankfulness, express gratitude; Insight, read something uplifting, insightful, positive, intriguing; Meditate, spend fifteen minutes alone breathing, visualizing or with sound; Exercise.

Being intentional about how we begin the day makes a difference in our ability to be patient: not jumping to respond to that e-mail we did not want to receive and just want to be done with, taking a moment to say hello to a colleague and having a quick chat about their weekend rather than rushing to our office, or greeting people with a genuine smile and creating a tone, before the conversation has even begun, of openness and congeniality.

How we step into each day makes a difference in the quality of our everydays, and our everydays make up our lives, as a well-known quote reminds us. However, not just our everyday lives, but our entire lives, even the magnificent moments, are amplified when we invest, little by little, with authentic gestures, and build a community we want to be a part of. If we extend kindness — because that is who we wish to be rather than because of whom we feel we have to be — we create an environment of positive energy that people want to be around, and we enjoy our own company as well.

Extend kindness. We often hear such a suggestion, which we generally assume refers to how we engage with others. But remember to extend it to yourself as well and, when it comes to your daily routine, how you begin your day. Consciously start the day well, and you give the rest of your waking hours a greater chance of turning out well.

Petit plaisir Make chocolate almond praline cookies — one of my favorites. The recipe combines chocolate, caramelized roasted almonds, and a savory pairing of salt that tickles your taste buds and makes it hard to eat just one.

Explore further thesimplyluxuriouslife.com/december18 (recipe for chocolate almond praline cookies)

December 19
Mindful Transitions

In August 2019, I found a new home, in Bend, Oregon. Because of the moving truck's schedule, I had to wait a week before officially moving in, so the week leading up to the official move was unique.

Whenever a transition arrives in our lives, whether we seek it out or not, it is fraught with new or less familiar emotions. Navigating them, observing them, and trying to make sense of them can be perplexing, but on the flip side, transitions are rich with reasons to celebrate, for a new and unknown next chapter is ready to begin.

As much as I wanted to move into my house, I appreciated the week in limbo to settle in gently, thoughtfully, with intention — from wrapping up affairs at the rental that had been my home for four years, extending my gratitude to those who gave more in kindness and neighborly friendship than they had to, and simply savoring the luxuries living in my rental had afforded.

I understood I had many new luxuries awaiting me where I was going, but trying to remember and acknowledge what most likely will never be again is one approach that helps along the journey, so that we do not fail to appreciate all we have and, in so doing, toss away the good we have found.

I also put into place details so that the first weekend in my home would be as welcoming as possible for the boys as much as for me. On day one of my ownership of my new house, the first dog door I have ever had was installed. Oscar took time to adjust to the new approach to entering the yard, but Norman was game. A new favorite French candle was waiting to be enjoyed, as well as a new journal to record plans, dreams, and dinner party menus.

Settling into Le Papillon exceeded my earlier giddiness levels as I had been longing to own my own home in Bend for four years and to begin cultivating my sanctuary. But the peace of mind that we bring with us, whether we are moving into a new home or not, is the best companion we can have to cultivate rich and wonderful everydays. As I put the door back on its hinges, complete with its new dog entrance, the rain began to fall, and by the end of the day, it was raining as well as thundering. A beautiful evening indeed, and I savored every sweet scent of the rain-filled fresh air.

It can be tempting to race through moments in your life when you are confident that what you are racing toward is far better than where you are or is the culmination of years of effort. But you reveal your confidence in the future when you slow down to savor what surrounds you right now.

Petit plaisir To pick you up and keep you going through your day, listen to Vivaldi's Trumpet Concerto in B-flat Minor.

Explore further thesimplyluxuriouslife.com/december19 (how to minimize the stress of a major life transition)

December 20
Design Your Own Life

The changing of the seasons approaches yet again. The shortest day of the year for the Northern Hemisphere, and the longest for the Southern (perhaps a more meaningful day than New Year's Day), presents an opportunity to ponder and assess the design of your life and how it is built.

As you reflect on the days that have made up the past year, how would you describe them? Were they full of hope, excitement, and productivity, or frustration, questions, and tears? With all my heart, it is my wish that you are looking back on a year that was full of more ups than downs, more moments of joy than hurt, and more reasons to celebrate than to shake your head.

The beauty of those 365 days is that we have a choice each day as to how we will live them. Tomorrow, more light gradually, yet steadily will begin to fill our days, a change we can think of as symbolizing the clarity we have gained if we have chosen to be honest about our journey thus far. There will be times when frustration confronts us, but thankfully there will be times when complete exhilaration fills us. How we choose to see each experience will determine how we will emerge on the other side. It is so easy to be cynical and negative, but who has ever accomplished something because they did not think it would happen? I can pretty much guarantee the answer is no one.

In order to accomplish, in order grow, in order to shine, we must turn our face to the sun and strive. We must squeeze out the goodness, wherever we can find it, and we are fortunate to have 365 days each year. How will you spend them?

    I cherish the last days and weeks of the year. It is always a good idea to examine your growth, to ponder the obstacles that have stood in your way and how you handled them. Hopefully, you will see strength that you were not aware you always possessed. Recognizing that strength will boost your confidence, reminding you that you will and can be even more content in the coming year as you consciously live the life you have designed so well.

    Petit plaisir   Listen to Vince Guaraldi's *A Charlie Brown Christmas* album, and play your favorite track on repeat. Mine is "Skating" — I cannot help but tap my toes and dance about each time I hear it.

    Explore further   thesimplyluxuriouslife.com/december20 (a simply luxurious holiday playlist)

December 21
Opportunity

If opportunity knocked one minute from now, what would you do? Would you recognize it, would you doubt it, would you ignore it, or would you step gladly forward without any promise of deeper contentment?

    The simplest and most accurate definition I have found for "opportunity" is preparation crossing paths with our life journey — a force that is beyond our control to slow down or speed up or pause in order to get ready.

    Opportunity keeps chugging along at its own comfortable pace. Sometimes that pace is Mach 80, and in other instances, it is a leisurely, steady 30-minute mile. Fortune — by which I mean opportunity — has crossed my path more than a few times, for which I am grateful, but I did not always see it for what it was. However, when I finally learned to say yes without hesitation, what made it easier was that I was eager, ready, and prepared to share, pounce, and communicate. Preparation is the key.

    The funny thing about preparing is that often we do not know all that we are preparing for. It may be only in hindsight that we recognize that having a certain experience or learning a particular skill came in handy when opportunity presented itself.

    As much as we may want to know the future, seeking such knowledge is futile and wastes energy better spent in the present. In order for something positive to occur, we have to begin the preparations with a hopeful heart.

Examine what you are preparing for. What goodness are you opening your life up to, so that when it does cross your path — even when others may say, "There's no way you could make that happen" — you know that you actually are more than ready because you have been preparing and waiting for this moment to arrive.

Petit plaisir Signify a pride of place when it comes to your home by either choosing a name for your abode (no matter how large or petite), and add a simple symbolic object that is not glaringly obvious but that speaks to your choice (case in point, I have a butterfly doorbell on my front porch).

Explore further thesimplyluxuriouslife.com/december21 (five ways to make your dreams come true: five "bills" to expect)

December 22
Success in Ordinary Hours

When you expend great effort and have patience, the life you have imagined and thoughtfully curated will begin to become your reality. It will often be so gradual that it may take a particular moment, one that spotlights all that is going well in your life, for you to realize how it truly is coming together.

Henry David Thoreau was right that we will "meet with a success unexpected in common hours." The success we seek, which will be unique for each us, does not arrive at a grand soirée we have planned, a special event where we anticipate something extraordinary happening. No, it happens often in our everydays, when we pay attention to all we have begun to build, accumulate, and bring together to create what we once only dreamed about.

The first holiday season I spent in Le Papillon was my favorite thus far. To an onlooker, it would not seem all that extraordinary. Only each of us, living our lives thoughtfully, will know if indeed our dreams are coming together. The dream might simply be peace of mind, or it might be finally understanding what true contentment is and reveling in it each and every day.

Understanding your full potential rests at the foundation of living a life of quality over quantity — a conscious appreciation of what is found within yourself rather than seeking applause from external

sources. While the journey that leads to this destination takes place gradually, when you do it intentionally, you will arrive, and you will know when you do.

Petit plaisir Share some holiday cheer with your neighbors, whether by sharing a homemade favorite treat from your kitchen, delivering a note of appreciation, or doing anything that expresses your gratitude for the neighborliness you share.

Explore further thesimplyluxuriouslife.com/december22 (how to harness your inner voice and reach your full potential)

December 23
Thoughtful Decorating: A Shift in Approach

Leading up to my first winter holidays at Le Papillon, I went through my four boxes of holiday decorations and pared them down to three. While it is true that I want less stuff to store overall, my primary desire in paring down is that I want to store what I truly love and actually look forward to using each year when the holidays arrive.

I also took a closer look at the color scheme I wanted to work with in my house, and that required me to let go of certain items; some reflected a different me, and others I had kept partly out of a sense of obligation.

Likewise, this year, I changed how I decorated my tree. I let go of trying to make it "perfect" (admittedly, it never was, but I always unconsciously tried to make it look like the trees in the magazines) and hung for the first time in many years ornaments that speak to my journey and welcomed details handmade by my maternal grandmother, as well as a handful of ornaments I made from pine cones that had fallen outside my new home. I am not crafty, but it was fun to create something that would be part of my story and different from other tree décor.

How you celebrate and decorate for the holidays evolves and moves with your life as it too evolves, grows, and meanders. So long as you do not continue to be tied to what no longer brings joy to you or others in your life, or to decorations that remain only out of obligation, you can be sure to experience a festive, warm, and memorable season.

Petit plaisir Take a nap and wake up refreshed to enjoy a festive evening — large and gregarious or small and intimate — that perhaps lasts late into the night.

Explore further thesimplyluxuriouslife.com/december23 (twelve simple winter holiday décor ideas)

December 24
Priorities

In November 2019, following Thanksgiving, I arrived home to about six inches of snow. The first snow shoveling of the season! Yes, I was excited. And what this made clear was that, when tasks that need tending to (in this case, snow shoveling), which others may loathe, bring us giddiness (as was my case) or at the very least contentment, we must pay attention, as life is revealing what brings us joy. What such a feeling reflects is something much deeper, something about what we are investing our time in beyond the present moment and the direction we need to keep traveling, regardless of whether others understand.

When a task engenders excitement or, at the bare minimum, resolution and determination to see it through well, we reveal to the world what we prioritize — whether we are caring for our home, investing in our neighborhood, supporting our health with a regular workout routine, investing in a special relationship, or becoming frugal with our finances in order to save up for something more important.

We are not always aware of what we are prioritizing in our lives, and when we look closely, we may realize that what we are prioritizing aligns exactly as we would want. However, it is also possible that we may realize we have been investing in a way of life that does not align with what we hope will materialize in our near or distant future. Such a discovery is a gift. When we acknowledge the misdirection, we can correct, and when we correct, we become cognizant about how to proceed in the right direction.

As the new year inches closer, taking time to assess how you prioritize your time, energy, and finances will confirm or correct your path forward and ensure that what materializes in the new year is all you have hoped for and perhaps more.

Petit plaisir Make a classic French *chocolat chaud* (hot chocolate) and pour it into an espresso cup to sip and savor while sitting next to a crackling fire, preferably outside in the snow.

Explore further thesimplyluxuriouslife.com/december24 (recipe for *chocolate chaud*, plus two additional holiday desserts)

December 25
More Wonderful Because of the Hiccup

In my household, it is a simple, yet special morning. The boys' (my dogs') stockings are stuffed full of toys and treats, I prepare a decadent meal, and the tree glows as I wander down the hall from my slumber. Just as important as the opening of gifts, the breakfast has been planned in advance, and I will place homemade croissants (made in advance and defrosted overnight in the refrigerator) into the oven to not only tickle my taste buds, but to create a sweet smell for Christmas morn. Along with some bacon, special eggs, and black tea, the morning will be for lounging, followed by a walk through my snow-covered neighborhood. And in 2015, my first year in Bend, a new tradition began: touring (aka Nordic, classic, or cross-country skiing).

For my first winter in Bend, I rented skis and found the trail, and the boys bounded beside me as we reveled in the festive day. It was not until I arrived back at my car that I realized I had lost my keys somewhere out in the snow. Yes, we were locked out of our car and our home on Christmas day. Yet, even three hours later, after a taxi took us back to our house, where I found my spare car key (after climbing through my bedroom window), we were back in the car, heading home to enjoy a festive meal, and warm ourselves with our paws and feet up. The best gift I have ever received, having dreamed about it since 2005, was to live in Bend. Losing my keys in the snow on a major holiday did not dampen the day in any way.

Now that that dream has been granted, I feel as if I am living in my own little fantasy land. That year, the snow had been falling for nearly two weeks, and local venues offered holiday plays and movies. And while walking outside a few nights before in downtown Bend after a screening of *The Christmas Story*, I looked up to see a brilliant full moon offering a backdrop to the glistening snow. Yep, a dream come true.

Dare to dream, and when that dream, after much patience, persistence, and effort, becomes your reality, choose to welcome any perceived hiccup. Let it be part of what makes your dream, and now your life, uniquely special and all the more worth savoring.

Petit plaisir Take a walk with a loved one or many, two-legged and/or four-legged, and hold yourself in the present moment, in the company, the beauty of Mother Nature, and savor being alive to experience it all.

Explore further thesimplyluxuriouslife.com/december25 (seven reasons to spend time with nature)

December 26
Between the Years

In 2019, a TSLL reader, Hanna, who lives in Germany, shared with me the phrase *zwischen den Jahren*. Her explanation of what translates as "between the years" caught my attention.

While I was teaching, the two weeks of holiday that end one year and begin another were a treasured time, a fertile time for ideas to rise to the forefront of my attention. Following the first year of the blog's creation, beginning in 2010, I took the last full week of the year off, and I continue to do so, even now that I no longer teach. While I have experienced the value of this time "between the years," I did not know how sacred the final week of the year was in many cultures.

This special time offers freedom to let the mind wander and dance about, entertaining new ideas without the pressure of deadlines. Having an abundance of free time can also be difficult for some if their muscles are not prepared to dance and dance well or simply relax and relax well.

The holiday hangover can be real and take a day or two, or maybe more, to be alleviated. If we are not aware that such a state exists, we may think we are stuck. The good news is, we are not.

I have experienced this feeling; however, with each year, my awareness of the realities of the emotional ebbs and flows during a cherished time of year has enabled me to shorten the "holiday hangover." The process of successful transition follows this order: (1) Examine, then apply what is helpful life fuel and toss unnecessary fodder in your mind or in a journal (perhaps on the plane, train, or car ride home). (2) Slip into bed for a deep, restful night's sleep. (3) Wake up with a fresh mind, take restorative deep breaths, and enjoy a day you make your own for rejuvenation.

Now the "between the years" time begins, yours to savor and linger in while you acknowledge your unique journey, appreciating but not being consumed with others' ways of living that do not align with yours.

I enjoy spending the time "between the years" writing, creating, planning, organizing, seeking out inspiration, sleeping, and reading, each in the amount necessary, which can change by the hour.

Beginning today or on another of the final days in December, savor this special gift that arrives but once a year.

Petit plaisir Settle in and let yourself savor the time "between the years." Reflect, savor, plan, settle in, whatever brings you calm, cultivates reason for celebration and appreciation, and enables you to begin anew on January 1.

Explore further thesimplyluxuriouslife.com/december26 (ten ideas for making the most of "between the years")

December 27
Surprises

When it comes to surprises, I am somewhere in the middle as far as enjoyment is concerned. Like most people, I love good surprises but abhor bad ones.

In June 2018, I experienced four surprises, which fell on a continuum ranging from not good at all to absolutely magnificent. First, on the bad surprise side: a mouse (whom I quickly escorted out of my house in the wee hours of the morning). Then, on the very good side: the arrival of the first-proof copy of my second book.

Yep, the book I absolutely could not wait to share with readers of TSLL was real. After I opened the package, I sat on the floor and took it all in: the smell of the pages, the sharpness of the cover, the content laid out as it should be, chapter by chapter. A reader of the blog who described it as my "book baby" was absolutely correct.

Sometimes the biggest surprise is that your dream comes together as you had wished, even though you know how much work and time it took. However, it never feels real until it shows up in its completed form.

The questions I asked myself included: "Is it possible to enjoy any type of surprise? Is it possible to appreciate the not-so-wonderful surprises?" As for the latter, I am going to say probably not as much as the good ones, but what I learned from the not-so-welcome ones that week was that the way I handle them will determine future opportunities or setbacks.

When I saw the mouse, the first thing I did . . . yes, I will admit it, I screamed. Then I started to strategize. I wanted it out of the house, not just back in its hole or wherever it came from, so I got out my broom, and made a clear passage to the wide-open back door. The boys were half asleep and did not see it (perhaps this was a reason to welcome a cat into my life), so I made sure they were out of the way and then gently showed the tiny rodent the door at broom's length.

While the two examples I share with you today, on either end of the spectrum, are far from extreme, I found that the ways we handle surprises can be seen as opportunities for growth and deeper appreciation.

Perhaps you also had a surprise or two recently. I hope that whatever happened turned out well, but if it did not, take a moment to consider how to apply the lesson in order to seize a future opportunity

rather than squander what hopefully will never happen again. And if indeed it was a very good surprise, why not savor it a little bit longer?

Petit plaisir Visit a local independent bookshop and spend as much time as you desire. Welcome home one book that speaks to you and to where you are heading in the new year.

Explore further thesimplyluxuriouslife.com/december27 (view the new year as a reset: five areas to examine)

December 28
Your Authentic Life

When you were younger, if you were like me, you had created in your mind's eye an idea of how your life would unfold. As an adult looking back, I see that my ideas were shaped by what I saw around me. It is extremely difficult to seek what we do not know exists. So what I saw — school, teachers, married parents, women with children, and small-town bliss — was initially what I pursued. However, within me was a curiosity that would not settle for this presented path.

I did not see many roles for women besides wife, mother, and teacher. I often wonder what I would have chosen as a career path if I had not become an English teacher, but it was not until I was well immersed in my career that I came to realize there were paths that were more desirable, better suited to my tastes, predilections, and talents. No matter how I tried to convince myself, the marriage-and-mother path — at least not the traditional path I had witnessed — did not ignite or elicit the positive emotions other directions and options have. Thankfully, I had not stepped into those roles before I had these *aha* moments.

We can unconsciously limit the idea of designing a life that is congruent with who we wish to be, who we are most comfortable being, and who we have the potential to evolve into, but if we choose to be curious about life, if we choose to ask "Why?" or "Why Not . . . ?" we gradually begin to discover the right path for ourselves regardless of society's expectations and "safe" or "acceptable" paths.

Along the way, others may either stray from us because they cannot understand us or they uncomfortably cling to us because something about our path piques their curiosity. Sometimes we will be tempted to revert to the "acceptable" path because it is easier and we don't have to keep explaining ourselves, but being "safe" when it comes to a life's journey, and dismissing or ignoring our yearnings never allowed anyone to reach their full potential.

The life I have the good fortune and opportunity to live today causes me to pinch myself. When I was young, I did not see models of women living life on their own terms and being content, at peace, and confident doing so. A lot has changed, in society as well as with my understanding of how I most enjoy living. Significant progress has enabled more and more women to choose freely the life they live, and while more progress certainly needs to be made, thankfully, improvement has occurred. For some people, my life path will never make sense, but for others, it will be the example they need, proffering different ideas of living well. Hopefully, they will be assured that they too can make the journey.

Sometimes the role models who provide inspiration for how to live our best life cross our paths and catch our attention, but sometimes, we do not see or meet the people we are capable of becoming. If that is true in your case, do not be deterred. When we do not see what we need, we can become what we needed to look up to and, in so doing, become a role model for someone else's life journey to reach true contentment.

Role model or not, dare to discover your unique path. Along the way, you may be surprised by the person you become. Respect who you find, be kind to yourself, but keep striving forward, even if you don't have a model to follow.

Petit plaisir Begin planning your garden for next year — seeds, new spring plants, etc. It is the equivalent to preparing one's upcoming seasonal wardrobe — preparing what we need, what will fill the gaps, and what will last for years and be worth the investment.

Explore further thesimplyluxuriouslife.com/december28 (sixteen benefits of self-reliance)

December 29
A Life of Contentment

Once we know what dream to pursue, no matter how small or large, adrenaline and excitement fuel our engines. Throughout the duration of our journey of building a life of contentment, we may have moments of doubt, but so long as we know in our hearts that what we are doing is sincere and a true passion, the doubts quickly subside.

As we near the realization of our goal, the doubt that occasionally creeps into our lives can grab on with more force, more seriousness, with its attempts to invoke fear — that what we have spent time and energy doing is not worth it, that it will not work out as we had hoped, that it will be received differently and more negatively than we could have imagined.

December

That fear calls for a moment in which we calm ourselves and remind ourselves of all we have done and why we have done it.

There will always be critics, but we need not be among them. After all, often our harshest critics respond from a place or instance of pain in their own lives that we have triggered by what we have succeeded in doing. They may not know this themselves, and it can be hard to believe their criticism likely has nothing to do with us.

The critiques to consider are the ones from those we trust, those who understand what we are trying to accomplish and have our best interests at heart. Even then, we must trust ourselves, because if we have done the homework required to get to know ourselves, we know best about what brings us joy and, ultimately, contentment.

Once we have found contentment, it becomes less likely that we will be rocked from our calm seat of quiet confidence. We may remain open, we may adjust, and we are always in motion to some degree, but the critics are less likely to inflict real pain.

We follow dreams because a good life is made up of living with curiosity, pursuing the unknown, and embracing the opportunity to do what we love. If we follow our dreams, we are living a life that is our own reality, and how sweet is that? Critics will try to inflict a wound or two, but we have armor to protect ourselves: knowledge of who we are, what we are doing, and why we are doing it. Applause would be great, but trying to please everyone can pull us off track.

When you embrace your true self, those who connect with you and your journey will step forward because when you are igniting, it is hard not to inspire others to find what ignites them as well.

Petit plaisir Listen to Gretchen Yanover's "Suddenly I Felt Joy" and be reminded of how simple joy can be experienced.

Explore further thesimplyluxuriouslife.com/december29 (eleven life-truths about contentment that seem impossible until we experience them)

December 30
What We Seek, We Find

Little by little, a life of true contentment comes together. And even though our lives are dynamic, when we remain grounded in the moment, holding our mind open, what we experience will continue forward in our memories, to be treasured and make us smile when we reflect upon them. We do not ask them to be anything more than what they could be.

The Road to Le Papillon

Knowing this truth serves as a reminder to be fully present, and to savor, savor, savor and appreciate, appreciate, appreciate. But we must also remember to be patient, to keep our eyes open, to say yes — to become more comfortable with life not unfolding as we had expected, and to realize that the universe may be looking out for us better than we can look out for ourselves.

Recently, I discovered a pedestal dining room table, one I had been trying to find, and purchased it. My new-to-me round oak table would not be everyone's choice, but for years, I have been certain this type of table would work best for my lifestyle and aesthetic preferences. I did not expect to find it when I did, but it was meant to be mine when I saw it. Seconds after inquiring about what I wanted, the shop owner told me he might have something I would be interested in. One month later, it was in my home, purchased for a very reasonable price.

I had found the table, and finding a house of my own followed a year later. I had expected the order to be reversed, but it turns out, the universe had other plans. Patience, Shannon, patience.

While the table I once had was not sturdy enough to travel with me, nor large enough, I was thankful to have had it for as long as I did. Now someone else who would welcome it into their home would enjoy it, and I could not be more tickled that it will continue to be appreciated. I could not have imagined I would find such a perfect table for where I was in my journey, and also at an unbelievably affordable price. But I did, and I am buoyant about this find.

Conversely, I also did not expect to be renting for as long as I did (four years), but all worked out for the best as my house, Le Papillon, was not ready for me yet. Prior to buying Le Papillon in 2019, I exercised the opportunity to trust life. Since arriving in Bend, my patience and confidence continues to deepen, trusting that it is the universe's way of helping me navigate in a manner that will benefit me so long as I remain conscious and aware, and continue to strive forward when opportunity presents itself.

If you find yourself not quite where you hope your journey will lead, take today, this very moment, to remind yourself that you are precisely where you need to be if only you will savor where you are, no matter how small the goodness may seem. Extend gratitude, and let yourself sit with ease, knowing that while events may seem to occur out of order, life is not static and, in fact, is progressing, so long as you keep striving forward.

Petit plaisir Let newly formed ideas ripen. Trust your inner compass to know when to harvest.

Explore further thesimplyluxuriouslife.com/december30 (how to ensure a bountiful harvest in life)

December 31
Living Simply Luxuriously

While one of the most important lessons to learn as early as possible is to understand that living a fulfilling life is simple, it is not easy to reach this realization and maintain this clarity. Once we grasp the essentials in life that make it most rewarding, we must be vigilant and strong, and ignore those who try to lead us down the wrong path for their benefit and not ours.

    The decisions we make determine our fulfillment. The ones that unnecessarily make life more complicated include decisions that bring instant gratification, that please our family or friends, that put money in the salesman's pocket, and those that are contrary solely to be contrary, not to honor our sincere path.

    However, when we make decisions that stay true to what we most value (love, sincerity, kindness), we eliminate unnecessary burdens and create more self-respect, peace of mind, and stability.

    After a day of "sorting out the home," as Beth Kempton coined in *Calm Christmas and a Happy New Year*, the filter in the dishwasher is clean and ready for a new year of sparkling up my dishes and pots and pans, the refrigerator gleams, awaiting fresh food and drink, the fire alarms have been tested, mattresses flipped, the holiday decorations packed away for their eleven-month rest, and the Christmas tree prepared for pickup by the Boy Scouts. The house seems to breathe easy; it feels lighter, expansive, and open to a new start. And the boys and I are packed up to visit the Pacific Ocean and welcome the new year.

    Not long after settling into our tiny cottage two blocks from the beach, waves, and seagrass, a place we have reserved at least once a year since 2012, I began to crave being home for New Year's Eve and Day if only because Le Papillon had become my tailored glove of comfort. This is not to say the oceanside cottage was not delightful and cozy. Each time we visit, I appreciate our regular respite by the ocean as there are no tasks tempting me; instead, I am content just to be, to sit, to nap, to read, to write, to be still, as nothing immediate or necessary (besides eating) requires my attention.

    However, the full first year at Le Papillon has taught me how to just *be* in my own home and how to revel in my own company without the need for a grand occasion or socializing with others, and without apology.

The Road to Le Papillon

Simultaneously, I learned that I can accomplish much and arrive at a place of peace and contentment when I make time to just *be* regularly. When I am at peace in my home, I savor my life and my ways of moving through my days, my sleep is deeper and uninterrupted, my relationships and conversations spark delight and joy rather than worry and pain, and I can let go of what is out of my control with far more ease and speed.

What a lovely lesson and place to reach — to desire to return home, a home that is mine, tailored to the way I enjoy my days — and to know that, after welcoming the new year (having turned in at 9:00 p.m.) with walks on the sand in the drizzling rain that seems to wash away the old and enable new possibilities and clarity of direction, I will pack up to drive back to Bend and be welcomed by the sight and comforts of Le Papillon.

Let yourself revel in your time at home, even if the world nudges you to step outside. Knowing that you engage in events and people outside your home in an amount that feeds your social self, do not dismiss but instead honor your need to enjoy time in your sanctuary.

Petit plaisir Nestle in, close your eyes, and listen to Mark O'Connor's "Butterfly's Day Out," featuring Yo Yo Ma and Edgar Meyer. Be reminded that your Le Papillon wishes to fly as well. I have no doubt that you will nurture it to do so.

Explore further thesimplyluxuriouslife.com/december31 (a simple life lived well *is* luxurious living. Let me explain . . .)

Conclusion
A Twenty-Two-Year Journey to Le Papillon

Without knowing it, upon leaving Wallowa County days after graduating from high school at age eighteen until the summer of my fortieth year, I was on my journey to Le Papillon.

On this journey, with myself as my constant companion, I chose to listen to my voice, not knowing for some time what language I was speaking or how to translate it, but doggedly looking for lessons after many mornings and nights of asking, "Why isn't it clicking?" and "What else can I do?" and "How is this supposed to be helpful?"

I stepped into an unspoiled clearing of contentment when I acquired the keys to Le Papillon during the late summer of 2019. In *The Book of Awakening*, Mark Nepo teaches:

> There are two basic ways to feel the fullness of life, and both arise from the authenticity of our relationships. One is from our love of life, and the other is from our love of each other.
>
> Often, in our solitude, we can discover the miracles of life, if we take the time and risk to be alone until the glow of life presents itself. This is the reward of all meditation. It's like taking the path of our aloneness deep enough through the woods so we can reach that unspoiled clearing.
>
> We can also reach that unspoiled clearing by taking the time and risk to be thoroughly with each other. This is the reward of love.
>
> But our most frequent obstacle to experiencing the fullness of life . . . is the hesitancy that keeps us from being either fully alone with life or fully alone with each other.
>
> Being half anywhere is the true beginning of loneliness.

I risked being alone, as Nepo writes, as a result of a core determination to find peace — a peace within myself, a peace to fuel inner strength to finally just be Shannon without apology, without shrinking, without passively accepting limiting labels to bolster someone's else's self-esteem. But it took time. The "deep enough" Nepo writes about when we honor our time alone can become more than just uncomfortable; it can be painful until we near the "unspoiled clearing," and contemplating retreat is understandable but will not lead us to contentment, only loneliness.

My first step into the woods began the summer leading into my sophomore year of college. I chose to stay in the small college town in an apartment I had moved into with my roommate, who would not be staying in town that summer but would return in the fall (yet, thankfully, still paying her half of the rent). One of the first nights of being alone in that apartment, I felt painfully alone. So much so, I slept on the floor of the dining room (we didn't have a table yet) with my comforter and pillow — why, I am not sure, but I knew it was out of feeling confused by my decision to stay on my own.

The perplexing reality of my life to that point was that I enjoyed being in my own company during my entire childhood, but upon reflection, someone — my mother usually, but other people as well — were usually in the vicinity, doing their own thing as I went about doing what engrossed my attention. For the first time in my life, I was entirely physically alone, without a person or a pet.

However, I had chosen it, and that summer was the worst of it. As we sometimes do when we do not know how to heal ourselves from within, we reach out to and for others, so I reached out and ended up in a relationship with a sweet boy who knew me from the success of my high school athletics. The relationship was not destined to last, but it was not until I was on the brink of the altar that I gathered up my innate courage, finally started to pursue my curiosities in and around campus, and ended what I knew, somewhere inside of me, was not my journey.

Author of *Awaken the Happy You* and meditation teacher Richard Paterson writes, "A spiritual awakening is a coming home to yourself, a return to your original nature . . . a spiritual awakening gives us a glimpse behind the curtain of the 'person' to behold the splendor of what lies beyond — the True Self . . . In India, they call it Sat Chit Ananda — Truth, Consciousness, Bliss."

In his book *The Three Marriages*, David Whyte explores what we discover during a spiritual awakening: "We reach a certain threshold where our freedom to choose seems to disappear and is replaced by an understanding that we were made for the world in a very particular way and that this way of being is at bottom nonnegotiable. Like a mountain or the sky, it just *is*. It is as if we choose and choose until there is actually no choice at all . . . the only question is whether you will respond."

With each exploration over the past two decades, I gradually returned to the person who knew how to be content with her own company, who knew how to explore and wander and inquire and engage, standing up when required and sitting still to observe, learn, and listen, and letting go when necessary.

During my twenties, I pursued the goal the American culture touts as supreme — happiness. But Henry David Thoreau's wisdom rang true when I stopped pursuing and started engaging with the life around me: "Happiness is like a butterfly: the more you chase it, the more it will evade you, but if you notice the other things around you, it will gently come and sit on your shoulder."

Eventually, the butterfly of happiness gently introduced itself and shared the gift of contentment. I willingly gave my thirties to the exploration of what contentment consists of and how to carry it with me each and every day. The genesis and growth of TSLL during its first decade was my exploration.

Which leads me to my forties. In many ways, my house, Le Papillon, embodies the arrival of the butterfly. I had stopped searching and straining and narrowly defining what life *had* to be for me to be at peace. I found my way to myself, to being at home with myself, honoring my well-being, and acknowledging my true self.

Moving in to Le Papillon gave me a safe, inspiring sanctuary, just as my house in Pendleton, Oregon, had done thirteen years ago — in that case, to begin TSLL, to let my defenses down and breathe more deeply, exploring what wanted to be understood, known, and bravely shared. When I finally got my footing, I found the courage to let go of all that was meant to be part of my journey for only a limited time.

Yes, Le Papillon is a structure, a house, but I have lived in houses and apartments before, none of which gave me the ability to find my inner peace. What makes Le Papillon different rests solely on who I was when the house crossed my path. I saw, and knew in my bones that Le Papillon, as I would eventually call it, was meant to hold my life.

With its ode to Britain's Arts and Crafts architecture, my American Craftsman–style home extends homage to my predilection for British country living. Its garden design uses limited outdoor space to include vegetables, berries, and fruit trees as landscaping elements, and I noticed the French approach to gardening, the *potager*, during my first walk-through of the exterior.

The location in a small, friendly neighborhood in proximity to Mother Nature's beauty allows me to enjoy fully each of the four seasons, and I even have a taste of my childhood home on Alder Slope in Wallowa County.

All three — Britain, France, and Wallowa County — have contributed to my life and have enabled me to blossom, but I had to be either reminded of or taught such life lessons over the past twenty-two years. Le Papillon brought me home to Shannon, and it brought deep contentment to my everydays.

If, as I stood at the brink of the road to Le Papillon, I had been cautioned that twenty-two years would unfold their lessons before I would feel at ease living my life every single day, I am not sure what my response would have been. Part of me, the impatient, short-sighted teenager, may have been hesitant to proceed, but the other part of me — I would like to say the wiser part — would have been grateful there was a destination worth journeying toward.

Because, indeed, it was more worthwhile than words can describe, but I have tried to do that in the book you hold in your hands.

The Road to Le Papillon

Just when the caterpillar thought the world was over, it became a butterfly.
— Barbara Haines Howett

Epilogue

To travelers on the road to their Le Papillon...

We delight in the beauty of the butterfly, but rarely admit the changes it has gone through to achieve its beauty.

—Maya Angelou

My choice of the French word for butterfly to name my home had everything to do with the four stages a butterfly passes through to become a butterfly, revealing a beauty that awes onlookers.

My affection for France led to the name Le Papillon. Had Spain or Germany or any other country captured my heart and broken me open, as my time spent in France did, I might have named my house La Mariposa or Der Schmetterling, but it was France, and so the name became Le Papillon.

Traveling the road to your Le Papillon may begin with only the vaguest hope that something beyond your comprehension for how you wish to live your life is possible, as tiny as a butterfly's first stage — the egg, too small to be seen with the naked eye. For me, feeling small was growing up in a geographically isolated place, Wallowa County, whose name few could pronounce and fewer could locate on a map. Your first stage may be that others cannot fathom the dreams you hold in your heart; but you know they are there, and your courage allows them to come to life. Hold fast to them. Listen to them. Trust them.

The second stage in becoming a butterfly is the caterpillar, scuttling along the ground, a tree trunk, or a blade of grass. It grows and sheds skins, much as we are cast into situations we did not choose, do not enjoy, or do not understand. Through these life chapters, we learn who we are, what speaks to us, who or what hurts us and what and whom we are drawn to. We move — from one activity, one academic level, one job, one relationship to another — while learning and applying the knowledge we have gained. We shed old selves and behaviors that no longer fit, and bravely continue to explore, inching toward our desired destination even if we do not know how it will all materialize, or when.

The third stage will be unavoidably painful but is absolutely necessary to our transformation. What we are transforming into is not made clear which is why we may hesitate or question whether we should step forward and subject ourselves to something full of apparent unwanted discomfort. Author Octavia F. Raheem, author of *Pause. Rest. Be.: Stillness Practices for Courage in Times of Change* speaks to the necessity of the third phase in order to become the magnificent thing that is the butterfly:

> "Like caterpillars making their way to their cocoon . . . it is unclear what we are becoming. Caterpillars must enter a liminal space to grow their wings. In that space, they literally dissolve into goop. In that soup of slime, there are cells that will become the magnificent thing that kisses flowers in bloom: A butterfly. Those cells are called imaginal cells. The mystery of imaginal cells is that they are not assigned to anything in advance. They may become an eye, a wing or an antenna . . . Between endings and beginnings, our old self vanishes. Our vision is often challenged in liminal spaces . . . Here we are at a departure and arrival point exhaustedly realizing that what worked in the past will not work here in this environment. It's messy and we may cry a lot. Each tear is an imaginal cell. We may endlessly sigh. Each breath is an imaginal cell. We may writhe, rage, moan and kick about. Each movement unleashes an imaginal cell . . . Rest and stillness allow the imaginal cells to slowly form into the signposts, paths, and vessels that point us forward . . . We have been deconstructed in order to put ourselves back together in a way that not only heals us but also our families, community and world . . . Without [liminal space] there are no beginnings, no metamorphosis or transformation. Without it, we have no wings to rise."

The third stage along the journey to becoming a butterfly is the pupa or chrysalis, attached to the underside of a leaf, hidden away, looking like a part of something else or nothing identifiable. Yet a transformation is taking place, gradually and steadily. The cells reassemble themselves; new ones emerge, while old ones die away. The caterpillar's transformation into a butterfly happens as though by magic.

My arrival in Bend, Oregon, was the beginning of my third stage. In many ways, my hiding away, though I did not realize it at the time, was teaching at a high school where I had felt fortunate to be hired to teach what I loved. I threw myself into my work as an AP Language and Composition teacher. I sacrificed my social life in order to give 100 percent at school, which gave me the peace of mind to give 100 percent to my writing once I left the school building. There was no room for anything else. But the transformation had begun and did not conclude until just before the book you hold in your hands went out into the world in early 2022 as the pandemic continued to keep me in my cocoon for the preceding two years where I gradually became aware that indeed a transformation was happening, and finally I stopped fighting the change that I unconsciously longed for, a change that felt as natural as taking breath. I let myself be still, let myself rest when my mind and body needed rest, and with the support of trusted people, I encouraged myself to apply the skills I had for so long wanted to understand so that I too could find peace, connect lovingly with others and deepen the quality of the one and

Epilogue

only life I was given. I let myself feel emotions I had long protected myself from, nudging myself to be more vulnerable, more open, more fully Shannon than I had been since I was a young girl. I let myself grieve fully in order to move through the transformation process to discover and savor fully the joy, no matter how it arrived or presented itself, on the other side.

Your third stage may have also taken place partially or entirely during the pandemic, or it may have been the death of a loved one, an injury, or an illness requiring you to halt your life and the way you partake in your work and relationships. Or perhaps it was a job loss, a divorce, any shift that requires a pause, implores you to reflect, and needs you to let yourself grieve. To not do so, to avoid any and each of the needs your life journey calls for at this unwanted moment prohibits the transformation process that is the prerequisite for reaching the fourth stage, Le Papillon. It is when we entirely step into and through the third stage that we become able to transform.

When we enter the third stage, we might spend less time with friends and family; we may even unconsciously push people away as we need more time with ourselves, to know ourselves, to find the courage to set out in a new direction. We do this with confidence in the true selves we have been all along, yet only now fully understand and embrace. Rather than linger in the pain of being hidden, we navigate through the suffering we must experience and understand. This changes us. We can never be the same, as we have acquired new knowledge, new awareness that influences our decisions moving forward. We ask questions along the way, let ourselves feel our emotions fully, and reach out to trusted sources when we need support, guidance, and reminders that we are heading in the best direction for our well-being, peace of mind, and true contentment.

Finally, the fourth stage. The butterfly emerges, resplendent in its unique, stunning beauty. Breaking free from the transformational cocoon, it immediately seeks out connection as floral scents draw it to its food source. We emerge from our third stage of solitude ready to live fully, to engage; we are grounded, but without assumptions or expectations. When we emerge, when we apply all we have learned, our strengthened courage sits well with the unknowns, not clinging, but opening our hearts to the possibilities we are ready to experience.

Your butterfly self will look very little like your caterpillar self, and that is something to celebrate. You have grown and been courageous, and the world, in each of its everyday moments, is yours to savor deeply. You have arrived at a place of true contentment. And because the journey was neither simple nor pain-free, your appreciation of your newfound mode of travel — with contentment as your grounding vehicle — ensures that you will not forget what it took for you to arrive. You now carry wisdom with you, and no matter what events or emotions arise, you have the skills to navigate through them well, with the healthy connections, loving exchanges, and life successes you had dreamed about at the first stage of your journey.

Bon courage and *bon voyage*,

Shannon

Quick Guide to Recommended Books

And I Shall Have Some Peace There by Margaret Roach (June 8)
Appetite for Life: The Biography of Julia Child by Noel Riley Fitch (August 4)
The Alchemist by Paulo Coelho (February 19)
The Art of Possibility by Benjamin Zander (October 22)
At Elizabeth David's Table: Classic Recipes and Timeless Kitchen Wisdom by Elizabeth David (July 11)
Attached: The New Science of Adult Attachment and How It Can Help You Find — and Keep — Love by Amir Levine and Rachel Heller (September 28)
Bibliostyle by Nina Freudenberger (July 10)
Big Magic by Elizabeth Gilbert (October 19)
Bonjour, Happiness by Jamie Cat Callan (July 26)
The Book of Awakening by Mark Nepo (August 27)
Books for Living by Will Schwalbe (September 7)
Calm Christmas and a Happy New Year: A Little Book of Festive Joy by Beth Kempton (November 30)
Calm Clarity by Due Quach (April introduction + November 16)
The Code of the Extraordinary Mind by Vishen Lakhiani (September 15)
The Courage to Be Disliked by Ichiro Kishimi and Fumitake Koga (February 1 + June 7)
The Course of Love by Alain de Botton (April 30)
The Creative Habit: Learn It and Use It for Life by Twyla Tharp (November 10)
Daily Rituals: How Artists Work by Mason Curry (April 27 + September 12)
Daily Rituals: Women at Work by Mason Curry (April 27)
DailyOM: Inspirational Thoughts for a Happy, Healthy, and Fulfilling Day by Madisyn Taylor (November 23)
Dinner with Edward by Isabel Vincent (October 26)
The Edible French Garden by Rosalind Creasy (August 23)
The Edible Herb Garden by Rosalind Creasy (August 23)
Everyone Can Bake: Simple Recipes to Master and Mix by Dominique Ansel (September 25)
Fashion as Communication by Malcolm Bernard (September 3)
The Four Agreements by Don Miguel Ruiz (June 22)
Four Thousand Weeks: Time Management for Mortals by Oliver Burkeman (August 5 + August 22)
The French Art of Not Trying Too Hard by Ollivier Pourriol (February 11)
The French Chef in America: Julia Child's Second Act by Alex Prud'homme (August 4)
The French Exit by Paul DeWitt (May 3)
A French Garden Journey: The Road to Le Tholonet by Monty Don (January 20)
Happiness by Design: Change What You Do, Not How You Think by Paul Dolan (June 22)

The Road to Le Papillon

Happy Ever After: Escaping the Myth of the Perfect Life by Paul Dolan (September 26)
The Healing Self by Deepak Chopra (April 7)
Herbs by Judith Hann (August 23)
Hotel du Lac by Anita Brookner (December 8)
A House in the Country (1942) by Jocelyn Playfair (August 2)
Daring to Trust: Opening Ourselves to Real Love and Intimacy by David Richo (September 19)
How to Be an Adult in Relationships: The Five Keys to Mindful Loving by David Richo (September 19)
I Am Invincible by Norma Kamali (March 9)
In a French Kitchen, inspired by Susan Herrmann Loomis (August 9)
The Irresistible Introvert by Michaela Chung (September 26)
Joie de Vivre: Simple French Style for Everyday Living by Robert Arbor (August 23)
Julia Child Rules by Karen Karbo (November 8)
Keep Going: 10 Ways to Stay Creative in Good Times and Bad by Austin Kleon (January 10)
The Last Lecture by Randy Pausch (October introduction)
Limitless by Laura Gassner (February 9)
Little Women by Louisa May Alcott (September 30)
Long Live the Queen: 23 Rules for Living from Britain's Longest-Reigning Monarch by Bryan Kozlowski (April 10)
Loving What Is: Four Questions That Can Change Your Life by Byron Katie (September 29)
Man's Search for Meaning by Viktor E. Frankl (October 5 + October 16)
Mastering the Art of French Cooking by Julia Child, Simone Beck, and Louisette Bertholle (August 4)
Miss Buncle's Book by D. E. Stevenson (March 26)
My Life in France by Julia Child (August introduction)
The Mystery of Mrs. Christie by Marie Benedict (January 20)
A New Earth by Eckhart Tolle (February 9 + March 14)
Nonviolent Communication: A Language of Life by Marshall Rosenberg (November 24)
Notes from the Larder and *Kitchen Diaries* by Nigel Slater (May 30)
The One Thing: The Surprisingly Simple Truth Behind Extraordinary Results by Gary Keller (December 14)
Outliers: The Story of Success by Malcolm Gladwell (September 23)
The Paradox of Choice by Barry Schwartz (July 21 and October 13)
Pause. Rest. Be.: Stillness Practices for Courage in Times of Change by Octavia F. Raheem (Epilogue)
The Person You Mean to Be by Dolly Chugh (June 2)
Plat du Jour by Susan Herrmann Loomis (February 12)
Provençal Mystery series by M. L. Longworth (August 14)

Guide to Recommended Books

The Queen's Gambit by Walter Tevis (November 22)
Quiet by Susan Cain (September 26)
The Road Less Traveled: A New Psychology of Love, Traditional Values, and Spiritual Growth by M. Scott Peck (August 8)
Simple French Food by Richard Olney (August 6 and November 13)
The Tao of Pooh by Benjamin Hoff (January 3 + December 13)
A Taste for Provence by Helen Lefkowitz Horowitz (July 8)
Think Like a Monk by Jay Shetty (March 24 + September 15)
The Three Marriages: Reimagining Work, Self and Relationship by David Whyte (introduction to the book)
Thrive: Finding Happiness in the Blue Zones by David Buettner (July 23)
The Thursday Murder Club by Richard Osman (November 28)
Tiny Habits: The Small Changes That Change Everything by BJ Fogg (October 25)
To Kill a Mockingbird by Harper Lee (September 22)
Tuesdays with Morrie by Mitch Albom (June 20 + September 21)
The Untethered Soul: The Journey Beyond Yourself by Michael A. Singer (June 1 + August 26)
Walden by Henry David Thoreau (January 18, August introduction + August 4)
The War of Art by Steven Pressfield and Shawn Coyne (September 24)
The Way of Integrity by Martha Beck (January 4 + February 2)
When: The Scientific Secrets of Perfect Timing by David H. Pink (April 28)
Year of Wonder: Classical Music to Enjoy Day by Day by Clemency Burton-Hill (introduction to the book)

Quick Guide to Recommended Musical Selections

Abel: Symphony in F Major, op. 1, no. 4 (November 12)
Albinoni: Concerto for Two Oboes in F, op. 9 (allegro) (November 16)
— — —: Sinfonia for Two Oboes in G Major (May 7)
— — —: Trumpet Concerto in B-flat Major (December 5)
C.P.E. Bach: Flute Concerto in A Major, Wq 168 (September 22)
J. S. Bach: Brandenburg Concerto no. 2 in F Major, BWV 104 (June 18)
— — —: Cello Suite Gigue 6.6, arranged by Peter Gregson (June 30)
— — —: Cello Suite no. 1 in G Major (January 9)
— — —: Concerto in C Major for Violin and Oboe (November 20)
— — —: French Suite no. 4 in E-flat Major (July 2)
— — —: Oboe Concerto in F Major (April 5 + August 20)
— — —: Orchestral Suite no. 3: Air on the G String (June 10)
Basie: "April in Paris" (March 20)
Basie Orchestra: "Let It Snow" (December 17)
Benda: Flute Concerto in E Minor (August 29)
Coltrane: "Body and Soul" (October 24)
— — —: "Giant Steps" (January 15)
— — —: "My Shining Hour" (November 15)
Davis: "So What" (October 15)
Debussy: Arabesque no. 1 in E Major (November 6)
Einaudi, Ludovico: "The Days" (July 30)
— — —: *Primavera* (June 13)
Ellington and Coltrane: "Sentimental Mood" (October 28)
Farrenc: Etudes, Book 1: no. 12, Moderato (August 12)
— — —: Nonette in E flat Major, op. 38.
Fitzgerald: *The Lost Berlin Tapes* (February 17)
Gardot: *Sunset in the Blue*, especially "From Paris with Love" (August 6)
Grappelli: "Sweet Lorraine" (November 11)
Guaraldi: *A Charlie Brown Christmas* album (December 20)
Handel: "The Arrival of the Queen of Sheba" (May 11)
— — —: Concerto Grosso, "Alexander's Feast," Andante non presto (July 12)
— — —: Concerto Grosso in B-flat Major, op. 3 (November 1)
— — —: Water Music, Suite no. 2 in D Major (December 3)
Haydn: Symphony in D (*London*), no. 104 (June 24)
— — —: Symphony no. 22 in E-flat Major (April 15)
Heinichen: Concerto in F, SBL 234 (June 21)
— — —: Concerto no. 7 in G Major, S. 214 (July 26)
Holst: "Jupiter, the Bringer of Jollity," from *The Planets*, op. 32: IV (March 3)
Hot Sardines: "French Fries and Champagne" (October 14)
— — —: "Wake Up in Paris" (October 14)

Marsalis: "Winter Wonderland" (December 10)
Fanny Mendelssohn: Overture in C-major (August 26)
Felix Mendelssohn: Symphony no. 5, *Reformation*, in D, op. 107, second movement (September 18)
Monty Python: "Always Look on the Bright Side of Life" (March 26)
Mozart: Clarinet Quintet in A, K. 581 – 4. Allegretto con variazioni (June 29)
— — —: *Eine kleine Nachtmusik*, K. 525, first movement (Allegro) (September 2)
— — —: Oboe Concerto in C major, K. 314 (January 17)
— — —: Piano Quintet in E-flat Major for Piano and Winds, K. 452 (February 13)
— — —: Piano Sonata no. 12 in F, K. 332 (October 31)
— — —: Symphony no. 20 in D Major, K. 133 (September 27)
— — —: Violin Sonata no. 21 in E Major, K. 304 (February 24)
O'Connor: "Butterfly's Day Out" (December 31)
Platti: Oboe Concerto in G Minor (September 13)
Giacomo Puccini: Nessun Dorma! from *Turandot*/Act 3 (August 8)
Saint-Saens: "The Swan" ("Le Cygne") from *Carnival of the Animals*
Satie: *Gymnopédies* (March 7)
Simone: "Feeling Good" (October 20)
Johann Strauss II: "Morgenblätter" ("Morning Papers Waltz") (September 10)
Telemann: Flute Quartet in G, TWV 43 G10 (August 1)
— — —: Viola Concerto in G Major (June 28)
Van Wassenaer: *Concerti Armonici* (March 5)
— — —: Concerto Armonico no. 6 in E-flat Major (October 2)
Vivaldi: Cello Concerto in C Major, RV 398 (October 8)
— — —: Concerto for Three Violins in F, RV 551 (February 5)
— — —: Concerto for Two Guitars in G Major, RV 534, Allegro (May 1)
— — —: Concerto for Diverse Instruments in C Major, RV 558 (July 17)
— — —: Flute Concerto *Il Gardellino* (The Goldfinch) in D, RV428, Allegro (March 20)
— — —: *Four Seasons: Winter* (*L'Inverno*) (January 3)
— — —: Trumpet Concerto in B-flat Minor (December 19)
— — —: Violin Concerto in D Major (op. 3, no. 9) (September 4)
Yanover: "Blossom and Cadence" (February 20)
— — —: "Suddenly I Felt Joy" (December 29

~find the full playlist on the blog at
https://thesimplyluxuriouslife.com/3rdbookplaylist

Acknowledgments

The gift of time I have found through the journey of bringing *The Road to Le Papillon* to publication is arguably the most amazing gift to receive.

When given wholly, without distraction, without a schedule looming, without keeping one eye on the door, the recipient of our time — a person or persons, a project — receives something priceless. The next minute, the next day, the next year is never promised, so we savor what is given, and when we give something of such high value, we communicate whom and what we cherish.

I had written many of the first drafts of the entries beginning in 2010, but it was during the one year full of time at home in 2020 that I told myself to bring the idea of a daily meditations book together, as I did not know when I would again have such an abundance of time to do so.

The work began, and the time and effort given by the following people is something I will always be grateful for, whether for their expertise, their attention, their time, their support, their full presence, thank you. *Mille mercis.*

To Patricia Fogarty, my fearless, talented, and straightforward guide through the entire process, from the seed of an idea, to how to organize, what to keep, what to cut, and how to bring it all together into a book readers would hold in their hands, my editor since I began publishing, thank you for your patience with me. Thank you for wrestling with the many ideas I sent your way, and thank you for your gentleness and kind words of support during life's heart-hurting moments.

To Sarah Löcker, your illustrations and thoughtful, creative attention to the detail in each one that appears in this book tell a part of the journey to Le Papillon my words could not alone convey. You first, without inquiry or expectation, sent two sketches of my boys a few years ago, and for each piece, I am grateful more than you know. For your enthusiasm for what you do, sharing your world with me as we worked together, thank you for saying yes to being part of this project.

To Dash Creative, J, Mike, and Jeremy, the reason the book is able to be published is in no small part due to the visual aesthetics and functionality you bring to TSLL blog, the online home of simply luxurious living. Thank you as well for designing the cover of *The Road to Le Papillon*, and to J for being my trusted Eagle Scout web coding expert. With every hope and question I have about TSLL as it has grown over the years, you work your magic, and I am grateful for your friendship, kindness, and expertise.

To the people who have stood beside me along this journey to Le Papillon, the list would be an entire new book, but most notably it begins

The Road to Le Papillon

with my parents; includes my Great Aunt Betty and her devoted Junior, my Great Uncle Rufus; teaching colleagues and administrators who understood my respect and dedication for education while lovingly seeing a fire burning for something more — Doug M., Tom L., Mary T., Nancy F., Matt K., Nina S-B; my contractors, who treated my pups as kindly as they treated the direct-speaking client who loves France and loves to cook (whether they always liked what I gave them to nibble on I am not sure, but their kind words when they did enjoy it made me smile), Kris, Marc, Mike, and especially Jeff; my friend Veronique, your *joie de vivre* is a breath of fresh air; to my counselor, Lynne, for your guidance leading me back to my true self; my real estate agent, Greg, who patiently worked with me for five years before we found Le Papillon, and then we found it!; and to the two heartbeats in my life, one for nearly seventeen years and one who continues to bring a strong beat of steadiness for going on twelve years, Oscar and Norman, my boys, my companions, the cover stars of this book.

And, finally and most certainly, to those without whom this book would not exist, TSLL's weekly newsletter subscribers. Thank you for your time shared each Friday over the course of ten years, whether with a cuppa at home or on your lunch break at work as the week came to a close and the weekend beckoned, thank you for your continued interest in finding your own journey that sings the song of your true self. Thank you for trusting me, and thank you for your gentle kindness.

Made in the USA
Monee, IL
23 March 2022

2efd5f39-114a-431c-86a2-dc5effe82553R01